The Complete Book of

MODERN FLY-FISHING

Edited by Larry Solomon

DBI Books Inc., Northfield, Illinois

STAFF

EDITOR
Larry Solomon

COVER PHOTOGRAPHY
Boyd Pfeiffer

PHOTOGRAPHY
Larry Solomon
Larry Green
Boyd Pfeiffer

PRODUCTION MANAGER
Pamela J. Johnson

ASSOCIATE PUBLISHER
Sheldon L. Factor

PUBLISHER
Milton P. Klein

I would like to give special thanks to George Mowbray for his quality developing, printing and photographic advice.

Larry Solomon

Copyright © MCMLXXIX by DBI Books, Inc., 540 Frontage Rd., Northfield, Ill. 60093, a subsidiary of Technical Publishing, a company of the Dun & Bradstreet Corporation. All rights reserved. Printed in the United States of America. No part of this book may be reproduced, stored in a retrieval system, or transmitted in any form or by any means, electronic, mechanical, photocopying, recording, or otherwise, without the prior written permission of the publisher.

The views and opinions contained herein are those of the authors. The publisher disclaims all responsibility for the accuracy or correctness of the authors' views and opinions.

ISBN 0-695-81312-9   Library of Congress Catalog Card Number 79-91651

CONTENTS

Introduction

WELCOME TO THE wonderful world of fly-fishing. A world of beauty and mystery, excitement and serenity, challenge, frustration and gratification. A world filled with all the things that make any outdoor sport fascinating and attractive.

Fly-fishing is an activity that enhances whatever aspect of angling you are currently involved in—whether it be bait fishing, spinning or plug casting. Fly-fishing is not difficult. It only appears to be so. The fact is, fly-fishing can be quite easy if only a few certain steps are followed, as we shall see.

Though fly-fishing represents a very small minority of anglers when compared to the rest of the fishing world and other sports as well, there are, strangely enough, more books written on this subject than any other. It may be due to the great versatility fly-fishing offers in addition to the vast amount of knowledge that can be learned when an individual becomes involved in the game. Many fly-fishing books go into specific detailed subjects such as entomology, types of imitations, styles of casting and so forth. For any novice to attempt to learn it all in a short period of time would be a mistake. It is too complex. Yet, if it were taken one step at a time, and enjoyed while it is being learned, it becomes an endless joyous pursuit. That shall be the purpose of this book. To lead you step by step into the world of fly-fishing. To allow you to grow while you are having a good time in acquiring both the technique and the knowledge.

An angler-author I know said that we fly-fishermen are the product of our angling literature. For the most part, I believe him to be correct. There are very few anglers I know who have gone through the full evolution—from bait fishing on up to acquiring, from their own experiences, the knowledge necessary for serious fly-fishing. Most of us have just never had the opportunities or the available time to do so. Therefore,

Just a few of the books written about fly-fishing and flytying.

One of the beautiful and serene trout environments.

most of our learning has come from the written experiences of others who have learned their game well and shared their knowledge through their own books or through articles written for the various outdoor sport and fishing magazines.

The purpose of this book is to let you share the vast knowledge and experiences of several individuals who I consider it an honor to know. They are widely recognized as some of the foremost authorities in the sport of fly-fishing. I know them all to be extremely talented and creative anglers. Each will discuss one aspect of fly-fishing in detail in a way that should enable you to understand that aspect and to perform properly so that you can catch fish, have fun doing it and, at the same time, enjoy the environment around you.

The area of bass and panfishing will be covered by

Larry Green.

Larry Green. Larry lives in San Bruno, California, and is a native of that state. He was previously employed by the California Department of Fish and Game and has always been involved with fishing, hunting and the outdoors.

Since 1962, Larry has published over 700 outdoor related photography supported articles for just about every major outdoor, fishing and hunting publication. For many of these magazines he has served in a staff position—Field Editor, west coast for *Field and Stream;* Contributing Editor for *American Bass Fisherman;* and Contributing Editor for *Angler Magazine.* Larry recently authored the book, *10 Secrets To More Productive Fishing* (BMC, 1978), and has contributed to numerous other books on angling.

As if the written word was not enough, in 1975, Larry started the "Fisherman's Forecast" radio show, which is broadcast in San Francisco on KCBS 7 days a week to an estimated 1 million listeners. They certainly know the name of Larry Green out West.

Besides being prominent in the fishing world, Larry has led significant movements in the field of conservation and was instrumental in blocking the construction of two dam projects and the banning of the use of DDT in California.

The use of a camera is always an enhancement to an outdoor writer, and this is just another one of Larry's accomplishments that make him super-qualified to show you the world of fly-fishing for bass and panfish.

Boyd Pfeiffer, a resident of Phoenix, Maryland, is another well-known angler-author-photographer. Boyd will be covering the wide and exciting world of saltwater fly-fishing. Over the last 18 years, Boyd has been a significant contributor to *Field and Stream, Sports Afield, Salt Water Sportsman* and about 30 other publications. He is currently the Contributing Editor to the "Salt Water Update" column of *Outdoor Magazine.* Besides contributing to Stoeger's *Angling Bible* for 2

Boyd Pfeiffer.

opened his current operation, The Rivergate, in Cold Spring, New York. It is known nationwide as one of the most respected mail-order operations for the fly-fisherman and flytier. Actually, that word respect is what follows Eric wherever he goes. I had the pleasure of co-authoring with Eric, *The Caddis and the Angler* (Stackpole). In addition to many articles for various fishing magazines, his other books include, *Fly Tying Material* (Crown) and *The Complete Book of Flytying*

One of the few men I know who is involved in as many outdoor activities as myself is my good friend **Eric Peper,** who was raised in Rockland County, New York, and now resides in Burnsville, Minnesota. Eric currently writes the "Fly of the Month" column for *Field and Stream* magazine. In this book he will put in proper perspective for you the subject of trout fly pat-

years, and being the Outdoor Editor for the *Washington Post* newspaper for 6 years, Boyd found time to co-author *Field & Stream Fishing Guide* (1972); *Tackle Craft* (Crown, 1974); *Shad Fishing* (Crown, 1975); and *Field Guide to Outdoor Photography* (Stackpole, 1976). As a member of the Outdoor Writers Association of America and the Photographic Society of America, Boyd has received numerous awards for his talents—all the better in enabling him to give you a comprehensive view of saltwater fly-fishing.

Eric Leiser is one of the true gentlemen of the fly-fishing business. Eric, born in Brooklyn, New York, was a songwriter for many years. However, his interest in the world of fly-fishing was too strong to keep it just as a hobby. In 1966 Eric opened the Fireside Angler in Huntington, New York, and quickly made it a known name for fly-fishing and flytying equipment and supplies. He then moved on in association with the Fly-Fisherman's Bookcase. In April, 1977, Eric

Eric Peper.

terns, both suggestive and imitative. Eric was the Editor of the *Field & Stream* Book Club for several years. He has also written articles for several of the prominent outdoor magazines, has contributed to *Advanced Fly Tying Techniques* by Ken Bay and has co-edited, *Fishing Moments of Truth* and *Hunting Moments of Truth*. Eric's creativity and imagination are two assets that I have always admired.

With the knowledge that I have acquired from my own angling experiences over the past 25 years, and with what I have learned from some of the true masters that I have had the pleasure and fortune to fish with, I will discuss the areas of trout and salmon fishing.

All of the contributors are experienced and have fished the North American continent—east, west, north and south. Our objective will be to relate to you the areas of fly-fishing that are available, the most up to date and practical techniques that have been developed and how to perform to best enjoy them. If there was any one suggestion I could give you while you are learning, regardless of what level of experience, I would say be very observant and experiment with your new ideas. That's the key to learning the game.

Eric Leiser.

Larry Solomon

No life so happy and so pleasant as the life of a well governed angler . . . .
Izaak Walton

CHAPTER 1
What Should I Know About Fly-Fishing?

I FIRST BEGAN fishing when I was 8 years old. I remember attaching a piece of string to a stick and using a bent pin for a hook. A friend and I dug up worms which we impaled on the pin. My first venture astream was on a piece of property owned by a Mrs. Garnell. Word had spread that there were a number of trout in the pool behind her place. What kind of fish they were did not matter, only that they were there. Our baited pins were flung haphazardly into the water, and the anticipation of just sitting there observing the surroundings of a new environment and waiting for the unknown was unforgettable. We caught some fish with lovely coloring which I later learned were trout. I brought them home in a pail and put them in the bathtub.

That experience was my introduction to a way of life I've never been able to change. Nor do I intend to. Each time I went out I learned something new. I was fortunate in being able to progress through the various stages of fishing one by one, a step at a time. This evolution involved bait fishing of all kinds, plug casting and spinning. Each one was different, requiring new techniques and approaches. Each was a challenge. Each was fun and exciting.

I don't recall when I first started using a fly rod, only the circumstances. A friend and I were fishing for bluegills with worms and a bobber and doing only fairly well, while an angler in a boat waving a long rod was consistently hooking fish. I later asked him about his equipment and why he was doing the certain things he did which resulted in so many caught fish.

He was a fly-fisherman and like most of them was only too eager to explain not only the technique and

The use of spinning, plug casting and fly equipment requires different techniques, but each has its purpose.

9

equipment involved but the fun that could be had doing it. I've met many an angler who did not have, or would not take, the time to instruct a youngster, much less talk to him. This time I lucked out. Soon thereafter I was the proud possessor of a new fly rod, reel and line and on my way to a new experience, and a new challenge.

Though I did not give up my other methods of fishing (and I still use some of them today), I learned that I had more fun with the fly rod under the right circumstances than with any other type of equipment. Not only did I learn the capabilities of a properly used fly rod, but I also learned there was much more that needed absorbing in this new field. Technique, equipment, presentation and their development were in direct proportion to success. After 25 years I'm still learning, still enjoying the challenge, and still going fishing with a fly rod every chance I get.

In order for you to get the best start and be prepared for the different areas you will be learning about, I will try to anticipate any questions you may have before you have a chance to ask them.

Question: *Why fly-fish?*

Because it makes you a complete angler. There are certain situations in all kinds of waters where the use of a fly rod and fly is the most productive method at the time. For example, when a hatch is taking place on a trout stream, fish are not interested in bait such as worms, spoons or plugs which imitate minnows or other hardware. At that time they will feed exclusively on

natural flies which are hatching, or on a very close resemblance of the natural. There is no other way to approach them except with a fly rod.

Another example is bass fishing the surface of a shoreline from a boat. A good fly rodder can present a bass bug under a low overhang to where the fish are simply because the line can be cast flat, not in an arc as is the case with a spinning rod and lure. Incidentally, approximately five casts can be made into different lies in the same amount of time it takes a spin fisherman to retrieve his lure. Another case I might cite is the one which occurs in certain saltwater bays when striped bass are in a surface mood. I have witnessed a good fly rodder take up to 50 school bass while his spinning counterparts did not so much as get a strike. And, if you ever intend to fish for salmon in some of the Canadian streams, a practical aspect of the fly rod is the fact that it will be the only method they will allow you to use.

So you see, there are a number of good reasons why it behooves you to learn the art of fly-fishing, the most important of which is to become a *complete* angler.

Question: *How is fishing with a fly rod different from using a spinning rod or casting rod?*

For the fisherman who started by using either spinning or plug casting equipment, which is probably almost everyone, you are used to casting something at the end of the line that has weight. That could be a spinning lure, a plug, a heavy piece of live or dead bait, or a light piece of bait together with a weight or a

Proper timing with rod and line makes fly casting seem effortless.

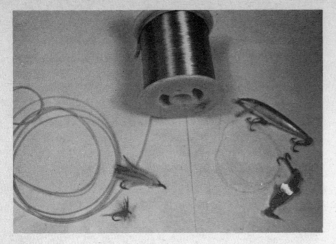

The weight of a flyline is needed to cast the almost weightless flies, while weighted lures are necessary to cast the almost weightless spinning or casting line.

to #15 which is the heaviest. The size of line that is used will usually relate to the type of fishing you will do, the species of fish you are going after, the size fly that will generally be used and, of most significant importance, the size and strength of the rod to be used. Using the proper size line for the particular type of fishing and equipment will enable you to cast and perform with maximum efficiency. It all comes down to having a balanced outfit.

Question: *What is a balanced outfit and why is it important to have one?*

Fly rods are made in different actions. Some are light; some heavy. Some are soft or slow; some are fast or stiff. This all refers to the way that they bend and cast a line. For example—a #5 line, which is fairly light, would properly work or bend a light, soft rod but would not do well on a heavier, stiff one. That stiffer rod might require a #7 or #8 weight line to work it properly.

Weights of flylines are listed in numbers.

bobber. In those cases, it was the weight at the end of the line that carried the lure you were casting to your target. In order for that weight to cast far, the line on spinning or casting outfits is of insignificant weight. In fact, it is often the object of many casters to use as light a line as possible in order to get the most distance in the cast.

The principle of fly casting is the exact opposite. For the most part, the fly has very little weight. Therefore, in order to be able to get some distance in the cast, the weight is put in the line. The contrast then is, with spinning or casting tackle, you are casting the lure, while in fly casting, you are casting the line with the fly attached to the end of it by means of a leader.

Question: *Is it difficult to learn to cast with a fly rod?*

No! The main thing is to understand the basic principle behind fly casting, which is allowing the line, while you are casting, to exert its weight against the rod. This gives the rod its action which casts the line and fly where you want it. The problem most beginners have is that they become more concerned with just waving the rod in the air than how the line is working with the rod. It is a question of timing which can easily be developed with a bit of instruction and some practice. Once you have mastered the basics, you can get involved in many different techniques. However, as with most activities, the basics are the most important. We will cover the basics in detail in Chapter 2.

Question: *I hear people talking about different line weights. What are they talking about? Is it something that I should know about, and will it make a difference?*

As I mentioned before, the flyline has the weight and it is what makes the rod work. The weights of these lines are standardized among the various manufacturers and are listed as numbers—#1 being the lightest, up

All rods are labeled by the manufacturer as to what weight line or lines (sometimes two or three) will work best with that particular rod to give it proper action and performance. When you are casting, the line is working at the tip of the rod, creating a moving weight. Since your hand is on the handle, arcing the rod back and forth, it would not be comfortable for very long with all that weight at only one end. One of the purposes of the fly reel, besides holding the flyline, is to act as a counterbalance. The reel should be heavy enough to offset the weight generated by the line. With relatively light outfits, such as those using #4 or #5 lines, this is a relatively small problem. However, as the outfit gets heavier, this balance becomes more significant. One of the mistakes many people make with larger outfits is that they often use a reel that is too light for the rod and line. How and why does this mistake happen? Many think that the way to see if a rod and reel are balanced is to place the front of the handle across one extended finger. If the rod with reel attached balances, then all is well. If it falls backwards from the reel, then the reel is too heavy. If it falls forward from the tip, then the reel is too light. That is what most people are taught, and it could apply to most lightweight outfits but not to the heavier ones. If you were casting and had about 30 or 40 feet of a #8, #9 or heavier line working in the air, that weight would far overcome what appeared to be a good balance before the line was stripped off the reel and the casting begun. Therefore, in larger outfits, the reel should be a bit heavier. To test for proper balance in the heavier outfits, place the middle of the handle across one extended finger. The heavier reel will eliminate adverse strain on the hand and makes for more comfortable and enjoyable casting. I think it would be proper to say that you could have the best rod made, but if you don't have the correct line on it, it will not work well. On the other hand, an inexpensive rod with a properly balanced line and reel can be used enjoyably and will function well.

Question: *If I have a balanced outfit, can I use one outfit for all fishing?*

The question is an easy one. However, the answer has a few variables. I guess if a man had an 8-foot or 8½-foot balanced outfit that could handle both #6 and #7 weight lines, he would be able to fish for, hook and land probably every species of fish that is approachable with a fly—both fresh and saltwater. Remember, I said every species, not every size. That is one of the variables.

When I first started to fly-fish, I think my first rod was an 8-foot glass rod that took a #6 line. I originally got it for fishing in lakes and ponds for bluegill and bass. It worked pretty well for the most part, considering my lack of ability to cast well at the time. We usually used relatively small #12 hooks for the bluegill and small bass. These flies, having very little weight and offering no resistance, were not hard to cast. However, one day I was given a deer hair bass bug tied on a size #1/0 or #2/0 hook which was just the thing for a trophy size bass. Well, I was all excited and naturally had to go out and try it right away. It really looked like a big piece of meat, and I could see why a big fish would take it. To my dismay, with my rod and the #6 line, that bug cast as though I had a parachute attached to the end of my line. It went no place. The problem was that this fly was much heavier and much more air resistant than my rod and line was able to handle. I needed a stronger rod that would handle about a #8 line to generate enough power to be able to properly cast and control a fly that size. I also should have used a shorter leader. This didn't mean that I would not be able to catch any good size fish with that outfit, because I did take some up to 4 pounds. I just was limited to the size of the fly that I was able to use. Another point to consider is that my 8-foot rod for

(Above) Balancing outfit at front of handle is only practical for lightweight lines and short casts.

(Below) Balancing outfit in middle of handle is proper for mid and larger weight outfits.

The line that casts a small size #16 fly will probably not be able to cast a larger more wind resistant bass bug. A heavier rod and line would be needed.

(Left) Large rods and heavier lines are necessary to properly cast larger saltwater flies and fight larger fish.

(Below) Small 6-foot to 7-foot rods are advantageous for small brush covered streams.

the #6 line was adequate to play and land those average size bass that would stay in the open water. However, a bigger fish that would go into the weeds would make you wish that you had a telephone pole and a winch to get him out. So looking back at our discussion, you have two things to consider as to the practicality of the outfit. First, the size of the flies that you will be casting, and secondly, the size of the fish that you will be catching and how they fight.

The same thing applies to saltwater. You can fish for baby or snapper bluefish that weigh up to 2 or 3 pounds, or for tarpon weighing up to about 8 or 10 pounds and use that same 8-foot or 8½-foot rod with the #6 or #7 line comfortably, both in casting, since you don't need a big fly, and in fighting the fish. However, if you get into the good sized bluefish, from 8 to 16 pounds, or those tail walking tarpon, from 50 to 100 pounds and bigger, you will be using flies that are considerably larger, about 3 or 4 inches long on size #1/0 to #4/0 hooks. You will also be hooking fish that could bend that relatively light rod into a pretzel. The fish would be in control of you rather than you controlling the fish.

Even with trout fishing, where the fish in the river and streams will average from ½-pound to 2½ pounds with the occasional trout 3 pounds or better, there can be a need for a heavier outfit if you are fishing big rivers such as the Yellowstone or Madison in Montana. On these rivers you are often using very large flies, both wet and dry. That requires a larger outfit than usual to function properly. On the other hand, there are times when it may be advantageous to go to a small outfit such as a 6½-foot or 7-foot rod for #4 or #5 line in order to properly fish small brush covered streams.

So basically, the answer is "Yes," you can use one outfit to catch almost any fish species. However, there are many occasions where a different size outfit is required to properly fish the existing conditions or handle the bigger fish.

It is important to have control of the line at all times while casting.

It is often necessary to make long casts when fish are farther out than you can wade.

Question: *How far must I be able to cast in order to fish properly?*

I guess the easiest answer to give is—whatever it takes to get to the fish. However, that doesn't really tell you too much since the distance you must be able to cast can vary depending on the species you are fishing for and the water conditions. If I were to pick a 10-foot range that would cover the majority of fly-fishing, I think that it would be from 30 to 40 feet.

There is a great tendency among fishermen, especially when trout fishing and quite often salmon fishing, to overcast—to try to cast farther than is necessary. It always seems that an angler on one side of the river feels he has to cast to the other side. The truth is that most often there are many good fish at half that distance and even sometimes within 15 to 20 feet of the angler. What is most important is that the farther you cast, the less control you will have of the line and, more importantly, the fly. The key is to be able to make the fly do what you want it to do. Generally, the shorter the line, the easier it is to control.

There are situations, mainly in saltwater or if you are fishing from the shore of a lake, where you will sometimes have to reach distances of up to 70 or 80 feet in order to get to the fish. That is another reason for a larger outfit with a rod sometimes up to 9 feet or more with lines #9, #10, or #11.

The main thing to consider in casting is control. You should not be trying to cast any farther than what you can control. That could be 30 feet to one person and 60 feet to another. The idea is to work your way up. Learn to cast and control up to 30 feet well. Then slowly increase your ability in 5-foot lengths. You will find that this will require slightly different techniques and timing, a subject we will discuss in Chapter 2 on casting.

Question: *How long should a fly rod be?*

The best answer that I could give is that the rod should be the proper length to let you fish as easily and as comfortably as possible with the line you are using and in the type of water you are fishing. As I mentioned before, you can use one rod for many types of fishing. But under what circumstances should you use an 8- or 8½-foot rod rather than 6- or 10-foot?

There are occasions where a 6-foot rod would be quite pleasurable and even valuable, such as on shallow small streams where you are fishing with small flies and making casts that are relatively short. However, under most conditions, it would be more practical to use a longer rod. One of the facts of fly casting is that up to a point the higher the line is above the water or ground while you are casting, the easier it will be to cast farther and with more control. Therefore, if you were fishing a larger river or body of water where you might be wading up to your elbows, a short rod would be a disadvantage if you had to cast any distance. Also, the more line that you can keep off the water surface after the cast is made the more control you will have when manipulating or working your fly and when working a fish after it strikes.

Looking at the other end, a 9½- or 10-foot rod could be a distinct advantage while salmon fishing where you have to make 60- and 70-foot casts while wading deep using a #8 or #9 line and a good size fly. Besides being able to keep the line high above the water or the weeds on the river bank while casting, you will also be able to keep the hook high enough above you so that, as you make your forward cast, it doesn't take your hat off or snag your ear. Sometimes however, the fact that the long rod keeps the line a good distance away has some disadvantages. When the flyline, especially a heavy one, is working in the air in preparation for a cast, it creates leverage and stress on your hand. We attempt to offset this by using a properly weighted reel to counterbalance this stress. However, the longer the rod, the greater the stress on your hand. I have always found that I can cast more comfortably for a longer period of time with rods under 9 feet than with rods over 9 feet. Another point is that the longer the rod, the less accuracy you are likely to have in placing your fly where you want it. This is not always important. If you are blind casting an open body of water, accuracy is insignificant. However, if you are fishing for rising trout or trying to place a bass bug in a small hole in the weeds, you will want pinpoint accuracy. I feel that much of this is lost with rods over 9 feet. I think you will also find that a slightly faster action rod will usually be more accurate than a slow action rod.

So, for your first rod select one that will give you the most flexibility and enable you to fish the majority of situations. As your ability increases and you have a desire to become more selective, you can get into different outfits of different weights and actions. For now, just learn the basics, catch some fish and have fun.

One important point I should mention. When you go to buy your first rod, reel and line, or any outfit for that matter, make sure that you buy the equipment at a place where they know what they are talking about, or take someone along who does. If your first outfit is mismatched or off balance, it can be a bit frustrating, create some problems and offset the pleasure of a truly enjoyable and fascinating sport.

Question: *Besides the different weights in flylines, are there different types of flylines. What are their uses and is it important for me to know about them?*

Yes, there are different types of flylines. The differ-

Fly-fishing shops know how to outfit you properly.

ent types are designed to best suit the various fishing and water conditions that you are likely to encounter in this vast fly-fishing world. I will list and explain them briefly below.

Level floating line—Although it is the least expensive, it is not generally recommended for good casting. This line is the same diameter throughout its entire length. It is best used in sizes #1 and #2 as a running line for heavier shooting heads (see below).

Double taper floating line—This line is similar to the level line to the extent that it is the same diameter throughout most of its length. The difference is that at each end the line tapers down to a smaller diameter. It may not seem like much, but it makes a big difference as to the way the line turns over and in the delicacy of control. This is an excellent line for fishing dry flies, nymphs and wet flies for most of your trout fishing conditions. Personally, I also prefer the double taper for most of my long cast Atlantic salmon and greased line fishing, which will be discussed in Chapter 6 on salmon and steelhead fishing.

Weight forward floating line—This line is almost the same as most double taper lines for the first 30 feet. The weight forward then tapers down to a small diameter for the remaining 60 feet or so, sometimes referred to as the running line. This enables the caster to have a relatively small amount of line in the air while casting (20 to 30 feet), yet "shoot" or cast a considerable additional amount of the smaller diameter "running" line for a longer cast. This line is the most popular all-purpose line available. It is also an

Different type and weight lines are listed on boxes in a standard code.

excellent line for casting a slightly larger fly or casting into the wind, since the majority of the line weight is up front giving maximum line speed.

The shooting head—This is approximately 30 feet of line, made (by the manufacturer or made by yourself) from either one end of a double taper line or the front end of a weight forward line. The rear end of the shooting head is made into a loop which in turn is attached to the loop of a lightweight running line. This combination allows the caster the ability to make very long casts. It also allows the angler to change the shooting head, for example from sinking to floating line, by just interchanging the loop-to-loop connection.

The above four variations are the basic types of lines that are used. However, there are different densities of lines which let it sink or float in order to enable you to fish different depths of the water. These are listed and explained below.

Floating—As the name indicates, this line is designed to float on the surface of the water. Modern flylines are manufactured with a plastic coating over a nylon core of varying densities. With the floating line there are many air bubbles sealed within the plastic covering along with a low density core. This line is best for fishing dry flies and for wet flies in shallow to moderate depth.

Sinking tip—All but the first 10 feet of this line is a floating line. The first 10 feet sinks. This line is valuable when you are fishing moderate depth water and you want to fish wet flies and nymphs closer to the bottom and not have them come up to the surface as the line swings with the current.

Sinking—The entire line is of a much higher density with a core of either dacron or even lead. They are made in three varieties—slow sinking, fast sinking and extra fast sinking—depending on how fast you want the fly to get to the bottom and the depth of water you will be fishing. These lines are good for fishing larger, deeper rivers and lakes or saltwater for the time when you really want your fly to get down and stay there.

Question: *Do I need more than one line with me when I go fishing?*

That word "need" is pretty strong. You can get by for the majority of your fly-fishing with a floating line. Even if you want the nymph or wet fly to sink, you can use a weighted fly or put some weight on your leader. However, that does not always get the job done properly. There will be many situations where you will be better off with an alternate line. Considering that you have a floating line, let's look at a few examples where

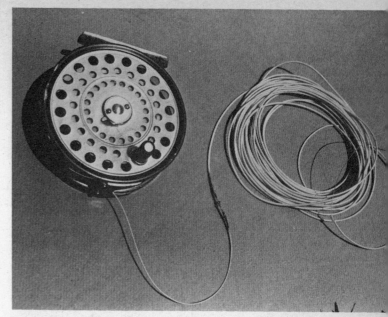

Shooting head lines are attached "loop-to-loop" to a lightweight "running" line.

It is advantageous to have an extra spool for the reel.

the alternate, obviously a sinking tip, would make the difference of whether you catch fish or not. The first thing is to realize why the floating line often fails when you really want to fish your fly down deep. It's a simple law of angling physics. What's at the end of the line will go where the line goes. If your fly at the end of the leader is weighted, or if the leader is weighted, or both, the fly and leader will sink as long as it is allowed to dead drift, free from the drag. However, with the floating line on the surface, when you retrieve it or when the current causes the line to swing or drag, the fly will also come up to the surface.

There are times when this action is what you may want, and you should be aware of those times. Unfor-

Having the flexibility to switch to the proper line often results in a successful day.

Dealers in Fly-Fishing Equipment

Dan Bailey
209 West Park Street
Livingston, MT 59047

Creative Sports Enterprises
2333 Boulevard Circle
Walnut Creek, CA 94595

Hunter's Fly Shop
Valley View Lane
New Boston, NH 03070

Robert Jacklin
West Yellowstone, MT 59758

Jack's Tackle
1262 Valley Forge Road
Phoenixville, PA 19460

Kaufmann's Streamborn Fly Shop
13055 SW Pacific Hwy.
Tigard, OR 97223

Bud Lilly's Trout Shop
West Yellowstone, MT 59758

The Orvis Company, Inc.
Manchester, VT 05254

Rangeley Region Sports Shop
Rangeley, ME 04970

The Rivergate
Route 9
Cold Spring, NY 10516

Hank Roberts
1035 Walnut Street
Boulder, CO 80302

Thomas & Thomas
23 Third Street
Turners Falls, MA 01376

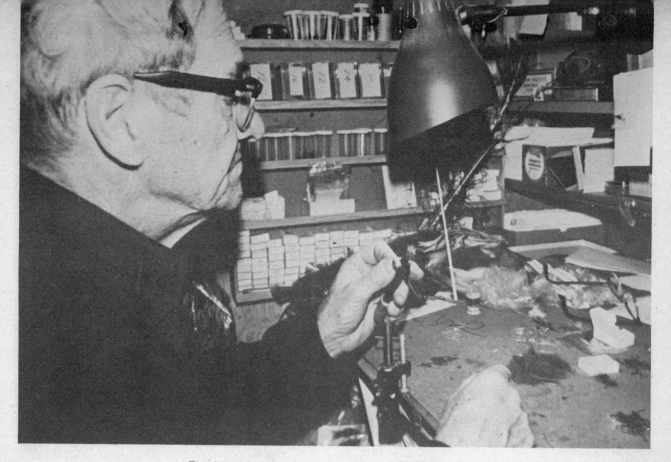

Flytying enhances your appreciation of the fly-fishing world.

tunately, when the fish are feeding down below, it is best to keep the fly there. Let's say you take a trip to your favorite bass lake to fish with surface bugs early one morning. You had one or two fish come to the fly just at daylight, but now they just aren't playing the game the way you had hoped. If you have fished for bass before, you know how fickle they can be. When you meet another fisherman who has caught a dozen decent size fish by fishing his lure on the bottom, you know that you have been using the wrong approach. However, how can you keep your fly on the bottom when your line is on top. You can't! By using a sinking line or at least a sinking tip line, the fly will not be brought to the top when retrieved, since the line is also down deep. This same situation applies to most types of fishing, whether it be in saltwater for bluefish or striped bass, fishing in a lake, or fishing for trout, bass or salmon in a river. Naturally it is more exciting to get the action on the surface and have the fish take a floating bug or fly. However, fish feed mostly below the surface and if you want to get them, that's where you will have to work your fly if they want it there. The answer then to the original question is "no," you don't necessarily need more than one line when you go fishing in order to catch fish under many situations. But, an additional line will give you considerable flexibility and will enable you to fish the fly properly under almost all situations, resulting in more fish caught and a more enjoyable time.

This is easily done by having an extra spool for the reel with you that is already filled with an alternate line. It can be easily interchanged in less than a minute.

Question: *Is it necessary to be able to tie flies in order to become a good fly-fisherman?*

The answer here is twofold. You do not have to learn how to tie your own flies to become a good fly-fisherman. There are many excellent fly rodders who do not tie their own flies. However, if you do learn how to tie your own, you will have a distinct advantage over the individual who does not. Here are a few reasons:

1. After an initial expense you will be able to tie your own favorite patterns at a fraction of what it would cost to buy them. A finished fly including hook and material will cost approximately 5¢ as opposed to 75¢, 80¢ or $1.

2. You will be able to obtain the exact pattern you want, tied the way you want it. Many times (because there are so many kinds of patterns) a sporting goods store will not carry the fly you want, or he may be out of stock on a popular pattern.

3. Because you tie your own, you will find that you will be more inclined to study exactly what trout and other fish are feeding upon in order that you may imitate it more perfectly. Quite unintentionally you will also be acquiring a knowledge of stream life.

Larry Solomon

18

CHAPTER 2
Assembling Your Outfit and Learning to Fly Cast

FLY CASTING IS, in my opinion, the most important part of the fly-fishing game. The presentation of the artificial fly is usually more important than the fly itself. If the fly is not dropped in a spot where there are fish, if the fly doesn't get to the fish in an appealing manner, or if you don't have contact with or control of the fly after the cast is made, it almost doesn't matter which fly you are using. I have always contended that the fly-fisherman who best casts and presents his fly will consistently catch more fish. In fact, even if the fly is not exactly what the fish are looking for, he will still catch more fish than the fisherman who has the perfect fly but cannot get it to the fish properly.

A person who handles a fly rod well is a thing of beauty to watch. A graceful ballet of rod and line in the air, a good fly cast appears so effortless, yet is so effective. It is simply a matter of understanding the principles of casting techniques, the function of the rod and line, and your part in utilizing them. Fly casting is just like any other sport that requires some finesse and technique, such as golf or tennis. The rod and line can be likened to the golf club or the tennis racquet. I have always been amazed while watching professional golfers, tennis players and baseball players at how effortlessly they would swing, yet how hard or far the ball

was hit. Most inexperienced or unpracticed participants of the same sports seem to exert enormous energies for minimum and inconsistent results. Assuming that the equipment is adequate, the answer then is timing and form—getting the maximum response and results for the minimum amount of effort by properly coordinating your body movement to the equipment that you are using. One of the most important factors is properly understanding the principles of the game and how the equipment functions.

ASSEMBLING YOUR CASTING OUTFIT

I can remember years ago the difficulty that many people had when they tried to learn how to cast. One of the main problems then was the lack of uniformity in equipment. It was much more difficult to get a properly balanced rod, reel and line. As a result, even if the caster was performing well, he might not get the proper results. This was often discouraging and in many instances caused the fisherman to become frustrated and abandon his great anticipations. Today, fortunately, the manufacturers of fly-fishing equipment are doing an excellent job of making it easy for an angler to get started in fly-fishing correctly. Fly rods are made of various materials—bamboo, graphite or fiberglass.

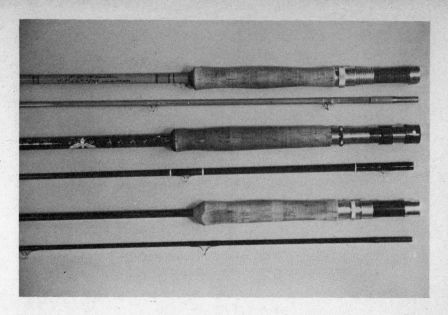

(Top to bottom) bamboo rod; fiberglass rod; graphite rod.

Some rod manufacturers are experimenting with combinations of different synthetic materials, e.g. a mixture of graphite and fiberglass, to try to get the "perfect action." When a rod is produced, it is labeled for the line that will balance it correctly. For example, a particular 8-foot rod weighing 3½ ounces may call for line weight #5. That means that in order for the rod to balance and cast properly, you should be using a #5 line. A rod may often call for two lines such as #5-#6 weight. This means that both lines will work properly and give additional flexibility in your fishing.

The big breakthrough was in flylines. Not too long ago, lines were classified in relation to their diameter, and these diameters were given letter designations—A, B, C, D, etc. Unfortunately the line diameters varied in weight from one manufacturer to another. The diameter of the line is not what makes the rod work properly, it is the line weight that does the job. Today, lines are classified by weight and are manufactured to standard specifications as established by the American Fishing Tackle Manufacturer's Association. The significance of this is that if a particular rod calls for a WF7F or DT7F line, then you can use any line from any manufacturer that is so designated and feel confident that it will match the rod in casting weight. I will say again here that it is important to buy your equipment at a store where they know what they are talking about or to take someone with you who does.

In order to get started, I suggest the following for your first basic outfit:

1: A fly rod either 8 or 8½ feet in length calling for a #6 or #6-#7 line.
2: A flyline of corresponding weight either in weight forward or double taper. It should be a floating line at first.
3: A single action fly reel that will hold the flyline and anywhere from 50 to 100 yards of approximately

15-pound dacron backing. It is important that the reel be the right weight together with the line to properly balance the rod.
4: A 100-yard spool of approximately 15-pound test dacron backing (remember dacron not nylon).
5: Preferably a 9-foot tapered leader. You may as well get three of them to start. They should have a butt diameter of about .020 and taper down to about .007 at the tippet. These measurements should be marked on the package.

Now that you have everything you need, let's put it together properly so they function correctly.

The first thing that you have to do is to attach the backing to the reel. You should make sure that the knot you tie is a good one and will not pull loose. I prefer to

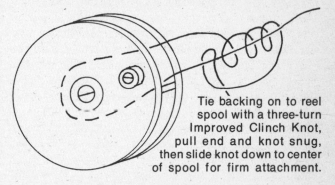

Tie backing on to reel spool with a three-turn Improved Clinch Knot, pull end and knot snug, then slide knot down to center of spool for firm attachment.

use a three-turn Improved Clinch Knot as illustrated.

Once the backing is fastened to the spool securely, wind it on evenly making sure that there are no loose loops. You want it to provide a good even base for the flyline. You also want it on evenly in the event you hook a big fish that takes you into the backing, which you want to pay out smoothly without tangling or causing unnecessary resistance.

The amount of backing you put on the spool will

depend on the size of the reel and whether you are using a double taper or a weight forward line. You can get more backing on a reel using a weight forward line than if you used a double taper. This is because the double taper has the wider diameter for approximately 80 percent of its line length, while the weight forward has the wider diameter of line for only about 30 feet or approximately 33 percent of its line length. The remaining 66 percent of line is a much smaller diameter running line.

Some tackle manufacturers list specifications with the reel which tell you how many yards of a certain pound test backing you can put on the reel using a specific weight and type of line. For example, it might say: If you are using a WF6F you can add 90 yards of 15-pound test backing; or if you are using a DT5F you can add 50 yards of 15-pound test backing. However, if

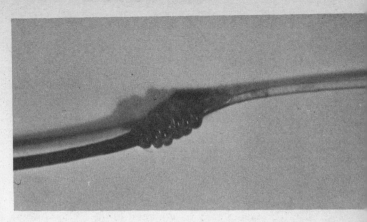

Coating the knots joining the backing to the line or the leader to the line with "pliobond," makes a smoother junction that will slide through the guides easily.

THE NEEDLE KNOT

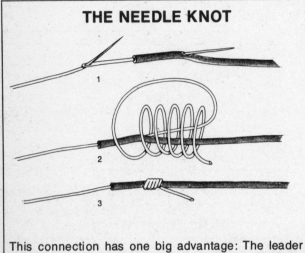

This connection has one big advantage: The leader comes out the center of the flyline, which minimizes the hinging effect between line and leader. **1.** Using a new razor blade, slice the end of the leader butt to a hairlike point that will pass through the eye of a small needle (no larger than half the diameter of the flyline tip). Insert the needle through the center of the flyline and out one side. **2.** Grip the needle point in a pair of pliers and pull the needle and about 8 inches of leader through the line. Tie a "Nail-less" Nail Knot. **3.** Trim leader tag and apply rubber-based cement.

THE NAIL-LESS NAIL KNOT

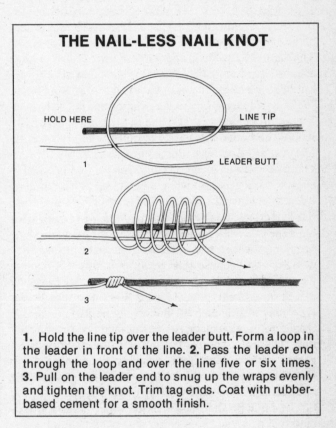

HOLD HERE   LINE TIP

LEADER BUTT

1. Hold the line tip over the leader butt. Form a loop in the leader in front of the line. **2.** Pass the leader end through the loop and over the line five or six times. **3.** Pull on the leader end to snug up the wraps evenly and tighten the knot. Trim tag ends. Coat with rubber-based cement for a smooth finish.

there are no specifications listed, and if the store where you purchase your equipment can't help, you may just have to experiment. The end result that you want is a full spool with only about 3/8-inch left empty to the edge of the spool. A full spool lets the line come off the reel smoothly. A shallow spool creates much more drag as the line comes off. Experiment by putting 50 yards on the spool if you are using a double taper or 75 yards if you are using a weight forward. Then, without using a permanent knot from the backing to the line, put the line on the spool. If it just about fills up the spool you are in good shape. If it fills up too much, you have to take

some backing off. If it does not fill up enough, remove the flyline and add additional backing. When splicing the backing together, use a simple four-turn Blood Knot and trim the ends close. (See Chapter 4 for an illustration of the Blood Knot.)

Now that you have the proper amount of backing, the next task is to attach the backing to the line. I prefer to do this with a Nail Knot since it makes a small strong knot with no loose line ends to catch on the guides as the line comes in or goes out. It is a good idea to coat both this knot and the one that joins the line to the leader with one or two coats of "pliobond." This seals the knots even more and smooths out the junctions, allowing the line to run in and out of the guides as easily as possible.

Assuming that your line is now properly on the reel, the next step is to attach the leader to the line. It appears that manufacturers of flylines put a bit more taper on the line than is actually necessary or even sometimes advisable for ease of casting. Many experienced fly-fishmen suggest cutting 2 or 3 feet off the end of the flyline before attaching it to your leader. This will allow the line to turn the leader over a bit easier during the cast.

Most ready-made tapered leaders have a loop at the butt. The leader may be attached to the flyline one of three ways—by using the leader loop, using the Nail or Needle Knot or by using a "leader link." If you want the smoothest knot for sliding through the guides, cut the loop of the leader and tie the Nail or Needle Knot as illustrated on page 21. However, if you are looking for the simplest and quickest means to make the attachment, use the illustrated Line-to-Loop or Wedge Knot. This knot also makes it very easy to remove and change leaders. An item called "leader link" can also do the job of connecting line and leader in a simple manner.

Now this next point is very important to the balancing and matching of the flyline to the leader. The point where the line and leader join must bend consistently just as the line or the leader alone does. The type of knot you use will not make any difference. If this consistency is not there, you will get what is called a "hinging effect" which will make it quite difficult for you to turn the leader over correctly and make a good cast. This happens quite often when the angler is not aware of the problem. Leader materials are made of varying stiffnesses. Just because the butt of two different leaders may be .021 in diameter does not mean that they will match the same flyline. If leader A is softer than leader B, A may be fine on a #6 line, while the stiffer leader B would not work well on the #6 but might be fine on a #7 line. The only way to find out is to tie them both together with a quick knot, possibly the Line-to-Loop Knot, and perform the "bend" test. To perform the bend test grasp the line with the fingers of one hand and the leader with the fingers of the other hand approximately 3 or 4 inches on either side of the joining knot. Then slowly bring your hands toward each other for a few inches. This will cause the line and leader to bend at the knot. It is the way they bend that tells you whether or not the leader is correct for the line. If they both bend the same in a gradual curve then the line and leader match. If the line has almost no bend but the leader bends sharply, then the leader is too soft. If the line bends sharply but the leader has almost no bend, then the leader is too stiff. The last two conditions will cause some casting problems and should be corrected by using either a stiffer or softer leader, whichever is appropriate in order to obtain the correct curve. This may seem like a minor point, but it is quite significant

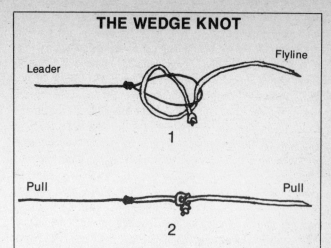

THE WEDGE KNOT

Leader

Flyline

1

Pull

Pull

2

1. Put the end of the line through the leader loop, completely around it, and under the line itself and then back through the loop between the leader and the line where it enters the loop. **2.** Work the knot tight, not cutting the excess end too closely.

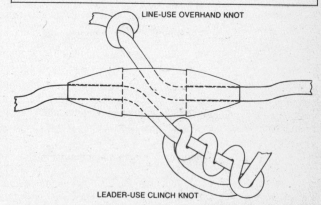

LINE-USE OVERHAND KNOT

LEADER-USE CLINCH KNOT

To use a leader link insert line through end of link and out side slot. Tie overhand knot. Insert butt of leader through other end of link and out opposite side slot. Tie Clinch Knot (see illustration above). Pull knots tight using pliers. Cut tag ends close. Press knots into slot and pull hard on line and leader to test.

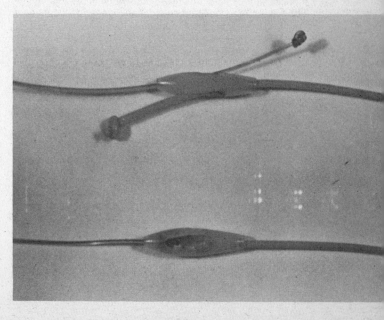

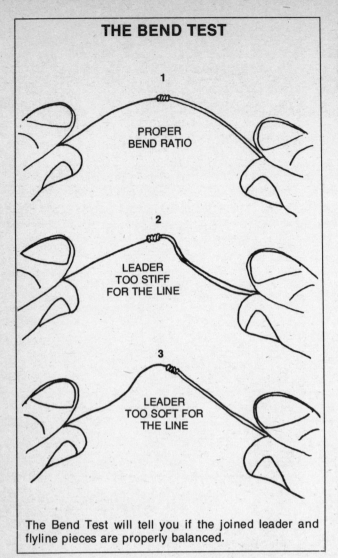

THE BEND TEST

1

PROPER
BEND RATIO

2

LEADER
TOO STIFF
FOR THE LINE

3

LEADER
TOO SOFT FOR
THE LINE

The Bend Test will tell you if the joined leader and flyline pieces are properly balanced.

of brightly colored yarn and tie the leader to it. The yarn will act the same at the end of the leader as would an actual fly. Being bright in color, the yarn will also be easy to see and will aid in determining the quality and accuracy of your casting.

Now that you are ready to start casting, there are a few important points you should remember:

1. You must allow the weight of the line to work against the rod. That weight is what makes the rod work, and the working rod makes the line cast.

2. The line will travel in whatever direction that you move the rod tip. If you move the rod tip straight back, the line will move straight back. If you drop the rod tip on the backcast so that it moves toward the ground, the line will go in the same direction. Therefore, remember to feel the movement of the rod tip, and you will feel the movement of the line.

3. There are three parts to the basic forward cast—pickup, backcast and forward cast. Each part is dependent on the other and you are the controlling factor. Timing and form are the key principles to good casting, not how much effort you put into it. Master the principles and form first, then you will be able to use the power properly when needed.

A fully completed cast consists of the backcast (a rearward movement of the rod and line), followed by the forward cast (the forward movement toward the intended target of the rod and line), allowing the line and the fly to land on the water.

Periodically, I will refer to a "false cast," which is the same rearward and forward movement of the rod and line, but the motion is not stopped, and the line and fly do not fall into the water. Quite often, especially when dry fly-fishing, one, two or three false casts are made before the final cast is executed. They should all be performed in a continuous fluid movement.

for proper line, leader and fly coordination. In order to get the fish to take, the fly has to get him properly. The entire outfit is attached from your hand on the handle to fly at the end of the leader. They all have to work properly together in order to get the best results.

When you put your rod together, make sure that the guides are evenly aligned so that the line will slide smoothly through them. The best way to put the line on the rod is to double up the line, not the leader, and thread it through the guides. This makes it difficult to miss a guide, and if you let go of the line, it won't slide back through all the guides.

LEARNING TO FLY CAST

Now that you have a properly balanced outfit, you are ready to cast. Before you go through the motions of the cast, you should have something at the end of the leader to simulate a fly. The reason you should not use an actual fly when you first learn is so that you don't accidentally hook yourself. However, if you happen to have a fly that you don't like, you can break off the hook point and tie it on. As an alternative, take a 1-inch piece

BASIC CAST 1

BASIC CAST 2

The Basic Cast

During any and all casts, it is most important to keep tension on the line. This is important so that the weight of the line can make the rod work. If the tension is relaxed during the cast, the action dies and so does the cast. The hand that is not holding the rod is responsible for keeping tension on the line. One of the main errors that the beginner commits is to move the free hand or "line hand," (left hand, assuming a right-handed caster) toward the rod as the rod is moved forward. This reduces the tension and causes the line to collapse. So when you are practicing, try to be conscious of keeping tension on the line with the "line hand" at all times.

1: To begin you should let out about 20-25 feet of line and leader (or the amount of line you feel you can control) by stripping it off the reel and working it through the guides. The first move of the cast is the pickup of the line from the water with the rod. From position **1** to position **2**, the wrist is NOT USED AT ALL. The action is initiated with the forearm, and the rod is held as an extension of the forearm. Note that the left hand holding the line is at about waist level at this time.

2: Note how the weight of the line has "loaded" or put stress on the rod so the rod can work. It is at this

BASIC CAST 3

BASIC CAST 4

point that the power stroke is applied with a minimal action of the wrist and forearm combination. You should try to feel that you are throwing the rod tip toward the tops of trees behind you, not down toward the ground. Note that although the rod hand has lifted the rod up and toward the rear, the line hand has remained in the same position in order to maintain line tension.

3: The arc the rod travels assumes the hour positions of a clock, with 12 o'clock directly over your head, 9 o'clock in back of you and 3 o'clock in front of you. You will note that after imparting the power stroke, the rod

has traveled to the 10 o'clock position. It should not travel any farther back than this "time" position. If it does, you will most likely be throwing the line down toward the ground. At this point, the line should be moving in a straight back and slightly upward direction. Note also at this point that the line hand has moved up toward the rod as the weight of the line pulls to the rear. This will also allow the line hand to be brought down with the forward cast to accentuate the tension of the line on the rod.

4: The rod is moved from position 3 to position 4 with the movement of the forearm. Again, the wrist IS NOT

BASIC CAST 5

BASIC CAST 6

USED initially. The power stroke forward is now made with the wrist driving the rod tip FORWARD, not down. Note that the line hand has pulled the line down. It is done in the same tempo as the movement of the rod, in order to maintain the tension of the line on the rod. An accentuation of this movement can increase that tension, as is done with the "double haul" cast.

5: The power stroke has been completed and the line is in the process of moving toward the target. Note that the rod has been stopped at the 2 o'clock position. This way the line and fly will be cast to stop above the water surface, then drop down gently. If the rod is thrown

farther down to the 3 o'clock or 4 o'clock position, the line and fly will be forced down on the water surface prematurely. If you wish to add length to the cast and utilize the extra line that is being held in the line hand, it should be released to "shoot" at this time.

6: Although the line has unfolded and is about to drop on the water, the rod is still maintained in that 2 o'clock to 2:30 position. If you are making false casts, which is usually done with dry flies before the line and fly are allowed to drop on the water, the entire procedure is repeated in a smooth, fluid movement.

The Steeple Cast

Often there are times when you have an obstruction behind you—trees, bushes, a wall or anything of that nature that would inhibit your backcast. There are two casts that are used in this case. The first is a variation of the standard cast and is called the "Steeple" cast.

1: The rod is picked up in a similar nature as the basic cast. With this cast, it is even more important to utilize only the forearm and not the wrist. The wrist will automatically apply some action without you trying. You should feel as if you are trying to throw the rod tip straight up to the 12 o'clock position.

2: Notice that the movement has been stopped at the 12 o'clock position, and the line is moving high towards the 1:30 or 2 o'clock position.

3: With the line and fly high above the obstacle, the rod is now moved forward toward the intended target.

4: The rod is stopped at the 10 o'clock position for the forward cast, and the fly is allowed to drop on the target or is picked up again if a false cast was intended.

STEEPLE CAST 1

STEEPLE CAST 2 ▶

◀ STEEPLE CAST 3

STEEPLE CAST 4

The Roll Cast

This cast is also used when there are obstacles behind you or when you do not wish to make a backcast. It is quite often used when fishing with wet flies, nymphs or streamers. It is not as practical with dry flies, although it is sometimes used, as this movement does not remove the water from the fly well.

1: Bring your casting arm and rod up to the 1 o'clock position and let the line hang along your side. Your line hand is also brought up to the rod in preparation for a downward pull.

2: Simultaneously, the rod is forced downward sharply, and the line hand pulls the line in the same direction in order to maintain the tension. The action of the rod forces the line to roll over and forward toward the intended target.

3: To insure the maximum action from the rod, the rod should be thrown as far down and forward as possible.

ROLL CAST 1

ROLL CAST 2

ROLL CAST 3

Upstream Hold or Reach Cast

One of the problems with most rivers and streams, for the average fly-fisher, is that the flow of water is never of a uniform speed from one side to the other. Usually the center of a stream flows faster than the sides, but there are, in many stream situations that you may face, as many as four or five variations of current speed at a given point.

The problem this presents to the angler, of course, is the ability to obtain a drag-free float. The conventional straight-across stream won't do it since the center current will wisk the heavier line downstream faster than the leader and the fly. Therefore, to offset and counterbalance the faster stream flow, many anglers will, after the cast has been made and the line is on the water, mend* their line so that it falls upstream of the current, attempting to give the leader and fly a headstart and assuring a certain number of feet of natural flotation. This can be somewhat effective with wet flies and streamers, but it usually does not work too well with dry flies. Mending the line when using a dry fly causes loss of control and contact with the fly, and the fly is pulled away from the line of drift, generally creating an unnatural movement.

Many times you may wish to impart some action, in the form of a twitch, to the fly. To do so properly, your fly should be cast down or down and across to the fish.

Also, by fishing downstream to the fish, the fly will get to him before the leader or the line.

The best method I know that assures the most line control is a cast called the "upstream hold" or the "reach" cast. I find that I use this cast for the majority of my stream and river fishing. This technique will allow the fly to land directly on its intended target without having to overcast or make unnecessary mends or movements after the fly is on the water. Line adjustment is taken into consideration before casting.

Here's how it works. There is a fish rising down and across stream from your position. You must land the fly 2 or 3 feet above the lie of the fish and get a drag-free float to approach him naturally. You will need to strip about 6 feet of shooting line from the reel to compensate for the extension or reach that you will make with the rod. This will enable you to keep the main part of your line upstream and give your imitation a head start. This sequence assumes the current is flowing from right to left.

1: Make your normal false casts so that your fly is directly over the target. Now strip an extra 5 or 6 feet of line from the reel and hold it loosely beside you with the line hand. The backcast is made just as though you were making a normal basic cast.

REACH CAST 1

---

*See Chapter 4 page 105 for an illustration and explanation of the mend the line technique.

2: Then make your forward movement as you normally would, by pointing the tip of your rod toward the target area. This will give the line and fly the direction desired.

3 and 4: As the forward cast is unfolding, allow the extra 5 or 6 feet of loose line (which you held) to slide through the guides as you bring the entire rod, butt leading, then tip, upstream (to the right or the left, depending on which side of the stream you are fishing) as far as you can. This should be accomplished in a smooth and fluid motion: There is no pause throughout the execution of this cast. The 5 or 6 feet of loose line which has been allowed to slip through the guides during the maneuver of bringing the rod upstream, acts as a slide. If you did not allow the loose line to pass through the guides as you moved the rod upstream, you would pull the fly away from its intended target.

REACH CAST 2

REACH CAST 3

REACH CAST 4

5: Your flyline has landed considerably upstream from you. As your fly and line move downstream in a dead drift, follow the movement with the rod at the same speed as the current. This will enable your fly to drift drag-free, and at the same time allow you to have direct contact without any slack line, so that you can strike in the event of a rise.

6 and 7: These photos show the position of movement with the rod if the current was coming from left to right.

8 and 9: These photos show the executed positions of the rod if the upstream hold cast is made directly downstream.

Larry Solomon

REACH CAST 5

REACH CAST 6

REACH CAST 7

REACH CAST 8

REACH CAST 9

CHAPTER 3
How to Tie Your Own Flies

NOT TOO MANY years ago, flytying was considered a fairly difficult and mysterious art. There was very little literature on the subject, and few of the knowledgeable flytiers of the time were inclined to share their knowledge. It was as if the art of flytying were almost deliberately being kept a secret.

Times have changed. There are more books on the subject of flytying today than on most of the major hobbies in the world. Suddenly it is no longer mysterious or secretive. Most importantly, we've learned IT IS NOT DIFFICULT. Anyone can learn to tie a highly effective fly pattern in a single evening.

Flytying is not only an end to a means, namely flyfishing, but also an end unto itself. Once you have learned the basics, you will find that you enjoy tying flies almost as much as fishing. It, in itself, becomes a rewarding, thoroughly relaxing, creative hobby. Its boundaries are as limitless as your own imagination.

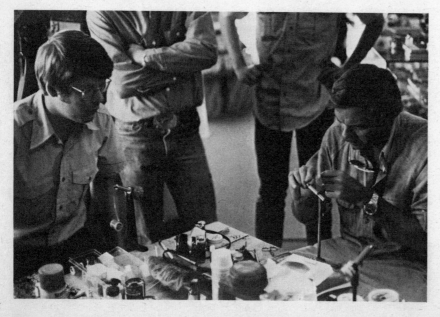

An experienced tier intrigues spectators.

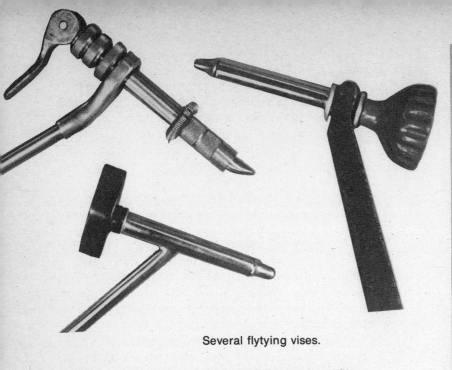

Several flytying vises.

Various hackle pliers.

Before we begin the actual basics of tying some flies, there are a few things you should know before you decide to go out and purchase the necessary tools, hooks and materials.

TOOLS AND MATERIALS

Any hobby or craft can be made easier if the proper tools are employed. A poorly constructed piece of equipment can be, to say the least, discouraging. You do not need many tools in order to tie your flies. However, the few that you will be using should be well made. They should not only perform the function they were designed for, but they should also last you a long time.

There are five primary tools you will need. They are:

1: VISE. The vise is designed to hold the hook on which you will be tying your materials. It should perform this function without slippage. A good vise will take hook sizes ranging from 1/0 to 28. The easiest, and fastest vises to use are those manufactured with a lever

Types of scissors used in flytying.

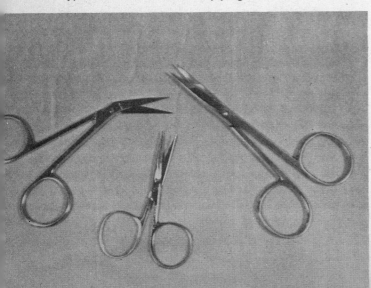

action, as opposed to a screw knob, that opens and closes the jaws. It should have a C-clamp which will allow you to raise or lower the vise to the desired height in addition to being able to offset the angle of the jaws for specialized flytying such as double hooks. A good vise will cost you approximately $15 to $30. (There are excellent higher priced models available, but those will depend on your individual budget.)

2: SCISSORS. The scissors should be sharp and finely pointed and approximately 3½ to 4½ inches in length. A good pair can be obtained for about $6.

3: HACKLE PLIERS. This item is used to hold the tip or butt of a feather as it is being wound on the hook shank. The way to test a good pair of hackle pliers is to insert a hackle feather between the plier jaws and try to pull it out. If the hackle breaks off, the pliers are good. If the hackle can be pulled out, the tool is inadequate. Some manufacturers serrate the inside jaws of their pliers. This may tend to cut the hackle. The best I've used are those originated by Herb Howard. Herb would serrate one side only and leave the other smooth. This type seemed to have the best gripping power. If you have a pair from which the hackle constantly seems to slip out, try putting a small rubber band around one of the hackle plier jaws, or use epoxy and cement a small rubber pad on the inside of one of the jaws. Hackle pliers are relatively inexpensive costing approximately $2.50 to $3.

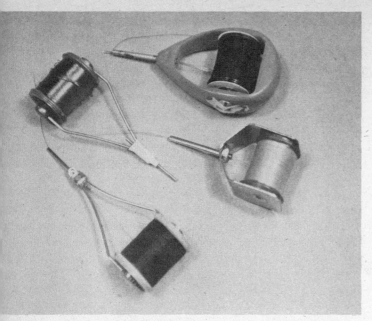

Different types of thread bobbins.

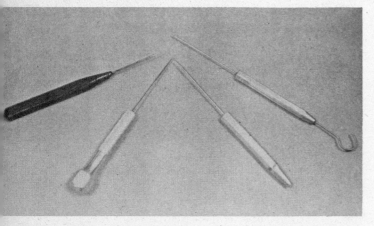

Various dubbing needles.

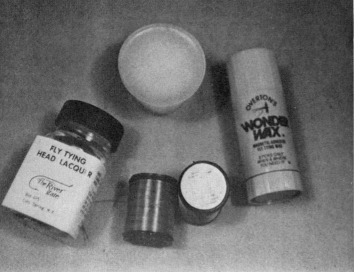

Other materials used in flytying — thread, wax and head lacquer.

4: BOBBIN. The bobbin is a device which has a metal tube at one end while the other end holds a conventional sized spool of thread. Both ends of the tube should be smooth so they will not cut your thread while it is being used. That part which holds the thread should be tension adjustable to allow for free unspooling of the thread. Some of the best I've seen are the Matarelli, Renzetti and S&M type bobbins. Prices range from about $2.75 to $5.25.

5: DUBBING NEEDLE. This tool is nothing more than a sewing needle embedded in wood, plastic or metal. The pointed end is used to pluck out dubbing fur on scraggly nymphs and poke out wayward hairs that have been accidentally tied down. It is also used to apply head cement to the head of a completed fly. Price on this item is nominal ($1-$2). If you want to take the time, you can make one for yourself using a sewing needle and a piece of wood.

Once you have the basic tools required for the proper tying of flies, you will also need various hooks and materials. You will also need such non-materials as thread, cement and wax. As you progress you will find that flytiers are an odd lot, and there is almost nothing that cannot be used in the art. To make a list here of all the items that can be used would take too many pages. Therefore we will cover the materials and items which you will be needing before the beginning of each fly.

I will briefly state, however, that many of the feather and fur materials used in flytying can be obtained at no cost at all if you know where to look. I have often made the statement, "If it flies or walks, it can be used for flytying." That does exclude lizards, frogs and snakes doesn't it? Every bird and animal, whether it is wild or

Much of the materials used for tying flies can be obtained while hunting, from friends who hunt or from animals killed on the road.

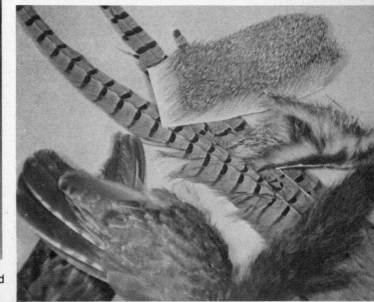

domestic has some plumage and hair or fur which can be utilized.

Do you hunt? Do you have friends that hunt? Do you know that all legally shot game such as pheasant, quail, grouse, ducks, geese, rabbits, deer, squirrels, and others are used in the tying of many of our flies. If you hunt, save every piece of feather and fur. If you do not, ask your friends who do hunt to save them for you.

Also if you do not hunt, there is one form of hunting you can do which does not require a license (please do check your state game laws on this) and that is what we flytiers call *road hunting*. All that is required is a good pair of eyes to spot an animal that has been hit by a vehicle along one of our roads. What you will usually find, depending on the region in which you live, are groundhogs (excellent material), squirrels, foxes, and various birds. The fur and feathers found on these animals will only rot away and be wasted unless you salvage the material. If you take a look in any catalog which lists the various feather and fur materials, you will see how much can be saved simply by picking up your own. You will have to skin, wash, stretch (tack up on a board) and dry each skin. Or, in the case of birds, pluck the plumage. (*Caution:* It is possible to contract rabies, lice and possible skin diseases from handling dead wild animals. Be sure and take the proper precautions, eg. wearing gloves, if you use this method to acquire flytying materials.)

Another area you will find a few free (or for a very small charge) scraps is your local taxidermist. Even common house pets such as cats and dogs have some material to offer. However, do your snipping selectively or whoever owns the pet may let you know in no

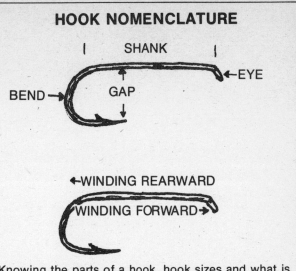

HOOK NOMENCLATURE

SHANK

BEND — EYE

GAP

← WINDING REARWARD

WINDING FORWARD →

Knowing the parts of a hook, hook sizes and what is meant by "winding forward" will help you when you begin to tie your flies. Hook sizes are designated by numbers with the numeral 1 in the center. Going up the scale, hook sizes become smaller as the number becomes larger. For example, size 28 would be the smallest in the following sequence: 1, 2, 4, 6, 8, 10, 12, 14, 16 18, 20, 22, 24, 26, 28. For larger saltwater or salmon hooks a reverse scale with a zero added is used. For example, a size 5/0 would be the largest in this sequence: 1, 1/0, 2/0, 3/0, 4/0, 5/0.

uncertain terms that he does not prefer Felix or Rover running around with bald spots.

Basically there are four types of classifications of flies—nymphs, wet flies, streamers and dry flies. The nymph patterns are designed to imitate a form of underwater insect—usually the immature stage of a mayfly, stonefly or caddisfly. The nymph is a sub-surface fly designed to ride on or just above the bottom of moving water. Most wet fly patterns are designed to imitate drowned insects and move with the current along the bottom. Streamer flies are a type of wet fly designed to imitate small fish and are again a sub-surface fly. As the name implies, dry flies are fished on the surface of the water and designed to imitate various insects.

HOW TO TIE A NYMPH

If you have come this far, it's fairly certain that you at least intend to try and tie your own flies. And, we shall assume you have purchased, or borrowed, the proper tools for the purpose.

The best way to start flytying is to select a pattern that will be relatively simple yet one you will be able to fish with. The pattern I've selected is called the *Gold Ribbed Hare's Ear*. It can be tied both as a wet fly or a nymph. We'll tie the nymph version first. This pattern, incidentally, is perhaps the most popular of all sub-surface imitations fished in the United States. Take my word for it, you will take trout and other fish with it even if your casting is not what it's supposed to be and your

Some different hook types. Clockwise from 12 o'clock — ring-eye, down-eye, up-eye, loop-eye.

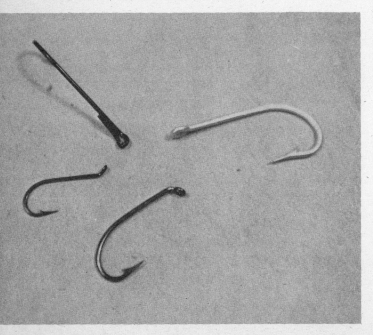

Shank length for flytying hooks can vary greatly. At the top is a turned up eye, 5X short shank hook. The middle hook is a turned down eye, 1X long shank hook. The hook on the bottom, best suited for tying streamers and bucktails, is a turned down, loop eye, 6X long shank.

Specialized flytying hooks. At top is a short shank, ball eye, heavy wire hook best suited for steelhead flies. In the center is a black finished, turned up, loop eye salmon hook traditionally used in tying Atlantic salmon patterns. At the bottom is a ringed eye, long, humped-shank hook made especially for building bass bugs. The hump prevents the bug body from twisting on the hook shank.

Turned down eye, sproat bend hooks—3X long shank above, 1X long shank below. These are excellent wet fly and nymph hooks.

Turned down, ball eye, sproat bend hook is shown on the left. On the right is a turned up, tapered eye, model perfect. The left hook is usually preferred for wet flies and the right hook for dries.

Flytier's Glossary

Barb—Needle sharp projection facing opposite direction of hook point to keep fish from escaping.

Bend—Round part of hook curving from shank to barb and point.

Bobbin—Device that holds spool of tying thread controlling feed of thread through a narrow tube.

Body—This is the part of the fly tied on the shank of the hook. It is made of various materials such as floss, wool yarn, tinsel, chenille, fur, hair or combinations of two or more of these materials.

Butt—Made of wool or chenille tied on at end of shank just before the bend of the hook. Also called an egg sac by many tiers.

Cement—Usually thick, fast drying lacquer used to secure the tying thread, chenille, wool, tinsel and other materials to hook.

Chenille—Looks like a caterpillar without legs. It is made by weaving silk or rayon fibers between two threads. It comes in many colors and is used for the body on dry or wet flies or nymphs.

Egg Sac—Extra piece of wool or chenille tied on hook at the end of the shank just before the bend. Is of larger diameter than body. Also called the "Butt."

Eye—Round loop at the end of the hook used to attach leader or line.

Floss—A loosely woven thread having a high lustre. Furnished on small spools of two or four strands. Two or four strands unwind at the same time. Used mainly to build up fly body of all types of flies.

Fur—Used for fly bodies. Usually comes from small animals such as rabbits, moles, badgers, beavers, muskrat and others. Some animals like beavers and badgers provide both hair and fur, the fur coming from an area close to the skin.

Hackle—A small, but long and narrow feather from the neck area of domestic fowl or wild ducks, geese or upland birds. It is tied into a fly pattern just behind the eye of the hook. The tip is tied to the shank of the hook and then the rest of the feather is wound around it and secured with a half hitch and cement. The hackle is also used on the body of a woolly worm being interwrapped with chenille along the entire length of the shank. Most flies, both wet and dry, have a hackle of some kind.

Hackle pliers—A small clamp type tool for holding hackles or thread in an out-of-the-way position while working on another part of the fly.

Half-hitch—A simple loop made with the tying thread to hold it in place without cutting the thread. It allows the tier to continue wrapping the same thread to secure other parts of the fly.

Hair—Stiff bristly fibers from polar bears, deer, squirrels, moose, calves, badgers or skunks. Used mainly for wet flies or streamers.

Head—Area just behind the eye of the hook made with several wraps of the tying thread. It is either cemented or lacquered.

Lacuer—A fast drying, clear synthetic liquid having a high cellulose content. Used as cement when thick, as a paint when thinned and colored.

Legs—Made from thick bristles or rubber strips to imitate insect legs.

Ribbing—Usually made with tinsel. Is wrapped leaving spaces between turns. Applied to body of fly often over wool or chenille.

Shank—Part of hook between eye and bend.

Silk—Tying thread. Sometimes nylon thread is used.

Tag—Tied on rear end of hook at the start of the bend. Made of wool or tinsel.

Tail—Three or four hairs tied at rear of hook. Extends from one-half to one inch to the rear of shank.

Thread—Same as tying thread. Made of silk or nylon. Used to attach most parts of a fly pattern.

Tinsel—Flat metallic tape in gold or silver and other colors. Comes in widths from 1/16- to 3/8-inch.

Vise—Tool used to clamp hook in position at convenient working height.

Wax—Beeswax or paraffin wax. Used to coat the thread and make it adhere lightly to hook.

Wing—Part of fly made to imitate insect wings. Made from hair or from actual sections of wing feathers.

Wool—Yarn like that used in knitting. Used to make fly bodies by wrapping around shank of hook.

A flytier's table showing the results of some good work.

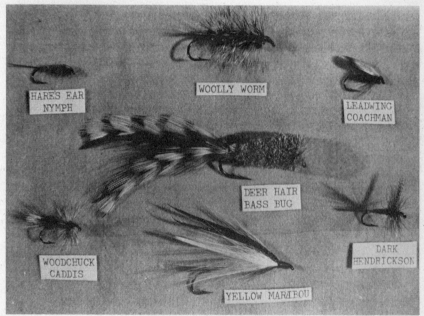

HARES EAR NYMPH

WOOLLY WORM

LEADWING COACHMAN

DEER HAIR BASS BUG

WOODCHUCK CADDIS

DARK HENDRICKSON

YELLOW MARABOU

Here are seven patterns which you will be shown how to tie in step-by-step construction in this chapter.

knowledge of the water is still to be learned. It is a highly effective fly.

In addition to our tools we shall need the following items:

1 bottle of head cement to be used when the fly is completed
1 spool of black (or brown) thread size 4/0
1 cake of wax
1 pack of hooks Mustad Model No. 9671 size 12
1 piece of hare's mask dubbing (You can substitute chipmunk or red fox squirrel skin.)
1 brown hackle neck (or loose feathers of the same color from a rooster)
1 spool of fine oval gold tinsel
1 pair of duck quills from a mallard, pintail, widgeon (or any other duck having gray wing feathers)

The hook you will be using, the Mustad Model No. 9671, is a heavy wire hook slightly longer than standard. It is designated as 2XL, which means 2 Extra Long. The reason we're using a longer shanked hook is because the insect form that we are imitating has a long body.

Place the hook in the jaws of the vise so that the barb and point are covered. (Once you become advanced and have tied a number of flies you can leave the point and barb exposed.) The hook should be perfectly horizontal.

I've recommended a size 4/0 thread which is slightly thicker than the 6/0 size most commonly used. Novices have a tendency to break a finer thread because their fingers have not yet become educated in the proper tension application. After you've tied a few dozen flies, switch over to the finer 6/0 thread.

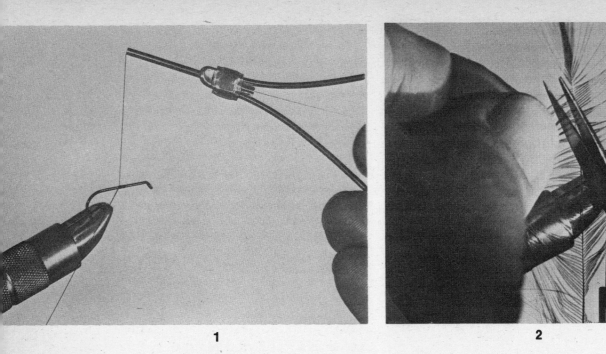

1

2

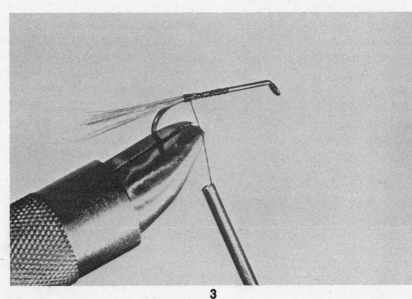

3

Holding the bobbin containing the thread in your right hand (all procedures are reversed if you are left-handed) wind the thread onto the middle of the hook shank and also over itself. (Fig. 1) All turns of thread, with or without materials, should be made in turns going away from you. Wind the thread almost to the bend of the hook. Hook and thread are now in position to accept the first material which will make up the tail of our fly.

Hare's Ear Tail

The tail of this fly is made from the hackle fibers taken from the neck feathers of a brown rooster. Take one of the feathers and hold it by the tip. Stroke the fibers downward with the thumb and forefinger of your free hand so they stand out from the stem at a 90-degree angle.

With your scissors cut 6 to 8 fibers from the stem being careful to keep the tip alignment even. (Fig. 2) Measure them along the top of the hook shank so the tips extend approximately ⅜-inch past the bend.

Having determined the proper position, hold them between the thumb and forefinger of your left hand on top of the shank and bring your thread over and around them thus fastening them to the shank. Two or three turns of thread should do it. However, continue making turns of thread toward the eye of the hook until you have reached the bare shank of the hook, then come back to your starting point. By taking turns off the area of a material that you are tying in, you will lock the fibers in place since the thread now has secured itself to another area. (Fig. 3) The thread should be left hanging at the first point you started to tie down the tail.

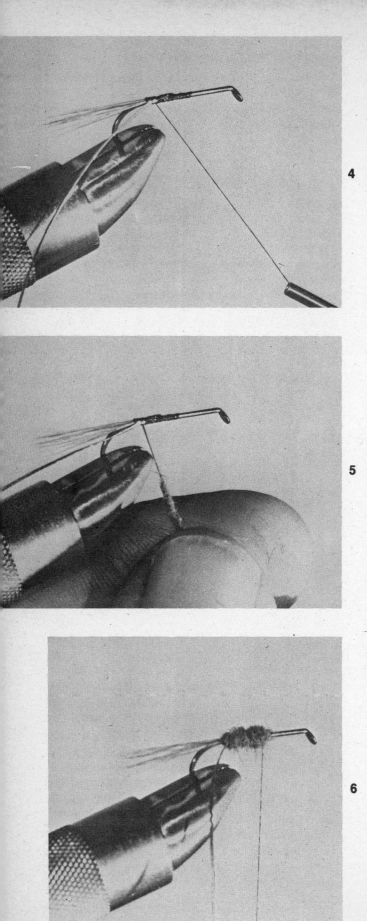

Hare's Ear Body and Rib

The next item of material to be tied in is the rib which consists of a 4-inch section of fine oval gold tinsel. (Oval tinsel is nothing more than a fine metal wound over a cotton core.)

4 Cut a 4-inch section of tinsel from your spool and tie it in to the hook shank where you left off with the tail. Once it has been secured forget about it. We won't be tying in the tinsel until the body has been finished. (Fig. 4)

The body of this pattern is made from the fur and hair of an English hare. You can substitute the hair and fur from a chipmunk or a red fox squirrel. What you should be looking for is a coarse type of fur which has both soft fur and guard hairs mixed in.

(**Note:** What flytiers refer to as *DUBBING FUR* usually means the soft fur which comes from the inner skin of an animal. When they refer to *HAIR,* it means the outer fur which is made up of actual hair type fibers, some long, some short, depending on the animal.)

When tying a pattern like the Gold Ribbed Hare's Ear, I like to cut some of the softer fur from the lower face and some of the short stubby guard hairs found on the ears. Mixed together they give the fly a very scraggly appearance. Prepare a small amount of this

5 hare's fur mixture and lay it aside.

You will now need that cake of wax we mentioned earlier. In this instance, the stickier the wax, the better because of the coarseness of the fur involved.

Take your cake of wax (an excellent type is the Overton Wonder Wax which comes in a large deodorant type of tube) and apply a liberal amount of the wax to your thread.

Now take a very small amount of the hare's fur you've prepared and spin it onto the thread. You will have to hold the bobbin thread tautly (not tightly) as you do this. Spinning fur onto thread is accomplished by holding the fur on the thread with your thumb and forefinger and slipping your finger off your thumb while using tension. Have you ever snapped your fingers to make that clicking sound? Use exactly that maneuver using your left or right hand. One important point, and that is, when tying a fly always spin in one direction only. (Fig. 5)

As you spin the fur onto the thread try to keep the

6 section of thread nearest the shank in a thinner coat of fur. This will help your taper. Spin only about a 1-inch section of thread with your fur.

When you have spun (or "dubbed") fur onto the thread, take the thread and wind it around the shank of the hook toward the eye. (Fig. 6) The idea is to fill two-thirds of the hook shank from the bend toward the eye with fur. The furred thread should have a gradual taper enlarging as it approaches the foreward area. Exactly as if it were a natural insect.

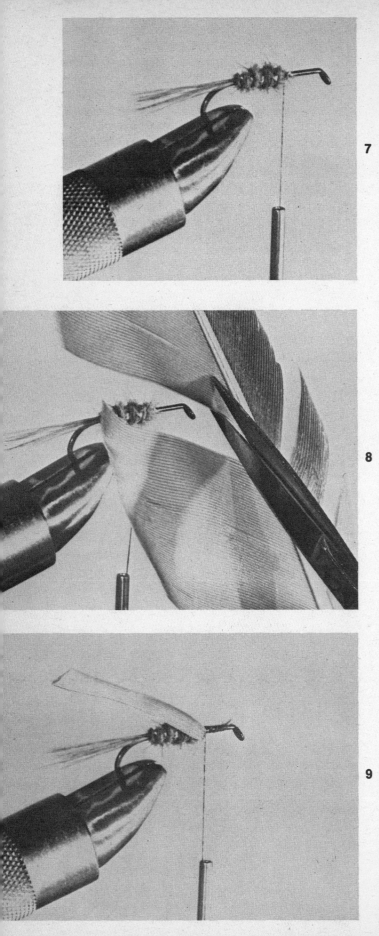

When you reach the area one-third before the eye of the hook, allow your thread to hang from its bobbin and forget about it for now.

Go back and grasp that section of oval tinsel which you tied in previously and in an oval spiral wind it to where the thread has been left hanging. Upon reaching the thread, take the thread and tie down the oval tinsel. (Fig. 7) Cut away any excess tinsel with your scissors.

Hare's Ear Wing Case, Thorax and Legs

The wing case on a nymph represents that part of an insect from which the undeveloped wing will eventually emerge. It appears to be somewhat of an elongated lump. In our pattern the wing case is tied in first and formed later. The wing case can be made from a number of types of wing quill section. The most commonly used is that taken from a mallard duck.

Take a mallard duck flight feather (or widgeon, pintail, or other natural gray duck quill, or gray goose wing quill for that matter) and cut a section from it measuring approximately $3/16$-inch in width. (Fig. 8)

Lay it on top of the hook shank with the tip end toward the eye of the hook. The underside (shiny side) should be facing up. Tie it down with your thread. (Fig. 9) Forget about the wing case section for now.

At this stage of our operation we have to build the thorax area. This area is fuller and heavier than the rest of the body. (Again, to simulate the natural insect.)

Therefore, wax your thread, spin more hare's ear dubbing mixture on it and wind the thread around the fore third of the shank which has thus far been left uncovered.

When you achieve the fullness of that shown in the photograph wind your thread to a point just behind the eye of the hook. (Fig. 10)

10

9

Now go back and grasp that wing quill section previously tied in and pull it forward over the thorax and past the eye of the hook. Use your right thumb and forefinger to accomplish this.

While holding the wing case fairly tautly with your right hand digits take the bobbin with your left hand and wind a couple of turns of thread over the wing case section just in back of the hook eye to secure it in place. Once the wing case has been secured snip the excess butts protruding past the eye of the hook. (Fig. 11)

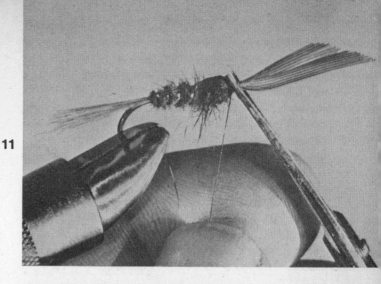

11

At this point we shall need to tie the thread off with a knot so that the fly does not unravel. The knot we will use is called the Half Hitch Knot.

Take a ball point pen with the writing portion retracted and hold it against the thread while you are holding your bobbin in your left hand.

Bring the thread around the pen for one complete turn. (Fig. 12) Now lift the pen and hold the hollow point of it to and onto the eye of the hook. Swing the bobbin to the left and allow the thread to slip off the pen onto the hook shank just behind the eye. Repeat this procedure three or four times. This is the simple Half Hitch Knot. Having made the number of knots required on this fly, cut away the remaining thread. Your fly is almost complete.

12

Pick up your dubbing needle and poke out some of the guard hairs and fur from under the thorax area (the fore third of the body nearest the eye). This plucking out of hairs and fur will give the semblance of legs and will make the fly move and vibrate when fished. (Fig. 13)

Once that has been accomplished all that is necessary is to use the same dubbing needle in applying a touch of varnish or head cement to the finished fly. This will assist in keeping the final thread windings secured. (Fig. 14)

You've just completed your first fly—a Gold Ribbed Hare's Ear Nymph. If it does not quite meet your own standards compared to the one in the photograph, don't hesitate to use it on the stream. This pattern, regardless of how it has been tied, will still take fish. In fact, the more scraggly it looks, the more effective it is.

13

Some fly-fishermen like to add weight to their nymphs. To achieve this effect it is a very simple matter to wind some fine lead wire onto the shank of the hook before beginning to tie the fly.

Should you desire to weight your nymph, the turns of lead wire on the shank should be closely adjoining and cover a distance that will give even distribution of weight between the bend and the eye. Once wire has been wound on the shank it should be liberally coated with head cement and the thread passed back and forth over it for additional security.

14

I might add here that it is sometimes better to weight your leader while it is being fished rather than the fly itself. Weighting the fly could slightly inhibit its movement and life-like action.

HOW TO TIE A WET FLY

Wet flies are also generally easy to tie. The first sample I've chosen is among the five most popular wet flies being fished today. It is taken by trout and other fish not only as a nymph but as a variety of larval insect forms. Other than the normal non-materials you will require are the ones listed in the following pattern description.

BLACK WOOLLY WORM (Tied in sizes 2-14)
HOOK: Mustad Model 38941 or 79580
THREAD: Black
TAIL: Red hackle fibers
RIB: Medium flat silver tinsel
BODY: Black chenille palmer with grizzly hackle
HEAD: Black

Many of our western tiers prefer this fly to be weighted because of the deeper water found in some of that country's wide and brawling streams. I suggest you first learn how to tie this pattern and then if you wish to add some fine lead wire to the shank, by all means do so.

The hooks used for this pattern are a little longer than standard because of the shape we are trying to imitate. Both the Mustad Model Nos. 38941 (3XLong) and 79580 (4XLong) are ideal and the most commonly used.

For our purposes we shall tie a size 6 Black Woolly Worm. Therefore, affix such a size and model hook in your vise. Spiral some thread onto the shank terminating at the end of the hook.

Woolly Worm Tail

For the tail we will be using a rooster neck hackle which has been dyed a bright red. Cut a few fibers from such a feather and tie them in on top of the shank so that the tips extend past the bend for approximately ¼-inch. The procedure here is exactly the same that you used to tie in the tail of the Gold Ribbed Hare's Ear Nymph. Upon completion the thread should be left hanging at a point just in front of the bend of the hook. (Fig. 1)

Woolly Worm Rib

Our flat silver tinsel rib is tied in first and wound through the body later. When you tie in this type of tinsel, which is to be used to form the ribbing through a body, always (after you have initially secured it to the hook shank) take a few turns of tinsel around the shank (in turns away from you) and then secure it with the thread. This will program the tinsel to wind in the proper direction when it is later needed.

Leave both the tinsel and thread dangling from near the bend of the hook. (Fig. 2)

Woolly Worm Body

Since the body consists of black chenille which is palmered (ribbed in an open spiral) with a grizzly saddle hackle feather, we must first tie in the hackle.

We've selected a saddle feather because it is generally longer than a neck hackle. A long neck hackle can also be used if the fibers radiating from the stem are not too long. A grizzly hackle is one which has white and black barring. It comes from a breed of chicken called the Barred Plymouth Rock.

Select a long saddle hackle and stroke it downward so that the fibers extend from the stem at right angles. Tie the tip of the hackle to the hook. You will have to separate the fibers near the tip so that you have a small area to use as your tie-in point. (Fig. 3)

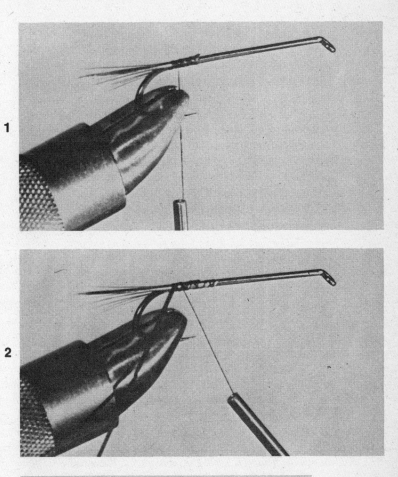

1

2

3

4

5

Wind your thread over the tip end of the hackle to secure it well and then cover it with thread along the shank of the hook as far as the tip lays forward toward the eye. Once it has been secured, bring your thread back to its starting point near the bend.

At this point you will have two materials, the saddle hackle feather and the tinsel, waiting in line to be used after the body has been wound on the shank. Before we begin with the chenille body, place a liberal amount of head cement on the hook shank. It will help hold the body in place more permanently.

Chenille comes in various sizes. It is designated in the following manner:

00—very fine
0—fine
1—medium
2—large
3—extra large

The larger the number, the larger the diameter of the chenille. For our hook size we shall use a 2, or large sized chenille.

Chenille itself is nothing more than fine rayon fibers wound on a cotton core. Before we tie our chenille to the shank of the hook it is a good idea to remove the rayon fibers from one end. This will expose the cotton core. We will need about a 5-inch section for our body.

Tie the chenille to the shank of the hook by winding the thread over the cotton core just exposed. (Fig. 4) When it has been secured to the shank, bring the thread forward in an open spiral and leave it hanging at a point just behind the eye of the hook.

Now go back and grasp the chenille, and in turns going away from you, wind it around the shank of the hook in closely connecting turns up to the thread. Tie it down with the thread and cut away the excess. (Fig. 5)

Go back and grasp the tinsel previously tied in and wind it in an open spiral to the thread. Tie it down also and clip the excess. (Fig. 6)

6

7

8

Go back one more time and grasp the saddle hackle previously tied in. If you can't handle it with your fingers only, attach a pair of hackle pliers to the butt end. This grizzly saddle hackle feather must be wound through the chenille body of the fly between the ribs of tinsel. Starting at the bend, the hackle should be wound up to the eye where the thread is waiting to tie it down. The easiest way I've found to do this is to force the hackle on its back during the winding process. In other words, the shiny side should face the chenille body. As you wind the hackle through the chenille you will find that the fibers spring out from the body. (Fig. 7)

Wind the hackle all the way to the thread. Tie it down

with the thread and snip off the excess butt. Take enough turns of thread around the area just before the eye to cover any exposed material while at the same time building a neat conical shaped head.

When the head has been completed whip finish or half hitch your thread and cut it. Place a dab of head cement over the thread windings. That does it for the Black Woolly Worm. (Fig. 8)

Should you desire to tie larger or smaller Woolly Worms, remember that the size of the chenille should be adjusted to the hook size. Woolly Worms can be tied in any color you want. Some of the most common are the yellow, brown and olive.

As far as classic wet fly patterns go, the Leadwing Coachman is right at the top of the list. It is also among the top five wet fly producers in the world. If I had my choice of only one wet fly, I would be hard pressed between the pattern we are now going to tie and the Gold Ribbed Hare's Ear. As a budding flytier it will give you additional techniques which will be useful in the tying of other wet fly patterns. The description reads thus:

LEADWING COACHMAN (Sizes 4-16)
HOOK: Mustad 3906
THREAD: Black
BODY: Peacock herl full
HACKLE: Brown
WING: Mallard duck or equivalent

You'll notice that this pattern is tied in a wide range of hook sizes. The larger sizes such as the 4, 6 and 8 are used primarily for night fishing—very effectively I might add.

Spiral some fine black thread onto the shank of a size 12 hook. Let the thread hang at a point almost, but not quite, to the bend.

Leadwing Coachman Body

From an eyed tail feather of a peacock (see description of the tail itself in the section dealing with the Yellow Marabou Streamer) pluck two fibers from just below the "eyed" portion of the feather. (Fig. 1)

Hold them by the tips and stroke them downward with your fingertips so the tiny flues extend from the fiber stem at right angles. Place the butt ends diagonally under the hook shank between the thread and the shank and tie them in. The butts should extend forward along the shank of the hook almost to the eye. In an open spiral wind the thread forward over the butts and then back once more to your starting point. Now bring your thread forward to a point just behind the eye of the hook.

Grasp one of the herls and wind it in connecting turns to the thread. The tiny flues should stand out from the shank. Upon reaching the thread with the first herl, tie it down.

Bring your thread rearward in an open spiral to the point where the other herl has been left waiting and then foreward once more to a point behind the eye. This will secure the first herl so that if the second, or outer one, is broken while fishing you will still have one herl to work with.

Grasp the second herl and wind it to the thread also in closely connected turns. Tie it down with the thread and clip away any excesses. (Fig. 2)

Leadwing Coachman Hackle

The hackle on this fly can be tied in either as a throat or a collar. The latter is the most commonly used, and since we will be tying a throat in the next fly, let's tie the collar style here.

Take one soft brown hackle feather from a rooster or hen on which the fibers will reach from the eye to the point of the hook after being tied in.

Hold the feather by the tip and separate the fibers on the stem at a point near the tip. Tie the hackle to the shank at that point on the hackle where the fibers have been separated. (Fig. 3) Wind the thread over the tip portion toward the eye to secure it and then back to your starting point. Clip the excess tip.

1

2

3

Grasp the hackle feather by the butt with your hand, or, if it is a short one, with a pair of hackle pliers. Wind the hackle around the shank toward the eye of the hook three times. Each turn should be forward of the first. As you make your turns stroke the fibers of the hackle rearward with the fingers of your left hand so that they slant to the rear.

Upon completion of the hackle turns hold the hackle up vertically from the hook with your right thumb and forefinger and tie it down with thread using your left hand. Two or three turns of thread should do it. Clip the excess butt feather.

Leadwing Coachman Wing

The wing of the Leadwing Coachman is made from the flight feathers of a mallard duck or a similarly colored duck. You will need one feather from the left wing and one from a right wing in order to have a matched pair. The best feathers to use are the third and fourth feathers in from the outer pointers. Cut a section of fibers from each of the feathers measuring slightly less than ⅛-inch wide. (Fig. 4)

Take the section of fibers cut from the left wing and place it along the far side of the hook shank. The concave side of the feather should be facing the shank. The tip of the feather should curve upward in mirrored relationship to the downward bend of the hook. (Fig. 5) Take one turn of thread over the quill section and let the weight of the bobbin hold it there.

With your fingers, or a pair of tweezers, whichever works better, place the second section of quill against the near shank of the hook and measure it so that is exactly the same length as the first. The concave side should also face the shank. (Both feathers are cupped against the hook shank).

When the second feather has been measured to match the first, hold both feathers in position with your left thumb and forefinger and remove the turn of thread used to hold the first in position. Both sections of quill should partly cover the body of the fly and partly ride above the hook.

Bring your thread over both feathers, down the far side, under and straight up the near side of the shank. Pull straight up. Take another turn of thread around the area. (Fig. 6) You may find that the feather on the far side has been crimped. If this happens, the next time you do it allow your thread to follow the natural curve of the quill section before you cinch up on it. Just a little practice will take care of this problem. Once the quill sections forming the wing have been secured clip the excess butts protruding beyond the eye.

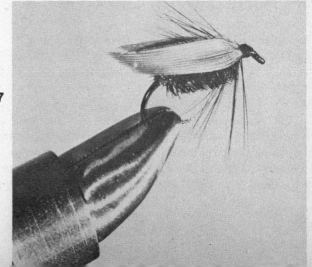

Finish the head of the fly with only enough turns to cover any exposed portions of quill. Try for a tapered but very small head.

Whip finish or half hitch the fly and apply a touch of head cement. Does it look like the one in the photograph? If not tie another. Eventually it will. (Fig. 7)

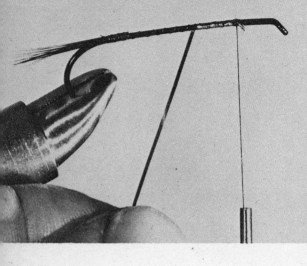

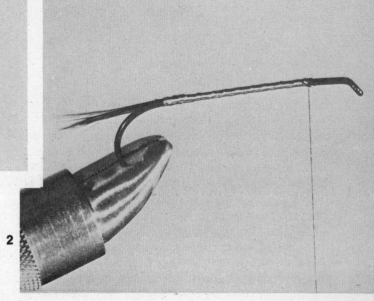

HOW TO TIE A STREAMER FLY

In order to catch fish with a streamer fly it is extremely important that it be presented properly. In this case that means the proper action must be imparted for any of these patterns to be effective.

There is only one streamer fly which, if fished improperly, will perhaps still be effective. That streamer is of the marabou type, regardless of color.

Marabou, by its very nature moves, undulates and pulses even while standing still in a stream. For our example we are going to tie a Yellow Marabou streamer. The pattern description is thus:

YELLOW MARABOU (Sizes 2-14)
HOOK: Mustad Model 9575
THREAD: Black
TAIL: Red hackle fibers
BODY: Flat silver tinsel or silver mylar tubing
THROAT: Red hackle
WING: Yellow marabou topped with peacock herl
HEAD: Black

The hooks used in most streamer flies are long—usually 1½ times longer than standard. One of the best hooks to use is the model number listed above simply because it has a looped eye. A looped eye hook is one on which the shank comes back on itself after forming

the eye. It will not cut a leader and will form a neater head.

Place a size 6 hook in your vise and spiral some black thread onto the shank terminating at the bend.

Yellow Marabou Tail

Here again, the tail consists of hackle fibers that have been dyed a bright red. Tie them in. Bring your thread forward to where the shank of the hook ends.

Yellow Marabou Body

Tie in a 10-inch section of flat (medium) silver tinsel at the point you left your thread hanging. (Fig. 1)

Wind it rearward toward the bend in turns going away from you. Each turn of tinsel should be directly next to the preceding one. They should connect, not overlap. Upon reaching the bend (you will be covering the butts of the tied-in tail fibers) reverse yourself and wind the tinsel back toward your starting point. Again, these should be connecting turns, not overlapping. Upon reaching the thread tie down the tinsel with four or five turns of thread. Cut away the excess tinsel with your scissors. Take a few more turns of thread over the area to cover any exposed tinsel butts. Place a touch of head cement on the windings. (Fig. 2)

Yellow Marabou Throat

From the same hackle feather you dyed red, cut the

4

3

same amount of fibers you used for the tail. These will be used for the throat of our pattern.

While bait fish, which is what we are imitating, do not have throats, the red hackle fibers coming from under the hook shank will give the impression of gills, or blood. They are effective.

Remove the hook from your vise and re-insert it into the jaws in an upside down position. Place the hackle fibers on the underside (which is now the topside) of the hook shank so that the fibers extend rearward for about ¼-inch. Tie them in with your thread.

As you take your turns of thread securing the fibers, take one or two turns of thread around the shank but *under the red hackle fibers* very closely to the first turns of thread. This will force the fibers upward.

Once the fibers have been secured clip the excess butts and reverse the hook to the normal position in your vise once more. Now the hackle fibers should be pointing downward. We have thus formed the throat of this pattern. (Fig. 3)

Yellow Marabou Wing

Marabou, which forms the main ingredient of our wing, comes from a turkey. These fluffy body feathers come in various sizes from short (1 to 2 inches) to long (4 to 6 inches). I personally prefer to tie all my marabou streamers with the short type since these seem to be undeveloped feathers which have no center stem. You

can actually tie a larger fly with the short "blood" feathers.

Select one such feather and measure it along the top of the hook shank so that the tips extend as far rearward past the bend as the tail does. Hold the feather in your left thumb and forefinger and secure it with your thread. Three or four turns should do it.

Now take two or three turns of thread over the shank of the hook but under the butt ends of the marabou just tied in. This will help wedge the material in place. Take two or three more turns over the marabou and hook shank.

Cut away the excess butts which protrude past the eye. However, when you do so, cut them just in back of the eye and at a slant toward the thread. (Fig. 4) The effect we are trying to get here is that of a tapered slope going downhill from the tie down area to the eye. This will allow you to build a neater head later.

To top off the wing and give it a little more resemblance to a bait fish, we shall need 5 or 6 strands of peacock herl.

A peacock eyed tail is a long brilliantly colored green bronze and gold feather which comes from the tail of a male peafowl. I'm sure you've often seen such feathers used as decorations or in floral arrangements. Most likely you've observed a few of these birds in a local zoo.

The fibers we require from this feather are those long

ones which begin somewhere below the eye. Do not use those within the first 2 or 3 inches just below the eye. Save this section for such patterns as the Leadwing Coachman, Royal Coachman, or any pattern which calls for use of peacock herl for the body. This section has fuller flued herl and is not as plentiful. Many tiers use what is sold as "Strung Peacock Herl" for their streamer wings since it is of the narrow variety.

Cut six of the peacock herl fibers and measure them along the top of the hook shank so that they extend past the bend the same distance as the marabou wing. Tie them in directly on top of the marabou. Clip the excess protruding past the eye. (Fig. 5)

Wind your thread around the shank in front of the eye so that it covers any exposed material while at the same time forms a neatly tapered conical shaped head. Whip finish or half hitch and cut away the thread.

Use a bottle of black lacquer and paint the thread head with it. Allow it to dry and give it a second coat. It should come out nice and glossy. That completes the Yellow Marabou Streamer. (Fig. 6)

(**Note:** An alternative to forming a very realistic body on marabou streamers is to employ the use of mylar tubing. Mylar tubing is a synthetic tinsel which is braided around a cotton core.

The idea is to cut a 1-inch or so section of the tubing [depending on the size fly you tie] and remove the cotton core with a pair of tweezers.

When the tail of the fly has been tied in, the mylar tubing is slipped over the eye of the hook and all the way to the bend where it is tied down with the thread. Incidentally, red thread is used for this procedure.

Once the tubing has been secured to the bend, the thread is cut after a whip finish knot or a few half hitches. Black thread is then tied to the fore end of the hook shank and the other end of the mylar tubing.

After the excess tubing has been snipped away, all processes follow in exactly the same manner as the conventional marabou tied above.)

Marabou streamers are tied in many colors, the most popular of which are yellow, black, white and yellow, and red and white and black. The multicolored ones give a nice effect and are as easy as the solids. You lay one section over the other for the effect you desire.

5

6

HOW TO TIE A DRY FLY

Thus far, the flies we have learned to tie are imitations designed to be fished beneath the surface of the water. Hence their names, *wet fly, nymph, and streamer*. A dry fly is designed to be fished on top of the water. Its name implies that it should float dryly, or, without becoming wet.

We both know that anything that is thrown into the water will become wet. In the case of a dry fly it is a matter of degree and a matter of what kind of water is being fished. For example, a sparsely tied dry fly may float like thistledown on the surface of the slow moving waters of a pool but be submerged in the faster currents of a riffle or rapids.

What makes one dry fly float better than another is the material that goes into its makeup. In addition to hooks made of lighter wire, we employ the use of feathers and furs, wherever possible, to assist the pattern in its buoyancy. We also specialize our construction for particular situations. It does get a little complex. However, don't worry about the entire picture at this time. The subtle changes you will be making in the future can be added as you progress in both tying and fishing. Actually, most of them are just plain common sense.

For now, what I do want you to remember is this. Always use a natural fur for the bodies of your dry flies. Though there are many synthetics on the market today in a great variety of colors, and many of these synthetics are easier to dub than natural fur, *don't use them for the body of a dry fly*. They do not float as well as natural fur,

feather fiber, or duck and goose down, regardless of how they are advertised.

I also do not recommend the use of synthetics for wings. There is something unnatural about them in addition to their misbehavior when being cast.

Nature has endowed us with more than enough material to produce any of the thousands of dry fly patterns ever devised by the flytier. Stay and tie with natural materials when tying a dry fly.

We have saved the tying of the dry fly for last for two reasons. (1) It is just a little more difficult than the flies you've already learned to tie. (2) It is a known fact that almost 90 percent of a trout's diet (or other fish for that matter) is found beneath the surface. Our intent in this brief treatise on flytying is not only to get you to tie your own flies but to take fish with them.

Strangely, though most of the food for trout is found beneath the surface (and it is easier to catch them that way), most of the flytying and fishing supplies sold are for the use of a dry fly. The reason for this is simple. Most of us prefer the excitement of seeing a trout rise and strike our lure. It is a visual thrill. You not only feel what's happening, *you see it*.

The first dry fly we are going to tie is not among the top 10 successful dry flies fished. I shall give you that list later.

Our pattern, however, does exemplify standard dry flytying procedure. It is also a much less costly fly to tie since it uses a light brown rooster neck for the hackle. The fly I am talking about is the Dark Cahill. Its pattern description is as follows:

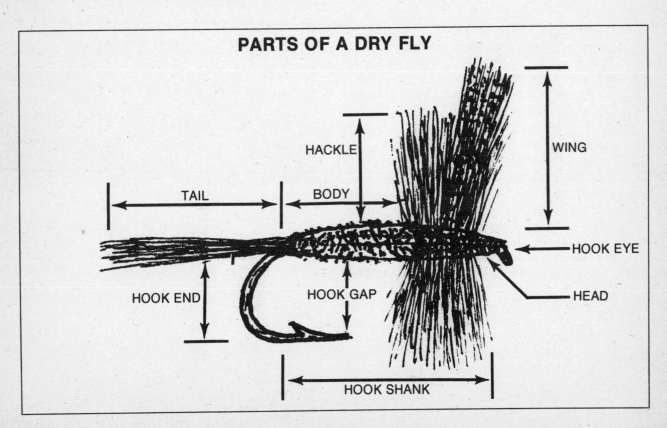

PARTS OF A DRY FLY

HACKLE

WING

TAIL

BODY

HOOK EYE

HOOK END

HOOK GAP

HEAD

HOOK SHANK

DARK CAHILL (Sizes 10-16)
HOOK: Mustad Model 94840
THREAD: Black
WING: Woodduck flank, or mallard flank dyed woodduck
TAIL: Dark ginger (light brown) hackle fibers
BODY: Muskrat dubbing
HACKLE: Dark ginger

The hook we are using for this pattern is manufactured with fine wire. It has less weight and will thus assist the materials tied upon it to float better. There are other models of dry fly hooks which are even finer. Some are designated as 1Xfine, 2Xfine and even 3X-fine. They will help float the fly even higher in the water but, except for the larger sizes (size 10 and down), I don't recommend them because they have a habit of straightening out on a good fish.

Clamp a size 10 hook in your vise. Spiral some fine black thread onto the shank commencing just behind the eye and winding ⅛-inch rearward. Bring the thread forward again for one or two turns so that it hangs from the thread base you've just formed.

(**Note:** At this stage of your flytying you should try using a size 6/0 thread. Your fingers will have gotten used to handling the 4/0 you used in the previous flies and should be able to handle the finer thread without breaking it. The 6/0 thread will take up less space while making the necessary turns. A thread I highly recommend is the one originated by Herb Howard and is now sold by various companies under the trade name of "Flymaster.")

Except for rare occasions, the wing of a dry fly is *always tied in first*. This is extremely important. The wing is the most difficult operation for almost any dry fly pattern, and it also sets up the proper proportion for the rest of the given pattern, regardless of the hook used. If you get the wing tied-in properly, the rest should follow quite easily.

Dark Cahill Wing

The wing of the Dark Cahill calls for the fibers from the flank feather of a male woodduck. Though some supply houses do list them, they are fairly scarce and rather expensive. (Some houses have listed them at 40¢ a pair.) I suggest you use mallard flank which has been dyed a lemon brown. This will look much like the color of a natural woodduck feather. Do this at least until you've become accustomed to tying this type of wing and you're lucky enough to procure some of the natural. Natural woodduck, incidentally, is often called "Fly Tier's Gold." (If you know any duck hunters, ask them to save you the skin or some feathers.)

Take one of the flank feathers and hold it between your right thumb and forefinger with the slightly convex (topside on duck) side facing you.

With your left thumb and forefinger bend the tips downward so that they are perfectly aligned. (Most such feathers have an oval curved shape and if you cut the fibers from the main stem the tips would be staggered unevenly.) When they have been aligned, cut a section of fibers from the feather measuring approximately ⅜-inch wide. (Fig. 1) The length of our wing should be as long as the hook shank.

Fold or roll the fibers so they form one solid clump and hold them on top of the hook shank so that the tips protrude beyond the eye of the hook.

Your left thumb and forefinger should be holding the clump of fibers and also be resting or slightly hugging the shank of the hook at that point from which the thread is hanging.

Grasp your bobbin with your right hand and bring the thread up along the pad of your thumb, over the hook shank, then downward against the pad of your forefinger, then under the hook shank and finally upward once more. Now pull straight up and tighten the clump of fibers against the shank. Take two or three more turns around the same area. You can now let go of the clump of fibers. (Fig. 2)

1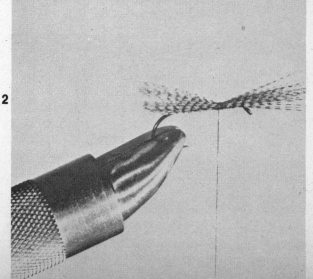

2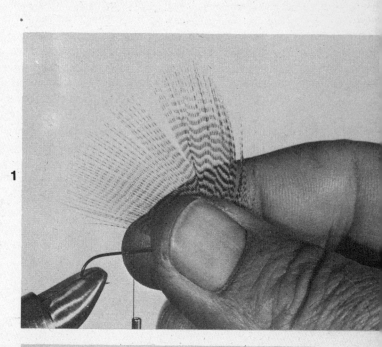

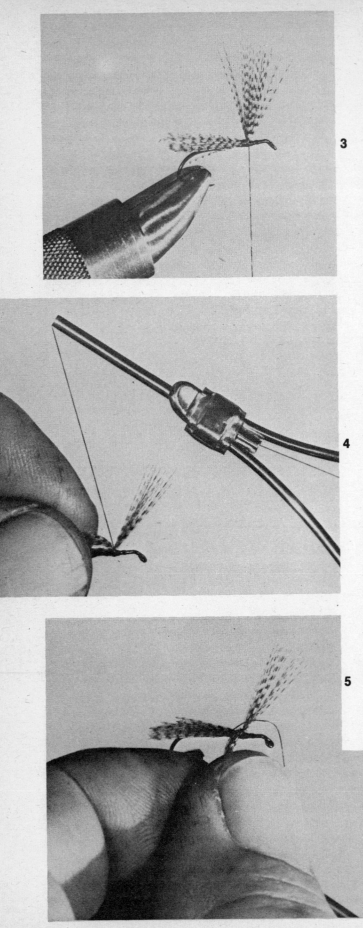

With your left thumb and forefinger lift the clump of fibers extending over the eye to a vertical position. With your right hand take enough turns of thread in front of the clump of fibers so they stand erect, or nearly so. (Fig. 3) The wing is now ready to be divided.

With your fingers separate the fibers in the vertical clump so there is an equal (approximately) amount on each side. Bring your thread through the division just formed. This is a diagonal movement from front to rear. (Fig. 4) Now bring it around and under the hook shank in back of the divided clump and then forward through the divided fibers once more. This is a diagonal movement from rear to front. (Fig. 5)

What you have just done is make a figure eight of thread through the clump of fibers, thus dividing them and forming what will now be called the wing.

Now bring the thread around the shank of the hook in back of the wings for one or two turns. The wing is complete and in place.

At this point the thread must be brought rearward so that we can tie in the tail. However, before we do so the excess butts of the clump must be cut.

When you cut the excess butts of the wing cut them at staggered intervals. This will form a natural under taper upon which you can build your body later. (Fig. 6) Once the butts have been trimmed, bring the thread to a point almost to the bend.

Dark Cahill Tail

The tail for the Dark Cahill is made from a hackle feather taken from the neck of a dark ginger (light brown) rooster.

It is prepared in the same manner as those you used in the previous flies. However, its length should be as long as the shank of the hook (or as long as the wing is high).

When it is tied in, the butt ends of the tail should butt up against the butt ends of the wing in order to make an even connection and lay an even foundation for the body which will follow.

For a size 10 hook you may have a little difficulty in obtaining a proper hackle length fiber. The long fibers are found along the sides of the rooster neck. A top grade Indian neck usually has more of the smaller hackles for tying smaller flies. These are good necks but lack some of the larger feathers needed for tailing a fly this size. Many supply houses have barrels or boxes containing large oddball cluckers. Most of them will be of the brown shade. Dig through some of these and pick yourself a couple of rooster necks just for tailing material. If you should also see some large creams or whites, take those also since they can be used for other patterns. Prices on these "barrel" necks should cost you no more than $1 or $2.

Tie in your tail. When it has been secured, bring your thread to the center of the shank and let it hang there. (Fig. 7)

Dark Cahill Body

The body of the Dark Cahill is made from muskrat underfur. If you don't have muskrat (easily obtainable) any medium gray fur will do.

The fur should be plucked from the skin and spun onto your thread. It will be much easier to dub than the fur in the first fly you tied because it is much smoother. You may find that some of the longer guard hairs seem to get in the way when you try to remove the underfur. Do what I do. First pull out the guard hairs from a small area and then pluck your underfur.

Use a very small amount of fur to spin on your thread. Keep the section of thread nearest the body very sparsely dubbed. (Fig. 8) When the thread has been spun with fur, wind it rearward toward the bend. Try to time your turns so that when you approach the point just before the bend that section of thread which has the start of dubbing upon it will be wound around the shank. What you are trying to do is obtain the narrowest effect of threaded fur at the rearmost section of the hook shank so that you will have the beginnings of a neatly tapered body.

Wind your thread forward to a point behind the wings, leaving a very small space in which the hackle of your fly is to be tied in. (Fig. 9) Let your thread hang at that point for now, because it is time to prepare your hackle.

Dark Cahill Hackle

The word *hackle* in a dry fly refers to the feather which forms the collar of fibers radiating from the hook shank in front and in back of the wing area. It is this hackle collar that primarily keeps the fly sitting upright on top of the water. When you hear advanced flytiers talk in terms of *good stiff hackle,* they mean that the fibers on the hackle feather itself are very firm and stiff. A soft hackle would bend or collapse under the weight of the hook. A stiff hackle would keep the fly sitting upright.

In addition to stiffness of fiber, the size, sheen and color are also important. You will pay more for a top grade hackle cape* than a second or third rated one.

How can you tell if a hackle cape is of good quality? When you pick up a hackle cape, bend it slightly with the fingers and thumb of one hand and hit the fibers with the fingertips of your free hand. It's a sweeping motion similar to brushing dust or ashes from a particle of clothing. If the feathers have bounce, that is, if they spring back rapidly, the fibers themselves are usually stiff. Look at the entire neck itself. Does it reflect light? Is it shiny? That usually indicates primeness. If it's the color you want, does it have the hackle sizes you need for tying your flies? For some tiers a number one neck is the kind that will tie a size range from 14 to 18. For another tier who is going salmon fishing his preference may be one containing sizes from 6 to 12.

The more rooster necks you look at, the better you will become in grading the necks you buy. So take every opportunity to look through as many necks as you can. Most reliable shops will allow you this privilege.

Some shops carry loose hackles in packets. I don't recommend these for dry flies because it is often very difficult to find the proper size hackle for the pattern you are tying. Generally the quality of these loose hackles is not up to standard. Some of the dyed ones which are sold in packets can be used for throats on wet flies and streamers, but that's about all they are really good for.

For our fly we will need a light brown (dark ginger) hackle feather which, when wound around the shank, will have a radius equaling three-quarters the length of the wing.

Some suppliers sell hackle gauges for measuring hackle size. A good one I know of is called the *Walt Dette Hackle and Wing Charts.* It not only measures hackle size but streamer wing length and upright wing length as well.

If you don't have a hackle gauge, all you need to do is hold one of the hackle feathers against the hook shank by the center stem and see how far out the fibers protrude.

Once you have located the area on your neck from which to pluck a size 10 hackle, remove two such feathers. Just pull them from the skin. Look at the hackle feathers themselves. Do you notice the *web* extending along each side of the feather shaft and gradually disappearing as it approaches the tip? *Web* is that softer more opaque portion shaped like a feather inside your feather. The wider the web, the faster the feather will soak up water.

At the point where the web begins to disappear (generally about half way up the feather on a good cape) cut the fibers from the center stem on both sides working toward the base. Do this with both feathers.

Many tiers strip these excess fibers with their finger tips. However, if you strip away the fibers as opposed to cutting them off, you leave a very smooth and slippery stem which has a tendency to pull out after you've tied them in.

Once you have prepared the hackle feathers lay them back to back (shiny side to shiny side) so that they flare away from each other. Excess butt ends should be trimmed so they are only ⅛-inch long.

Place both feathers against the shank of the hook with the butts pointing diagonally downward toward the eye. Take two turns around the hackle butts in back of the wing and two turns around them in front of the wing. Clip any excess butts at a point directly behind the eye. The dull side of one feather should be facing you and should be mirrored in the other direction by its counterpart. (Fig. 10)

10

---

*Hackle feathers come from the neck and back areas of various birds. Usually hackles are sold on the skin or as loose feathers in a packet. A hackle cape is the neck or back skin of a bird with the feathers intact.

With a pair of hackle pliers grasp the tip (including part of the center stem) of the hackle feather nearest you. Wind it around the shank of the hook in back of the wing so that the fibers stand directly out from the shank. If they should lean toward the rear don't be afraid to twist the pliers and the feather to make them behave the way you want them to.

On a size 10 hook you will need about 3 to 4 turns of hackle in back of the wing and the same in front. (It is better to have any unintended extra turns of hackle in back of the wings rather than in front of them.)

The turns of hackle are made so that one falls directly in front of the other as you work toward your thread which has been left dangling just behind the eye.

When the proper turns of hackle have been made, lift the hackle by the tip with your hackle pliers and bring two turns of thread around that section where it leaves the shank. In other words, tie it down. Clip the excess tip. (Fig. 11)

Go back and grasp the second hackle feather by the tip and wind it through the fibers of the first hackle. As you make your turns, give a little wiggling motion so

that the second hackle works nicely and snugly into the first. The second hackle will spread the fibers of the first hackle just a bit but that's what you want. When the proper turns have been made, tie the second hackle down also and clip the excess.

Whip finish or half hitch the head. (Do not build a head of thread on a dry fly. Only use enough thread to do the job.) Apply a touch of head lacquer to the windings. Your Dark Cahill is completed. (Fig. 12)

Because you have learned to tie the Dark Cahill (at little materials expense) you can now tie the following flies using exactly the same procedure. The only changes you will be making is the color of the materials. The flies you can now tie are: Light Cahill (second most popular fly used in dry fly-fishing), Light Hendrickson and Dark Hendrickson.

The one most popular fly throughout the United States is the Adams. Perhaps you've heard of it. You can also tie this pattern if you just add the tying technique called a *hackle tip wing*. Why don't we tie a hackle tip wing just so you can tie this highly effective pattern.

The pattern description for the Adams is as follows:

ADAMS (Sizes 10-18)
HOOK: Mustad 94840
THREAD: Black
WING: Grizzly hackle tips
TAIL: Grizzly and brown mixed
BODY: Muskrat dubbing
HACKLE: Grizzly and brown mixed

The wing of the Adams consists of two grizzly hackle feather tips. A grizzly neck as we've learned is from a chicken called a Barred Plymouth Rock. It is black barred with white.

Pluck two of the medium to large sized feathers from the middle of the neck. (Smaller hackle feathers slim down too much for a pronounced wing.) Place them back to back (shiny side to shiny side) so that they flare away from each other. Separate the fibers from the tip of the two feathers so that the tips will be as high as the hook shank is long.

With the tips protruding out over the eye of the hook place them on the shank which has been prepared with a base of thread (as with the Dark Cahill) and tie them in.

Once they have been secured to the hook shank lift the tips to a vertical position. You will notice that quite a number of fibers are protruding from the center stem and still laying almost flat along the shank. (Fig. 1) Cut these away with your scissors. Now take enough turns in front of the hackle tips to keep them propped erect.

Pass the thread through the two hackle tips in a figure eight. Don't be afraid to push and pull a bit on your hackle tips to make them sit properly divided. Bring your thread to a position just behind the wings. Clip the excess butts. (Fig. 2)

Take your dubbing needle and place a small drop of head cement at the base of the divided hackle tip wing. It will firm up the base but not lose the wing freedom.

Complete the rest of the fly according to the pattern description. It should look like the photograph. (Fig. 3)

There are other types of dry flies you will want to tie but certain other techniques will be involved. Build a library as you progress through the various stages and add these patterns to your repertoire.

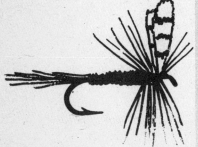

One rough water fly very similar to the Adams which you can tie with the knowledge you've gained already is the AuSable Wulff. Here the wing calls for the use of white calf tail. You will have to align the tips of these fibers before you tie them in but they are tied to the shank using the same technique as the Dark Cahill. It, like the Adams, is a universal producer. The pattern description reads thus:

AUSABLE WULFF (Sizes 8-18)
HOOK: Mustad 94840
THREAD: Fluorescent red
WING: White calf tail divided
TAIL: Woodchuck fibers from tail of woodchuck
BODY: Tan amber fur
HACKLE: Grizzly and brown mixed

One other standard type of dry fly you should be familiar with is an imitation of a caddisfly. Unlike a mayfly, the wings of a caddisfly lie flat along its body thereby presenting a different shape. Should caddisflies appear on the stream surface, we want to imitate this shape.

One of the simplest and most effective types of caddis imitations tied is the Hairwing Caddis. It can be made of deer hair, or mink, or woodchuck guard hair fibers.

My own personal favorite is that using the guard hairs of a woodchuck (groundhog). It is tougher than deer hair, floats as well or better and has more break-up in color than mink. Here is a pattern description:

CHUCK CADDIS (Gray) (Sizes 10-18)
HOOK: Mustad 94840
THREAD: Gray
BODY: Muskrat dubbing
WING: Guard hairs from the back of a woodchuck
HACKLE: Grizzly and brown

Chuck Caddis Body

Place a size 12 hook in your vise and spiral some fine gray thread onto the shank terminating at the bend.

Spin some muskrat fur onto your thread (exactly as you did for the body of the Dark Cahill) and begin winding it around the shank of the hook (Fig. 1) However, for the body of a caddisfly build the taper in reverse. In other words keep the thicker section of fur near the bend and taper to almost zero as you approach the head area. (Fig. 2)

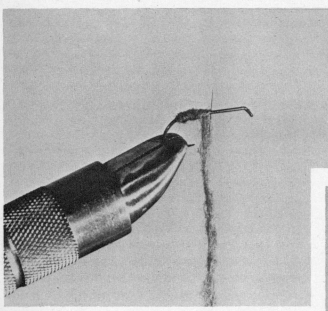

1

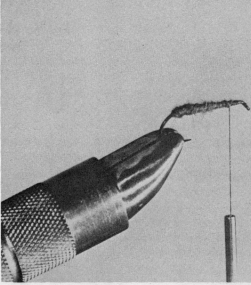

2

Chuck Caddis Wing

Our pattern calls for the use of woodchuck guard hairs. The hair fibers you want are those taken directly from the back of a groundhog. They are black with white cream tips.

The groundhog is readily available in many of our states and is a common "road-kill." It is also unprotected in many states. Therefore you should never have to buy any of this material if you keep your eyes open and are willing to do a bit of skinning, tacking and drying.

You will find that when you use the guard hairs of a woodchuck you will have little trouble aligning the tips. They seem to grow very uniformly. One little tip I will offer to you here. The hairs near the rear end of a chuck have shorter white tips than those from the middle back or shoulder region. The hairs with the narrow barred white tips should be saved for the smaller flies and those from the upper area for the larger ones.

Grasp a section of about 12 fibers from a piece of woodchuck. Align the tips first then cut the section from the hide. Try to keep the tips aligned evenly. Remove the softer underfur from the clump of hairs you have just cut.

Place the woodchuck fiber clump on top of the hook shank and measure it so that the tips extend approximately one-third of the hook shank length past the bend.

Tie them in. Incidentally, when working with silky hairs such as woodchuck and mink, it is always a good idea to place a drop of head cement on the base threads on which you tie in the hair. If you have tapered your body properly the woodchuck fibers should lay flatly on top of the hook shank. (Fig. 3)

Trim the excess butts extending past the eye to a point just before the eye. Cut them at an angle. This will allow for a smooth head later. Bring your thread rearward over the fibers to a point one-third of the shank from the eye. (Fig. 4)

Chuck Caddis Hackle

In this case our hackle will not be wound on a bare shank. It will be wound over the base of the woodchuck fibers. Because the woodchuck fibers have already been tied in, the diameter of the hook shank and fiber base upon which we will wind our hackle will have expanded. Therefore the hackle you should tie on a size 12 caddis should be a standard size 14.

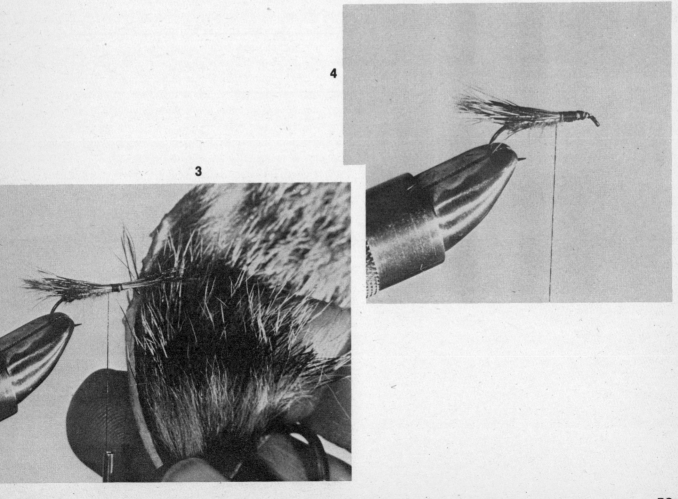

Pluck one grizzly and one brown hackle feather from their respective necks (of equal size in fiber length) and tie them in where you left your thread. (Fig. 5)

This time you will not have a wing to work around. You simply wind the hackle so that it radiates from the hook at right angles. First the one, then the other through it in conventional manner.

Clip the excesses and whip finish or half hitch your thread. A touch of head cement completes the fly. (Fig. 6) Easy, wasn't it?

The particular caddisfly you've just tied can be var-

ied in body color to match a natural on the stream. Some of the ones used are black, olive, yellow and brown in addition to the gray bodied one just tied.

Strangely, my favorite of all is one tied with a dirty orange (medium gray fur dyed orange) body color. While it does not seem to imitate any insect in particular, it works best as an all-purpose pattern.

Hook sizes are also changed to match any of the naturals. Frankly, the hook size is more important than the body color. In all instances the wing and hackle shades remain the same.

With a reasonable amount of practice you should be able to tie the few flies that have been featured in the preceding pages. The techniques acquired during the processes of their construction will also allow you to tie quite a number of other patterns listed in this and other books. The key word, however, *is practice*. There is not a one of us who does not have the time to tie at least two or three flies each day. If you can do that, you will be well on your way to a rewarding and enjoyable hobby.

5

FLIES FOR BASS FISHING

While all of the flies you have learned to tie in the preceding pages can be used for bass (and definitely for panfish), there are times you will wish you had something bigger, something that resembles the large spinning lure and casting plugs that so often take a trophy specimen. Another reason for having an out-size fly or bug is to prevent many of the smaller fish from taking it before a good bass has a chance.

For the fly-fisherman the answer lies in the tying and shaping of what is called a *deer hair bug*. Deer hair bass bugs can resemble anything you want them to though generally they are tied to imitate mice, frogs and large tadpoles. One of my own favorite, resembling a cross between a mouse and a blunt faced tadpole, is the Pusher Bug. It is easy to tie, and although it is made of deer hair, you can pop it through the water like a conventional cork popper. Let's tie one.

6

PUSHER BUG (Sizes 1/0 to 4)
HOOK: Mustad 7948A or 7957B
THREAD: Gray, size 2/0
TAIL: Two hackle feathers on each side of shank from bend (1 each grizzly and dyed red)
BODY: Natural gray deer hair trimmed to shape

The hooks I've selected here are made of heavier wire, similar to the wet fly and nymph hooks used earlier. However, they have a slightly deeper gap, which is a preference on my part because of the nature of fly tied and fish sought. Actually, you can use most other hook models of the same size and shank length.

Our thread is gray simply because it matches the color of the deer hair, and won't tell on you if you've made any mistakes in spinning the deer hair.

Pusher Bug Tail

Place a size 2 hook in your vise. Spiral your gray 2/0 thread onto the shank beginning just before the bend and wind to the bend. (It is easier to spin deer hair on a bare shank than one which is covered with thread or materials.)

Select a pair of grizzly hackle feathers which are fairly wide and at least 3 inches long. Also select a pair of hackle feathers which have been dyed red. It does not matter if the feathers come from the neck or saddle, cock or hen, as long as they are fat and long enough for the job.

Trim the excess fibers from the center stem working toward the butt. This is exactly the same method you used to prepare hackles for a dry fly. Your completely trimmed feathers should be 1½ inches long.

Place one red feather against one grizzly feather. They should snug against one another. Tie this pair as a unit to the far side of the hook shank with the grizzly hackle as the outer feather. (Fig. 1) Tie the remaining two feathers onto the near shank so that they mirror the first two. Trim the excess butts. Secured butts and thread should not occupy more than ⅛-inch of space from bend forward. (Fig. 2)

Pusher Bug Body

The spinning of a deer hair body can be fun. That is, after the method has been practiced and mastered. Therefore, though it may be a little frustrating at the start, be persistent. The rewards far outweigh the learning process.

The reason we use deer hair (and also caribou and antelope) is the fact that it is hollow. When you tie deer body hair to a hook shank, the thread which compresses the fibers, causes it to flare. We want to use this fact to our advantage and make the hair flare, or spin, completely around the hook shank.

Cut a section of fibers 1/16-inch thick from the base of a piece of deer hide. (The hair must come from the back of the deer. Tail and leg fibers are not as hollow and will not flare too well.)

Remove the fuzz from the butt end section of the fibers by poking the points of your scissors through them, or use a fine toothed comb and comb them out. (Fig. 3)

Trim the tips from the clump of fibers you've just cut. You won't need them. All you should have left is a section of fibers approximately ¾-inch long.

1

2

3

Lay them directly on top of the hook shank. Bring the thread over them, under the shank and pull straight up. The fibers will flare. However, they will not flare all the way around the shank because of the thread and feather butts on that portion of the shank. (Fig. 4) Bring the thread through the flared fibers and down the far side. Let it hang there for now.

Cut another section of deer fibers of the same size. This time hold them under the hook shank in exactly the same area behind the bend and bring your thread up the near side, over the shank and pull down on the far side. What you are doing is filling in the bare space under the shank of the hook. Grasp the flared deer hair with the fingers and thumb of your left hand and hold them rearward while you take two turns of thread directly in front of them.

If you have not completely covered that section of hook shank which has a base of thread and feather butts, you will have to add more deer hair using the methods just described.

Once you have only a bare shank to work upon we are ready for the spinning of deer hair for a full 360 degrees around the shank. To spin deer hair on a bare shank cut a section of deer hair fibers just slightly thicker in diameter than those used before. (You will know exactly how much to use after you've tried it a few times.) This time place the section of fibers diagonally on the shank of the hook. Take two loose turns of thread around the hair and the shank and pull the thread taut. (Fig. 5) *Don't stop but continue winding* two or three more turns of thread through the hair fibers that have begun to flare and radiate around the shank.

When you make this maneuver, it will feel as if the hair is going to slip and pop and fly all over. It won't as long as you make one continuous motion winding the thread around the shank.

After the additional two or three turns of thread through the fibers you will notice that the hair has stopped spinning. At this time grasp the flared fibers, hold them rearward with your left thumb and fingers and bring your thread directly in front of them. Take two turns of thread directly in front of them.

Apply a touch of head cement to the fibers where the thread was left hanging. Cement should be applied after every two sections of fibers have been spun on the shank.

Repeat the process and add another section of spun hair in front of the ones just spun on. When you have completed this section of fibers, place your left thumb and fingers on top and around the hook shank at the bend and press them against the shank. Use your right thumb and forefingers and push the flared fibers at the fore end rearward. In other words, compresss the fibers so they form a tighter unit. (Fig. 6) Many tiers use the casing of a ball point pen to accomplish this packing of deer hair.

The pushing and packing of deer hair should be done with every alternate two sections of deer hair when the head cement is not applied. For example, after you've spun one section of deer hair, apply head cement, after the next, push and pack, after the next, cement and so on. Keep building the shank with spun deer hair until the entire shank has been covered.

Upon reaching the eye of the hook whip finish or half hitch your thread and cut it away. Place a final drop of head cement on the thread windings. (Fig. 7) You now have one fluffy puff ball resembling nothing. It will have to be shaped.

Remove the deer hair puff ball from the vise. Hold it upside down and with a pair of scissors trim most of the fibers from the bottom. That section of fibers on the bottom of your fly should be trimmed fairly close to the shank so that when it is fished it will not only ride upright but also give you enough gap clearance to strike the fish properly.

Now place the blunt edge of your scissors against the feather tail and cut the fibers in front of the tail. If you keep the blunt edge of your scissors against any material you don't wish to cut, you won't cut them accidentally. Work around the bend of the hook clearing the fibers in that area. In other words try to free the tail feather area. (Fig. 8)

Angle your scissors and trim the rest of the fibers of the bass bug body to a cone shape with a blunt head. Trimming a deer hair body is akin to sculpturing. The idea is to cut away that material which does not resemble the intended finished object.

When your trimming has been completed your bass bug should appear something like the one in the photograph. (Fig. 9) If it does not, don't be concerned. It will fish just as well as one tied by a professional. Each attempt you make will be an improvement. Again, the most successful ingredient in flytying is *practice, practice, practice.*

Once you have mastered the technique of spinning deer hair, you can be as creative as your imagination. Color, shapes and sizes can be varied and the nice part is that all of your creations will catch fish.

7

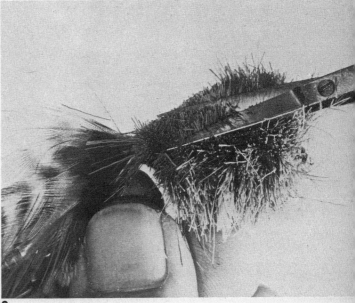

8

9

SOME POPULAR FLY PATTERNS

The list that follows describes the pattern recipes for some of the more popular fly patterns used today. You will be able to tie many of them using the techniques acquired in the preceding pages. Some of them, however, will require other methods and processes not covered. For that information I've recommended a few books on the subject which will complete (almost so) any knowledge you wish to add to your repertoire. If your budget allows, purchase these books one at a time, absorb their contents slowly and proceed as far as you wish.

DRY FLY PATTERNS

BLACK GNAT (Sizes 12-18)
HOOK: Mustad 94840
THREAD: Black
WING: Mallard duck quill
TAIL: Black
BODY: Beaver or mink dyed black, or black mohlon
HACKLE: Black

BLUE WINGED OLIVE (Sizes 12-18)
HOOK: Mustad 94840
THREAD: Olive
WING: Pale dun hackle tips
TAIL: Dark dun
BODY: Olive gray muskrat or beaver
HACKLE: Dark dun

BROWN BIVISIBLE (Sizes 10-16)
HOOK: Mustad 94840
THREAD: Black
TAIL: Brown
BODY: Brown hackle palmered length of hook shank and collared with white hackle

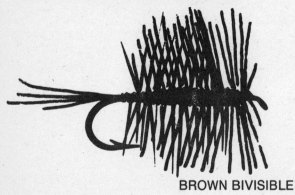

BROWN BIVISIBLE

CREAM VARIANT (Sizes 12-16)
HOOK: Mustad 94836 or 94838
THREAD: Cream
WING: None
TAIL: Dark cream hackle fibers
BODY: Quill stem from cream rooster
HACKLE: Dark cream hackle tied oversize

DARK HENDRICKSON (Sizes 12-18)
HOOK: Mustad 94840
THREAD: Gray
WING: Woodduck flank
TAIL: Medium dark bronze dun
BODY: Muskrat
HACKLE: Medium dark bronze dun

DUN VARIANT (Sizes 12-16)
HOOK: Mustad 94836 or 94838
THREAD: Olive
WING: None
TAIL: Dark dun
BODY: Red quill stem from furnace neck
HACKLE: Dark dun

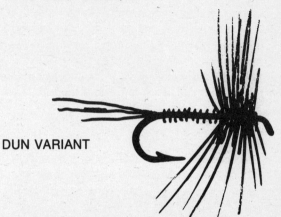

DUN VARIANT

FEMALE BEAVERKILL (Sizes 12-16)
HOOK: Mustad 94840
THREAD: Gray
WING: Mallard duck quill or equivalent
EGG SAC: One turn of extra fine yellow chenille
TAIL: Dark ginger
BODY: Muskrat
HACKLE: Dark ginger

GINGER QUILL (Sizes 12-18)
HOOK: Mustad 94840
THREAD: Yellow
WING: Mallard duck quill or equivalent
TAIL: Golden ginger
BODY: Stripped peacock quill
HACKLE: Golden ginger

GINGER QUILL

GRAY FOX (FLICK) (Sizes 12, 14)
  HOOK: Mustad 94840
  THREAD: Primrose (Pale yellow)
  WING: Mallard flank
  TAIL: Golden ginger
  BODY: Fawn colored red fox fur
  HACKLE: Light cast grizzly and golden ginger mixed

GRAY FOX VARIANT (Sizes 12-16)
  HOOK: Mustad 94836, 94838
  THREAD: Primrose yellow
  WING: None
  TAIL: Golden ginger
  BODY: Quill stem from dark cream rooster neck
  HACKLE: Golden ginger, dark ginger and grizzly mixed and tied oversized

HUMPY (Sizes 10-16)
  HOOK: Mustad 94840
  THREAD: Red
  TAIL: Deer hair natural gray/brown
  UNDERBODY: Red floss
  BODY: Natural deer hair pulled over
  WING: Deer hair
  HACKLE: Brown and grizzly mixed

HUMPY, EASTERN (Sizes 12-16)
  Same as above except that woodchuck guard hairs are used in place of deer hair.

IRRESISTIBLE (Sizes 10-16)
  HOOK: Mustad 94840
  THREAD: Gray
  TAIL: Woodchuck guard hairs from back of animal
  BODY: Natural gray deer hair clipped and shaped
  WING: Woodchuck guard hair
  HACKLE: Brown and grizzly mixed

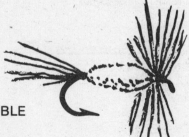

IRRESISTIBLE

LIGHT CAHILL (Sizes 10-18)
  HOOK: Mustad 94840
  THREAD: Yellow
  WING: Woodduck flank
  TAIL: Dark cream to golden ginger
  BODY: Creamy red fox, cream fitch (polecat) or cream opossum
  HACKLE: Dark cream to golden ginger

LIGHT HENDRICKSON (Sizes 12, 14)
  HOOK: Mustad 94840
  THREAD: Gray
  WING: Woodduck flank
  BODY: Urine stained fox belly, or equivalent
  TAIL: Medium bronze dun
  HACKLE: Medium bronze dun

LITTLE SULFUR DUN (Sizes 16, 18)
  HOOK: Mustad 94840
  THREAD: Yellow
  WING: Pale dun hackle tips
  TAIL: Dark cream (straw)
  BODY: Creamy yellow fitch or opossum
  HACKLE: Dark cream

MARCH BROWN (Flick) (Sizes 12, 14)
  HOOK: Mustad 94840
  THREAD: Orange
  WING: Mallard flank, bronze tinge
  TAIL: Dark ginger
  BODY: Red fox belly mixed with sandy hare's ear
  HACKLE: Dark ginger and grizzly mixed

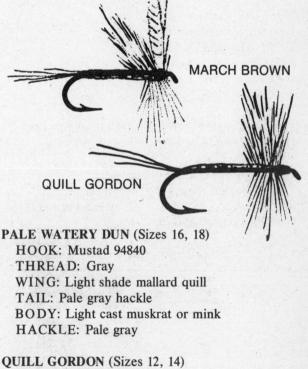

MARCH BROWN

QUILL GORDON

PALE WATERY DUN (Sizes 16, 18)
  HOOK: Mustad 94840
  THREAD: Gray
  WING: Light shade mallard quill
  TAIL: Pale gray hackle
  BODY: Light cast muskrat or mink
  HACKLE: Pale gray

QUILL GORDON (Sizes 12, 14)
  HOOK: Mustad 94840
  THREAD: Gray
  WING: Woodduck
  TAIL: Medium to dark dun
  BODY: Stripped peacock quill
  HACKLE: Medium to dark dun
  Note: For durability of peacock quill, counterwrap body with 6/0 white silk thread and apply clear varnish.

RAT FACED McDOUGALL

RAT FACED McDOUGALL (Sizes 10-16)
HOOK: Mustad 94840
THREAD: Gray
TAIL: Dark ginger
BODY: Gray caribou trimmed to shape
WING: Chinchilla or grizzly hackle tips
HACKLE: Dark ginger

RED QUILL (Sizes 12-16)
HOOK: Mustad 94840
THREAD: Gray
WING: Woodduck flank
TAIL: Medium bronze dun
BODY: Quill stem from brown rooster
HACKLE: Medium bronze dun

RENEGADE (Sizes 10-16)
HOOK: Mustad 94840
THREAD: Black
BODY: Peacock herl
HACKLE AFT: Brown
HACKLE FORE: White

ROYAL COACHMAN HAIRWING (Sizes 10-18)
HOOK: Mustad 94840
THREAD: Black
WING: White calf tail or equivalent
TAIL: Golden pheasant tippet fibers
BODY: Peacock herl divided by band of red floss
HACKLE: Brown, dark

ROYAL COACHMAN HAIRWING

SOFA PILLOW (Sizes 6, 8)
HOOK: Mustad 9671
THREAD: Yellow
TAIL: Yellow duck quill section or equivalent
BODY: Yellow floss
WING: Gray squirrel tail to tip of tail
HACKLE: Grizzly, full
HEAD: Yellow

MIDGE FLY PATTERNS

ADAMS MIDGE (Sizes 20-24)
HOOK: Mustad 94859 (Ring eye)
THREAD: Gray
TAIL: Grizzly
BODY: Muskrat
HACKLE: Grizzly and brown

BLACK MIDGE (Sizes 20, 22)
HOOK: Mustad 94859
THREAD: Black
TAIL: Black
BODY: Black
HACKLE: Black

BLUE DUN MIDGE (Sizes 20, 22)
HOOK: Mustad 94859 (Ring eye)
THREAD: Gray
TAIL: Dun
BODY: Muskrat
HACKLE: Dun

BROWN MIDGE (Sizes 20, 22)
HOOK: Mustad 94859
THREAD: Brown
TAIL: Brown
BODY: Brown fur
HACKLE: Brown

CREAM MIDGE (Sizes 20, 22)
HOOK: Mustad 94859
THREAD: Primrose yellow
TAIL: Dark cream
BODY: Creamy yellow fur
HACKLE: Dark cream

OLIVE MIDGE (Sizes 20, 22)
HOOK: Mustad 94859
THREAD: Olive
TAIL: Olive
BODY: Olive fur
HACKLE: Olive

WULFF FLY PATTERNS

BLACK WULFF (Sizes 8-14)
HOOK: Mustad 94840
THREAD: Black
WING: Black calf tail
TAIL: Black calf tail
BODY: Pink fur
HACKLE: Black

GRAY WULFF (Sizes 8-14)
  HOOK: Mustad 94840
  THREAD: Black
  WING: Natural brown calf tail
  TAIL: Natural brown calf tail
  BODY: Muskrat
  HACKLE: Medium blue dun

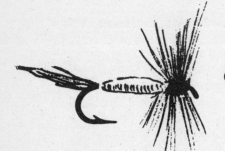

GRAY WULFF

GRIZZLY WULFF (Sizes 8-14)
  HOOK: Mustad 94840
  THREAD: Gray
  WING: Dark brown calf tail
  TAIL: Dark brown calf tail
  BODY: Yellow fur or mohlon
  HACKLE: Grizzly and brown

WHITE WULFF (Sizes 8-14)
  HOOK: Mustad 94840
  THREAD: Black
  WING: White calf tail
  TAIL: White calf tail
  BODY: Cream wool
  HACKLE: Light badger

WHITE WULFF

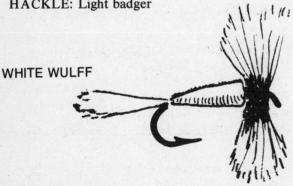

TERRESTRIALS
BEETLE (Sizes 16, 18)
  HOOK: Mustad 94840
  THREAD: Gray
  UNDERBODY: Brown hackle palmered on shank and trimmed top and bottom
  BODY: Natural gray deer hair over shank as shell
  HEAD: Clipped ends of deer hair
  Note: Deer hair must first be tied in, then the hackle palmered through, then butt section of deer hair fibers pulled forward and secured.

BLACK ANT (Sizes 14, 20)
  HOOK: Mustad 94840
  THREAD: Black
  BODY: Fuzzy fur dyed black
  HACKLE: Black at center shank dividing body

CINNAMON ANT (Sizes 18, 20)
  HOOK: Mustad 94840
  THREAD: Brown
  BODY: Fuzzy cinnamon dyed fur
  HACKLE: Dark ginger at waist

DEER HOPPER (Sizes 8-12)
  HOOK: Mustad 9672
  THREAD: Light brown or yellow
  TAIL: Red hackle fibers
  BODY: Yellow deer hair trimmed to hopper shape
  RIB: Brown hackle palmered and clipped
  WING: Turkey wing quill sections shaped down-wing
  HACKLE: Brown and grizzly mixed

INCH WORM (Size 14)
  HOOK: Mustad 94831
  THREAD: Green
  BODY: Green deer hair tied down and reversed
  RIB: Green thread (overhang from original tie-in)
  HEAD: Peacock herl

LETORT CRICKET (Sizes 12-16)
  HOOK: Mustad 9672
  THREAD: Black
  BODY: Black mohlon or fur
  WING: Black deer hair
  HEAD: Spun and clipped black deer hair

WOODCHUCK HOPPER (Sizes 8-12)
  HOOK: Mustad 9672
  THREAD: Light brown or yellow
  TAIL: Red hackle
  BODY: Yellow deer hair clipped to shape
  RIB: Brown hackle palmered through body and clipped
  WING: Guard hairs from back of woodchuck slightly spread
  HACKLE: Brown and grizzly mixed

CADDIS DRY FLY PATTERNS
DELTA WING CADDIS (Sizes 10-22)
  HOOK: Mustad 94840
  THREAD: Gray
  BODY: Gray fur
  WING: Dun hen hackle tips tied at 45-degree angle
  HACKLE: Bronze dun

DELTA WING CADDIS, OLIVE (Sizes 10-22)
HOOK: Mustad 94840
THREAD: Olive
BODY: Olive fur with gray cast
WING: Dun hen hackle tips tied at 45-degree angle
HACKLE: Dark ginger

FLAT WING CADDIS, BLACK (Sizes 14-20)
HOOK: Mustad 94840
THREAD: Black
BODY: Dark gray fur (almost black)
RIB: Black hackle trimmed top and bottom (palmered)
WING: Mottled quill section trimmed to "V" shape past bend
HACKLE: Black, trimmed on bottom

FLAT WING CADDIS, GRAY (Sizes 14-20)
HOOK: Mustad 94840
THREAD: Gray
BODY: Muskrat
RIB: Brown hackle trimmed top and bottom
WING: Mottled quill section (turkey or other) to "V"
HACKLE: Brown, trimmed on bottom

FLAT WING CADDIS, OLIVE (Sizes 14-20)
HOOK: Mustad 94840
THREAD: Olive
BODY: Olive fur
RIB: Grizzly hackle trimmed top and bottom
WING: Mottled quill section trimmed to "V"
HACKLE: Brown, trimmed on bottom

FLAT WING CADDIS, TAN (Sizes 14-20)
HOOK: Mustad 94840
THREAD: Light brown
BODY: Beige/tan fur
RIB: Brown hackle trimmed top and bottom
WING: Mottled quill section trimmed to "V"
HACKLE: Brown, trimmed on bottom

HENRYVILLE SPECIAL, BURNT ORANGE BODY (Sizes 12-18)
HOOK: Mustad 94840
THREAD: Gray
BODY: Burnt orange floss
RIB: Grizzly hackle palmered through floss
UNDERWING: Woodduck flank fibers
WING: Slate mallard tied tent
HACKLE: Brown

HENRYVILLE SPECIAL, OLIVE BODY (Sizes 12-18)
HOOK: Mustad 94840
THREAD: Gray
BODY: Olive floss
RIB: Grizzly hackle palmered through floss
UNDERWING: Woodduck flank fibers
WING: Slate mallard tied tent
HACKLE: Brown

HENRYVILLE SPECIAL, FLUORESCENT GREEN (Sizes 12-18)
HOOK: Mustad 94840
THREAD: Gray
BODY: Fluorescent green floss
RIB: Grizzly hackle palmered through floss
UNDERWING: Woodduck fibers
WING: Slate mallard tied tent
HACKLE: Brown

SID NEFF HAIRWING, BROWN (Sizes 12-18)
HOOK: Mustad 94840
THREAD: Brown
BODY: Light brown fur
WING: Tan gray deer hair
HEAD: Clipped deer hair
Note: Wing tilts upward on all Sid Neff Hairwings

SID NEFF HAIRWING, GRAY (Sizes 12-18)
HOOK: Mustad 94840
THREAD: Gray
BODY: Muskrat
WING: Deer hair dyed dark gray
HEAD: Clipped dark gray deer hair

SID NEFF HAIRWING, OLIVE (Sizes 12-18)
HOOK: Mustad 94840
THREAD: Olive
BODY: Olive fur
WING: Tan brown deer hair
HEAD: Clipped deer hair

SOLOMON'S HAIRWING, GRAY (Sizes 12-20)
HOOK: Mustad 94840
THREAD: Gray
BODY: Olive fur with hint of muskrat gray
WING: Tan/gray fur (#2 in Solomon/Leiser blend)
HACKLE: Dark ginger

SOLOMON'S HAIRWING, OLIVE (Sizes 12-20)
HOOK: Mustad 94840
THREAD: Olive
BODY: Medium olive fur
WING: Natural brown deer hair (#3 in S/L blend)
HACKLE: Bronze dun

SOLOMON'S HAIRWING, PALE YELLOW (Sizes 14-20)
  HOOK: Mustad 94840
  THREAD: Beige or light brown
  BODY: Pale yellow (#4 in S/L blend)
  WING: Tan deer hair
  HACKLE: Ginger

SOLOMON'S HAIRWING, TAN (Sizes 12-20)
  HOOK: Mustad 94840
  THREAD: Beige or light brown
  BODY: Tan ginger
  WING: Tan brown deer hair
  HACKLE: Cream

WRIGHT SKITTERING CADDIS, MINK BLACK (Sizes 12-16)
  HOOK: Mustad 94840
  THREAD: Black
  BODY: Black fur
  WING: Black mink tail guard hairs
  HACKLE: Dark rusty dun

WRIGHT SKITTERING CADDIS, MINK BROWN (Sizes 12-16)
  HOOK: Mustad 94840
  THREAD: Brown
  BODY: Dark brown fur
  WING: Dark bronze dun mink tail guard hairs
  HACKLE: Bronze dun

WRIGHT SKITTERING CADDIS, MINK CINNAMON (Sizes 12-16)
  HOOK: Mustad 94840
  THREAD: Orange
  BODY: Burnt Orange/Gray fur
  WING: Dark brown
  HACKLE: Rusty dun

WRIGHT SKITTERING CADDIS, MINK GREY (Sizes 12-16)
  HOOK: Mustad 94840
  THREAD: Gray
  BODY: Gray
  WING: Blue dun mink tail guard hairs
  HACKLE: Rusty dun

WRIGHT SKITTERING CADDIS, MINK GRAY (Sizes 12-16)
  HOOK: Mustad 94840
  THREAD: Olive
  BODY: Medium olive
  WING: Dark brown mink tail guard hairs
  HACKLE: Rusty dun

CADDIS LARVA FLY PATTERNS

GILL RIBBED LARVA (Sizes 14-20)
  HOOK: Mustad 37160
  THREAD: Black
  BODY: Green floss
  RIB: Peacock herl counter wound with fine gold wire
  HEAD: Peacock herl

LATEX LARVA, CREAM (Sizes 10-16)
  HOOK: Mustad 37160
  THREAD: Cream
  UNDERBODY: Cream floss
  BODY: Cream latex
  HEAD: Peacock herl

LATEX LARVA, OLIVE (Sizes 10-16)
  HOOK: Mustad 37160
  THREAD: Olive
  UNDERBODY: Dark green or olive floss lacquered with clear cement
  BODY: Cream latex wound over wet body
  HEAD: Peacock herl

CADDIS PUPA FLY PATTERNS

JORGENSEN FUR CADDIS PUPA, GRAY (Sizes 8-14)
  HOOK: Mustad 3906B
  THREAD: Gray
  BODY: Gray sealex blend #117
  WING SLATS: Mallard quill
  HEAD: (See Jorgensen Caddis pupa, olive.)

JORGENSEN FUR CADDIS PUPA, OLIVE (Sizes 8-14)
  HOOK: Mustad 3906B
  THREAD: Olive
  BODY: Olive sealex blend #119
  WING SLATS: Mallard quill
  HEAD: Natural gray/brown rabbit fur with guard hairs roped and spun wet fly style as collar and pulled downward so most of hairs form tuft of beard under thorax.

JORGENSEN FUR CADDIS PUPA, TAN (Sizes 8-14)
  HOOK: Mustad 3906B
  THREAD: Light brown
  BODY: Tan sealex blend #118
  WING SLATS: Mallard quill
  HEAD: (See Jorgensen Fur Caddis Pupa, Olive.)

SOLOMON'S CADDIS PUPA, GRAY (Sizes 8-14)
  HOOK: Mustad 3906B
  THREAD: Gray
  BODY: Gray fur or sealex
  RIB: Brown monocord
  WING SLATS: Mallard quill
  LEGS: Partridge or substitute
  ANTENNAE: Partridge or substitute
  HEAD: Peacock herl

SOLOMON'S CADDIS PUPA, OLIVE (Sizes 8-14)
  HOOK: Mustad 3906B
  THREAD: Olive
  BODY: Olive fur or sealex
  RIB: Brown monocord
  WING SLATS: Mallard quill
  LEGS: Partridge or substitute
  ANTENNAE: Partridge or substitute
  HEAD: Peacock herl

SOLOMON'S CADDIS PUPA, TAN (Sizes 8-14)
  HOOK: Mustad 3906B
  THREAD: Brown
  BODY: Tan fur or sealex
  RIB: Brown monocord
  WING SLATS: Mallard quill
  LEGS: Partridge or substitute
  ANTENNAE: Partridge or substitute
  HEAD: Peacock herl

NYMPH FLY PATTERNS

BREADCRUST (Sizes 8-16)
  HOOK: Mustad 3906B
  THREAD: Orange
  BODY: Hot orange seal's fur, or sealex over orange wool
  RIB: Center quill stem from brown rooster
  HACKLE: Grizzly as wet fly collar

DUN VARIANT NYMPH (Sizes 10-14)
  HOOK: Mustad 3906
  THREAD: Olive
  TAIL: Three strands of peacock herl tied short
  BODY: Claret seal fur or equivalent (sealex)
  LEGS: Grouse or partridge hackle

DARK HENDRICKSON NYMPH (Sizes 10-16)
  HOOK: Mustad 9671
  THREAD: Gray
  TAIL: Woodduck flank
  BODY: Muskrat
  WING CASE: Dark gray mallard quill
  LEGS: Woodduck flank or equivalent

DARK HENDRICKSON NYMPH

GOLD RIBBED HARE'S EAR NYMPH (Sizes 10-16)
  HOOK: Mustad 3906B
  THREAD: Brown
  TAIL: Brown hackle fibers
  BODY: Hare's mask dubbing
  RIB: Fine gold oval tinsel
  WING CASE: Gray goose or duck quill
  THORAX: Plucked guard hairs from hare's ear

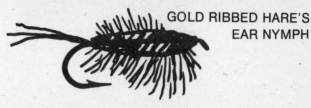

GOLD RIBBED HARE'S EAR NYMPH

HENDRICKSON NYMPH (Flick) (Sizes 12-16)
  HOOK: Mustad 9671
  THREAD: Olive
  TAIL: Woodduck flank or equivalent
  BODY: Blend of fox belly, beaver and claret seal fur (grayish brown)
  RIB: Fine gold wire
  WING CASE: Light gray goose or duck quill
  LEGS: Partridge or equivalent

LEADWING COACHMAN NYMPH

LEADWING COACHMAN NYMPH (Sizes 10-16)
  HOOK: Mustad 9671
  THREAD: Black
  TAIL: Brown hackle fibers
  BODY: Peacock herl
  HACKLE: Dark brown
  WING PAD: Mallard quill cut to shape

LIGHT CAHILL NYMPH

LIGHT CAHILL NYMPH (Sizes 10-16)
  HOOK: Mustad 9671
  THREAD: Yellow
  TAIL: Woodduck flank
  BODY: Creamy yellow opossum fur or equivalent
  HACKLE: Dark cream to buff
  WING PAD: Mallard flank cut to shape

MARCH BROWN NYMPH (Flick) (Sizes 10-14)
  HOOK: Mustad 9671
  THREAD: Gray
  TAIL: Three strands of ringneck pheasant tail fibers
  BODY: Amber seal (or sealex) blended with fawn fox
  LEGS: Partridge
  WING CASE: Section of fibers from short ringneck tail

MONTANA NYMPH (Sizes 6-12)
  HOOK: Mustad 9672
  THREAD: Black
  TAIL: Three crow fibers (or black hackle)
  BODY: #00 black chenille
  THORAX: #2 yellow chenille with black hackle palmered through for legs
  WING CASE: #00 black chenille pulled over

MONTANA NYMPH

MUSKRAT NYMPH (Sizes 10-16)
  HOOK: Mustad 3906B
  THREAD: Gray
  BODY: Muskrat dubbing
  BEARD: Finely marked natural guinea hen
  HEAD: Black ostrich herl

OTTER NYMPH (Sizes 10-14)
  HOOK: Mustad 9671
  THREAD: Black
  TAIL: Mallard flank fibers
  BODY: Tan otter fur
  THORAX: Tan otter fur to shape
  LEGS: Speckled light gray guinea hen or grizzly hen
  WING CASE: Mallard flank

STONEFLY NYMPH (Sizes 6-14)
  HOOK: Mustad 38941
  THREAD: Orange
  TAIL: Dark brown or black horsetail
  BODY: Dark brown seal or rabbit
  THORAX: Dark brown seal or rabbit
  LEGS: Grizzly neck hackle dyed light brown
  WING CASE: Dark brown turkey

TUPS INDISPENSIBLE (Sizes 12-16)
  HOOK: Mustad 9671
  THREAD: Primrose yellow
  TAIL: Pale dun hackle tip
  BODY: Light yellow floss
  THORAX: Honey, red and sulfur fur mixed

ZUG BUG NYMPH

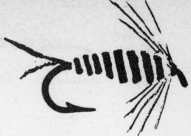

WHITLOCK NYMPH, BLACK (Sizes 4-10)
  HOOK: Mustad 79580
  THREAD: Black
  TAIL: Two black peccary or porcupine fibers
  BODY: Black seal's fur (or sealex)
  RIB: Fine oval silver tinsel
  WING CASE: Peacock herl (several strands)
  HACKLE: Black
  FEELERS: Same as tail
  HEAD: Black

ZUG BUG (NYMPH) (Sizes 10-16)
  HOOK: Mustad 3906B
  THREAD: Black
  TAIL: Three peacock sword fibers tied short
  BODY: Peacock herl
  RIB: Silver oval tinsel
  WING PAD: Mallard flank cut square
  LEGS: Brown hackle tied as collar

BLACK GNAT

COACHMAN

WET FLY PATTERNS
BLACK GNAT (Sizes 8-16)
  HOOK: Mustad 3906
  THREAD: Black
  TAIL: None
  BODY: Black chenille
  HACKLE: Black
  WING: Slate duck quill

COACHMAN (Sizes 10-16)
  HOOK: Mustad 3906
  THREAD: Black
  TAIL: None
  TAG: Flat gold tinsel
  BODY: Peacock herl
  HACKLE: Brown
  WING: White duck quill

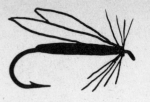

COWDUNG

COWDUNG: (Sizes 12-16)
HOOK: Mustad 3906
THREAD: Black
TAG: Flat gold tinsel
BODY: Dark olive floss
HACKLE: Brown
WING: Cinnamon tan peacock wing quill, turkey, or
   equivalent

DARK HENDRICKSON (Sizes 10-16)
HOOK: Mustad 3906
THREAD: Black
TAIL: Woodduck flank
BODY: Muskrat
HACKLE: Medium bronze dun
WING: Woodduck flank

GINGER QUILL (Sizes 12-16)
HOOK: Mustad 3906
THREAD: Gray
TAIL: Golden ginger (buff)
BODY: Stripped peacock
HACKLE: Golden ginger
WING: Slate mallard quill

GOLD RIBBED HARE'S EAR (Sizes 10-16)
HOOK: Mustad 3906
THREAD: Black
TAIL: Brown
BODY: Coarse and soft fur from hare's mask
RIB: Fine gold tinsel (oval)
HACKLE: Plucked out guard hairs from hare's ear
WING: Mallard quill

GOLD RIBBED HARE'S EAR

GRAY HACKLE (PEACOCK) (Sizes 10-14)
HOOK: Mustad 3906
THREAD: Black
TAIL: Red hackle fibers
BODY: Peacock herl
HACKLE: Grizzly
WING: None

GRIZZLY KING (Sizes 10-14)
HOOK: Mustad 3906B
THREAD: Black
TAIL: Red duck or goose quill section
BODY: Green floss
RIB: Fine flat gold tinsel
HACKLE: Grizzly
WING: Mallard flank

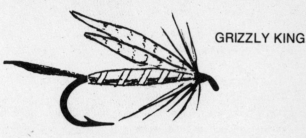

GRIZZLY KING

LIGHT CAHILL (Sizes 10-16)
HOOK: Mustad 3906
THREAD: Yellow
TAIL: Woodduck flank fibers
BODY: Cream fox or equivalent
HACKLE: Dark cream
WING: Woodduck flank

MARCH BROWN (Sizes 10-14)
HOOK: Mustad 3906B
THREAD: Brown
TAIL: Speckled grouse or woodduck flank
BODY: Hare's mask dubbing
RIB: Yellow thread
HACKLE: Grouse or woodduck
WING: Speckled turkey quill or equivalent

MARCH BROWN

MONTREAL (Sizes 10-16)
HOOK: Mustad 3906
THREAD: Black
TAIL: Claret hackle
BODY: Claret floss
RIB: Fine flat gold tinsel
HACKLE: Claret
WING: Speckled hen or turkey wing quill

PICKET PIN

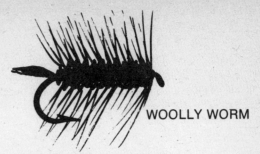

WOOLLY WORM

PICKET PIN (Sizes 8-12)
  HOOK: Mustad 9672
  THREAD: Black
  TAIL: Brown
  BODY: Peacock herl wound full
  RIB: Brown hackle wound through entire peacock
    body
  WING: Squirrel tail
  HEAD: Peacock herl wound full to form head

QUILL GORDON (Sizes 10-14)
  HOOK: Mustad 3906
  THREAD: Black
  TAIL: Woodduck
  BODY: Striped peacock
  HACKLE: Medium dark blue dun
  WING: Woodduck flank
  Note: Though black thread forms head, use yellow
    for body

ROYAL COACHMAN

ROYAL COACHMAN (Sizes 10-16)
  HOOK: Mustad 3906B
  THREAD: Black
  TAIL: Golden pheasant tippets
  BODY: Peacock herl split by band of red floss
  HACKLE: Brown
  WING: White duck quill

SULPHUR DUN (Sizes 12-16)
  HOOK: Mustad 3906
  THREAD: Yellow
  TAIL: Dark cream (straw shade if available)
  BODY: Creamy yellow fur
  HACKLE: Dark cream (straw)
  WING: Slate mallard quill (light shade)

WOOLLY WORM, BROWN (Sizes 6-12)
  HOOK: Mustad 38941
  THREAD: Black
  TAIL: Red hackle fibers
  BODY: Brown chenille
  HACKLE: Grizzly palmered through body

WOOLLY WORM, OLIVE (Sizes 6-12)
  HOOK: Mustad 38941
  THREAD: Black
  TAIL: Red hackle fibers
  BODY: Olive chenille
  HACKLE: Grizzly palmered through body

WOOLLY WORM, YELLOW (Sizes 6-12)
  HOOK: Mustad 38941
  THREAD: Black
  TAIL: Red hackle fibers
  BODY: Yellow chenille
  HACKLE: Grizzly palmered through body

STREAMERS/BUCKTAIL FLY PATTERNS
BLACK GHOST (Sizes 6-12)
  HOOK: Mustad 9575
  THREAD: Black
  TAIL: Yellow hackle
  BODY: Black floss
  RIB: Flat silver tinsel
  THROAT: Yellow hackle
  WING: Four white saddle or neck hackles
  CHEEK: Jungle cock (optional)
  HEAD: Black

BLACK GHOST

BLACK NOSED DACE (Sizes 6-12)
  HOOK: Mustad 9575
  THREAD: Black
  TAIL: Red wool tied short
  BODY: Flat silver tinsel
  RIB: Oval silver tinsel
  WING: White polar bear (or substitute), black bear
    hair and brown bucktail (or calf tail) in order
  HEAD: Black
  Note: Body of this pattern can be formed with mylar
    tubing

BLACK MARABOU MUDDLER (Sizes 4-10)
HOOK: Mustad 79580, 38941
THREAD: Black
TAIL: Red hackle fibers
BODY: Silver mylar tubing
WING: Black marabou topped with peacock herl
HEAD: Clipped black deer hair

Note: Fly is weighted for deep water

BLACK MARABOU (Sizes 6-12)
HOOK: Mustad 9575
THREAD: Black
TAG: Red hackle
BODY: Silver mylar tubing
WING: Few strands of red calf tail over which black marabou
HEAD: Black

GRAY GHOST (Sizes 4-12)
HOOK: Mustad 9575
THREAD: Black
BODY: Orange floss
RIB: Medium flat silver tinsel
THROAT Golden pheasant crest over which is tied white bucktail
WING: Golden pheasant crest feather over which are tied four bronze dun saddle hackles topped by 6 or 7 strands of peacock herl
SHOULDER: Silver pheasant body feather
CHEEK: Jungle cock eye or equivalent
HEAD: Black

HORNBERG (Sizes 6-10)
HOOK: Mustad 38941
THREAD: Black
BODY: Flat silver tinsel
WING: Dyed yellow calf tail tied upward at a slight angle and covered with two mallard flank feathers
CHEEK: Jungle cock or substitute
HACKLE: Grizzly and brown (tied as dry fly collar)
HEAD: Black

LLAMA (Sizes 6-12)
HOOK: Mustad 9575 or suitable
THREAD: Black
TAIL: Grizzly hackle fibers
BODY: Red floss
RIB: Flat gold tinsel
WING: Woodchuck guard hairs tied with color bands progressing from head to tail with black, tan, black and white tip
HACKLE: Grizzly tied as wet fly collar
HEAD: Black with black dotted white eye

MICKEY FINN (Sizes 6-12)
HOOK: Mustad 9575
THREAD: Black
BODY: Medium flat silver tinsel
RIB: Oval silver tinsel
WING: Yellow, red and yellow calf tail in order
HEAD: Black

Note: Body of pattern can be formed with silver mylar tubing

MUDDLER MINNOW (Sizes 2-14)
HOOK: Mustad 38941, 79580
THREAD: Gray
TAIL: Short section of turkey wing quill
BODY: Flat gold tinsel
WING: Gray squirrel tail with two turkey wing quill sections tied along side of shank and angling upward
HEAD: Clipped deer hair. Part of hair is flared along and around shank as collar

MUDDLER MINNOW

SUPERVISOR (Sizes 6-12)
HOOK: Mustad 9575
THREAD: Black
BODY: Medium flat silver tinsel
THROAT: White hackle fibers
WING: White calf tail over which are tied four light blue saddle hackles extending beyond bend
SHOULDER: Light green saddles covering one-third of blue saddles
TOPPING: Six to seven strands of peacock herl
CHEEK: Jungle cock or substitute
HEAD: Black

WHITE MARABOU (Sizes 6-12)
HOOK: Mustad 9575
THREAD: Red
TAIL: Red hackle fibers
BODY: Flat silver tinsel or silver mylar tubing
WING: White marabou topped with peacock herl
HEAD: Red

74

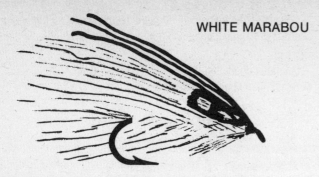

WHITE MARABOU

WHITE MARABOU MUDDLER (Sizes 4-12)
HOOK: Mustad 79580, 38941
THREAD: Gray
TAIL: Red hackle fibers
BODY: Silver mylar tubing
WING: White marabou topped with peacock herl
HACKLE: Natural deer hair collar tips almost to bend
HEAD: Clipped natural deer hair

Note: Also tied weighted

MATUKA STREAMER FLY PATTERNS

Note: On all matuka style patterns the body material should be such that the rib can bite into it firmly. Unyielding materials such as floss allow the hackle to slip. The ribbing material for these patterns should be fine but strong.

Note: On matuka patterns the wing length should be almost twice the hook shank length.

ADAMS MATUKA (Sizes 4-10)
HOOK: Mustad 9575
THREAD: Black
BODY: Red chenille, fur or sparkle yarn
RIB: Gold oval tinsel
WING: Two grizzly and two brown hackles
HEAD: Black

BADGER MATUKA (Sizes 4-10)
HOOK: Mustad 9575
THREAD: Black
BODY: Black (sparkle yarn, chenille or fur)
RIB: Oval silver tinsel
WING: Badger hackle
HEAD: Black

BLACK MATUKA (Sizes 4-10)
HOOK: Mustad 9575
THREAD: Black
BODY: Black (chenille, fur, yarn..)
RIB: Oval silver tinsel
WING: Black hackles
HEAD: Black

BLACK GHOST MATUKA (Sizes 4-10)
HOOK: Mustad 9575
THREAD: Black
TAIL: Yellow hackle fibers
BODY: Black fur or chenille
RIB: Oval silver tinsel
WING: White saddle or neck hackles
THROAT: Red hackle fibers
HEAD: Black

FURNANCE MATUKA (Sizes 4-10)
HOOK: Mustad 9575
THREAD: Black
BODY: Yellow sparkle yarn, chenille, fur
RIB: Oval gold tinsel
WING: Furnace hackle
HEAD: Black

GRIZZLY MATUKA (Sizes 4-10)
HOOK: Mustad 9575
THREAD: Black
BODY: Pink fur or sparkle yarn
RIB: Oval silver tinsel
WING: Grizzly neck or saddle hackles
HEAD: Black

GRIZZLY DYED OLIVE MATUKA (Sizes 4-10)
HOOK: Mustad 9575
THREAD: Black
BODY: Olive chenille, fur, sparkle yarn
RIB: Oval silver tinsel
WING: Grizzly hackle dyed olive
HEAD: Black

GRIZZLY DYED YELLOW MATUKA (Sizes 4-10)
HOOK: Mustad 9575
THREAD: Red
BODY: Light olive chenille, fur
RIB: Oval silver tinsel
WING: Grizzly hackle dyed yellow
HEAD: Red
Note: Wing hackles on all matukas should be as webby as possible.

SALMON FLY PATTERNS

AUSABLE WULFF (Dry) (Sizes 4-10)
HOOK: Light wire salmon
THREAD: Black
Same procedure as Wulff's dry fly (see same)

GRAY WULFF (Dry) (Sizes 4-10)
HOOK: Light wire salmon
THREAD: Black
Same procedure as Wulff's dry (see same)

ROYAL WULFF (Dry) (Sizes 4-10)
 HOOK: Light wire salmon
 THREAD: Black
 Same procedure as Wulff's dry (see same)

WHITE WULFF (Dry) (Sizes 4-10)
 HOOK: Light wire salmon
 THREAD: Black
 Same procedure as Wulff's dry (see same)

BLACK RAT (Sizes 4-10)
 HOOK: Mustad 36890 or English salmon
 THREAD: Red
 TAG: Oval silver tinsel
 TAIL: Golden pheasant crest
 BODY: Black seal fur (or sealex)
 RIB: Oval silver tinsel
 WING: Gray fox guard hairs
 HACKLE: Grizzly tied as collar
 CHEEKS: Jungle cock (optional)
 HEAD: Red

BLUE CHARM (Sizes 6-10) (Hairwing)
 HOOK: Mustad 36890 or English salmon
 THREAD: Black
 TAG: Oval silver tinsel and yellow floss
 TAIL: Golden pheasant crest
 BODY: Black floss
 RIB: Oval silver tinsel
 THROAT: Rich blue hackle
 WING: Bronze mallard overlayed with teal
 HEAD: Black

BOMBER (Sizes 2, 4)
 HOOK: Mustad 79580
 THREAD: Gray
 TAIL: Woodchuck guard hairs
 WING: Woodchuck guard hairs slanting forward at
  45-degree angle
 BODY: Natural gray deer body hair spun and
  trimmed to cigar shape
 RIB: Brown hackle palmered through body

BUCK BUTT (Sizes 6-12)
 HOOK: Mustad 38941, 9672
 THREAD: Gray
 TAIL: Fluorescent orange floss short
 BODY: Natural gray deer hair spun and clipped to
  trim cigar shape
 RIB: Brown hackle palmered through body and clip-
  ped fairly close to body

BUTTERFLY (Sizes 6-10)
 HOOK: Light wire salmon
 THREAD: Black
 TAIL: Red hackle
 BODY: Peacock herl

 HACKLE: Brown
 WING: White goat slanted rearward-divided wing
 HEAD: Black

COSSEBOOM (Hairwing) (Sizes 6-10)
 HOOK: Mustad 36890
 THREAD: Red
 TAG: Embossed silver tinsel
 TAIL: Olive floss short
 BODY: Olive floss
 RIB: Embossed silver tinsel
 WING: Gray squirrel tail sparse to end of tail
 HACKLE: Lemon yellow as collar
 CHEEK: Jungle cock, optional
 HEAD: Red

GREEN BUTT (Sizes 4-10)
 HOOK: Mustad 36890
 THREAD: Black
 BUTT: Fluorescent green floss
 BODY: Peacock herl
 WING: Black bear
 HEAD: Black

HAIRY MARY (Sizes 4-10)
 HOOK: Mustad 36890
 THREAD: Black
 TAG: Oval gold tinsel
 TAIL: Golden pheasant crest
 BODY: Black floss
 RIB: Oval gold tinsel
 THROAT: Bright blue hackle
 WING: Brown fitch tail
 HEAD: Black

MUDDLER MINNOW (Sizes 2-10)
 HOOK: Mustad 36890
 THREAD: Gray
 See description in Streamers and Bucktails

RUSTY RAT (Sizes 4-10)
 HOOK: Mustad 36890
 THREAD: Red
 TAG: Oval gold tinsel
 TAIL: Three peacock sword fibers tied short
 BODY: Rear half bright yellow floss; fore half
  peacock herl. Yellow floss forms a short wing from
  division of floss and peacock body and extends to
  middle of tail.
 RIB: Val gold tinsel
 WING: Gray fox guard hairs sparse (woodchuck
  guard hairs are a good substitute)
 HACKLE: Grizzly tied as collar
 CHEEK: Jungle cock, optional
 HEAD: Red

SILVER RAT (Sizes 4-10)
  HOOK: Mustad 36890
  THREAD: Red
  TAG: Oval gold tinsel
  TAIL: Golden pheasant crest
  BODY: Flat silver tinsel
  RIB: Oval gold tinsel
  WING: Gray fox guard hairs
  HACKLE: Grizzly tied as collar
  CHEEKS: Jungle cock, short, optional
  HEAD: Red
  Note: All salmon flies may be tied on the proper English salmon hooks if they are available.

SALT WATER FLY PATTERNS
ARGENTINE BLONDE (Sizes 1/0, 2/0)
  HOOK: Mustad 34007
  THREAD: Black
  TAIL: White bucktail
  BODY: Flat gold tinsel
  WING: Medium blue bucktail
  HEAD: Black

FRANKIE BELLE BONEFISH FLY (Sizes 1, 2)
  HOOK: Mustad 34007
  THREAD: White
  BODY: White chenille
  WING: Natural brown bucktail tied on underside of shank extending slightly (½ inches) past bend
  SHOULDER: One grizzly hackle on each side
  HEAD: White

FRANKIE BELLE POLY BONEFISH FLY (Sizes 4-8)
  HOOK: Mustad 34007
  THREAD: Red
  BODY: Fluorescent green chenille
  WING: (Hook is first turned upside down in vise) White poly yarn ¼-inch past bend shouldered with one narrow grizzly hackle on each side.
  HEAD: Red

BLACK BEAUTY BONEFISH FLY (Sizes 4-8)
  HOOK: Mustad 34007
  THREAD: Black
  BODY: Black mohlon or wool
  WING: (Hook is first turned upside down in vise) Six strands of fine flat silver mylar covered by black poly yarn extending ¼-inch past bend
  HEAD: Black

BROWN POLY BONEFISH FLY (Sizes 4-8)
  HOOK: Mustad 34007
  THREAD: Brown
  BODY: Beige/brown poly yarn
  WING: Beige/brown poly yarn to bend covered with brown poly yarn ¼-inch past bend.
  HEAD: Brown

COCKROACH (Sizes 2/0, 4/0) (Tarpon)
  HOOK: Mustad 34007
  THREAD: Red
  BODY: None, as such
  TAIL/WING: Six grizzly saddle hackles are tied in near the bend so that they extend approximately 2-2½ inches past the bend
  WING: Gray squirrel tail is tied in near the head and completely surrounds the shank and extends ¼-inch past the bend and blends into the grizzly saddle hackle
  HEAD: Red
  Note: This fly is also tied with a black head using Red Fox Squirrel tail fibers for the wing

GRASS SHRIMP (Stripers, Weakfish) (Sizes 1, 2, 4)
  HOOK: Mustad 34007 or 3407
  THREAD: Gray monocord
  TAIL: Olive saddle hackle tip tied down bend to imitate natural
  BODY: Dark olive wool over which is wound gray sealex
  SHELL: Strip of polyethylene bag
  RIB: Palmered olive gray saddle hackle heavy near eye and clipped on top
  SEGMENTATION: Rib of 6-pound test monofilament over shell in open spiral
  EYES: Burnt stubs of 20-pound test mono

GREEN BONEFISH FLY (Sizes 4-8)
  HOOK: Mustad 34007
  THREAD: Black
  BODY: Flat silver tinsel
  WING: (Hook is turned upside down in vise.) Six strands of fine flat silver mylar covered by bright green poly yarn extending ¼-inch past bend
  HEAD: Black

GOLDEN CLAW TARPON FLY (Sizes 3/0, 5/0)
  TAIL/WING: Two grizzly hackles covered by four hot orange hackles (three on each side) extending approximatley 2-2½ inches past bend
  COLLAR: Two to three turns of grizzly and hot orange hackle tied just forward of bend
  BODY SHANK: Covered by bright red thread to eye and lacquered
  Note: Most tarpon flies are tied with hackles at the bend so that they do not twist or foul around the shank

HONEY BLONDE (Sizes 1/0, 2/0)
  HOOK: Mustad 34007
  THREAD: Red
  TAIL: Yellow bucktail
  BODY: Flat gold tinsel
  WING: Yellow bucktail
  HEAD: Red

HORROR (Sizes 2-8)
  HOOK: Mustad 34007
  THREAD: Red
  BODY: Yellow chenille in two parts
  WING: Natural brown bucktail tied under shank of hook protrudes from split chenille body one-third distance from eye
  HEAD: Red

LEFTY'S DECEIVER (Sizes 2-3/0)
  HOOK: Mustad 34007
  THREAD: Red
  TAIL/WING: Six to eight white saddle hackles tied in at bend and extending past approximately 2½ inches. These are shouldered by 6-8 strands of silver flat mylar for half the distance of the saddle hackle
  BODY: Flat silver tinsel
  WING: White bucktail tied as collar surrounding shank and dense enough to form fish shape when wet. Hair extends to end of mylar strips.
  TOPPING: Eight-10 strands of peacock herl
  HEAD: Red

LEFTY'S DECEIVER, BLACK (Sizes 2-3/0)
  HOOK: Mustad 34007
  THREAD: Black
  TAIL/WING: Six to eight black saddle hackles tied in at bend and extending approximatley 2½ inches past. These are shouldered by six to eight strands of fine flat mylar tinsel for half the distance of the saddle hackle.
  BODY: Flat silver tinsel
  WING: Black bucktail tied as collar near head of fly surrounding shank and dense enough to form fish shape when wet. Hair extends to end of mylar strips.
  TOPPING: Eight-10 strands of peacock herl
  HEAD: Black

PINK SHRIMP (Sizes 2-8)
  HOOK: Mustad 34007
  THREAD: Gray
  TAIL: Pink bucktail
  BODY: Flat silver tinsel
  HOOD: Pink bucktail
  HACKLE: Palmered through body and clipped on top

PLATINUM BLONDE (Sizes 1/0, 2/0)
  HOOK: Mustad 34007
  THREAD: Red
  TAIL: White bucktail
  BODY: Flat silver tinsel
  WING: White bucktail
  HEAD: Red

STRAWBERRY BLONDE (Sizes 1/0, 2/0)
  HOOK: Mustad 34007
  THREAD: Black
  TAIL: Orange bucktail
  BODY: Flat gold tinsel
  WING: Red bucktail
  HEAD: Black

TARPON FLY (RED & YELLOW) (Sizes 3/0, 5/0)
  HOOK: Mustad 34007
  THREAD: Red
  TAIL/WING: Two red covered by two yellow saddle hackles off each side of shank at bend extending past it approximately 2½ inches.
  HACKLE: Two-3 turns of red and yellow hackle just aft of where wing-tail was tied in.
  Note: There is a very slight winding of thread forward, which is lacquered. About half the hook shank to the eye remains bare.

STU APTE TARPON FLY
  Same as above except that orange and yellow hackles are used.

RECOMMENDED BOOKS FOR FLYTIERS

The following bibliography will further aid you as you progress in the art of flytying. There are many other books, and there will be many others. Some will seem repetitious to you. However, no two authors think alike. Each one will have something new or different to impart.

The suggested titles have been commented upon regarding not only their specialized data but the degree of technology involved.

Almy, Gerald. *Tying and Fishing Terrestrials*. Harrisburg, PA: Stackpole, 1978.
  In depth coverage of terrestrial tying-advanced
Bates, Joseph D., Jr. *Atlantic Salmon Flies and Fishing*. Harrisburg, PA: Stackpole, 1970.
  A listing of patterns for salmon flies. No tying instructions included.
Bay, Kenneth E. *How To Tie Fresh Water Flies*. New York, N.Y: Winchester Press, 1976.
  Excellent book for beginners.
———. *Salt Water Flies*. New York-Philadelphia: Lippincott, 1972.
  Contains simplified tying instructions and patterns for saltwater flies.
Boyle, Robert H. and Whitlock, Dave. *Fly Tyer's Almanac* New York: Crown, 1975.
  Advanced. Covers new patterns and materials
———. *The 2nd Fly Tyer's Almanac*. New York-Philadelphia: Lippincott, 1978.
  Advanced. More new innovations.

Flick, Art. *Art Flick's Master Fly Tying Guide*. New York: Crown, 1972.
A number of experts compiled this book each his own specialty. Advanced.

Harder, John. *Orvis Index of Fly Patterns*. Manchester, Vermont: Orvis, 1978.
A listing of pattern descriptions of flies sold by the Orvis Company.

Hellekson, Terry. *Popular Fly Patterns*. Logan Utah: Perregrine-Smith, 1976,
Listing of patterns.

Jorgensen, Poul. *Dressing Flies For Fresh and Salt Water*. Rockville Center, N.Y: Freshet Press, 1973.
Beginner type of instructions.

———. *Modern Fly Dressings For The Practical Angler*. New York: Winchester Press, 1976.

———. *Salmon Flies, Their Character, Style and Dressing*. Harrisburg: Stackpole, 1978.
Specialized-Advanced

Kaufmann, Randall. *The American Nymph Manual*. Portland, Oregon: Frank Amato Publications.
All types of techniques on nymph tying.

Leiser, Eric. *Fly Tying Materials*. New York: Crown, 1973.
Details and describes all natural feathers, furs, synthetics, hooks and tools. A reference for all flytiers.

———. *The Complete Book Of Fly Tying*. New York: Knopf, 1977.
Excellent book for beginners as well as advanced. All types of flies and techniques covered.

Nixon, Tom. *Tying Flies For Bass and Panfish*. (Revised) New York: A.S. Barnes, 1977.
Tying of flies for panfish as well as hair bugs and cork poppers for bass. Beginner and advanced.

Rosborough, E.H. "Polly". *Tying and Fishing The Fuzzy Nymph*. (Revised) Harrisburg: Stackpole, 1979.
Simple advanced. Deals in specialized style for nymphs.

Solomon, Larry, and Eric Leiser, *The Caddis And The Angler*. Harrisburg: Stackpole, 1977.
Specializes in tying of caddis imitations. Covers larvae, pupae and adults. Advanced.

DEALERS IN FLYTYING MATERIALS

There are many retail shops throughout the United States and Canada which sell flytying materials and equipment the flytier needs for his hobby.

If, however, your local sporting goods store does not carry such a line, by all means urge him to do so. It is always better for a flytier to be able to select his tools and materials in person. Materials, especially, should be inspected so you can see what it is you are buying and obtain the best for your money.

In some cases your local store may not feel it is worth the time or space to carry such a line. For this reason there are listed below a number of reliable mail-order houses dealing in these items. Should you purchase through a mail-order house and you are not fully satisfied with the service or quality, do call it to their attention. Most of the firms dealing in this community are fair and honest and it is just plain bad business if they don't heed your compliants (should you have any).

Buz's Fly & Tackle Shop (Retail)
805 West Tulare Avenue
Visalia, CA 95277

E. Hille (Retail)
815 Railway Street
Williamsport, PA 17701

Hunter's (Retail)
Valley View Lane
New Boston, NH 03070

Kaufmann's Streamborn Flies (Retail)
P.O. Box 23032
Portland, OR 97723

The Orvis Company (Retail)
Manchester, VT 05254

Rangeley Region Sports Shop (Retail)
Rangeley, ME 04970

Reed Tackle (Retail and Wholesale)
P.O. Box 390
Caldwell, NJ 07006

The Rivergate (Retail and Wholesale)
Route 9, Box 275
Cold Spring, NY 10516

Thomas & Thomas (Retail)
22 Third Street
Turners Falls, MA 01376

E. Veniard, Ltd. (Retail and Wholesale)
138 Northwood Road
Thornton Heath, England CR4 8YC

Eric Leiser

CHAPTER 4
Fly-Fishing for Trout

WHEN YOU HEAR someone mention the fine art of fly-fishing, chances are they are talking about fly-fishing for trout, since that is where it all began. The trout and its environment were designed perfectly by

Typical mountain freestone stream, having many pockets, pools and riffles throughout its course of flow.

Mother Nature for the sport of fly-fishing—beautiful clear rivers and mountain streams that are usually wadable; the fish feeding selectively on insects and other stream life, both on top of and under the water's surface, making it a true challenge for any enthusiastic angler; and naturally the beauty of the fish itself with the marvelous combinations of colors and patterns which give the trout its distinct identification. The beauty of the fish is an aesthetic enhancement to the sport.

The history of fly-fishing as a sport began in England in the early 1400's, during the time of Dame Juliana Berners who is credited as being the author of *Treatise of Fishing With an Angle,* the first known book on fly-fishing. Fly-fishing in America became popular around 1800. At that time fly-fishing was done almost exclusively with wet flies—flies that are fished under the water's surface. The dry fly, an imitation fished on top of the water surface, gained its popularity from the mid to late 1800's. The popularity of the dry fly was stimulated by enthusiastic British anglers such as George Selwyn Marryat and Frederic M. Halford who were two of its biggest proponents. The major influence on wet or sub-surface fly-fishing was G.E.M. Skues, also from England. There were always conflicts of opinion among these gentlemen as to which method was the best.

The forefathers of fly-fishing in the United States had their geographic roots in the northeastern part of the

game is all about. The failure to understand the basic facts of this behavior and how to apply them to your fishing tactics is what often leads to some frustrating days on the stream. This chapter will attempt to give you the knowledge you need to know about the habits of the hungry trout, the food that it feeds on and how to adapt your fishing techniques to imitate that food in order to hook some fish.

I can remember many days of frustration when, because of not knowing what was happening, I maybe caught one or two fish rather than a dozen or more. The incident that sticks in my mind most vividly was the one that probably created my serious interest in fly-fishing. It was the end of June, 1959. I had just graduated from college and had decided that the next few weeks were all mine. My fly-fishing experience had been superficial for the past 4 years. Any fly patterns that I had accumu-

Classic limestone or spring creek, such as Armstrong Spring Creek as shown, maintains a relatively consistent level and temperature.

(Right) Just several of the many popular books that deal with fly-fishing for trout.

country. Theodore Gordon, Edward R. Hewitt and George LaBranche are names that are associated with the classic rivers in the states of New York and Pennsylvania, where they brought fly-fishing for trout to a practical reality through their experiences and writings.

The revolutionary changes in attitudes and techniques that have recently developed were stimulated by masters of the art such as Vincent C. Marinaro with his book, *A Modern Dry Fly Code*, (Crown, 1950), and Ernest G. Schwiebert, Jr. whose work, *Matching the Hatch* (Macmillan, 1955) really got us looking selectively at the insects that trout feed on. There were others such as Charles K. Fox, Art Flick, Preston J. Jennings and many more who were eager and willing to share their knowledge and experiences. During the past 20 years, the sport has mushroomed. Currently there have been more books written about fly-fishing than about any other sport. About 75 percent of those relate to fishing and tying flies for trout.

Fly-fishing for trout is unique from any other type of fly-fishing that you may get involved with. It is the most aesthetic and most challenging type of fishing you are ever likely to do. The areas and rivers that you travel to for trout are some of the most beautiful places in this country and in the world. That is definitely part of the pleasure. The behavior of the trout is possibly the most logical of any of the other fishes. At the same time it may also be the most complex. This logical complexity in the trout's feeding patterns and behavior is what the

lated were from what I had read about or been told about. I was only in the thinking stages of tying my own. I knew that a mayfly imitation was to look like a mayfly, but that was about it. I knew very little of why trout did what they did. My technique was to get the fly out there and hope that a trout was good enough, or should I say stupid enough, to take. Anyway, I decided to spend a few days on the famous Beaverkill River in Roscoe, New York, where a friend had taken me the summer before.

I arrived late in the afternoon and proceeded to fish a well-known piece of water called Junction Pool. I guess that because it was on a week day there was no one else around. It would have been great if I had been able to ask someone what was happening. The next hour of experimenting with several different flies brought only

Some of the necessary equipment that you will be using when you fly-fish.

A freestone stream, such as this section of the Beaverkill River in New York, has relatively clean, highly oxygenated water. The water level and temperature is greatly regulated by the amount of rainfall and weather conditions throughout the year.

one small fish. It was about ½-hour before dark when the water started exploding. Sharp splashes were occurring all over the pool. Trout were even coming clear out of the water. Some fish rose so close to me that I almost felt that I was under attack. What was evident, even for my inexperienced eyes, was that the trout were chasing and eating the heck out of a brown bug that was obviously hatching from the stream. The closest fly I had in my collection that looked like the natural was a brown stonefly or Marchbrown pattern. It's hard to remember now exactly which one. Anyway, I tied it on as quickly as I could and just started casting and stripping it back. There were some real monsters rising up to 18 to 20 inches, but the only fish that I could get to take my offering was one 10- to 11-inch trout. When it got too dark to see, I gave up. As I was leaving the river I could still hear the sharp splashes of feeding fish.

Now, I'm sure, or at least I would like to believe, that if I was in that same situation today I would have hooked at least a dozen of these good trout. I feel certain that any knowledgeable angler would have done fairly well. The problem was that I did not know four important points:

1—What the type of insect the trout were feeding on
2—How the trout were feeding on the insect
3—What imitation or artificial fly to use
4—How to properly present the imitation to the fish

All of the above are interrelated. The knowledge of one gives you the information necessary to know the other.

As you become more involved with fly-fishing for trout, you will find that you acquire a great fondness and respect for all your equipment—your rod and reel, your flies, your trout vest and all the little goodies that

you store in its pockets, your net, boots, favorite hat that you use only for trout, and all the other items associated with this joyous sport.

There is more skill involved in trout fishing than is required for any other type of fly-fishing. One reason is the vast amount of knowledge to be learned about what the trout eats and how to imitate that food with a fly. There is an unlimited amount of information that can be learned. However, it is not necessary to know too much in order to catch fish. It just depends on how proficient you wish to become and to what degree you want to get involved. The idea is to understand the trout's basic behavior, have a good variety of flies and learn how to cast and present the fly well. If you possess this basic understanding and fly casting ability, you will catch fish.

Another factor that requires more skill in trout fishing

is the ability to cast well in a variety of casting situations. It becomes a challenge which results in great satisfaction when you make a good cast to a trout that is in a difficult position and get him to come and take your fly. There have been many times that I didn't care if the fish even stayed on the line once I got him to take. After a while it seems that how you play the game becomes more important than the number of fish you have at the end of the day.

Trout are found in clean freshwater rivers, streams, ponds and lakes from coast to coast in the majority of the United States and Canada. The exceptions would be the southern-most states. Recently, however, trout have even been stocked in some experimental rivers in northern Texas.

The biggest enemies of the trout are a change of environment and pollution, both chemical and thermal. They thrive in cool water environments. Their preferred water temperature range is from 50 to 65 degrees. At that temperature range their metabolism is at its peak, and they feed most actively. When the water temperature gets above 75 degrees, the dissolved oxygen level in the water falls to a critical level for the trout. They will move to different parts of the river seeking cool springs and faster, more oxygenated stretches of water. However, some species such as the brown trout are more tolerant of water temperature. One of the exceptions and oddities is the Firehole River in Yellowstone Park, Wyoming. I have fished there when the water temperature, heated by the natural hot sulphur springs, was in the low 80's, yet the rainbow trout readily took dry flies and fought gamely.

Clean ponds and lakes that are properly managed and protected from pollution and misuse are excellent trout fisheries.

TROUT SPECIES

The brook trout, brown trout and rainbow trout are the three species that are found from coast to coast and are the ones that we are most concerned with. However, the cutthroat trout is equally as important in the western part of the United States and Canada. Most of the species feed similarly on both aquatic and terrestrial insects and other small stream and pond inhabitants, such as small minnows, crayfish, snails and freshwater shrimp. Large trout have been known to occasionally feed on mice, frogs, small birds and other small mammals. What we will be concerned with mainly is imitating the insects and bait fish.

Brook Trout (*Salvelinus fontinalis*)

This trout is actually a member of the char family. Its native range is northeastern North America from Georgia to the Arctic Circle. It has been introduced to the rest of the United States, Canada and other parts of the world where there is suitable habitat. This beautifully colored fish is rapidly decreasing in numbers in much of this country because of its low tolerance for

Brook trout

Rainbow trout

anything but the purist of waters. Most of the larger brook trout are found in the colder and larger rivers and lakes of the northern United States and Canada. The average size "brookie" that you are likely to encounter in most of our streams and ponds will be from 8 to 15 inches. A 15-incher is a prize. There are still many ponds and lakes in the New England states where some fine brook trout can be found. The state of Maine has some good water available. The states of Montana, Wyoming and Idaho also offer some big brook trout.

Some of the really fun brook trout fishing can be had in the small feeder streams of headwaters of larger rivers. These waters may only be from 4 to 8 feet wide and average 6 to 12 feet in depth with deeper holes here and there. You carefully fish the pockets and small pools with a relatively short line. The fish are usually hungry and eager to take your fly. It is not uncommon to spend 2 or 3 hours on a stream like that and hook 20 fish.

The brookie is not known to be a selective feeder as is the brown trout. Most of the patterns that have been tied specifically for brookies are quite bright and colorful, utilizing reds, blues and yellows. Flies like the Silver Doctor, Parmachene Belle and the Royal Coachman are old standards. The brook trout is distinguished by its red spots with blue aureoles on its sides. It has pink or reddish lower fins with white bordering the leading edge. It has dark wavy lines on the back and dorsal fin. Until the brown trout was imported in the 1880's the brook trout was *the* fish sought after by the fly-fisherman.

Rainbow Trout (*Salmo Gairdnerii*)

The rainbow trout is a native of the United States West Coast ranging from the mountains of northern Mexico, north to Alaska. Heavy plantings have well established the rainbow from coast to coast throughout the northern two-thirds of the United States and Canada. They are found in the fast water stretches of clean rivers and in cold water lakes and ponds. The rainbow trout is migratory in nature. If stocked in a small stream, they will gradually work their way down to the larger waterways or lakes. When Mother Nature says the time is right, they will work their way back

Successful angler with a 6-pound migrating steelhead. (Photo courtesy of Bob Linsenman.)

Brown trout

Well marked brown trout about to be released after putting up a good fight.

bles the lake dwelling form in color when it returns from the sea, but it is quite silvery and the rainbow line is less obvious. As it moves up river, the spots and colors darken. Eventually it will resemble the nonmigratory form. One of the important differences in the steelhead is that when it returns from the sea, it will be much larger than its nonmigrating cousins—averaging from 8 to 15 pounds and sometimes reaching up to 35 pounds. The techniques for catching the steelhead are usually different from the normal trout tactics and will be covered in Chapter 6 along with salmon, another anadromous species.

Brown Trout (*Salmo Trutta*)

The brown was the native trout of Europe. It was widely introduced into the waters of the United States in 1882, and subsequently to New Zealand, parts of Asia, South America and Africa. The brown trout has become a favorite of fly-fishermen the world over. It is much more able to resist environmental change than the other trout and seems to be able to tolerate and exist in warmer and more polluted water than its cousins. The territory of the brown trout is primarily the northern two-thirds of the United States from coast to coast. They can also be found in many of the southern states east of the Mississippi. I have also found them in New Mexico and Arizona.

Browns thrive in lakes, rivers and streams, although they are not found in the tiny feeder streams and creeks as are the brook trout. They will usually move out to the larger waters by the time they reach catchable size. The brown trout adapts extremely well to clean cold water lakes and reservoir systems, where they have been known to reach substantial sizes. Trout of 5 to 10

upstream to spawn. These spawning runs bring the larger fish, which live in the deeper downstream waters, up into the shallower river sections and make them available to the fisherman at that time.

The rainbow trout is known as a magnificent fighter, usually making long runs and spectacular jumps. A good size rainbow might reach 4 to 6 pounds. Under certain ideal water and food conditions they can be caught up to around the 15-pound mark. Like all trout, the rainbow is beautifully colored. It gets his name from the pinkish stripe that follows a lateral line along its sides.

The rainbow trout has another side to its family. This migratory species is known as the steelhead. It resem-

Large insect rich rivers such as the Madison in Montana, or New York's Delaware, shown here, produce large trout that are a test for any angler.

Large browns, such as this 7-pounder, are the occasional unexpected reward.

pounds are not uncommon to these big waters with occasional fish up to the 20-pound range.

What makes the brown trout so special are its feeding habits, its selectivity and its majestic appearance. It is ordinarily a more difficult fish to catch compared to the brook or the rainbow. This makes fishing for the brown more of a challenge and catching it more rewarding. When equal numbers of browns and brooks or rainbows were stocked in the same waters, for every brown trout caught, 4 or 5 brooks or rainbows were taken. The fact that it is difficult to catch accounts for the ability of the brown trout to obtain good size in many rivers. The average trout in most of our rivers would average between 9 to 13 inches. In good quality streams, maintaining adequate food and cover, brown trout of 14 to 20 inches are not that uncommon and provide an excellent test for the most experienced angler. The brown trout feeds freely on the surface for mayflies, caddisflies, stoneflies and terrestrials, thus becoming a significant quarry of the fly-fisherman. It is very active at night. As the brown trout gets older and wiser, he remains in hiding during the day and does most of his feeding in the safety of darkness. Some of the largest catches have been taken after dark.

The brown trout probably gets its name from the brownish-yellow base coloring on which are the characteristic red, black and yellow spots. The coloration will vary in different regions and water systems. This coloration intensifies and enhances their elegance as the fall spawning season approaches.

Cutthroat Trout *(Salmo clarki)*

Like the rainbow, the cutthroat is also a native of the West Coast. As the "brookie" is called the "native" on the East Coast, the cutthroat is similarly referred to as the "native" in many western states. The name "cutthroat" comes from the fact that most of the fish have a reddish slash mark on either side of their lower jaw. There are a great many crossbred varieties of the cutthroat, probably more than any other trout species. In many of the species, this slash mark is hardly noticeable. In others it is not there at all.

Like all trout, the cutthroat is beautifully colored, being light green on the back and having shades from pink to red along the lateral line, changing to very pale silvery green on the belly. They have sporadic spotting on their upper body increasing in density toward the tail.

In the inland waters the cutthroat will average 1½ to 3 pounds with an occasional catch of up to 5 pounds. The coastal sea-run species has been known to reach about 15 pounds. There are times when rainbows crossbreed with the cutthroat forming the "cutbow." They are better fighters than the pure cutthroat. The cutthroat itself is not too selective a feeder, and like the eastern brook trout, is much easier to catch than the selective brown or even the rainbow.

Delicate, lightly marked cutthroat trout.

TROUT FLY-FISHING EQUIPMENT

The Rod

The equipment that is used in fly-fishing for trout is some of the most delicate of any sport. It is also some of the most cherished and collected. Most of the original rods were handcrafted from bamboo. They were truly works of art and are now considered angling antiques of considerable value.

There are still many manufacturers producing fine bamboo rods today. They are beautiful effective pieces of equipment and are still highly cherished by their owners. However, although they may be worth the price, the beginner fly-fisherman may not wish to pay from $120 up to $400 for his first rod.

As fly-fishing became more and more popular, fishing tackle manufacturers experimented with different materials that could be used to make rods faster, easier and less expensive. I can remember one of my first rods being of tubular steel. It reminded me of a car antenna. I also had a rod that was solid fiberglass and quite heavy. These materials did not provide the proper action necessary in a good fly rod.

With the process of making rods from hollow tubular fiberglass, the rod making industry boomed overnight. The rods could easily be formed to any taper or action desired by varying the degree of taper and the thickness of the rod walls. These rods were also lighter than the bamboo rods which made casting easier on your hand with rods over 8 feet. One of the major advantages of the fiberglass rod was that it was considerably less expensive than bamboo. This made the sport of fly-fishing much more accessible to a larger segment of the population.

Although fiberglass is probably the most popular material currently being used for the manufacture of rods, tackle manufacturers have still not given up with their research. In the past several years they have been making rods of "graphite," a high-density carbon fiber, using basically the same process as that used with fiberglass. The action of these graphite rods is superior to most glass rods. The recovery response is faster and stronger, meaning that the same effort exerted will produce better results. Again, the graphite rods are significantly lighter than comparable glass or bamboo rods. This really makes a difference for rods of 8½ feet and larger which handle #7 weight lines and up. The use of graphite is a significant breakthrough which makes the game a bit easier.

The costs of trout fly rods vary considerably. Bamboo rods will vary from a bit over $100 to as much as $400 depending on the maker. Graphite rods will vary in price from a bit under $100 up to around $185. Fiberglass rods are the least expensive ranging in price from about $35 up to around $75. If you are handy at making things, there are many manufacturers and dis-

Three of the popular fly reels — upper left, Pfleuger Medalist; upper right, Orvis C.F.O.; bottom, Hardy Lightweight.

the rod and the flyline moving in the air. The purpose of this is to eliminate stress on your hand and make casting comfortable and controllable. The spool of the reel should be able to hold at least 50 yards of backing along with the flyline and leader. The reel also has another important function and feature—it is called the drag. The drag of a reel is the resistance it gives when you pull line off. It is very important that this drag be smooth. It should not be erratic or stick when line is pulled from the reel. An erratic drag could cause reel jamming, broken leaders and lost fish. The better reels have a drag that is adjustable. It can be made heavier or lighter depending on the strength of the leader tippet that you are using. The main purpose of the drag is in fighting the fish. When you hook into a good size trout, it is going to run. The larger the body of water and the larger the fish, usually the further that it will run. If you had no drag on the reel, and you did not control the spool with your finger, the line would overspool when the fish ran it out. It would then probably tangle and the fish would most likely break off. The drag allows the line to run out smoothly and at the same time creates a weight that the fish has to pull against. This tires the fish and helps you get him to the net quicker. The bigger the fish you are fishing for, the more important a good quality reel with a smooth drag is. It is not likely that 8- to 12-inch trout are going to run too far, but if you happen to hang into a 3- or 4-pound rainbow in a decent size river or in a pond or lake while you are standing on the shore, you can almost bet that he will take off all your line and be into your backing in about 5 seconds. You'll almost wish that you could run after him. You may also find yourself using this outfit for other types of fish that might aver-

tributors that will sell you the components necessary to put together your own rod. This can be fun. It will also save you close to half the cost of the rod. If you do a good job, it will also give you a great deal of pride when you use the rod and get good results. At the end of this chapter is a listing of tackle manufacturers, distributors and mail-order houses where you can get information and equipment. Many of them will already be represented in your local sporting goods store or fishing shop.

I had mentioned earlier that you could use one rod for all of your fly-fishing—to a degree, this is possible. If I had to choose one rod to fly-fish for trout, I would first try to evaluate the majority of the waters that I would be fishing. If I were going to fishponds, lakes and large to medium size rivers, I would probably select an 8½-foot rod that called for #6 and #7 weight line. If I were going to fish the medium sized rivers and small streams with an occasional trip to slightly larger water, I would probably go to an 8-foot rod for a #5 and #6 weight line. I would select a rod that had a medium action—not too fast and not too slow, so that it would be capable of handling dry flies, wet flies and streamers with equal ability. This is where it is important to have someone who knows what he is talking about to help you.

The Reel

Now that you have selected your rod, you will need a reel that will balance the rod and hold the flyline. If you recall earlier, we discussed the fact that the weight of the reel should offset the weight of the upper section of

Fly reel with extra spools.

age heavier than trout. So maybe spend an extra few dollars for a decent reel and you won't be sorry. It might also be a good idea to get a reel that you can buy an extra spool for in the event you wish to carry along another weight line or a sinking line.

The subject of lines was covered fairly well in Chapter 1 and in Chapter 2 on assembling your equipment. I would suggest that your first line be a floating one. For a beginner, I would suggest the weight forward type. I believe that it is a bit more forgiving than the double taper at first. As your casting improves, you might find that the double taper will give you better line control for a wider range of distances. If you want to pick up a second line of the same weight for the extra spool, a sinking tip for fishing deeper wet flies, nymphs and streamers would be a good choice.

The Leader

To the end of the line you will attach one of the most

anything is going to give, it will be the knot, unless you have a fray or some other weak spot in the leader. Since then I make five turns for my knots. It is very rare that I am left with a "pigtail" at the end of my leader, which is what happens when the knot comes untied.

Another incident that could even be more illustrative occurred while bass fishing when I was about 16 years old. My friend and I were in one boat and were having a contest with two others in another boat. Although I was using a spinning rod at the time, the principle is the same. Within the first 15 minutes I hooked a good bass that looked to be about 4 pounds on a surface popper. When I brought the fish alongside the boat, we noticed that we had forgotten to bring the net. Not knowing any better, I reached down, grabbed the line and lifted the fish out of the water. To my shocking surprise the knot came out and the bass swam away with my lure in its mouth. About ½-hour later I hooked another good fish about the same size and was horrified when the same

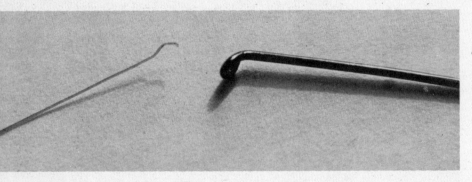

The type of "pigtail" left on the end of a leader where the knot has broken or been pulled out.

important parts of the outfit—the leader. This is also referred to as terminal tackle. The fat part of the leader that attaches to the flyline is referred to as the butt. The thin end to which you attach the fly is called the tippet. Since the leader is the weakest part of the line, the entire outfit is only as strong as the weakest part of the leader. Therefore, any knots that you tie in your leader should be made with extra care. More big fish have been lost because of an incorrect or hastily made knot than for any other reason. I can personally attest to that.

I used to think that I tied a fairly adequate knot. I had been told that four or five turns should be used when tying the Blood Knot joining the two pieces of leader together, or when tying the Improved Clinch Knot for tying on the fly. However, my feeling was that three turns were adequate. Every now and then the leader would part, but it happened so infrequently that it didn't register. The key was that in those days I caught very few big fish. I remember my first trip to Montana many years ago. It took four broken leaders at the knot, and the loss of four big fish in one morning on the Yellowstone River to give me a clue that the three-turn knot I was using was not adequate. When a fish strikes hard, the stress on the leader is maximum at that moment. If

thing happened. The knot I was using was a simple three-turn Clinch Knot—not even an Improved Clinch Knot. Three dollars worth of lures and two good bass was the price to realize that I should learn to tie a good knot, or in that case to at least remember to bring the darn net.

The leader should function as an extension of the line and, as I stressed in Chapter 2, should be balanced and bend equally with the flyline. If this does not occur, you have a hinging effect and the leader with the fly will not "turn over" or lay out correctly. You will have two strikes against you before you begin.

Many manufacturers make one-piece tapered knotless leaders. All stores or distributors that handle flyfishing equipment will have them. You should carry an extra one or two with you when you go fishing in case you damage or lose the one on your line. These leaders will either be 7½ or 9 feet in length. If you will be fishing small wet flies or dry flies of any size, I would suggest a 9-foot leader. As the fly you use gets smaller in size and you need a smaller diameter leader, you can add a piece to the tippet of your current leader, for example going from a 4X to 5X tippet. By doing this you will usually be making your leader longer. This should not be of any concern. If your line and leader are balanced, you should be able to cast and turn over a leader up to 15 feet long without much difficulty.

If you are going to be fishing big, heavy wet flies and nymphs or streamers, you may want to fish a shorter 7½-foot leader with a tippet of 2X or 3X. This would make it easier for you to cast those heavier flies. If you wish, you could cut back the 9-foot leader for this, then add back the additional pieces when you want to go to smaller flies.

The alternative to the one-piece knotless leader is constructing your own leader. Small spools of leader material are available in many different sizes. Tippet-leader material is categorized and listed on the spool in an "X" value which relates to the diameter of the monofiliment—8X being the smallest and 1X being the largest. All sizes larger than 1X are usually considered to be butt material and are just categorized by diameter listed in thousandths of an inch. Below is a chart of the relative "X" to diameter values.

Leader kit with spools of various size material.

TIPPET SIZE AND "X" VALUES	
"X" Value Listing	Diameter (in thousandths of an inch)
1X	.010
2X	.009
3X	.008
4X	.007
5X	.006
6X	.005
7X	.004
8X	.003

fly to work naturally.

The first step is to match a piece of butt material approximately 30 to 36 inches in length to the end of the flyline. (Refer to Chapter 2, page 23 for details and points of importance pertaining to this connection and the bend test.) Then you simply tie in progressively shorter pieces of material until you have tapered down to the desired diameter of tippet you want to use. It will take a little experimentation to end up with the size

Large air-resistant bass bug that requires a large strong leader to cast and turn it over properly.

The strength of the leader will vary slightly from manufacturer to manufacturer. The test strength of 4X at .007-inch will be approximately 4 pounds. Naturally the test strength will increase and decrease with the larger and smaller diameters. Although it is advantageous to have as strong a leader as possible, using the proper diameter is more important to the function of the leader during the cast and in the performance of the fly. I will discuss that in more detail shortly.

In constructing your leader the main consideration is for it to balance and turn over smoothly. With this in mind you need consistency in the material that you use. Therefore, for the majority of the leader, approximately the upper three-fourths, or that part of the leader that is largest in diameter, you should use the same brand of material. The tippet or end of the leader is the most critical and should be of the best material available. For most of your trout fishing you will be better off with a tippet material that is quite limp or soft. This allows the

90

tippet you want together with the length of leader you want. Don't let leader length scare you. The key is balance. If you were trying to make a 9-foot leader and it ended up being 10 feet it will be no problem. Illustrated below is a typical example of a construction progression.

light or too small for the fly, you will have difficulty in making the leader turn over properly and placing the fly where you want it. For example, a size #8 or #10 fly offers considerable air resistance when cast. If it were tied to a 6X tippet, the leader and fly would land on the water in a sloppy heap probably quite short of the

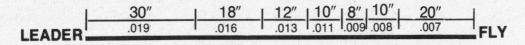

LEADER — 30" .019 — 18" .016 — 12" .013 — 10" .011 — 8" .009 — 10" .008 — 20" .007 — FLY

Total length of above leader = 9 feet

The above example is simply to give you an idea of basic construction. You can vary these measurements to construct the leader that you want. However, there are several important points to consider and remember:

1. Make sure that the junction from the line to the leader balances—use the "bend test." If it does not, the rest of the leader will not matter.

2. Do not have too much skip in diameter from piece to piece as you taper down or you will have the "hinging effect." A good rule is to skip .003 in the upper third of the leader, .002 in the middle third and .001 in the lower third. Use the "bend test" as you taper.

3. The next to the last piece should be slightly longer than the piece before it. The reason for this is, as you change flies, your tippet will get shorter and you will eventually have to change it. When you change it, you will be shortening the next piece slightly. If that second piece was short to begin with, it would not be long before you would have to change it also.

4. Make your tippet at least 18 inches to 20 inches long. There are two reasons for this. As mentioned above, as you change flies, the tippet will become shorter. You don't want to spend the day changing tippets when you could be fishing. Secondly and most importantly, a long tippet section allows your fly to function more naturally on or in the water. This especially applies to dry flies.

As I had mentioned earlier, the proper diameter of the tippet is quite important to the proper function of the fly—especially the dry fly. One of the main problems of dry fly-fishing is unnatural drag of the fly on the water surface. If the tippet is too heavy or too large for the size fly you are using, it will not allow the fly to drift naturally and will drag it. This drag often results in last second refusals by the trout, (most anglers think the trout missed the fly when this occurs). An example of this might be if you tied a size #18 hook fly to a 3X, .008 tippet. The size #18 fly would be more properly fished with a 5X or 6X tippet. Conversely, if the tippet is too

intended target. The 6X is just too weak to turn it over properly. It would take about a 4X tippet, possibly even 3X to properly control the cast. Another problem that you may have with too light a tippet is that you may break off and lose many flies while you are casting. Probably the largest tippet that you are likely to use for dry fly trout fishing will be 3X and the need for 8X is dubious. Therefore, I have listed below a practical guide for coordinating fly size to tippet size . . . . . .

Fly hook size	20-28	16-22	14-18	10-14	6-10
Tippet size	7X	6X	5X	4X	3X

When fishing with wet flies, nymphs or streamers, you can use leaders, if desired, that are a size or two larger for the corresponding hooks in the above scale. For example, a size 14 nymph could be fished on a 3X tippet, or large #6 or #8 wet flies or nymphs could be fished on 1X or 2X tippets.

Knots for Tying Your Leader: In constructing your leader, it is important to use good knots. The two that are most popular are the Blood Knot and the Surgeon's Knot. The Blood Knot is the most popular and has been the standard for making tapered leaders. Many fishermen, however, feel that the Surgeon's Knot is easier and quicker to tie. It also may be a better knot for joining leader strands of greater differences in diameter than in the Blood Knot. You should learn to tie them both.

Rainbows are known for their jumping ability.

Blood Knot

1. Lay one end of the tippet over the leader end to form an X. Allow 4 inches of each end to tie the knot.
2. Hold the X between your right thumb and forefinger. Using your left hand, make five turns of the leader end around the tippet, wrapping away from you. Bring the leader end back and insert it on the other side of the X. At this point, switch the knot to hold it between your left thumb and forefinger.
3. Using your right hand, make five turns of the tippet around the leader, wrapping toward you. Bring the tippet end back and insert it in the same opening that the leader end is in, but in the opposite direction. Now wet the wraps with saliva (this lubricates the monofiliment and allows the knot to tighten smoothly without too much friction) and tighten the knot by pulling the two standing ends.
4. Trim the tag ends for the finished knot.

Surgeon's Knot

1. Lay the tippet end over the leader butt.
2. Tie a big overhand knot, but don't pull it tight.
3. Pass the leader end and the standing part of the tippet through the loop again. Wet the knot and pull steadily on all four ends to tighten.
4. Trim the tag ends closely for the finished knot.

Improved Clinch Knot

The knots that tie the fly to the leader are as equally important as the knots that hold the leader together. Just about all of your needs can be handled with the Improved Clinch Knot.

1. Thread the tippet through the hood eye, and pull out about 4 or 5 inches. Make five turns with the tag end of the tippet around the standing part. Push the end through the loop created in front of the hook eye and then back through the big loop that was just formed.
2. Wet the knot and pull steadily on the tippet to tighten the twists against the hook eye. Trim the end leaving about $1/16$-inch for slippage.

Duncan Loop

The Duncan Loop is another knot that can be used effectively, allowing the fly to swing freely in the water.

1. Thread the tippet through the hook eye, and pull out about 5 inches. Bend the tag end of the tippet toward the hook eye to make a loop.
2. Wrap four or five turns around the top of the loop and the standing part of the tippet with the tag end.
3. Pull the tag end slowly until the knot starts to tighten. Then slide the knot to the desired position, and pull on the tag end to tighten the knot securely. Trim the tag end.

The loop will stay open allowing the fly to swing freely. When you hook a fish and weight is exerted, the knot will slide closed against the hook eye. After landing the fish, reopen the loop by sliding the knot back.

OTHER EQUIPMENT YOU SHOULD HAVE

One of the important items that you should have with you, especially in a river or stream, is a landing net. I will discuss the use of this later in the chapter. Nets are made of various materials. The least expensive models have an aluminum frame. As they get fancier and more aesthetic, they are fashioned from various types of wood. It is important for the netting to be a close mesh, so that fish cannot fall through the holes. If the material is of nylon, dacron or other synthetic rather than cotton, it will last much longer. The cotton or natural fiber has a tendency to deteriorate faster.

Another item that you will find a must once you become involved is a fishing vest. The vest holds everything that you need when you are at or in the river, from your leader tippet material to a spare reel spool and line that you might want with you, and all of your flies, to your lunch when you take a break ½-mile from the car. It should have LOTS of pockets. In the vest will be your boxes of flies; dry fly floatant to keep your dry flies from sinking; spools of leader tippet material so you can change your tippet when it gets too short, or when it breaks accidentally or when you change the size of your fly; insect repellent for the ones that want to bite you; a nail clipper to trim the ends off the knots that you tie in

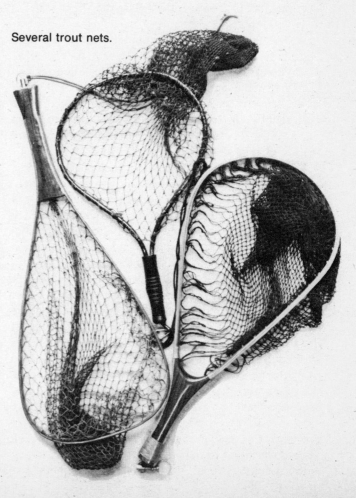

Several trout nets.

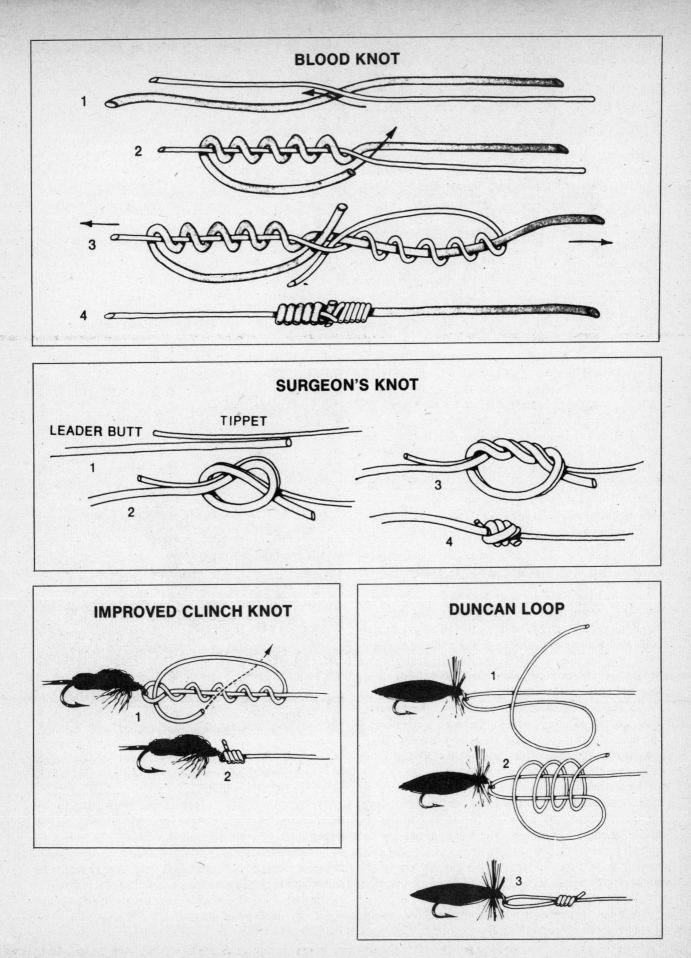

BLOOD KNOT

1

2

3

4

SURGEON'S KNOT

LEADER BUTT

TIPPET

1

2

3

4

IMPROVED CLINCH KNOT

1

2

DUNCAN LOOP

1

2

3

Typical trout vest with stuffed pockets.

Quite often a wading staff can be very handy for maintaining your stability in difficult to wade rivers.

the leader and tippet; a little plastic box (preferrably clear) to hold an insect that the trout are feeding on (you may want to examine the fly or imitate it when you tie your own); a hemostat to help you remove your fly without destroying it or the fish, when the trout has been hooked deep in the throat; anything else that you want to carry that either is useful or makes you happy.

A good pair of chest waders, not just hip boots are a must if you want to get to different parts of the river without getting wet. If they have felt soles or if you put felt on them (kits are available), they will not slip on the rocks.

BASIC TROUT BEHAVIOR

Now that you have organized the basic equipment to fish for the trout, it is important to understand the fish's behavior and the quality of its senses. The trout exists in its cold water environment for the purpose of reproduction of the species. However, that biological drive occurs for only a short time each year. Fortunately throughout the entire year the trout eats. This need for food is regulated to a degree by the water temperature. The ideal temperature range for the fish's metabolism is when the water is from 50 to around 65 degrees. When the water temperature falls much below 50 degrees or goes above 70, this feeding is reduced.

The feeding activity of the trout corrolates with the activity of what it feeds on. Other stream life and insects are much more available to the fish during the warm weather periods. Spring and summer are the times of the "hatches" which is when the acquatic insects make their transition from the bottom of the stream to the water surface. It is at this time that they are most vulnerable.

Trout are nearsighted and are only capable of seeing for up to about 30 feet. All objects beyond that distance are blurred. The fisherman should be aware that when he is in or near the stream, any fish within that 30-foot range is able to see him.

The trout's eyesight is designed marvelously for night vision. This is one of the reasons why many of the larger fish feed more actively after dark. The ability to discriminate colors and shapes is also surprisingly developed. The trout is quite often frustratingly selective and might reject slight variations from what it is actually feeding on. This selectivity is often controlled to some degree by the type of water that the fish feeds in. For example, the trout may be able to be extremely selective in discerning color variations in clear, smooth gliding water where it has ample time and water clarity to critically inspect the fly. On the other hand, fast choppy riffles greatly distort light and limit the fish's ability to be too critical. The trout often must make a spontaneous decision based upon a suggestive image created by the fly. In these conditions, size and silhouette seem to be the most important factors of your imitation.

I can remember fishing during a hatch on a Pennsylvania stream several years ago when the fish were feeding quite actively on the surface. There was a hatch of a certain insect, and the trout seemed to be keyed to it. I proceeded to fish the riffle at the head of the pool with a fly that I thought was a good imitation of the natural. After hooking several fish in succession, I moved to the slower section of the pool to work on three trout I saw feeding. To my dismay, the fly that had just taken three fish was totally rejected by these trout. It took trying two other slight color variations of the same pattern fly before I got one fish to take. It was no surprise to me, then, when I was able to catch one of the other two trout also. They wanted that particular fly. During the next hour I experimented in the different types of water and found that only that one color variation would take the fish in the slick clear water, while several variations worked equally well in the choppy riffles and runs.

When an insect or imitation fly is under the water, the trout can see it quite clearly. However an object on or above the water surface is quite different. The ability to see the entire object clearly is subject to the properties of light. As the light rays pass from the air into the water they are bent. This bending is called refraction. The amount of this refraction is directly proportional to the angle at which the light strikes the water surface. For example, light rays that enter the water perpendicular to the surface, are not bent or refracted at all. Those rays that enter the water nearly parallel to the surface are refracted at an angle of approximately 45 degrees. This means that the trout can see all objects that are above the surface since light enters the water from any direction. However, his ability to see and observe the outside world is restricted somewhat because the light rays are bent. As these rays are bent and enter the surface, they create circular holes called "windows" in the surface that the fish are able to see through. Those objects that are in the center of the window are very clear and distinct. As the objects drift from the center toward the edges, they become slightly distorted. Those objects at the edge are compressed and blurred. This window is the only place that the fish can see out of the water; the rest of the water surface acts like a mirror—what is seen is a reflection of the stream bottom and any objects that are underneath the surface film.

THE TROUT'S "WINDOW"

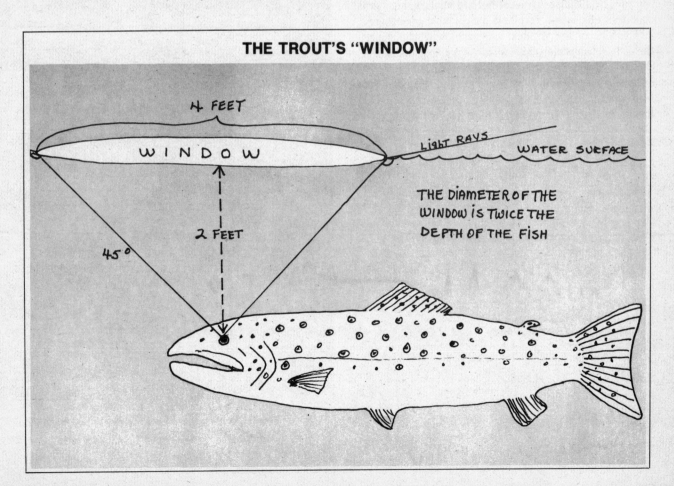

The white specks are large quantities of aquatic insects that are "hatching" from the water. This is when the feeding activity can often be frantic.

Because of this angle refraction, you can see why it might be necessary to stay low when approaching a spot where you know there are fish. It is quite advantageous to keep your silhouette at least in the compressed images at the edge of the window. Trout are quite wary and will spook at any unnatural movement. It is often advantageous to utilize available cover to break up your outline. Standing in front or behind bushes, high grass, boulders etc. is an excellent means of camouflage.

The size of the window increases with the depth of the fish in the water. The window is twice the depth of the fish. For example, if the fish is 12 inches under the surface, its window will be approximately 24 inches in diameter. If the fish is 3 feet deep, its window is 6 feet in diameter. Surface feeding fish usually hold closer to surface and concentrate their attention to

(Above) Slick, flat glides must be approached cautiously, so as not to spook wary trout.

(Left) Broken water riffles and runs do not require such a delicate approach.

96

Glassy water, such as this on Henry's Fork of the Snake in Idaho, reveals every little movement. The most delicate of presentations is often necessary.

It is often necessary for the angler to stay back from the water and use natural surroundings to keep from spooking wary trout.

what drifts into the water. At that depth, the window is quite small and, especially in fast water, the trout must make a quick decision whether to take or not. So you can see the importance of being able to cast effectively in order to place your fly in the right spot so it will drift into the fish's window where he can rise and take it.

If you are fishing a nymph, wet fly or streamer that is under the surface, the fish does not have its lateral vision restricted to the boundaries of the window. It is always better to make your cast so that the fly will drift as close to the trout as possible, but a trout will often move much farther to the side to take a fly underwater than if it were on the surface.

The trout's hearing ability extends to the lateral lines on its sides. This is a very sensitive system that detects

It is often valuable to observe and analyze the water and environment to get an idea of what the fish may be feeding on and how best to proceed.

vibrations. The fisherman should be very careful while wading and walking the stream banks so as not to create too many harsh vibrations that will scare the fish. Talking is no problem, since for all practical purposes, sound does not travel from air to water. The angler can sometimes utilize this vibration by fishing with a fly that simulates a minnow, working it in the surface so that the commotion imitates a natural crippled bait fish. This attracts the trout's attention, and it will often move considerable distances in pursuit of the fly. A Muddler Minnow is a typical fly pattern for this method.

ANALYZE THE FISHING ENVIRONMENT

Now that you have all your equipment in working order, we should take it to the water and use it for its

A piece of water like this is loaded with holding places for trout. Several positions are indicated by the "X's".

designed purpose—to cast a line and catch trout.

One of the most common faults of the beginning fisherman is that he is so anxious to get to the water and fish, he does not usually bother to really think about where the fish are. He just steps in and starts casting away—many times casting where there are no fish and walking in spots where the fish are. . . . or I should say were. The best trout fishermen that I know spend their first several minutes, after arriving at the water, especially at a spot they have never been to before, in observation and analyzation of the water itself for the purpose of determining where the fish would be and possibly what they might be feeding on.

Rivers and Streams

Rivers and streams are the most important and most exciting trout fisheries. They differ considerably from lakes and ponds which will be discussed separately.

With the exception of the relatively short period of time during which the trout reproduce, the fish will select a location in the stream that offers the maximum of both cover and food. The cover is protection from both predators and the strong current. With regard to the food, it would be a place near the edges of currents where it is easy to pick up food as it drifts by.

The idea is to examine a piece of water—a section of stream—and try to determine the most advantageous spot for a trout to be. You should be thinking to yourself when looking at the water, "considering the present water conditions, what would be the most likely place for a fish to hold that would offer considerable protection and at the same time be easy for it to feed." This could be a rock in the middle of the river, an undercut bank, a log or other object in the water, a sudden deep spot or hole. . . . anything that offers the cover and the food. Naturally the rocks would be the most natural and plentiful to look for. However, most of them are not sticking out of the water to be easily identified. They are under the surface creating pockets in the current which make it easy for the trout to hold. These current variations and pockets are easily discernible on the surface after a bit of experience. Where there is a large boulder, there will be a swirl on the surface just down stream from it. There will also be a considerable pocket of slack water downstream from the rock. This is an easy place for the fish to lie. The current that rushes on either side of the rock will bring food by the trout. He just moves in and out of his lie, picking up the morsels of

One large and one medium size trout hold their feeding positions on the upstream side of large rocks.

Small, insect rich streams, such as this Pennsylvania limestone, hold large quantities of healthy trout.

food as they are swept by.

Most people think that the best lie for a trout is behind a rock. This may seem logical, but I have seen more good fish holding in front of the rocks than behind. The nature of the current backing up in front of a large rock creates a condition that makes it easy for the fish to lie in. The fish also has a much clearer and less obstructed view of the food coming to it from in front of the rock than it would if it were behind it.

I can remember watching a section of stream from a high rock wall. I was able to see everything that was moving in the riffle down below. It always amazes me how when you first look at the water it seems vacant,

yet after careful observation fish seem to materialize out of nowhere. In this small stretch I eventually spotted six fish. Four of them were good size trout, one looked to be close to 15 inches. They were all in front of large rocks—each had his own. The other two trout were in the 8- to 10-inch class and were content to move casually from place to place picking up morsels as they went. They had one basic position, but strayed constantly, while the larger fish stayed put in front of the rocks moving slightly from side to side to side taking insects as they drifted by and occasionally rising to take one off the surface. It was a good lesson in learning some of the trout's behavior patterns. It was definitely time well spent and something that I would recommend to anyone who has the opportunity to do so. Anytime you are able to learn about the natural behavior of the fish that you are trying to catch, especially if you can watch it first hand, the easier it will be for you to understand how to function on the stream with your equipment. So, when you get to the river, pick out the best looking spots for a trout to be and concentrate your efforts there first. Start fishing the spot that is closest to you and work your way out toward the opposite bank, rather than casting almost to the other side, and probably scaring the fish that were close by.

One excellent way to learn a stream is to observe it at times of low water. This will usually be in mid summer. When the water is down, you can usually see the bottom structure much easier than during normal conditions. You should make note, at least mentally, of the large rocks, the deep pockets, undercut banks and any small streams or springs that may enter the large body of water. These are natural holding places and you will want to fish them during normal water conditions.

What happens when the water is high? High water creates new holding places—places where the trout could not or would not stay under normal conditions. High water is usually discolored for a period of time. This also provides a means of concealment to the fish, allowing him to lie in places he might not normally be. The fish will often move from the main current into the quiet water along the edges of the stream. This is especially true in the early season when the water, besides being high, is usually quite cold. The trout being cold-blooded does not care to contend with the currents at this time. They will seek the easy eddies which require much less energy.

Many fishermen make the mistake of passing up the spots near the shore during these high water times. They are missing out on some good action. Even during normal water conditions, I have seen trout lying in shallow water several feet from the shoreline. This is usually before the first people have come down to fish the stream that day. Invariably an angler will step in the river, without first looking, naturally scaring the fish that were lying there, and wade out about 30 or 40 feet into waist deep water. It is the smart and usually successful fisherman that stops to look at all the water before he starts to fish.

I remember early one spring morning telling an angler, who was about to wade into the depths, that he should try casting his fly near the shore first where a small stream trickled in and formed a pocket. He gave me a dirty look and ventured forth leaving muddy water behind him. I sat down on the bank, waited and observed. Within one minute, as the water cleared, I watched two trout move back into the pocket from where "bigfoot" had just spooked them. The water was only 10 inches deep, but the trout liked the fresh stream trickle.

I waited an ample time for the fish to calm down, then picked up my rod and moved cautiously below them. In three casts I had hooked the two trout. One was 11 inches, the other was 13. Needless to say, my deep water friend was in a huff. When he asked, "Where the heck did they come from?" I replied, "They were there all the time. You just didn't bother to look."

We were talking about high water before I went astray. One of the best places when the water is up and slightly dirty is at the tail of pools. Under normal water conditions the trout would lie in the riffles at the head of the pool down through the middle of the pool. That is where the food would be most plentiful. Also, the slightly broken water surface near the head of the pool would provide visual cover from above. However, when the water comes up and becomes discolored, the fish will often move down from the now heavier current

When the water is up (above), it is sometimes difficult to know exactly where the best holding places would be. The same section of stream in low water (below). It is easier to see the pockets. The fish would be concentrated in the different pockets. Mental notes should be made for when the water is up again.

into the easier current at the tail of the pool. These are areas anywhere from 5 to 15 feet from where the flat water turns into a choppy riffle again. Since the high dirty water is more difficult for the fish to see in, the quiet slower water at the tail gives the trout more time to see what drifts or swims by or over them, therefore making it easier for them to feed.

What about during low water conditions? Trout become extra wary during low water conditions, so it is often necessary to be a bit more careful when wading. Since the water is low, it is more common to be able to see the fish in the water. This means that the fish can see you easier also, therefore try to approach them from below or from the side. Low water will sometimes tend to concentrate the trout into a smaller section of the stream or river. Quite often low water is also warm water. Temperatures above 70 degrees are a concern to the trout. These high temperatures will often cause them to move to different sections of the stream that will offer more oxygen or cooler water. For example, they will often move from the pools up into the heavily oxygenated pocket water or riffles. Any places where a cool stream or a spring come into the main river would be a natural attraction and would have to hold fish.

I can remember several summers during serious low and warm water conditions when there were dozens of fish packed together at the mouths of cooler streams. These conditions make the trout dangerously vulnerable to predators of all kinds—man included. Abuse of these conditions can seriously hurt good trout populations.

Low, warm water conditions will cause trout to concentrate in large numbers at the mouths of cooler streams, or where cold springs trickle in.

In a pond or lake, a small 10-inch fish or a larger 20-inch trout quite often make the same dimple ring rise.

Lakes and Ponds

Lakes and ponds are a bit more difficult to figure out than rivers and streams. For the most part, all you see is the surface. You usually cannot see the formations on the bottom. This is where local knowledge can really help. If you know, or if you know someone who knows, where a stream comes into the lake or where there are natural springs, these would be very likely places for trout to congregate. Underwater structures, rocks and holes are also likely spots.

Trout do not usually hold as much in a pond or lake as they do in a river. They move around much more in search of food. Since there is no current to bring the food to them except where a stream flows into the lake, they have to go in search of the food. Early in the season, not too long after ice out in many parts of the country, trout can be seen cruising along just under the surface, every now and then making a gentle dimple type rise as they take an insect from the surface. There are several small insects that hatch early in the season in many lakes and ponds. The trout will simply suck them in as the insect pauses in the surface film to transform into a winged adult. The rise is usually the same regardless of the size of the fish. . . . just a little dimple. However, there could be a 20-inch fish under that dimple.

As I write this it brings to mind an incident that happened to a friend of mine. This story will also serve as an example of why it is always good to have backing

It is sometimes necessary to wait for the rise, then make a quick accurate cast to the fish.

Sometimes the most productive way to fish a pond or lake is to work the shoreline with a canoe. Quite often the fish will rise farther out than you can wade.

he was working and cast about 5 feet in front of him. When you thought the time was right, you gently twitched your fly. If the fish was near, you would see the dimple rise and feel your line tighten. "Got one," was usually the cry along the bank. I say the bank, because most of these lakes drop off too fast to be able to wade well. If you don't have a boat, you are left to walk the banks. Anyway, most of the fish we caught were from about 10 to 14 inches. Although we knew that there were big fish in the lake, it seemed that they were always caught on trolling streamers or with lures.

Joe pointed to a dimple rise and commented that it was just out of range. However, the next rise was about 5 feet closer. Joe had his line in the air and set the small fly on the surface about 3 feet short of the last rise form. Three twitches brought the rise, and the fish was

Dave Whitlock and Lefty Kreh discuss their plans as they prepare to float the White River in Arkansas in search of big trout.

on your reel. We were fishing Lake Glenida in Westchester County, New York. About 2 weeks after ice out there is usually a hatch of what we used to call the "ice fly" for lack of knowing what it really was. It really didn't matter what it was. We knew what it looked like, and we knew that the rainbow trout in the lake liked to eat them. The fly was a small black midge that could be imitated on a #16 or #18 hook. The idea was to wait until a feeding fish cruised to within casting distance. You would anticipate the direction in which hooked. Joe lifted the rod remarking that trout didn't feel too long. In fact, the line sort of went slack because the fish was swimming toward us.

As Joe reeled in line the fish must have realized it was hooked and gave us the surprise of our lives. It rolled on the surface about 30 feet from us. I would bet my best rod that it was better than 2 feet long. With that, it headed toward the middle of the lake. There was no stopping it. Unfortunately, there was no backing on the reel either. When the fish ran out all of the line, there was just that sickening "snap." Talk about a sad fisherman—I guess most people learn lessons the hard way.

Trout in lakes and ponds do prefer certain water temperatures. They will change their feeding levels as the temperature changes. In the early part of the season, many trout can be caught in relatively shallow

of the many patterns that are available, and they are some of the best. I don't think you should get too overwhelmed with too many patterns in the beginning. You should start with some good basics in different sizes and build from there as you gain knowledge and experience.

More importantly you should learn what to do with the patterns you have, how you should fish them and what size you should be using. In order to best understand why you should be fishing certain patterns and using certain techniques, it would be quite advantageous to have an understanding of what the trout feeds on, when he feeds on it and how he feeds on it. Now I just put that in one sentence, and it may seem incidental at this time, but there have been numerous books written on just that information alone. It is probably the key to understanding how you should function when you are

Natural and imitation Black Nose Dace.

water. As the season moves into the summer months, the angler usually has to go down deep for the fish.

TROUT FOODS

Now that you have a pretty good idea of where the trout might be, the next thing that you are going to think about is what fly should I fish with? It is always a big question, and one that does not always have a simple answer. There are certain basic good flies that are proven fish takers, for example, the Black Ghost or White Marabou in the streamer department; the Leadwing Coachman or Hare's Ear for the wet flies; the Zug Bug or Murcrat are good choices for nymphs; and the Adams or Goofus Bug (also known as Humpy) are excellent all around dry flies. These are just a sampling

fly-fishing for trout.

Let's take a look at the various basic foods that trout eat, how the trout feeds on them, how to imitate them and how to fish with the artificial flies that represent them. We will look at the bait fish, the mayfly, the caddisfly, the stonefly, and the terrestrial insects.

Bait Fish or Minnows

The bait fish is one of the largest pieces of food available to the trout on a year-round basis. They are always in the stream and available, but they are not always easy to catch. Unlike the insects that the trout feeds on which usually just drift by and are easy pickings, the bait fish can swim away quite rapidly and hide under a rock or other object. However, when a bait fish,

Fishing minnow imitations often results in a nice catch of large trout.

or minnow as I prefer to call them, is injured, for whatever the reason, and cannot swim properly, it is a prime target for any sizable trout to make a meal of. Remember that when you fish the imitation, make it look crippled, and you'll get action.

There are various types of minnows in the waters where trout live—dace, shiners, killies, chubs. Even the baby trout themselves are eaten from time to time. They are a choice target because they are a large piece of food. Think about the amount of energy expended and received when a trout goes after and eats a 1/4- or 1/2-inch long insect as compared with the nutrition it will get from eating a 2-inch minnow. It's a big difference. Besides reproduction, the only activity that the fish does in the water is hold itself in the current and move to catch a piece of food. "Mom Nature" has a rule of survival for fish—if you expend more energy going after your food than you get from eating it, you won't be alive very long. This is one reason why, as a fish gets larger, his diet changes also. Even though it will still feed on the insects, it will do so only when they are easy to get and will concentrate on the big ones. The minnow becomes a much more important part of a large fish's diet, because it gives the fish more for the work put out to get it. If you fish these minnow imitations diligently, you have a good chance of hanging into some hefty size trout.

Naturally, since there are different types of minnows, they all don't look exactly alike. They might look alike to many who just look at them as little fish, but some have marked physical characteristics. For example, dace have a dark stripe down their sides, while other minnows don't. Some shiners have a golden shine to them, while others, like killers, have a silver shine. If there are only one or two types of minnows in a particular piece of water, the trout might be keyed in to take

only something that looks like one of them.

Now, I'm not trying to discourage you, or make it sound difficult, I'm only trying to make you aware of the sometimes critical selectivity of trout, which is the reason that you can catch them one day and not the next. The answer is to have a few variations of imitations so that you can experiment and change if you are not getting the results that you expected.

There are several minnow fishing techniques that are effective. I will call them, the **crippled minnow,** the **swimming minnow,** and the **fleeing minnow.** The **crippled minnow** technique is effective and can be used throughout the entire season. It entails making your artificial look helpless in the water, therefore being a tantalizing target for the hungry trout. I have found this technique especially effective in the early season when, because of the still very cold water temperatures, the trout's desire to chase crazily around a river in pursuit of a little fish is not its favorite thing in life, yet it still values the minnow as an important food source.

The fly can be fished either weighted or unweighted. However, if you are fishing in the early season and wish the fly to work deep, as it should, you would be better off with a weighted fly and possibly a sinking tip line. The sinking tip is not a must, but it would be a help on larger rivers. The idea is to make your cast up and across stream. As the fly hits the water, make a big upstream mend. This will allow the fly to sink before the current creates drag on the line. (Another means of accomplishing this is to utilize the reach or upstream hold cast as discussed in Chapter 2.) As the fly and line swing by you, gently twitch your rod tip, about every 2 seconds, so as to make the fly jump forward and drop back a few inches at a time. This action gives the illusion of the minnow struggling to get some mobility. It often entices the fish to strike at something that may be trying to get away. As the fly swings down below you, the drag of the current on the line will start to bring the fly up toward the surface. It is at this time when the strike is most likely to occur. If it does not, allow the fly to swing directly below you and hang in the current for a few seconds before you retrieve it to make another cast. Sometimes a trout will follow the fly all the way in, and upon seeing it stop to rest, will hit.

It would be advisable to keep your rod tip slightly raised during the manipulation of the fly so as to absorb the shock in the event of a strike. Many leaders have been broken and flies lost when the rod tip is pointed at the striking fish. You can also use a pretty good size tippet, since the trout are not leader shy with a fly of this size.

The **swimming minnow** technique can also be effective throughout the entire season. One of the advantages of this method is that the water can be covered in a definite pattern, meaning that you can present the fly to the maximum number of trout if you work consistently. You make your cast across and downstream. The current on the line will move the fly across the current. A second after your fly hits the water, impart a similar type of twitching action with your rod tip as in the injured minnow technique—raising and lowering the rod tip every few seconds. Again, this will make your fly swim forward about 6 inches or so then drop back. At the end of the swing, again allow the fly to hang a few seconds before picking it up to cast again.

The third method, the **fleeing minnow** is the most exciting, because most of the strikes will be visible, since the fly is traveling in or just underneath the surface film. This technique is most effective from about the time that the river temperature gets above 50 degrees, through the rest of the season. It is especially effective when the water is dirty, on rainy days and just before and into darkness. My experience has been that it seems more effective for browns than other species.

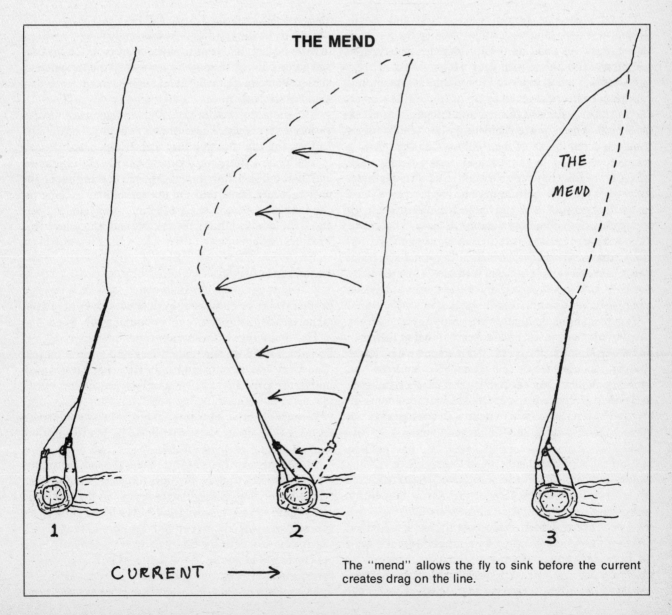

THE MEND

THE MEND

CURRENT ⟶

The "mend" allows the fly to sink before the current creates drag on the line.

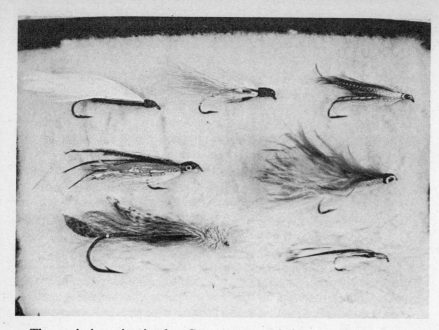

A typical assortment of bait fish imitations.

The technique is simple. Cast across and downstream, trying to land your fly as close to the far bank as possible. As soon as the fly hits the water, start stripping in the flyline with your left hand (if you are a right-handed caster) in 12- to 15-inch lengths. Again, it is important to keep your rod tip up or to the side a bit so that the hard strike that this method brings won't break the fly off. What you are simulating when you do this is a minnow coming out of the shallow water and fleeing across the stream. When fish hit it, it is a hard savage strike, since they have to move fast to catch it. In fact it seems that you only hook about one fish for every three strikes that you get. Sometimes the fish will miss the fly completely then come back and hit it again. Therefore, if the trout hits and misses half way through the swing, don't pick the fly up to cast right away, let it finish the swing. He may come around and nail it again. If he doesn't, make another cast to the same spot as the last one and be ready.

This technique can really save an otherwise fishless day when you have miserable weather that makes normal fly-fishing unsuccessful. I remember when I was guiding a couple that came from New York to fish Montana rivers. I had spent the previous week showing two other people ideal conditions and perfect water levels. Fortunately, the fish were also cooperative and we all had a great time. But, when Joan and Arthur came, they brought along a change of weather that was not too terrific. The temperatures went down and the waters came up. My friends wanted to fish the Big Hole River near Twin Bridges, Montana. It was known for good size brown trout and I had caught some of them the week before. Unfortunately, the first hour we fished produced nothing. We tried nymphs and wet flies but the trout didn't want any part of them. The water was still fairly warm, about 60 degrees, so I told them to put on a Muddler Minnow fly and fish it the way I described

above. I demonstrated first. My first cast produced a 14-inch trout and the fifth cast was hit by what appeared to be a serpent, but he missed it. Anyway, in 2 hours we had caught about 15 good trout up to 20 inches and had missed as many more. It saved the day and has done so many more since.

As I mentioned before, it is advantageous to have a variety of patterns. Three or four would be sufficient. In Chapter 3 on flytying Eric Leiser described how to tie the Yellow Marabou. Among the 10 other streamer and bucktail ties that are listed at the end of that chapter, there are three that are considered to be tops on any list. They should be part of your assortment. They are—the Black Ghost, Black Nosed Dace and the Muddler Minnow.

Major Insect Foods

The mayflies and caddisflies are the two insects most artificials imitate. They together with the stoneflies make up the majority of the average trout's diet.

The similarities of these three types of insects are that they all have both the underwater stage which is imitated by the nymph and wet fly, the adult stage imitated by the dry fly. Both stages are important to anglers.

We will examine each type of insect briefly by itself, then we will discuss how to fish both underwater and surface stages of the artificials.

The mayfly makes up one of the major portions of the trout's diet. They are of the Latin order *Ephemeroptera* (short-lived winged insect). This refers to the fact that, although the insect on an average lives for about 1 year, the winged adult only lives for an average of 1 to 3 days. However, it is during this period of emergence and transformation that some of the most exciting surface feeding activity and dry fly-fishing takes place.

This group of aquatic insects has been the most im-

Mayfly adult.

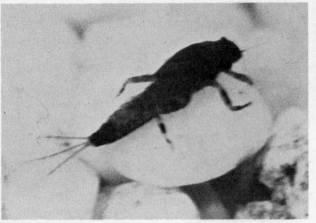

Mayfly nymph

(Above) Mayfly adult (subimago).

(Below) Mayfly adult spinner (imago).

portant link, throughout fly-fishing history and literature between the angler and the trout. There have been many volumes that dedicate themselves directly to the understanding of the behavior of mayfly species and how they affect the feeding habits of the trout.

These insects are found in rivers, streams, lakes and ponds all across the North American continent from coast to coast and in many parts of the South up through Canada. They range in size from as small as about ⅛-inch up to approximately 1½ inches in length. There are hundreds of species and a great variance in their coloration—from creams, yellows, pinks to gray olives and blacks. It is quite often that the trout becomes selective to a certain color mayfly, making it necessary to have an artificial that is close to the same coloration in order to catch the selective feeder.

As I mentioned, the typical mayfly lives for about 1 year. Almost all of its life, except for those few days that it becomes a winged adult, whose sole purpose is to reproduce, is spent on the bottom of the river or pond in the aquatic stage called a nymph. These nymphs are periodically available to the fish and are a very important food source.

There are three basic stages of the mayfly that we

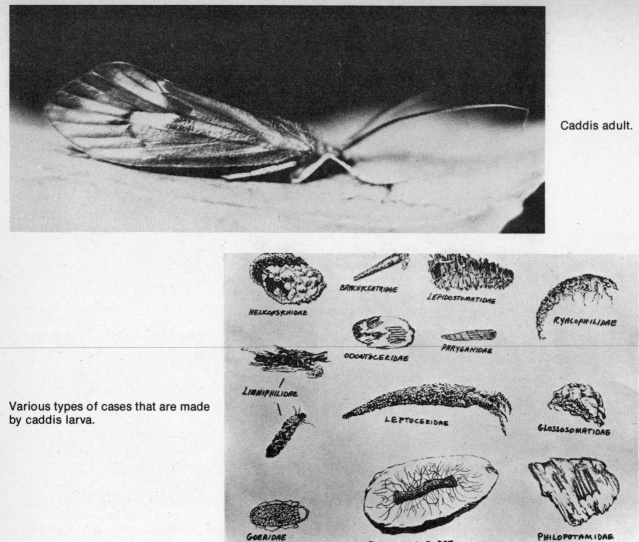

Caddis adult.

Various types of cases that are made by caddis larva.

have to be concerned with that provide food for the trout and that we should know how to imitate with our artificial flies and casting presentation. They are the *"nymph"* mentioned above, the *"adult"* or dun (properly referred to as the subimago) and the *"spinner"* or egg-laying adult (properly referred to as the imago). Each stage has its own importance as trout food and should be known by the fly-fisherman.

The **caddisfly** is equally as important as the mayfly in the trout's diet. In some areas, in fact, it has become more important as the water quality changes. The caddis seems to be more adaptable to environmental changes while some species of mayflies have disappeared or diminished in numbers.

The caddis are of the Latin order *Trichoptera,* which means hair wing, referring to the tiny hairs covering their wings. They are moth-like in appearance, having two sets of wings that lie tentlike over the body, but that is where the similarity ends.

Unlike the mayfly, which only has an adult life of from 2 to 3 days, as an average, the caddis adult has an average life of about 7 days, with some species living up to several weeks. Oddly enough, although the caddis is of equal food value with the mayfly, there had been very little written about it until *The Caddis and the Angler* (Stackpole Books) was published in 1977.

As are the mayflies, caddis can be found in rivers, streams, lakes and ponds across the North American continent, and also similar to the mayfly, they range in size from about ⅛-inch to almost 1½ inches in length. There are also hundreds of species among the caddis, but the color variations are not as varied as the mayflies. Although color selectivity is sometimes significant, the proper size and silhouette of the imitation is most important.

The major differences between the mayfly and the caddis, besides the basic physical structure, is the life cycle of the insect. It has an underwater stage similar to the mayfly nymph which is called the "larva." This

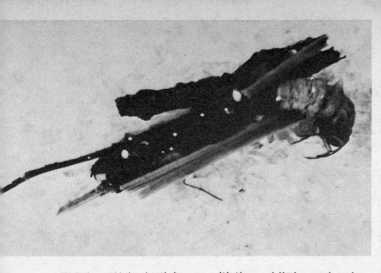

This is a 1½-inch stick case with the caddis larva showing.

Caddis pupa.

larva is referred to as nature's carpenters or stonemasons. Most but not all of the species build unique cases using grains of sand, pebbles, sticks and bits of vegetation. They are of various shapes and sizes and are the home of the caddis during its entire larval period. There are several species that do not have any case during their larval period. Some spin nets on the rocks, and others are known as the free-living species. These are the ones that are most important to the angler, since they are most available to the trout and the easiest to imitate with the artificials.

The next stage of the caddis is unique to itself as trout food. It is referred to as the "pupa." It is also the stage that the trout feeds on more than any other. It is very available to the trout during the emergence. Approximately 10 days to 2 weeks prior to the emergence and transformation to an adult, the larva seals off the end of its case. Those caddis larva which are free-living (don't build cases) build a cocoon at this time just for the purpose of pupation. During that 10-day to 2-week period, the insect goes through a major transformation, developing short wing pads and elongated legs. When the time is right, this pupa chews its way out of its pupal case and/or cocoon and makes its way to the surface to hatch into the adult caddis. This emerging pupal stage is unique to the caddis and is most important to the angler for his fishing activities. It is during this rise to the surface that the caddis pupa is most visible and vulnerable to the trout, therefore it is an important stage for us to imitate with our artificials.

The nature of this emergence is comparable to a large degree, to the rising to the surface of the mayfly nymph as it transforms into the adult. The speed at which the caddis emerges, however, is usually much faster than the mayfly. When the pupa leaves its case, it has some gaseous bubbles beneath its pupal sheath which separate the forming adult from the sheath. These bubbles aid the pupa in its ascent, as though you held an air filled balloon beneath the surface, then let it go. . . . it comes up rather quickly, as quite often does the pupa. Because it rises quickly, the trout also has to move quickly to catch it. This rapid movement by the trout causes a sharp or splashy rise form, which is so often associated with the caddis hatches. There are also species of caddis that rise slower to the surface, therefore not getting that splashy rise form. Being observant to this will give you an idea of how you have to fish your artificial.

When the mayfly nymph reaches the surface, it usually drifts in the film for a considerable distance as the adult emerges. The caddis does not afford itself this luxury. Upon reaching the surface, it is ready to fly, although not always with great stability at first. It can often be seen bouncing around the surface like a ping-pong ball in an effort to get itself airborne. This activity also stimulates the trout into making a crashing dramatic rise.

The adult is the stage that we imitate with our dry flies. However, the ovipositing adult, that is referred to as the "spinner" with the mayflies, is quite different, and is fished differently. . . . sometimes with a wetfly. This will be discussed later in the chapter.

The **stonefly** is about the largest aquatic insect that is available to the trout, with the possible exception of the helgrammite or dodson fly larva. The stonefly lives in clean cold water river systems and can often be found in great numbers, with some of its species reaching close to 3 inches in length. That provides a good mouthful for any hungry trout. Imitations of its underwater nymph stage are some of the most effective patterns for big trout in rivers, such as the Delaware in New York, the Madison and Yellowstone in Montana and many other freestone streams across the country.

Whereas most of the mayfly and caddis species emerge into the adult on the water surface, the stonefly usually crawls out of the stream to make this transition. It will crawl on to a rock or tree trunk or any object, usually after dark, where the nymph case will split and

Stonefly nymph.

Stonefly adult.

the winged adult will crawl out and fly to the trees and bushes. These nymphs have been known to crawl considerable distances before hatching. I remember setting up to a tent about 60 or 70 feet from shore one evening. Upon awakening the next morning, there were spent stonefly cases all over the tent and anything else that was out in the open.

Since most of the stonefly species emerge out of the water, you can see that the adult is not initially as important during a hatch as is the mayfly or caddis. There are some species, however, that do hatch in the water.

A good example is the early dark brown stonefly, tied at a size #14 hook, that hatches in many parts of the country just about the time that the trout season opens. Even though the water is still quite cold, the fish seem to take it readily as it lingers on the surface. Imitating this can be worthwhile. Again, it requires being observant as to what is happening on the water and to what the trout are feeding on.

The stage of the stonefly that can really bring the fish up to the surface is the ovipositing (egg laying) adult. The stonefly adults usually make their mating flights

when the air has warmed up in the late morning. At this time they will fly to the water and dip their abdomens into the water surface and deposit the egg masses. If it is a windy day, many of the large insects are blown onto the water, stimulating the trout into some voracious feeding. This activity is legendary for the quality of fishing that comes with it throughout the Rocky Mountain states, from the later part of June through early July. There are many other stonefly hatches from coast to coast at various times of the year that stimulate feeding activity. It takes a bit of knowledge of your area to know when they are.

UNDERWATER INSECT STAGES AND WET FLY IMITATIONS

Nymph Stage

The nymph is the first stage that grows from the egg of the mayflies and stoneflies, and the larva is the corresponding stage of the caddis. It is also the first stage that we anglers are concerned with imitating.

These insects feed mainly on algae and vegetative matter that is on the stream bottom. Stoneflies will also feed considerably on minute animal life, and sometimes

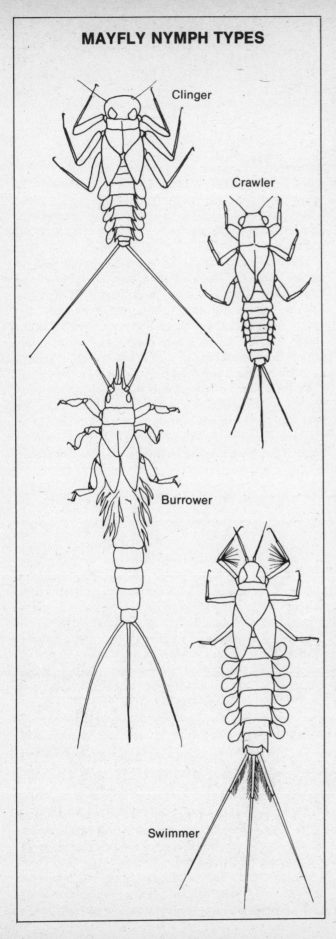

MAYFLY NYMPH TYPES

Clinger

Crawler

Burrower

Swimmer

even on other small nymphs. There are four basic types of mayfly nymphs. Some waters will have all of them—some may only have one or two. There is the flattened, heavy legged *clinging* variety that lives on and under the rocks in fast water sections of rivers and streams; the short stocky *crawlers* inhabit almost all parts of the rivers; the long, round bodied *burrowers* inhabit the slower silt and fine gravel sections of rivers and ponds, and are usually the larger species; and the torpedo shaped *swimming* nymphs. Although each type has its own specific characteristics, they all have the common gills on the upper section of their abdomen and one set of visible wing pads. This differs from the stoneflies that have two distinct wing pads.

The stoneflies have numerous species in their ranks, and although there is a great variation in size—from about ¼-inch up to almost 3 inches—and several variations in coloration, most of them have similar habits and characteristics. The stoneflies thrive in the same water as the clinging mayfly species—fast, well aerated sections of rivers and streams. They provide a big piece of meat for the trout, and many of the larger fish are caught on their imitations.

The caddis insects are basically of three types—the *casemakers,* which make up the majority of the species, the *net spinners,* and the *free-living* species. Although

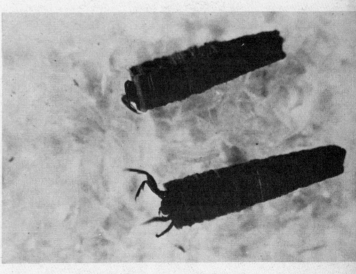

One-half-inch *Brachycentrus* caddis larva case.

One-half-inch *Psilitreta* caddis larva case with its bright green worm.

One-half-inch *Hydropsyche* net spinning caddis larva.

Three-quarter-inch "free-living" *Rhyacophila* caddis larva.

the casemakers are quite numerous and are often found in the stomachs of trout, case and all, most of them are not too important to the angler. The fish eat them by taking them off the rocks to which they are attached. The amount of time and effort spent in fishing that dormant, cased artificial compared to the results usually received is not really worthwhile. With regard to the larva, the attention should be focused on the net spinners and free-living species.

The net spinning species spin their webs on and between the rocks and stones on the stream bottom. They can, and often do, move in and out of these nets at will. They also periodically move to another place in the stream. All this activity makes the caddis larva, or worm, eligible to the trout to feed on. These net spin-

ners are usually various shades of dark green to grayish brown.

The free-living caddis larva are also important to imitate since the trout eat them and see them as the worm itself. They also move periodically. These larva have no case or net, they simply live on or under the rocks. However, at time of pupation, like all other caddis species, they will then build a case for that purpose. These free-living species are also various shades of green—some quite bright.

To get an idea of what kinds of nymphs are in your rivers and streams, you can look under the rocks. The best way to do this is with a piece of fine netting or plastic screening. You can do it yourself, but it works better if you have a friend working with you. It is best to

Collecting nymphs from the stream bottom to see what type of trout food is available . . .

work in about 12 to 18 inches of water. Have your friend stand about 4 or 5 feet downstream from you with the net in the water. (If you rig the net with a rod on either side it will be easy to keep it on the bottom.) As you stand upstream from him, kick over the rocks with your foot. This will dislodge many of the insects, and they will drift into the net below. Examination of the net's contents will give you an idea of what food is available to the trout and will help you decide what patterns you should fish with. The trout know that the nymphs are in the rocks and are ready to eat them whenever they are available. Periodically throughout the season, the nymphs go through a natural stream drift, at which time they will move from one place in the stream to another. At this time they become exposed and are vulnerable.

Nymph Fishing Techniques

Since these mayflies and other nymphs make up a large part of the trout's diet, it is obvious that using artificial flies that imitate them is quite productive. In fact, probably 80 percent of the trout's feeding is done underneath the stream surface. Also, the larger a fish gets, the more he feeds selectively near the bottom. A good nymph fisherman can catch more and larger fish, on the average, than the dry fly man. The nympher puts the food down below where the trout are usually looking for it.

The colors are usually on the drab side—grays, dark

olives, brown and tan for the mayflies and stoneflies, and shades of green or amber for the caddis. Sometimes, the size can be important, so it is a good idea to have several patterns in two or three different sizes. Early in the season the darker nymphs will be most effective. As the season progresses, the lighter shaded flies hatch, therefore lighter nymphs are productive.

Bottom Nymphs: The most important thing about fishing with nymph imitations, is to fish them properly. With the exception of the time that the nymph is swimming to the surface to hatch into an adult, it is on the bottom, either clinging to a rock or tumbling with the current to another spot. The bottom is where your fly

Several caddis larva imitations.

... gives the anglers an idea of what imitations to use.

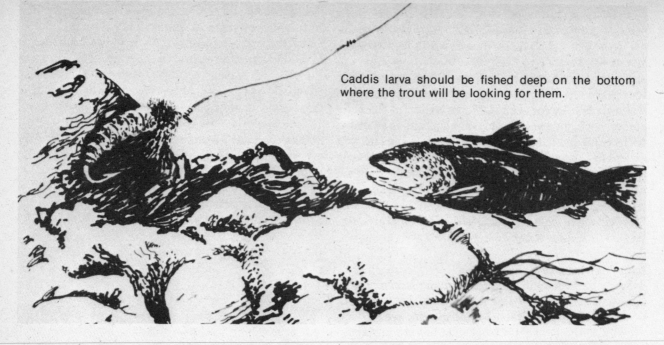

Caddis larva should be fished deep on the bottom where the trout will be looking for them.

should be. I would say that most fishermen do not fish their nymphs deep enough. The main reason for this is that they try to fish too far away from themselves. With a lot of line on the water the drag of the current will pull the fly toward the surface. The best nymph fishermen I know fish with a relatively short line. That could be 15 or 20 feet maximum. They fish under control and have what is referred to as "contact with the fly" at all times. That means that there is no slack in their lines, and they can feel what is happening with the fly. If it bounces along the rocks, they can feel it, but most importantly, when a trout picks the fly up softly, as often happens, they can feel that also and can strike before the fish spits it out.

It also helps to use a weighted fly to keep it near the bottom. A weighted fly has lead wire wrapped around the hook before the other materials are tied on. Another thing that can help is using "wrap-around." These are thin lead strips about 3 inches long that you wrap around your leader to help it sink. It is sometimes difficult to cast, but with some practice, you can control it. Naturally, the sinking tip or various sinking lines can also be effective.

There are two basic techniques that you should be familiar with. First there is the "dead drift" technique. This is where it is important to have that contact with the fly, because the trout usually picks the fly up softly. The idea is to pick a likely looking spot where trout would be lying. Position yourself to the side and slightly upstream of the spot. Make your cast so that your nymph lands in the current lane well upstream of the area you expect the fish to be. This will give the fly adequate time to sink before it gets to the fish. As your fly comes downstream, raise your rod tip to take up the slack. As the line swings by you, you can slowly drop

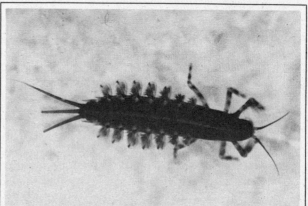

Natural *Isonychia* mayfly nymph.

Hand-tied *Isonychia* imitation.

114

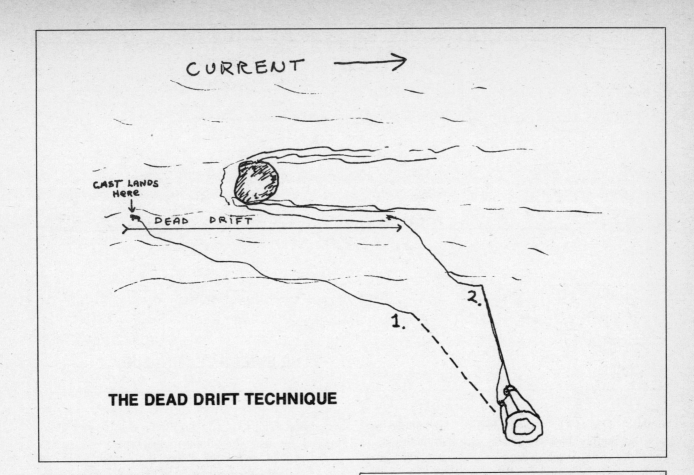

CURRENT →

CAST LANDS
HERE

DEAD DRIFT

1.

2.

THE DEAD DRIFT TECHNIQUE

the rod tip again to allow the fly to drift naturally. An experienced dead drift nymph fisherman can make his fly swirl around rocks with the current into pockets and eddies where the fish lie waiting. He is usually seen with a bent rod and a fish on his line. Again, the more line that you have out, the less control you will have on the fly.

There are times, especially in small streams, that you might want to cast almost straight upstream to a run of water that looks productive. When you do this, you must strip in the line as the fly comes downstream in order to keep that "contact." If you don't, and a fish takes, you will have too much slack to be able to strike and set the hook. Trout can spit a fly out immediately after taking it, and will if they feel that something is wrong. You have to hook them as soon as you feel or sometimes even see the take. When I say "see the take," I refer to watching the leader or end of your flyline. Sometimes fishermen even put a bright spot at the junction of the line and the leader in order to see it better. When your fly and line are drifting downstream and the fly is picked up by a trout, the line will stop short in the current. That is the time to strike. If you can see it, you can act faster than if you had to wait to feel it. Many times you may be hitting a rock, but you'll be surprised at how many of these "rocks" turn out to be fish and start to swim away with your fly in their jaws.

The other method you should use I call the "sweep"

(Above) Natural *Stenonema* mayfly nymph.

(Below) *Stenonema* nymph imitation.

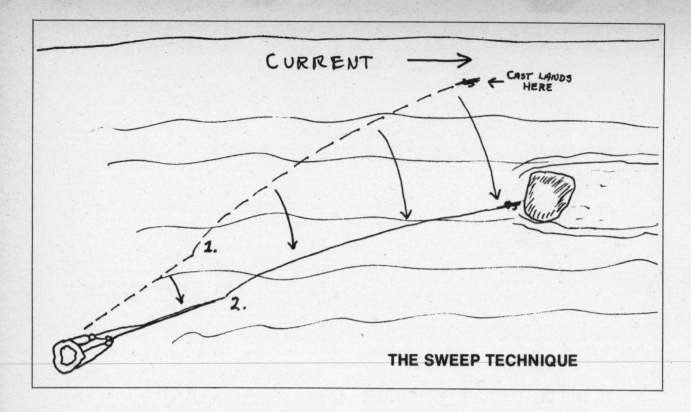

CURRENT →

CAST LANDS HERE

1.

2.

THE SWEEP TECHNIQUE

method. This is very similar to the "swimming minnow" technique used for fishing bait fish imitations. I call it the sweep method because you can cover a great deal of water in a pattern. It is a good locator. As the season progresses and the water gets warmer, this method becomes quite effective. The warmer water makes the trout more active, and they feed more toward the surface than when the water is cold (under 50 degrees). The sweep method works the nymph or wet fly closer to the surface than the dead drift technique. Quite often what you are imitating with the sweep, is a nymph that is emerging to the surface to hatch into an adult. The fish has to move a bit faster to get this nymph. Therefore, the strike is usually much sharper

Stonefly nymph imitation.

and more exciting. You don't have to worry about hooking the fish, they hook themselves.

The procedure for the sweep is to make your cast across and slightly downstream. I would suggest using that reach or upstream hold cast, or putting a mend in your line as soon as it hits the water. This gives you some initial slack which allows the fly to sink a bit before it starts that sweeping swing. The more slack you can give yourself as the fly hits the water, before it starts to swing, the better off you will be and the more fish you will catch. This starts the fly deeper in the water before it starts swinging up.

Any time during the swing, you are likely to get a hit, so keep the rod tip up a bit to absorb the shock of the strike. It is often a good idea to gently twitch the rod tip as the fly is swinging. This imparts a pulsating action which may be tantalizing and attract the trout's attention.

A very productive idea when fishing nymphs or wet flies is to fish a "cast" of flies or "droppers." This is an arrangement of two or more flies on the same leader. The additional flies other than the one at the tip of the leader are referred to as the droppers. The main advantage of using more than one fly is that it allows you to use different types of flies at the same time when you are not sure what to use. Then when you see which fly the fish are taking more often, you can concentrate on using that one. Another advantage is it also presents the flies at different levels and different angles to the fish. The only disadvantage of using a "cast" of flies is that you have to be careful while casting. There is a tendency for the two or three hooks to get tangled up with

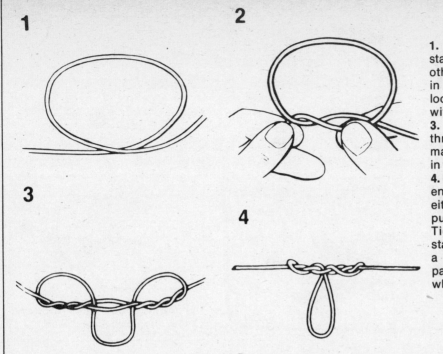

DROPPER LOOP

1. This knot forms a loop which stands out from line above sinker or other terminal rig. First, form a loop in the line. **2.** Pull one side of the loop down and begin taking turns with it around the standing line. **3.** After eight to 10 turns, reach through center opening and pull remaining loop through. Keep finger in this loop so it will not spring back. **4.** Hold loop with teeth and pull both ends of line, making turns gather on either side of loop. **5.** Set knot by pulling lines as tightly as possible. Tightening coils will make loop stand out perpendicular to line. Not a strong knot but serviceable for panfish and small saltwater species where such rigs are used.

each other. I would not recommend this technique when you are first learning to cast, but only once you have developed some control.

Many anglers have their own way of splicing leaders and making knots. I have illustrated here the knots and arrangements that I have found successful. The important thing is to arrange the cast so that the leader does not tangle unnecessarily. One rule is to make sure that the size of the dropper leader is about the same as the section of the main leader you are going to attach it to. It should not be of a smaller diameter or it will tangle more easily. Another point is to put the smaller flies at the tip of the leader and the larger flies closer to the butt. The flies should be approximately 24 inches apart. If you are unsuccessful with the flies that you are using,

change the sizes or the patterns of flies. Experimenting is usually one of the keys to success.

I think at this time I should mention the "wet fly." Although it is fished almost identically to the nymph, especially with the sweeping method, it resembles quite a different stage of the insect. In fact it imitates two different situations that relate to the mayfly and one that will be discussed later with the ovipositing caddisfly.

When a mayfly nymph emerges, it usually swims to the surface, drifts in the surface momentarily, then it splits at the wing case and hatches the winged adult. However, there are certain mayflies that leave their nymphal shucks on the bottom of the stream or on the way up. Therefore, they have their wings out as they are rising to the surface. The wet fly imitates this stage.

"CASTING" OF FLIES

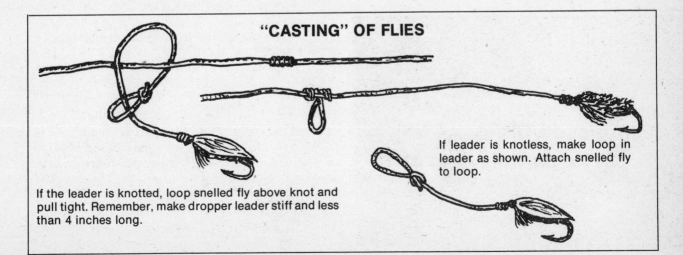

If the leader is knotted, loop snelled fly above knot and pull tight. Remember, make dropper leader stiff and less than 4 inches long.

If leader is knotless, make loop in leader as shown. Attach snelled fly to loop.

Typical collection of flies for the nymph fisherman.

Leadwing Coachman (top) and Hare's Ear (above) wet flies.

The other situations that the wet fly imitates is the dead or drowned mayfly. During a hatch, there are always some insects that are crippled or that get stuck in the surface film. The wet fly fished dead drift can imitate this drowned insect.

Floating Nymph: I mentioned that the nymph spends its life on the river bottom, and therefore that is where your imitation should be fished. There is one important exception. That is at the beginning of many hatches when the nymphs swim to the surface and pause on the surface as the adult attempts to emerge. At times, the trout will key on these floating nymphs, which are drifting helplessly in the surface film, and will take them in preference to the winged adult.

I remember several years ago when I was fishing on Nelson's Spring Creek near Livingstone, Montana.

This stream and its companion, Armstrong Spring Creek, are famous for their consistent daily hatches of #18 and #20 small, pale colored mayflies, sometimes referred to as pale olive duns. They start coming off the water at about 10 AM and last to around 1 to 2 PM. The fish rise and feed on the surface the entire time.

I had been there before and had done fairly well using small dry fly adult imitations. This time, I wasn't getting the response that I had hoped. Many fish were coming up to the fly, but would change their minds and refuse it. While I was pondering the situation, I observed a nymph floating by. I noticed that it remained in the surface for a long time, anywhere from 5 to 10 seconds, before the emergence of the adult took place. This made it extremely easy prey for the leisurely rising trout. It gave me an idea, and I searched my nymph box for any small flies that I had tied on a light wire dry fly

(Left) Natural nymphs hanging just under the water surface in preparation to hatch. They are extremely vulnerable to the trout at this time.

Floating nymphs tied on dry fly hooks.

hook. I had two that looked like the natural. I tied one on, dipped it in some floatant liquid so that it would not sink, and proceeded to fish away.

Well, I'll have to tell you that it was really the answer. I think I rose and hooked just about every fish that I cast to until I lost the two flies. If I remember correctly, I believe the count was 26 trout in 3 hours—and quite a few in the 15- and 16-inch range. These fish wanted the floating nymph in preference to the hatched adult. A case in point again for observation and experimentation being the key to success. The floating nymph is often quite productive when it appears that the fish are feeding on the surface. Sometimes the "rise form" (the manner in which the fish rises and breaks the surface of the water) can be an indication of what it is taking. The rise form will be discussed later in the chapter.

The main concerns when fishing the floating nymph are:

1. It is important that the artificial be the same size and of similar silhouette as the natural that you are trying to imitate.

2. Try to match the coloration as best you can. That will necessitate collecting some of the insects that are floating in the stream. It is advisable to carry with you a fish tank net with about a 4-inch opening to help you scoop them off the water or others out of the air. Remember when matching colors, a fly with dry fur or body material will usually be lighter in shade than when it gets wet. Sometimes the trout can be pretty fussy.

3. More importantly, allow the nymph to drag dead drift in the surface. You should look for and be aware of any unintentional drag that moves the nymph unnaturally. It will cause the trout to refuse your offering.

The Caddis Pupa Stage

A unique and extremely important activity that occurs under the surface pertains to the emerging caddis pupa. As I mentioned earlier, about 2 weeks prior to emergence or hatching the caddis seals itself in its case and goes through the transformation from larva to pupa. When the proper water temperature and light conditions for emergence have occurred, the pupa breaks open the end of its larval case at the head. When the hole is large enough, the pupa wiggles out of the case and is quickly on its way up to the surface. Just prior to leaving the case, the pupa develops gaseous bubbles which help to separate the pupal shuck from the body of the emerging adult. These gaseous bubbles are also instrumental in aiding the rapid ascent of most of the caddis species. The effect is like holding an air-filled balloon at the bottom of a pool, then letting it go. It comes up pretty fast. That is why trout and other fish have to move so rapidly to catch them. There are exceptions naturally. Some of the species rise slowly, similar to the mayfly emergence; others crawl along the bottom and hatch on land or on exposed rock. But the rapid

Caddisflies seal themselves in their cases in preparation for pupation.

Comparison of natural caddis pupa (top) and an imitation (below).

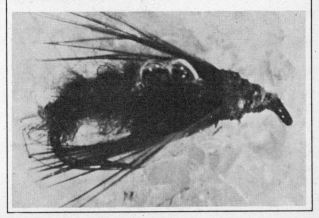

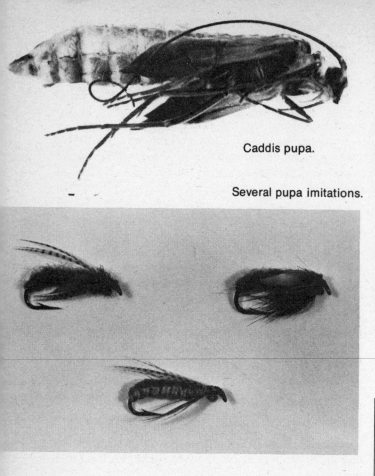

Caddis pupa.

Several pupa imitations.

There was a fair hatch of a particular caddis coming off, and I had expected to see some good rising activity. However, to my disappointment there were only two or three small fish working the surface. The section of water that I was fishing was about 5 feet deep. After catching one 7-inch trout, and seeing no other good surface activity, I decided to fish some stonefly nymphs that I knew were active at that time of the year (early May). In less than a dozen casts, I had a beautiful brown trout a bit over 16 inches. Deciding to keep him for dinner, I killed the fish, opened him up and examined the stomach contents to see what he was feeding on. I counted approximately 75 of the similar stonefly species that had been eaten by the fish not too long before. But surprisingly, the trout had accumulated about 200 of the emerging caddis pupa when they were probably about three-quarters of the way to the surface. I'm sure that the fish never broke water in the form of a rise. I switched to a double pupa arrangement on my leader and proceeded to take five more good fish. That was the answer—the good fish were leisurely taking the pupa in that deeper water. Another point for "observe

If the water you are fishing is less than 3 feet deep, the emerging caddis will reach the surface before the fish can get to it. This results in a splashy rise form. If the water is deeper than 3 feet the trout can usually catch the pupa before it reaches the surface.

WATER LESS THAN 3 FT. IN DEPTH

← WATER OVER 3 FT. IN DEPTH

ascent is very common, and the rise forms will usually tell very quickly how the pupa is behaving. Whether the pupa is rising slowly or rapidly, it is quite visible to the feeding trout and therefore more vulnerable in this stage than in any other. For that reason, fishing emerging pupa imitations is important to add to your bag of angling tricks. However, unless you have an actual caddis hatch on hand—minor as it may be—fishing the pupa is generally unrewarding. This does not mean that you cannot catch trout with it, but it is rare and is usually the result of a miscalculation made by a smaller trout mistaking the pupa for some other bit of food. However, once a hatch is under way, the initial feeding will be on the pupal stage—an opportunity for some fast and exciting fishing.

If the water that you are fishing is less than 3 feet deep, you will probably be able to see the rise of the trout, since the rapidly emerging pupa will usually reach the surface before the fish can get to it. This results in a splashy rise form, since the fish is moving quickly. However, in deeper water where the pupa has a much longer way to travel, the trout can usually catch it before it reaches the surface. In this case, it is not uncommon to see many insects coming off the water, but few or no rises.

An incident on the East Branch of the Delaware River in New York State brought my attention to this.

Angler working emerging pupa up in front of rising fish, marked "X".

A properly fished pupa imitation brings a nice brown trout to the net.

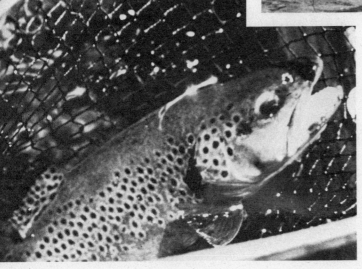

and experiment"—the key to learning some of the answers.

Incidentally, larger fish usually do not like to expend more energy than they have to when they feed. They will most often take the easiest prey available. In contrast, smaller fish will dart hither and tither to catch any morsel in sight. When they rise, it is usually a little splash.

Twitching Rod Technique for Caddis Pupa: Because the pupa emerges from the bottom in a unique manner, it is important to imitate, not only its size, shape and color, but also its motion. I have found it important to use flies that are weighted. If you want something to come from the bottom up, you first have to get it to the bottom. In addition to the weighted fly, you can also put some weight on your leader if you wish. For best control, fish with a relatively short line. The cast should be made up

and across stream. The fly and leader should be allowed to drift downstream with no drag so that the fly can sink. If you have to mend your line a number of times to obtain this effect, by all means do so. When the fly gets below you and begins to swing, help it along by lifting the rod tip gently in a pulsating movement. Most of your strikes will occur at this time. This cast and activity effectively imitates the rapid and erratic ascent of the pupa.

This technique can be quite effective through the first part of the hatch when you see trout rising to caddis with that splashy rise form. Pick a rising fish that is below you, then strip out just enough line to reach it. It is best to try to keep the distance between you and the fish less than 30 feet. Then make your cast upstream in the same current lane in which the fish is feeding and manipulate the fly in a dead drift down to the fish, allowing it to sink as much as possible. As the fly swings in front of where the fish rose, raise the rod, continuously twitching the tip as the fly comes up. This gives a life-like action to the imitation, and quite often results in a smashing strike. If you react too sharply, you may have some flies broken off. You must get accustomed to the feel of the technique. You can also use a slightly stronger leader tippet than used with the dry flies of corresponding size.

SURFACE INSECTS AND DRY FLY IMITATIONS

Adult Mayfly

The topic of the adult mayfly—how to identify it, how to tie it and how to fish its imitations—has been the topic of many books for over 100 years. It is fascinating because the insects are beautiful, and the manner in which the trout feed on them, coming up and taking them off the surface, is visually exciting. I will discuss

(Left) Natural mayfly.

Caddis (left) and mayfly (right) imitations.

the basics of how to identify them, how to imitate them and how to catch fish with these imitations. If your interest is stimulated and you want more information, refer to the list of books at the end of this chapter. You can get as involved as you wish with the identification of these insects and their relationship to the trout's behavior. You don't have to in order to catch fish, but it will enhance your enjoyment and understanding of the sport and will enable you to catch more fish at those difficult selective feeding times.

While I'm on the topic, I may as well go a bit further. Modern fly-fishing for trout has created a desire to learn more about the behavior of the insects that trout feed on. This in turn has resulted in the angler learning the proper identification of these insects by their Latin names such as *Stenonema vicarium*. Many of you may be saying to yourself right now, "What the heck do I want to get involved with that junk for? I can't even pronounce it. Even if I could, what good would it do me?" Well, when you are just a beginner fly-fisherman, it is best just to concentrate on the basic understanding

and function of the sport itself. However, as you progress, you begin to desire more knowledge to help you understand what the trout are doing at selective feeding times—why they wouldn't take your fly while the guy next to you was hooking them left and right, or the time you saw three or four different mayflies on the water at the same time and wondered which one the fish were feeding on and why. You may have fished imitations that looked just like the real insect, but you only hooked two small fish while you felt that you should have had a dozen good ones. It's times like those that make you want to know a bit more of what is happening in that mysterious world of "Mother Nature." Sometimes knowing just a little bit more can make a big difference. The reason for the Latin names is simply for proper communication and understanding, not to show off with some fancy pronunciation.

There is a difference between an insect and a fly in the world of fly-fishing. The insect is the real live natural bug that crawls and flies, the fly is the artificial that you buy or tie yourself to imitate the natural. The natural

Knowing the proper fly to use can make the difference during selective feeding situations.

Artificial *Tricorythodes* adult dun and spinner.

insects have specific names that classify them in the science of entomology, while the artificial flies have names that were given to them usually by the person who first created the pattern. It could be named after the person himself, or for a particular color combination, like the Blue Winged Olive or any other crazy name that someone dreamed up such as the "Royal Coachman" or the "Rat Faced McDougal." Anyway, the artificial names very rarely have any correlation with the names of the natural insects.

What happened over a period of time, was that the fisherman referred to the natural insects using the names of the flies that were tied to imitate them. For example, an insect that hatches in the East around the beginning of May is the *Ephemerella subvaria*. The artificial fly that is used to imitate it is the Hendrickson named after A.E. Hendrickson. If you were on an eastern stream about the first of May and asked what hatch to expect, someone would most likely tell you that the Hendricksons would be coming off at about 2:00 PM. Well, actually that is impossible, because the Hendrickson cannot hatch, it has to be tied.

Let me give you an idea why this can be confusing and misleading. The artificial called the Blue Winged Olive is one of the most popular patterns that was ever created. Why? Because there are many insects that have bluish wings and various shades of olive bodies. Whenever one of these insects would hatch, most fishermen would simply say that the Blue Winged Olives (B.W.O.) were coming off today. Now in a sense they were right because of the coloration similarity, but that did not tell you anything about the behavior of the insect, how the fish feeds on it, what the color shading of the insect was or what the correct size of the insect was. You could ask him what the size was, but some-

times three different people will give you three different sizes and opinions. Some insects do have two size variations, but if you know the insect, you know this.

Many of the insects that the B.W.O. imitates have specific characteristics that differentiate them from their cousins. For example, if a knowledgeable angler

Gentle rise form in the evening indicates fish are feeding on surface insects.

heard that the *Ephemerella attenuate* was hatcing, he would know: (1) the hatch was coming off in the morning usually around 10:00 AM; (2) the insect emerges from the bottom as a partially winged insect, therefore an emerger or wet fly pattern is effective at the beginning of the hatch and the dry fly later; (3) the color of the body of the emerging insect is a bright, yellowish olive which, upon reaching the surface and coming in contact with the air, turns to a darker grayish olive; (4) the insect has three tails and the wings are dark, almost charcoal gray; (5) the fly is usually tied on a size #16 hook. Or, if the angler heard that a #20 *Baetis* was hatching, he would know that the body is a dark olive with dark gray wings and two tails. He would also know that the nymph often floats in the surface film for a considerable amount of time before hatching, therefore, a floating nymph might work better than the adult dry fly imitation. All of that knowledge is conveyed by

nymph has reached the surface, and quite often with some species as the insect is on the way up, the wing case will split and the adult will start to emerge. This is what is classically referred to as a "hatch." During a "flush hatch," there could be thousands of insects emerging during a short 15- to 20-minute time period. Other hatches will be more sporadic, with the insect coming off here and there for an hour or two.

A hatch of an abundant mayfly species will usually occur about the same time each day, barring any drastic weather changes, for from 3 or 4 days to 2 weeks. There are some select species, such as *Tricorythodes*, a tiny mayfly that is imitated on a #24 hook, that hatch in large quantities each day for up to several months in certain parts of the country. The trout feed on them voraciously.

Once the first mayfly of the season hatches, the angler who possesses knowledge of the insects and their

Trout rises gently showing subtle rise form.

using the correct identifying name of the insect—information that Blue Winged Olive just could not convey.

I'm not saying that you have to learn the Latin names of the insects in order to be a successful trout fisherman, but you should not look down at their use as snobbery when you hear them. You may find that as you progress and learn more about this fascinating game, you may be asking someone how to pronounce *Ephemera guttulata* or *Paraleptophlebia adoptiva*.

Anyway, back to the adult mayfly. After the nymph has been in the stream for about 1 year, a combination of water temperature and light conditions, occurring approximately the same time each year, will stimulate the nymph to work itself to the surface. During this ascendance, the adult, which is inside of the nymph case, is separating itself from the case. Usually after the

behavior will know what to expect next and what flies to use, since these insects, under relatively normal environmental conditions will follow basically the same pattern and order of emergence each year. This knowledge is gained through experience, by reading the literature that has been written on the subject, and by inquiring at a local fly-fishing shop in the area of the river.

It is during these hatching periods that the mayfly is most visible and vulnerable to the trout. The blessing to the fly-fisherman is that this activity stimulates the trout into a feeding frenzy that we call a "rise"—when the trout swim up to take the insect either under or on the water surface. As the fish makes its rise, it creates a disturbance on the surface that is referred to as a "rise form." This could be anything from the most subtle dimple to a dynamic splashy rise with the trout coming clear out of the water. Quite often the nature in which

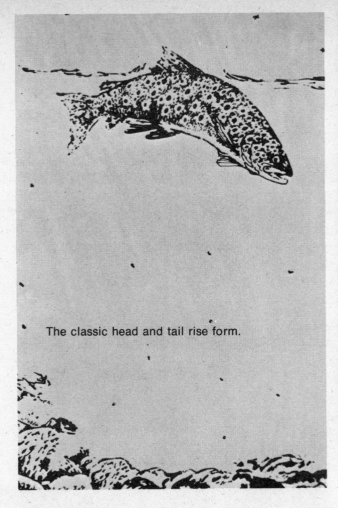

The classic head and tail rise form.

Splashy rise form usually indicates fish chasing something that is getting away.

the trout rises will be an indication of the type of insect or the stage of the insect that it is feeding on. That information would give you an idea what type of fly to use and even how to fish it.

The most subtle rise form is when the fish gently sips an insect from the water's surface. All that is seen is a small dimple followed by small rings from the rise. It is easily missed if the angler is not aware of this activity. The insect that is taken is usually flush in the surface film at a dead drift, making it a very easy target for the trout to take. When you fish your artificial to this type of rise form, make sure that the fly floats completely drag free. This rise form is very typically made for terrestrials (beetles, ants, etc.), spinners (dying ovipositing mayflies) or any insect that is helplessly caught in the surface film. With this rise form you quite often have no idea what size of fish is under that dimple, since the form will be the same whether made by a 10- or 18-inch trout. Many times I have been greatly surprised, upon setting the hook and anticipating an average fish, to find

THE "HOP SUDDEN INCH"

The "Hop" or "Sudden Inch" technique is used when you fish to a splashy rise form.

A "bulge" rise, where the trout does not show himself can often be an indication that he is feeding on emerging nymphs.

a trophy stripping line from my reel.

The classic rise form I call the "head and tail" or "roll." In this form first the head will appear, then the fish will gently roll in the surface and the tail will appear to complete the form. It is also an indication that the fish is taking an insect that is stationary and an easy target. However, this rise form is often to an emerging nymph that is just on or under the surface. Quite often if you look closely you will observe that the fish never actually sticks its head out of the water at those times. All that will be seen are its shoulders, dorsal fin and the top of its tail.

Any time that you see a splashy rise form, it is usually an indication that whatever the trout has taken or tried to take was moving or giving the fish the feeling that it was about to get away such as the emerging caddis pupa. It is often a good idea to use a high-riding dry fly and experiment by imparting a bit of movement to the artificial with a little twitch of the rod tip. This should make the fly hop about an inch or two. You don't want it to move any more than an inch or two or it will look unnatural. A bit of practice will help a lot.

The presentation of the dry fly is considerably more important than the imitation itself. There are times when having the exact imitation in size, shape and coloration can be quite important for selective trout, however if the imitation is presented poorly or sloppily, it probably won't matter how exact it is. I have often seen an angler, using only a mediocre imitation, but presenting it well, outfish by five to one the guy who had the exact imitation but could not cast it to the fish properly.

Nature is often quite consistent. If there are mayflies hatching, they are probably doing so in a similar way. In turn, the trout will key in to this particular behavior and be feeding in relation to it. If you present your fly so that it behaves drastically different from the natural, it will usually not be taken. Therefore, it is quite advantageous to observe the insects' behavior on the water surface and how the trout feed on them. It will give you an idea of how your imitation should perform.

For many years it was thought that the best way to present a dry fly was to cast it upstream to the fish and allow the fly to float dead drift downstream. Now there are certain conditions, such as small streams or in difficult currents, when that approach is necessary, but whenever possible, it would be to your advantage to present your fly to the trout by casting across and downstream using the "upstream hold" or "reach" cast as described in Chapter 2. There are several good reasons for this:

1. If you learn to control the upstream hold cast and present your fly across and downstream, you will be able to get a longer drag free drift with constant control of the fly than if you cast upstream.

2. If you observe the mayflies and many other in-

When a trout is seen rising with his head out of the water, it is obvious that he is taking something on the surface.

sects as they sit on the water, you will see that they almost always face upstream. Even when they fly, especially during their ovipositing flight, they usually go upstream. Therefore, if the fish sees the natural facing upstream, it would be to your advantage if your artificial did the same. If you make your presentation upstream, your fly will almost always face downstream, but if you make your cast down to the fish, you can face your fly upstream easily.

3. Trout are often known to be leader shy. This means that they can spook or refuse to take an artificial when the leader crosses above them or casts a shadow on them. When you cast upstream to a fish, the leader comes to the fish before the fly does. However, when your cast is on a downstream angle, your artificial will drift to the trout before the leader is seen.

4. As I mentioned earlier, it is sometimes effective to impart a little action to the fly and make it jump an inch or two. This movement should be upstream since that is what the natural insects do. However, if you cast upstream, you can only move the fly downstream or across the current. The downstream angle cast will allow you to make your fly twitch upstream.

Again I'm going to use those two words—observe

An indication that a hatch is in progress or about to begin is the appearance of trout just under the water surface, preparing to feed.

and experiment. This pertains not only to what is going on in the water, but with other anglers. If you see someone who is catching fish consistently, observe his technique and try it. You might ask politely what pattern and size fly the fish are taking or what insect they are feeding on. You will often find that a good fly fisherman is willing to share his knowledge with another enthusiast.

There are basically two occasions when you will be fishing dry fly imitations—either during a hatch with fish rising freely, or during nonhatching periods when you are just fishing the likely holding water trying to tempt trout to rise and take your offering. During the hatch, observe the trout as they rise. If all you see is their backs bulging in the surface, chances are that they are only taking emerging nymphs. However, if you see their heads come out of the water or if you can see the fish take a natural insect from the surface, you know that it is time for dry fly action. These hatching periods are often the most challenging. The trout can become extremely selective to feeding on not only a particular insect, but a particular stage of that insect. That selectivity could change as the hatch progresses. For example, as the nymphs are about to hatch, they get extremely active, crawling over the rocks, rising a few inches, then falling back. This is sort of a warm-up exercise in preparation for their swim to surface. This activity attracts the trout and stimulates feeding on the nymphal stage at the stream bottom. As the hatch progresses and the nymphs work their way up, the trout will key in on them as they pause in the surface film. This rise may look like the trout are feeding on the adults and is often misleading to the angler. Eventually the trout will concentrate their feeding on the surface adults for the remainder of the hatch. So you see, you have a change of feeding from nymph to emerging pattern then to the dry fly.

A hatch could last for 15 minutes or may continue sporadically for over an hour, depending on the species that is hatching and the weather conditions. When trout are rising to a hatching insect, although it is not always necessary, it may be an advantage to have a fly that closely resembles the natural insect in size, silhouette and coloration, in that order of importance. The more that you know about the insects available in the river, the better you can relate to this.

If you fish water that has a great variety of hatches and if you are a novice angler or a non-flytier, it could be a major project at first to accumulate imitations of every hatch. A good way to shortcut your quest of what flies to use is to consult a fishing shop in the area. They usually know what insect activity is on their local rivers, when the hatches occur and what artificials work best. Sometimes even more reliable are friends or fellow fishermen who have had several seasons of experience and are successful in their own fishing. One of the best ways to meet other anglers is through local fishing

One of the serious choices for the fly-fisherman, is the selection of the proper fly.

The use of a fish tank net will make it easier for you to collect and examine the insects that the trout are feeding on.

organizations such as Trout Unlimited, Federations of Fly Fishermen or your local rod and gun club.

When you see the fish starting to rise, inspect the water surface, look for the insect and capture it. It will be easier to catch if you have a small 4-inch square fish tank net, as I mentioned earlier. Once you have captured the insect, you can examine it closely and choose an artificial that most closely resembles it. There may be times that two or three different insects are hatching at the same time. This is where the game can get tricky. Quite often a trout will key in to one of these insects and will feed only on that one. It will reject the others. Many times the one that it selects may be the smaller of the two or three. Most anglers don't observe this selectivity and often become frustrated when they don't get results at times they believe they are fishing the correct pattern.

Several years ago I had a similar situation with two different caddis and one mayfly hatching simultaneously. I caught the first fish that I cast to, and naturally thought that I had the correct imitation and that the other fish would be easy. However, the next two that I cast to refused my offering. Upon inspecting the water, I observed the different insects and changed flies. Shortly after I caught another trout. During the next hour, I caught 6 or 7 more, but I constantly had to change flies from one to another, imitating the three

There is a definite difference between a caddis insect and a mayfly. The ability of the angler to tell the differences among the insects in the trout's diet can definitely help him catch more fish.

The Adams (left) and the "Humpy" or "Goofus Bug" (right) are two of the most popular and successful patterns from the East to West coast.

insects that were hatching. Apparently, the first insect that the first fish ate was what he was keyed in to . . . another fish 3 feet away may have taken one of the other insects first and was keyed into that one. It was an interesting lesson and one that can make the difference of whether you catch two fish or 10 during multiple hatches. Again—observe and experiment.

Trout also have a definite preference for certain hatches. I'm not sure if it's because a particular insect tastes so good or because it behaves in a certain manner that attracts the trout. However, I have seen situations where the fish were feeding on a relatively small insect while there were other considerably larger insects also in the water. You have to look closely and try to see just which one the trout is feeding on. You may see numerous insects in the air especially during some caddis mating flights, but upon close inspection see few or none on the water. In order for the trout to feed on the insect consistently, it must be on the water. Just spend a little time analyzing the situation before you fish it.

As a beginner, you may not necessarily wish to get totally involved in exactly matching the hatch. You might be better off starting with a small selection of imitations that will cover the majority of the hatches. Besides the flies that are tied as exact imitations, there are those that are known as suggestive patterns. They resemble no one insect in particular, but many in similarity. These patterns have been proven quite effective over the years and should be a major part of your initial collection.

As you progress, you can add to your collection when you have the need or desire. It is advisable to have a good suggestive pattern in several sizes, and to have two or three of each size. There is nothing more frustrating than having one of a fly, finding it to be just the one that the trout like, then losing it. If you have two or three, you can always tie on another and continue catching fish. A suggested assortment is listed at the end of the chapter.

Dry Fly Techniques

The majority of your dry fly-fishing will probably be with the drag-free, dead drift technique. The object is to observe the trout as it rises and determine where it is holding. If you see it rise several times in the same spot, then you know where you have to cast your fly. Make your cast so that the fly lands approximately 2 feet above the lie of the trout and let it drift *drag free* down to the fish. If all is right, it should come up and take it. I emphasize drag free because, if the trout are feeding on an insect that is quietly and calmly drifting in the current, your artificial must behave the same way. Varying currents quite often cause a pull or "drag" on the line or the leader. This in turn moves the fly unnaturally on the water surface, slight as the movement sometimes might be. This unnatural movement is enough for the trout to know that your artificial is not

Angler in full control and observation of his line and fly as they drift down to feeding trout.

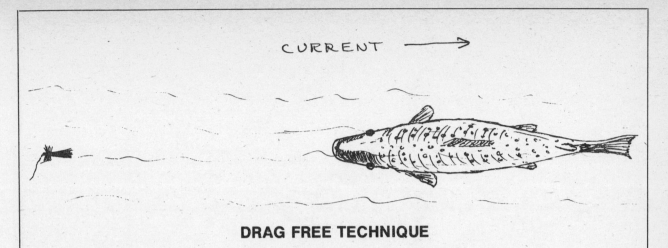

CURRENT ———→

DRAG FREE TECHNIQUE

The fly should land about 2 feet above and in the feeding lane of the trout and float dead drift down to him.

Angler executing a good control line cast across and downstream.

the real thing. If you have a fish come up to your fly and refuse it, the reason, other than the fly possibly being the wrong pattern or size, is probably unnatural drag. Try to watch your fly as it drifts in the current to see if it behaves as you want it to. You can often compare the drift of your fly with a bubble or leaf or bit of debris that may be floating close by. If your imitation is floating consistently with the other object, then it is probably doing fine. However, if it moves faster or slower or is pulled to one side of the object, there is some drag interfering with the natural drift. You may have to approach a particular piece of water from a certain angle, either downstream or upstream for example, in order to achieve the drift you want.

There are times when you might want to impart a bit of action to your fly in the form of a flutter or a hop on the water surface. This action is brought about by the fingers and wrist of the casting arm after the fly has landed. Accomplished correctly, the fly should bounce, skip and flutter on the stream surface, much in the manner of a natural insect that is having trouble getting airborne. This activity is especially pertinent to fishing the caddis hatches. Although this fluttering action has been utilized by many anglers over the years (often referred to as "skating"), Leonard Wright, in his book, *Fishing the Dry Fly as a Living Insect,* was the first to illustrate it, and bring it to the attention of anglers everywhere. He referred to it as "the sudden inch."

The cast is always made downstream or quartering downstream, and the fluttering motion is made to bring the imitation upstream, as a natural insect would behave. It is important that a good cast be made, giving you direct control and contact with the fly. Uncontrolled slack line will not allow you to perform the

131

A rapidly rising trout misses a caddis-fly.

function properly. The upstream hold or reach cast is perfect for this.

For example: You are presenting your imitation to a rising trout about 30 feet down and across stream from your position. The cast should be made so that your fly lands approximately 2 or 3 feet above, and in the feeding lane of the fish. The rod tip is held fairly high, and the tip is twitched gently just before the fly reaches the trout. This creates that "sudden inch" hop and attracts the attention of the trout. It creates the impression that the insect is about to get away and often stimulates a smashing rise. This twitching motion should not be overdone—a "flutter" is not a yank. The fly should only move an inch or two, not a foot. There should be a pause during which the fly is allowed to float naturally. If no results are obtained, another twitch may bring a strike.

However, keep in mind that standard procedures, especially with the caddis imitations, aren't always the answer. A case in point involves a method shown to me by a good friend, Ernie Maltz, from New Jersey. Ernie has been fishing with caddis imitations for over 30 years, and I usually learn much from what he tells me. He informed me that if a fish is seen rising regularly, you should be ready to drop your fly right on his nose as soon as he comes up. Even though the trout has just taken the natural, he will usually turn sharply for your artificial if your cast has been presented properly and accurately. The trout's instinctive thought may be, "Ah, there's another one."

The true value of this method is for the times when the trout is chasing the emerging pupa and misses it, which happens quite often. This situation is signaled by a sharp splashy rise followed by an erratic-flying caddis which has just emerged from the same spot. At these times the trout will momentarily linger just under the surface looking for the prey that has eluded it. The angler's immediate response in putting the fly right on the nose of the trout will result in taking that fish every time.

Persistence is the key word. I have observed Ernie in the stream making dozens of false casts at a time. The first time that I saw this, I wondered whether he was trying to catch a fish or a swallow. What he was really doing was keeping his line and fly in the air, at the ready, searching for a target. When the rise did come, Ernie's imitation would land in the circle of the rise form within a second, resulting in another hooked fish. When using this method, it is best to use a relatively short line. This is the most effective way to fish a dry fly when trout are chasing the emerging pupa.

Ovipositing Mayfly

The final stage of the adult insect that brings the fish to the surface is the ovipositing stage. This is when the insects lay their eggs on or in the water. The mayfly and caddis each oviposit in their own way, but whatever method, they are presenting themselves once more to the hungry mouths of the trout. The mayfly goes through a physical transformation from its newly emerged adult (subimago) stage to its ovipositing (imago) stage. At this time it will actually shed its skin. The remaining insect will have longer tails, almost clear glass wings (in most species) and a considerably darker

(Above) Angler making false cast with a short line, keeping his fly ready to instantly put it on the rise.

(Below) The results of a well placed cast.

starts to flatten out into the pool. The rise to the spinner is very subtle. The fish just sips in the insect. All that is usually seen is the ring of the rise. There are times when the trout will rise in the classic head and tail fashion. If you are not sure whether they are rising to spinners, all you have to do is look on the water surface. If you see a number of insects floating dead or dying in the water with their wings flat out in that spent manner, you can be fairly sure that the rising trout are taking them.

As you will be able to tell by watching the naturals, your imitation must float absolutely drag free. These insects often appear in fairly large quantities and are easy to catch. A spinner fall can coax some of the larger fish into surface feeding. Since the rise to the fly is pretty much the same regardless of the fish size, this often results in a surprise after you set the hook.

Ovipositing Caddisfly

The subject of the ovipositing caddisfly is significantly different than the habits of the mayfly. Since the caddis lives as an adult for a generally longer period of time than the mayfly, his appearance over the stream (other than during emergence or ovipositing) is quite common. Unlike mayflies, which go through that dramatic physiological change mentioned earlier, the caddis retains the same basic form and coloration through all of its adult phase. For this reason alone it is difficult to know when the caddis is ovipositing. Also, when trout are feeding on spent ovipositing mayflies, the dying insects are on the water in such quantities that the angler can recognize what is taking place. The caddis

Several of the popular caddis dry fly imitations. Top row (left to right): Henryville, Solomon's Deer Hair Wing, Len Wright's Skittering Caddis. Middle row (left to right): Flatwing Sedge, Delta Wing. Bottom row (left to right): Sid Neff's Deer Hair Wing, Quill Wing, Vermont or Hare's Ear Caddis.

body. This stage of the insect is referred to in the fly-fishing world as the "spinner." The majority of mayfly ovipositing takes place in the late afternoon or evening, although certain species are an exception. Weather conditions can also change the pattern a bit.

The spinners can be seen in numbers over the water, usually flying upstream. After the mating has occurred they will fall to the water, deposit their eggs and die. They lay flat on the water in a spent wing silhouette. This quite often occurs over the faster water riffles, but the best fishing is usually just below where the water

Ovipositing or egg laying mayfly "spinners" on the water surface.

"Spinner" or spent-wing imitation.

life cycle does not end in this manner. Rarely will you see large quantities or even smaller quantities of spent caddis on the water. The reason it is rarely seen is that it rarely happens.

After laying its eggs the caddis, in most instances, leaves the water and returns to the land. There are occasions when the caddis will mate two or even three times before expiring. They do not succumb to the rigors of mating and egg-laying, as in the case of the mayfly. What then is the value of the ovipositing caddis

if it does not collapse completely spent on the water, as the mayflies do, so trout feed on it? First, most caddis females do expose themselves to the trout in some way during the act of ovipositing, most often by flying close to the surface and dipping their abdomens into the water to release egg masses into the stream. More importantly, with some families of caddis, the female will actually enter the water, sometimes making its way to the bottom of the stream to deposit strings of eggs on the rocks and then *reemerge!* Obviously, this behavior is important to the angler as it presents the insect to the trout in still another situation.

Most of the caddis lay their eggs on or just under the surface. These insects may be imitated with various adult patterns, especially those that float flat in the film. It may be a good idea to clip the hackle off the bottom of the fly to accomplish this. The procedure for fishing the fly is pretty much the same as during the emergence period, although a bit more "dead drift" technique may be employed. The rise form will usually not be splashy.

In dealing with the insects that lay their eggs on the bottom of the stream we have a different situation. This discovery, for me, began with several puzzling experiences. The first was on a stream where I was fishing a particular hatch that I was pretty sure I had identified. The fish were obviously rising, but neither a pupa nor closely matched dry fly seemed to work. Evidently, the trout were seeing something that I could not. Then I read an article that reported findings of a test on the St. Lawrence River where they trapped insects and examined them every 4 hours to determine emergence periods. The test revealed that about 80 percent of all the caddis insects emerged between sunset and daybreak. However, the most interesting discovery was

Large swarms of mating or ovipositing caddis insects flying upstream at dusk.

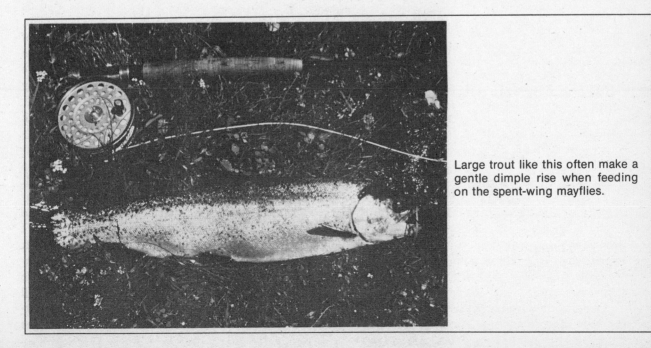

Large trout like this often make a gentle dimple rise when feeding on the spent-wing mayflies.

that many of the caddis insects captured were adult females that had just returned from ovipositing. An even more interesting fact was that the schedule of the returning ovipositing species was quite consistent with the period of emergence of the same species. That is, the ovipositing females returned during a hatch of pupa. That seemed to give me the answer to the frustrating experiences of the past. The only problem was that both the newly emerged adult and the returning from ovipositing adult appeared the same to the eye once they were out of the water and in the air. How then can you tell which is which? You can't! You and I will not be able to tell the difference, but the trout can. The difference is that the pupa will have short, stubby wings, cased in its shuck half the length of its body and slanting downward, while the returning female will have full mature wings, longer than the body and extending along the top. Now what good does it do us to know this if we don't know whether it is happening or not? The answer is that we have to experiment. If you are not getting the results using the conventional method of fishing the pupa or the adult caddis dry fly during a hatch, try imitating the returning female with a wet fly pattern.

The first time I encountered this phenomenon was during one evening fishing on New York's Beaverkill River. A mating flight of a large gray caddis, which was

Here is a close-up of a natural pupa (top) and returning from ovipositing adult (bottom).

There is a difference between the emerging pupa and returning from ovipositing. You may not be able to discern the difference, but the trout can!

emerged adults appear the same.

emerging pupa—wings ⅓ length of body.

emerging from ovipositing adult female—full-length wings.

Caddis lay their eggs either in strings on the bottom of the stream, or in a mass dipped in the water surface.

Comparison of natural returning from ovipositing (bottom) and artificial wet fly (below).

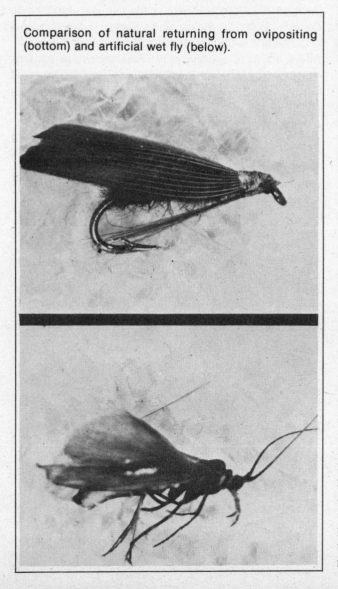

returning in great quantities, was in progress. There was little evidence of activity since few of the insects were on the water. As dusk approached, I noticed similar insects emerging from the surface. Shortly thereafter trout started to rise to what I thought was the emerging gray caddis. After many casts and only one fish, I decided to do a little collecting. While bending over in the stream, I noticed several slightly smaller, different caddisflies on the water, just above the water line. The insect was familiar to me. I selected a dry fly pattern that imitated it, but still got no results. Then the thought struck me. Maybe these were the returning flies of the same species. I switched to a down-winged wet fly pattern that was pretty close to the natural, and fished it similar to the emerging pupa. The results were astonishing—four, fat, brown trout were taken within 20 minutes. The trout were rising and taking it just as it hit the surface. I collected some samples of the insect species and was not surprised when I learned they were one of the families that laid its eggs on the bottom, then came back up.

This type of occurrence has repeated itself several times since that day. The imitation that I use is simply a standard wet fly without a tail, since the caddis has none. Naturally the size and coloration should be close to that of the natural insect for best results. Here again is a good time to try a cast of two flies, one at the tip and one as a dropper. Using an arrangement of one emerging pupa imitation and one returning wet fly on the dropper. If you take fish consistently on any one of the patterns, then that's your key.

Adult Stonefly

The ovipositing stonefly is most important on the western Rocky Mountain rivers, where certain species hatch in large quantities in the willow trees and bushes that grow on the banks. These insects are about 2 inches long and provide a big meal for a hungry trout. The Yellowstone and Madison and Big Hole Rivers in Montana and the Snake in Idaho are several rivers that are famous for these hatches and attract large numbers of anglers. These rivers, however, are only a few of the many free-stone rivers in that part of the country that have what is known as the "salmon fly" hatch.

The mating occurs usually during midday when the air has warmed. The large insects will fly over the river and mate. The female will then drop down to the water and deposit her eggs on the surface. She will sometimes remain on the surface for several seconds, providing an irresistible target to the waiting trout. The most frantic fishing is during a windy day when many of the stoneflies are inadvertently blown onto the water. I have caught fish during those conditions that have had full stomachs and live insects still in their mouths, yet they took my imitation for another. This type of insect activity brings up the largest trout on the river—the meal is just too good for them to pass up.

(Above) Spent-wing caddis.

(Below) Delta Wing pattern.

In the larger rivers, the trout will move in to the banks during this activity. If you are on foot, it is best to work your way upstream, casting with a relatively short line, working the pockets or the rises as you see them. Another popular way to fish these large rivers is by float trips. There are many guide services that provide these one day trips in many of the popular areas of the Rockies. Fishing by boat enables the angler to cover vastly more water than if he was wading, and cast to more fish in the process.

During the nonhatching periods, it is usually more difficult to get the trout to come up to the surface to take your dry fly. During these times the attention of the fish is concentrated on the stream bottom. However, once the water temperatures in the river have climbed above 50 degrees and some of the hatches have been under way, trout can be coaxed up to the surface. One method for this situation is to use an imitation of an insect that has hatched recently. The imitation should suggest that the insect was possibly crippled and unable to leave the water surface. It should float in the surface film and should be fished dead drift. This technique has been very successful for me relating to caddis hatches. Many of the caddis hatch during the night. Many times, while fishing early in the morning when there are no fish rising, I will use what I call a Delta Wing pattern. (See

Outfitters like Bob Jacklin, in west Yellowstone, Montana, guide float trips down the major rivers in the area.

138

Experimenting with new ideas often brings nice trout to the net.

Chapter 3 the list of Popular Fly Patterns for the materials needed to tie this fly.) This fly floats very flat on the surface and suggests one of the insects that didn't quite make it. The rises are always very gentle, and I have taken some good size trout this way.

In contrast, another method is to try to catch the attention of the trout by imparting some action to the fly, thereby stimulating him to strike. The sudden inch technique, mentioned earlier, using an imitation of an insect that had recently hatched, can be rewarding. In this case, the rises will usually be sharp. Many anglers are quite successful using a large heavily hackled fly. They are often referred to as skaters. They look like a big piece of meat jumping around on the water surface and quite often entice trout to rise to it. The fish often refuse this fly when they rise, but it serves as a great locator. After the fish has risen to the skater and refused or missed it, you can change to a smaller representative pattern and quite often catch that fish with it. Fish that new pattern both dead drift and twitching. The trout

may take it either way.

Another method is to use a pattern that looks like many different insects. Three of the best are the Adams, the Humpy or Goofus Bug and the Henryville. The idea is to make your cast so that the fly floats dead drift through the most likely looking feeding lanes of the stream. Hopefully, your fly will suggest an attractive enough piece of food that the trout will come up for it. From the mid season on through the summer months, terrestrial imitations, such as beetles and ants are fished in this manner.

One of the most exciting and often most productive methods in the later part of the season is fishing the "spider" type imitation in pocket water. As the water gets warmer, trout will often move into the turbulant heavily oxygenated pocket water. They will hold behind, in front of and alongside rocks and will take bits of food as they are washed by. The key here is to get directly below the pockets and, fishing with a short line and a short leader, work your way upstream. The short

Spider type dry fly.

and streams have already hatched. (The limestone and spring creeks are the possible exception to this.) However, the fish still have to eat and will forage for whatever is available. The bait fish also play an increasingly important role at this time. But, for the dry fly-fisherman, the terrestrials, especially the ant and beetle imitations often save the day.

The best place to fish these imitations is along any deep undercut banks or places with foliage overhanging good looking water. The trout here will be looking for

(Above) Typical stretch of pocket water.

(Below) Angler works pockets properly by casting and working them straight upstream.

line and leader give you maximum control for placement of the fly. It is extremely important with this method to have an absolute drag free float. The less line and leader you have on the water, the better off you will be. Try to come as close to having only the fly on the water as you possibly can. You will be casting straight upstream. Make your first casts to the bottom of the pocket, then work up, placing your fly on each side and in front of the rock. Since the trout in this type of water are used to the food going by rather quickly, they have to make instant decisions and move quickly. The rises are usually quite sharp. Since you are not trying to match any type of hatch, you should use a fairly large spider—size 8, 10 or 12—so that it will be sure to catch the attention of the fish. Remember, control of the line and fly are important.

Terrestrials

From mid-season, which I consider to be around mid to end of June in the East and Midwest and about early to mid July out West, till the end of the season, one of the most valuable imitations that the fly-fisherman can have in his box is the terrestrial. These are imitations basically of the ant, beetle, cricket and grasshopper. The more overgrown or heavily grassed or bushed the banks are, the more important and prevelant the terrestrial will be for the trout to eat. Also, at that time of the year, the majority of the aquatic insects in the rivers

(Above) Artificial ant (left) and beetle (right).

(Right) Typical grass and brush lined terrestrial water.

these insects. Any streams that meander through fields or meadows will also be excellent for terrestrials. The ants, beetles and cricket imitations seem to work well at any time of the day. The grasshoppers seem to be best from the late morning through the afternoon, after the air has warmed up allowing them to move about easily.

The procedure is simple. Just cast your fly into the likely feeding lanes and let it drift drag free in the current. The exception to the drag free might be with the hopper, where a gentle twitch now and then could be useful to entice a good fish to rise. Although a gentle presentation is advisable with the small ant imitations, it is not necessary to be delicate with the beetles, crickets and hoppers. In fact it is an advantage to have them land on the surface with a ''splat,'' since that is what the natural often does. This commotion can also attract the attention of the fish.

This type of fishing is actually prospecting for whatever hungry trout are available during these nonhatching periods and can often be rewarded with some large fish that were just waiting for a passing meal. You may find that, during a hatch when the fish are ultra selective to the proper imitation of the hatching insect, a chunky beetle or cricket will often tempt the selective trout into taking an offering that is considerably different from that hatching insect.

A good basic assortment of terrestrials would be:

ANTS: colors—black, cinnamon; sizes—16, 18, and 20.
BEETLES: colors—black, brown; sizes—14, 16 and 18.
CRICKET: colors—black; sizes—12 and 14.
HOPPER: color—brown/yellow; sizes—10 and 12.

YOUR OBLIGATIONS AS A TROUT FISHERMAN

With the equipment discussed, a knowledge of the trout's behavior, its food and feeding habits and a basic understanding and ability of how to relate to them with your fly-fishing techniques, you will be able to fish just about any type of trout water and catch fish. This will open up a new horizon of angling pleasure and aesthetic values.

The key to it all is having quality trout waters to be able to fish in. Fortunately, we still have quite a bit available, but it has not been without a fight and the efforts of many concerned people. A trout stream or pond is a freshwater eco-system that must have a balance of high quality water, oxygen and purity in order to maintain the necessary insect and fish life. Unfortunately, it does not take too much neglect or pollution to upset that balance and destroy the fishery. Once a fishery is ruined or polluted, if it can at all be

141

Patches of several of the top trout and fly-fishing organizations.

restored, which is often doubtful, it takes many years, and then it is never the same.

As you develop into a sincere trout fisherman, I hope you will develop an appreciation and concern for the environment that offers you so much enjoyment and then spread that appreciation to others. It is my hope that you will become associated with organizations such as Theodore Gordon Flyfishers, Trout Unlimited, The Federation of Fly Fishermen and The American League of Anglers to name a few. There are local mem-bership clubs across the country that offer angling comradeship and a unified effort to maintain quality trout fisheries. Become involved.

Other trout environment efforts that you are likely to encounter are the various types of stream regulations on different sections of water. For example, a section of a river may be regulated so that you may only keep two fish over 12 inches, or another may say that you may only keep four fish under 10 inches. Another, and one of the most popular and valuable for real quality trout

Sign showing special NO-KILL regulations on the Beaverkill River in New York.

fishing is the "NO KILL" or "FISH FOR FUN" regulations. These sections of rivers are usually open all year long for fishing, rather than limited to the season dates, but you must return all fish caught. What this means, is that there will always be a good population of trout in these waters and that they will have a good chance to reach a large size. Two of the best examples of the value of this regulation are the Beaverkill River in New York State, which has approximately 4 of its 20 miles as No Kill, and Henry's Fork of the Snake around Last Chance, Idaho, that has approximately 2 miles of No Kill water. The quality and number of fish in these sections are marvelous. The popularity of these regulations is evidenced by the fact that on almost any weekend during the main season, approximately 80 percent of all the fishermen on the entire system will be on that small section. In fact the problem now is that

you fly-fish, the more you will value the trout as a resource that is really too valuable to use only once. You might even find yourself putting them back in hopes of catching them again, even though the water does not call for that regulation. I know I often do.

Whether or not you intend to keep the fish, but especially if you intend to return them, one of the most useful items you should have with you is a landing net. It is relatively small and light and quite important for many situations.

In my early evolving years of trout fishing, I used a net to scoop the fish from the water, making sure it would not escape before I could stuff it into my creel. In those days, bringing home the evidence had some great importance. As I became more involved in fly-fishing, I began to appreciate the trout as a limited resource. The enjoyment of the game became the challenge of enticing

The number of fishermen on Henry's Fork of the Snake River in Idaho, is evidence of the popularity of the NO-KILL or FISH FOR FUN philosophy.

they get too crowded.

Not all rivers and streams are capable of maintaining various regulations adequately. The application of these regulations is done so only after careful and thorough study and evaluation of that water by local and state environmental and fishery departments. I guess the point that I want to make here is, that rather than looking at these regulations as a hinderance, they should be appreciated as an effort and means of increasing the quality of trout fishing for a steadily increasing number of trout fishermen who have a limited amount of water to fish. Unfortunately, as the number of fishermen increases, the amount of available water does not. In fact, if anything, it is decreasing, due to suburban development and pollution. This is what we have to be aware of and try to be progressive in regulating the water accordingly. You will find that the more

the trout and fooling him into taking my artificial for a natural insect. It wasn't long before I was releasing the fish I caught in order to give them another chance. With this feeling also came the attitude, "Who needs a net when I'm going to put them back. I'll look cool and professional, bringing them into my hand for a quick release." Unfortunately, that was an inaccurate assumption. It took several situations, when I wished that I had a net, to get me to change my mind. I've been using a net ever since.

Although most trout can be brought to the hand in average water conditions, it is far more logical to bring the trout into a net quickly and gently, especially if he is to be released. Let's look at the situation objectively. First, trout are fragile and, like all other fish, slimy. There is no way to hold a fish that wants to swim away without squeezing it tighter than you should. This could damage the fish. I have seen fishermen with a "death grip" on trout while trying to disengage a well hooked fly, followed by the half dead, returned fish helplessly tumbling in the current because the angler made no effort to resuscitate the trout before releasing it. Quite often, a fish handled in this manner never recovers and the purpose of returning the trout, to be fished for again, is defeated. If you intend to release fish, why not make the slight extra effort to assure its survival?

A trout in your net can be handled gently while holding your rod under your arm and the net and fish in the water. Remember, trout don't breath air. Keep them in the water, and handle with care. Too often, trout are seen in those "No Kill" regulated waters with their mouths torn. This restricts their ability to take in food properly. However, if you use barbless hooks or bend

another point. I am constantly amazed and dismayed by many anglers who feel it beneath their dignity to move more than a foot or two to land a fish. They seem to believe that, in order to be successful, the fish must be dragged to the net. A case in point occurred on a river when the water was quite high. Walking upstream to look at a particular pool, I passed an angler on the bank playing an apparently heavy fish. Upstream, the water was heavier than I liked, so I decided to return downstream. Fifteen to 20 minutes had elapsed since I had passed the hooked-up angler. I was therefore surprised to find him in the same spot with the same fish on. Upon inquiring, he said that it was a big fish, and he couldn't bring it back upstream. I asked if I could assist by demonstrating the proper way. When he agreed, I took his rod and had the 17-inch trout in the net in a

A fighting trout can be difficult to hold in fast water. The use of a net is helpful both to the angler and the fish. (Photo courtesy of Sid Neff.)

down the barb with pliers, you will be amazed at how easily the fly can be removed, saving wear and tear on both the trout and your fly. Think about and try it. You will seldom lose a fish using a nearly weightless, barbless fly. And think of how easily a barbless hook will come out if you hook yourself.

Back to the net. Two situations I recall, where I wished that I had had a net, concerned big fish in relatively heavy water. In both cases, after finally bringing the trout to within grabbing range, a futile attempt sent it dashing away again. Several more attempts of the same sort had the same result. Finally, the totally exhausted trout was unceremoniously skittered across the top of the water. Not a just reward for one of nature's most beautiful creatures, if he is to be put back.

The thought of bringing the fish to the net raises

shade over 1 minute. It was none to soon, as the fish was on his "last fins."

It is almost impossible to drag a heavy fish upstream against the current. What I did was nothing spectacular, just common sense. While holding the trout in position, I reeled in the line and walked downstream at the same speed. When I was alongside or below the fish, it was easy to bring it to the net with the help of the current. This holds just as true when you are in the river. Move down to the trout while holding it in position. When you get below the fish, bring it down to the waiting net. Don't stab with the net, just hold it in the water and bring the fish over it—then lift. It is much more of a feat to land the trout quickly and in good condition than to see how long you can prolong the fight until it is exhausted.

As anglers, we should have enough respect for the trout that we hold so dear and valuable to take the necessary precautions to keep them healthy if they are to be returned. A properly used net and barbless hooks are two simple means to this end. However, if you are going to keep some of the fish that you catch, they sure do taste good.

FLYS FOR TROUT FISHING

A suggested list of patterns that will allow you to cover a good portion of the situations that you will encounter is as follows:

Streamers or Bucktails
Yellow Marabou—sizes 6,8,10
Black Ghost—sizes 4,6,8,10
Black Nosed Dace—sizes 6,8,10,12
Muddler Minnow—sizes 4,6,8,10,12

Nymphs
Gold Ribbed Hare's Ear—sizes 6,8,10,12,14,16
Woolly Worm—sizes 6,8,10,12
Stonefly—sizes 4,6,8,10
March Brown—sizes 8,10,12,14
Muskrat Nymph—sizes 8,10,12,14,16

Wet Flies
Leadwing Coachman—sizes 12,14,16,18
Hare's Ear—sizes 12,14,16,18

Dry Flies
Adams—sizes 12,14,16,18,20
Light Hendrickson—sizes 12,14,16
Dark Hendrickson—sizes 12,14,16,18
Royal Coachman Hairwing—sizes 10,12,14,16
Light Cahill—sizes 12,14,16,18,20
Humpy or Goofus bug—sizes 10,12,14,16

Terrestrials
Brown or Black Beetle—sizes 14,16,18
Black Ant—sizes 14,16,18,20
Cinnimon Ant—sizes 16,18,20

The above list covers a lot of ground for your trout fishing. However, you may find certain hatches in your area that might not be covered by the above patterns. Make notes of your experiences. If you cannot find artificials commercially to match what you need, it's time to learn how to tie them youself. (See Chapter 3, the list of Popular Fly Patterns for the materials necessary to tie the above flies.)

BIBLIOGRAPHY

The listing of the following books pertain to Trout fishing and entymology or both.

Bergman, Ray. *Trout*. Rev. Ed., New York: Knopf, 1952.

Borger, Charles. *Nymphing*. Harrisburg, Pa: Stackpole, 1979.

Brooks, Charles. *Nymph Fishing for Larger Trout*. New York: Crown, 1976.

Brooks, Joe. *Trout Fishing*. New York: Harper & Row, 1972.

Caucci, Al and Nastasi, Bob. *Hatches*. New York: Compara Hatch, Ltd., 1975.

Flick, Art. *Art Flick's New Streamside Guide to Naturals and Their Imitations*. New York: Crown, 1970.

Koch, Ed. *Fishing the Midge*. Rockville Center, N.Y.: Freshet Press, 1974.

Marinaro, Vincent. *A Modern Dry Fly Code*. New York: Crown, 1970.

Meck, Charles R. *Meeting and Fishing the Hatches*. New York: Winchester Press, 1978.

Merritt, Richard W. and Cummins, Kenneth W. *An Introduction to the Aquatic Insects of North America*. Dubuque, Iowa: Kendall/Hunt, 1978.

Schwiebert, Ernest. *Matching the Hatch*. New York: Stoeger, 1978.

———. *Nymphs*. New York: Winchester, 1972.

———. *Trout*. New York: E.P. Dutton, 1978.

Swisher, Doug, and Carl Richards. *Fly Fishing Strategy*. New York: Crown, 1975.

———. *Selective Trout*. New York: Crown, 1971.

Solomon, Larry and Eric Leiser. *The Caddis and the Angler*. Harrisburg, Pa: Stackpole, 1977.

Talleur, Richard. *Fly Fishing for Trout: A Guide for Adult Beginners*. New York: Winchester.

Wright, Leonard. *Fishing the Dry Fly as a Living Insect*. New York: E.P. Dutton, 1972.

Larry Solomon

CHAPTER 5
Trout Flies
for the Rational Angler

AS YOU READ through this chapter, you'll note that most of the remarks are addressed to the flytier. This approach will undoubtedly disappoint some readers, but I cannot help but feel that flytying is a natural step in the evolution of the fly-fisherman. The inability to tie flies is not a significant barrier to obtaining the pattern types described in the following pages because most are available commercially. The non-tier will simply have to search as vigorously for suppliers of flies as the tier searches for sources of materials.

If you have never tried tying your own flies, you should try soon. The savings you'll realize in the cost of flies will be far outweighed by the indescribable joy you'll get from catching trout on a fly you've tied yourself. If you have tried flytying and given up in frustration, try again but read the next few lines before you do.

To get started properly in flytying, find a tier whose work you admire and respect, and get that person to teach you. This is the only way you will attain competence with any degree of speed. It is possible to learn to tie from books and pictures, but the process is slow and frustrating. Next, be sure you are working with the best tools and materials you can afford. Let your mentor help you to acquire the essentials. Do not purchase tools or materials unless an experienced tier is with you

to guide your selections. Trying to tie with poor tools or materials will frustrate the novice more quickly than any other obstacle. If you'll follow these two rules, you'll be tying your own flies more quickly than you ever believed possible. And, you will have begun what I feel is one of the most satisfying and rewarding endeavors associated with fly-fishing.

Whether you tie or buy, there are a couple of facts that should guide you both in selecting your fly patterns and the manner in which you fish them. A trout is a relatively simple organism. It has only three needs in life: food upon which to exist; cover or concealment from its enemies; and comfort—water of proper temperature and flow. Places where these three conditions are met are places where you should cast your fly. The better these conditions are met, the larger the trout will be that occupies that place.

Ideally, your fly will imitate the food forms found where the trout lives. To determine what food forms abound, you should do a bit of research—turn over a few rocks, seine the flow of the stream with some screen wire, and be observant. Watch for insects and insect cases on land, in the air, and in the water. Watch for small fish and note their size and coloration. What you see is what your flies should imitate. After all it

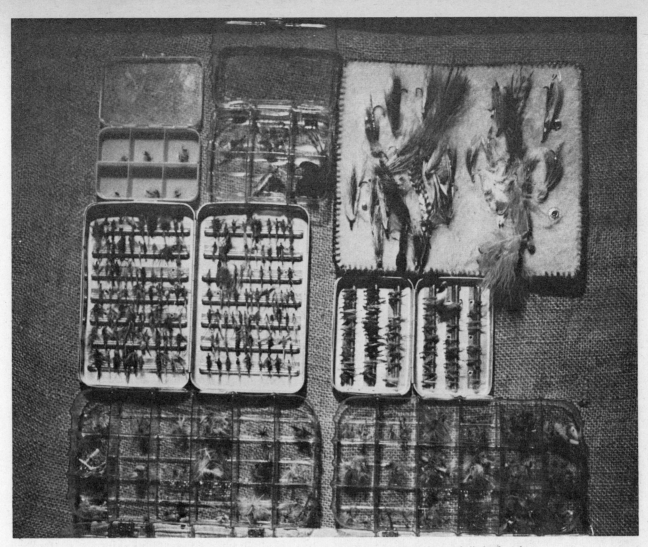

A "few" of the fly boxes carried by a fly-fisherman planning a full day's trip.

does no good to fish a stonefly imitation in waters where there are no stoneflies—at least in most cases it will prove fruitless. The kinds of flies you tie or buy to imitate the food forms found in the water you fish may take many forms. With the words and pictures that follow, I hope to give some guidance to your selection.

DRY FLIES

The trips through my fishing notes that I make during the closed season of each year never fail to depress me. Why? Because I invariably discover that most of the fish that I have caught have been taken on a relatively small number of the fly patterns that I carry, and I suspect that others have the same experience. There are several possible explanations for this, including times of the day or year that I fish, fishing to hatches more often than fishing blind, loyalties to given patterns and so on. What truly bothers me is that I cannot satisfactorily answer the question, "Why do fly-fishermen carry so many patterns to begin with?" So,

bear with me as we jointly try to answer that question in this discussion.

The first reason that I can identify for having so many kinds of flies is that I enjoy tying them, and this is coupled with the second reason which is that I hate throwing any fly away—even for the purpose of recycling the hook. Now, while digging through my fishing vest I discover that I have nine different dry fly patterns for *Ephemerella subvaria,* the popular Hendrickson, and these patterns are tied in two different sizes and a couple of subtly different color variations. The flies have been tied over a period of several years, and in total they represent about two and a half dozen flies. Now, I think we are beginning to find one of our first answers, and the nice part of this answer is that it applies to all the mayfly imitations in the fly box. Let's analyze my collection, and find out why it exists.

First, there is the classic woodduck-winged, dun-hackled, creamy-bodied, Light Hendrickson. This is in the box because it is the traditional pattern for the

The traditional Hendrickson.

The thorax tie.

The variant.

result of close examination of the behavior and shape of the natural mayfly. The two body segments (abdomen and thorax) in the thorax-style tie are more representative of the mayfly body configuration, and the pattern is used when the trout are a bit more selective. The fly is durable. It rides well on the water, and it, too, works.

Next, there is a wingless, variant tie, with dun hackle and a pale body. This pattern is used in high wind and fast water. It rides very high and is used during the hatch to tempt those trout feeding at the ends of pools in which Hendricksons are emerging where the water runs just a bit faster. The variant tie bounces over the riffles and gives the illusion of a dun about to escape. It has resulted in some exciting, splashing rises.

Now we move toward the more realistic patterns. There is a cut-wing, thorax-tied pattern, with spread "pontoon" tails and clipped bottom hackle. This fly is a

classic Catskill waters on which I learned to fish with flies. It is pretty, delicate, easy to tie, and it works. It has earned its place in the angler's collection over 50 years, and it deserves to be there. Next, there is a pattern tied with exactly the same materials, except that the hackle and wings sit a bit further back on the body, and there is a fur thorax tied just forward of the wing and hackle assembly. This variation has also earned its place, but this is a modern modification evolving as a

The cut-wing Dun.

The Comparadun (Caucci-Nastasi).

variation on the Marinaro thorax-style pattern, and it is used in more critical angling situations where the water is relatively calm, and there is no wind to riffle the surface. The fly sits right on the surface film and the high wing, cut from a webby hackle section gives a very "honest" picture in the trout's feeding window. The fly has proved to be deadly in several situations over the years.

Next we have the Caucci/Nastasi deerhair-winged Comparadun. This is a real favorite during dense hatches where the trout have established feeding loca-

tions and are taking eagerly. There is no hackle on this pattern, and the fly floats beautifully due to the spread tails of mink guard hairs and the supporting semicircular deerhair wing. The picture that drifts into the trout's window is super-realistic and ideal for critical feeding situations. Its durability results in fewer fly changes and more fishing time.

For the *most* critical feeding situations there is the Swisher/Richards no-hackle with duck quill segment wings and spread tails. This gives the most accurate representation of the natural dun mayfly and is perfect

The parachute dun.

The Swisher-Richards no-hackle.

The soft-hackle, or spider, wet fly imitates both caddis and mayflies in their sub-surface life stages. (Photo courtesy of *Field and Stream*.).

for still water conditions. It is used when none of the patterns listed above will elicit consistent rises. I prefer not to use the pattern at all times because trout mouths shred the realistic but somewhat fragile quill wings. One Comparadun, on the other hand, has lasted for as many as 20 fish.

All of the patterns listed above reside in my fly box in sizes 12 to 14 to imitate the dun or sub-adult stage of *subvaria*. The body colors range from cream to creamy pink to a mixture of brown, yellow and red furs, which imitates the male *subvaria* dun. In addition to the imitations of the duns, there are three patterns I use to imitate the adult or spinner stage of *subvaria*. There are two spent-wing patterns, one with polypropylene wings and one with clipped hackle wings. In addition there is a large, full-hackled variant tie. The bodies for all three spinner patterns are the same, a palmered brown hackle clipped so that only stubs remain. This body is the result of experimentation, and it has proved to be both durable and effective.

I have selected the Hendrickson as the example for this discussion, but I have similar arrays of patterns for all the major hatches that I fish. My fishing notes tell me that I use the Comparadun more often than any of the rest, and this is supported by the fact that I have a preponderance of this pattern in the collection. Yet, I know that there are times and places where each of the other patterns either works more effectively or gives me more pleasure to fish. As a result, they will probably all remain there. Your choice is up to you, but I submit that the longer you are in this game, the more you will find that you move toward a variety similar to that just described.

NYMPHS

Let's look now at the nymph patterns where your imagination can really run wild. With dry flies we are at least limited to where they are fished. They must float. With nymphs we add a weight problem to our collection. These may be fished near the bottom; in virtual mid-level suspension; or near the surface to imitate an emerging insect. In trying to meet the first two conditions the fly's body conformation is identical, but once the insect begins to emerge, we have by definition the challenge to imitate the emerging wing. For purposes of continuity, let's limit the discussion to the Hendrickson.

The first pattern I come across is a home modifica-

The stiff-hackled emerger. Note splayed tails. (Photo courtesy of *Field and Stream*.)

tion of the traditional Hare's Ear. This is tied on a number 14, 2X Long hook. It is tied both weighted and unweighted to cover the first two subsurface conditions mentioned above. It consists of nothing more than woodduck tails and a roughly dubbed body of Hare's Ear ribbed with a very fine gold tinsel. I have let this pattern evolve itself at my vise by simply eliminating details such as wings, wing pads, and legs from the original pattern. None of the eliminated parts was ever missed by the trout. It has become the pattern I use in a variety of colors for imitating all mayfly nymphs. It has no top or bottom or side. It looks exactly the same from any angle. And, it works like a charm.

But what of all the fun you can have tying nymphs by putting on realistic looking legs, beautifully designed wing pads, gossamer like gill structures, realistically designed tails, and so forth. I tie those too, and there are plenty of them in my fly box. People admire them when we compare flies, and I just enjoy the heck out of tying them. But I don't fish them too often. Why? Because the simple pattern described above has proved over the years to be more effective. When I lose one, all that I have lost is about 4 minutes at the vise and 3¢ worth of materials. We reach a more complex problem when we design mayfly emerger patterns. Here the features to be imitated are the emerging wing and the body attitude in the water. The fly must drift in roughly 6 inches of space below the surface film. There must be enough weight to sink the fly but not so much that the fly's mobility is affected or that it sinks too deeply. I use three different patterns to achieve three different goals. First, there is the classic soft-hackled fly or spider tie. This consists of nothing more than a tail, a body, and a very soft and sparse hackle. It has good water penetration, and it has an alive, impressionistic appearance as it drifts along just under the surface. This pattern, too, looks the same from every angle. I tie it with highly absorbent materials such as a wool body, and webby hen hackle or partridge hackle.

Next, is the subsurface emerger pattern, tied with a woodduck tail, hare's ear body, and a clump of dun-colored down from the base of a hackle feather for a wing. Again, the pattern enters the water easily, is very light so it doesn't sink deeply, and the filmy clump of down feathers imitates an emerging wing quite well.

I also tie a surface emerger. The pattern is identical to the one just described, with the addition of two widely spaced turns of dry fly hackle in the thorax area. The hackle is clipped top and bottom, but there are adequate fibers to keep the fly floating just in the film. It is most effective when cast to a feeding fish, when you can see the rise, because the fly itself is almost invisible to the angler due to its low float in the water.

The foregoing covers the mayfly imitations that I regularly use. It is easy to see from this discussion how flies can begin to accumulate. If memory serves, we have named 12 different patterns used to imitate the

(Above) Caddis larva.
(Below) Typical caddis larva tied on Mustad #37160. (Photo courtesy of *Field and Stream*.).

three life stages of a single species of mayfly. Six of those patterns were carried in two different sizes, making a total of 18 flies even if only one of each was carried. Assuming that we would carry at least three of each, we now have 54 flies for one hatch. I don't know about you, but I try to fish at least six major mayfly hatches each season, so to be even reasonably well equipped I now have over 300 flies in my fly box. But let's turn now from mayflies to that very prevalent little devil, the caddisfly.

I admit to a higher tolerance for impressionism when I begin to match caddisflies, as there are so many species and so much less study has been done on them. I try to restrict myself to matching general areas of color, size, and behavior in the caddis families, and, of course, once again there are three different life stages to imitate. Let's start at the bottom of the stream and work our way to the surface in this discussion.

The first (from the anglers standpoint) important life stage in the caddis is the larva. For practical purposes we'll call this the caddis worm. My favorite imitation begins with the Mustad 37160 bait hook. The tie is nothing more than a body segment and a thorax segment with the body roughly four times longer than the thorax. The materials I use span a wide range from latex to plastic to wool and fur for the body. The thorax may be peacock or ostrich herl, fur, or wool. I tie the worm in a variety of colors, sticking mainly with natural "earth" tones of green, tan, brown, black, and cream. In each case the thorax is darker than the body. In some of the larger sizes, I will add "feelers" of hackle, herl, or picked-out dubbing to the thorax section, but I feel these are probably more for my gratification than the fish's.

As with mayflies, the pattern problem with caddis grows more complex as we head toward the surface. The next life stage is the pupa. In this stage the insect's wings and legs are becoming evident and should be represented either realistically or impressionistically in the imitation. I generally choose the latter, because the soft-hackle tie mentioned in our mayfly discussion serves very adequately as an imitation of the caddis pupa. But, my love for tying leads me to the more creative realistic patterns, and many of these reside comfortably in my fly boxes as well. These range from the Jorgensen caddis pupa, using duck quill segments for the stubby side wings, fur guard hairs for legs, and coarsely dubbed fur for a thorax; to the Solomon pupa with similar wing structure and partridge feather legs and feelers; to Gary LaFontaine's Sparkle caddis, which uses sparkle yarn to imitate the air bubble surrounding an emerging caddis. All of these patterns have worked for me at one time or another, thus each has earned its place, and generally each is represented in several sizes and colors, as well.

It is worth noting at this point that if the angler is not carrying caddis patterns in his fly box, he is missing out on an awful lot of trout fishing. Caddis are by far the most prominent insect in my two favorite midwestern trout streams, and this is also the case on the classic waters of New York's Catskills where my angling teeth were cut. During the late spring and summer when mayflies hold back their emergence until the more propitious hours of evening and night, the caddis often obligingly emerges during daylight hours and provides enjoyment for the observant angler. The next two patterns discussed should be carried in some quantity by every trout angler.

Happily, representation of the adult stage of the caddisfly does not take on the degree of complexity (at least for me) that the sub-adult and adult stages of the mayfly do. I carry but two patterns, albeit in many sizes and colors, and both were designed by Larry Solomon. The first of these started life some 8 years ago as the "Boeing" caddis, but Solomon, fearful of trademark difficulties, renamed it the Delta Wing caddis. The pattern consists of a chunky body, two hackle tip wings tied in a plane with the body and forming a "V" and a standard dry fly hackle with the bottom portion trimmed off. This pattern forms a very acceptable imitation of a floating adult caddis. In addition, I have found (and I think Larry will agree) that this is an excellent exploring pattern when no insects are in evidence.

The other adult caddis pattern that I use regularly is Larry's Hair-Wing caddis. Hackle and body are the same as for the Delta Wing, but the wing itself is formed from a small bunch of deer body hair, tied to form a tent over the body and extending just past the bend of the hook. I prefer to use this pattern during the height of a hatch as it is more mobile than the Delta Wing, and as a

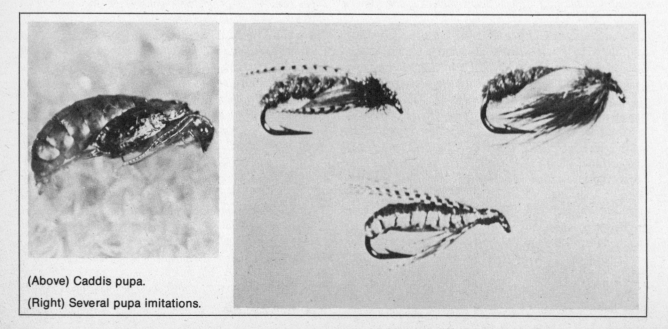

(Above) Caddis pupa.

(Right) Several pupa imitations.

The Delta Wing caddis, a good imitator and an excellent "searching" pattern. (Photo Courtesy of *Field and Stream*.)

The Hairwing Caddis. (Photo courtesy of *Field and Stream*.)

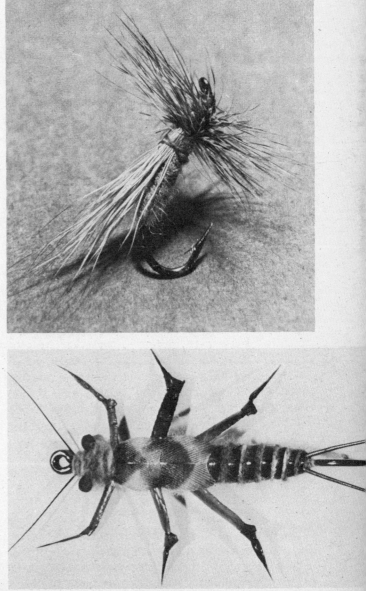

result is easier to maneuver in a manner similar to the bouncing caddis naturals.

I once wrote a caddis article in which I said, "Watching a caddis hatch is like watching a bunch of activated ping-pong balls in an enclosed space." And this points out a feature worth noting about fishing an adult caddis imitation. Because the flies are so active and their flight so erratic, rises to them are likely to be fast and savage. Many rises are missed by the fish, and this leaves the observant angler an excellent opportunity. It is wise to cast precisely to the spot where you have just seen a fish rise, and to get that cast there as quickly after the rise as possible. To do this, keep your fly in the air by false casting, and the instant you see the rise, slap your fly as close to that spot as possible. Don't worry about presentation. If you get the fly there soon enough, you're almost certain to get a rise.

The next aquatic insect family getting prominent space in my fly box is the stonefly. Only two life stages are represented, the nymph and the adult. I have, after much experimentation, settled on only one type of nymph pattern, and for this I thank Charles Brooks, author of *Nymph Fishing for Larger Trout*. Stonefly nymphs are generally weighted to fish near the bottom, and Charles maintains that because the fly is twisted and turned by the current, it is important to imitate only the insect's back color. Thus, all his stonefly patterns are tied with back and belly identical, and with a hackle collar that is symmetrical. I discovered the validity of this inadvertently during a western trip some years ago when I tied some imitations of the nymph of the giant Montana stonefly (salmon fly) which consisted of nothing more than a black cigar-shaped body, a gold rib,

(Right) Ted Neimeyer's Quillstone, an example of fine art in stonefly imitations.

and a black hackle collar. The flies were incredibly successful on the Firehole, and I and two friends had every evening of our trip occupied tying duplicates for our four non-tying companions. (Needless to say, the patterns were also heavily weighted, and as a result more than a few are still clinging to rocks in the Madison, Henry's Fork and Firehole.) Since that time and after having my initial suspicions confirmed by Mr. Brooks' observations, I have restricted most of my nymph tying to that one simple pattern in many imitative sizes and colors.

As with caddis pupa imitations, however, there is the desire and the motivation to become more creative in one's tying efforts for stonefly imitations. Driven by the beautiful imitations tied by such artists as Ted Niemeyer and Paul Jorgensen, several of my own feeble efforts toward realism occupy space in my fly box. Some of them have worked on occasion, and far more haven't. That does not mean I'll stop tying them for my own pleasure, but I hope the bulk of my efforts reflect a bit more realistic attitude if not a more realistic collection of flies.

Imitations of the adult *Pteronarcys californicus,* the salmon fly, or giant Montana stonefly, predominate in catalogs from western shops. But, imitations of other stoneflies found in eastern and midwestern streams are rarely seen. Because the resting attitude of the stonefly is similar to that of the caddis, however, I have found that the adult caddis patterns mentioned in the previous discussion work very well if tied in natural-matching color combinations. My first experience with this pattern occurred on the upper reaches of the Willowemoc in New York's Catskill mountains in late summer of 1975. A little yellow stonefly emerges almost every evening during August on that stream, but I had not paid it any attention because of heavy insect activity from caddis and mayflies at the same period. During one period in August, however, the trout were showing a marked selectivity for the stonefly, so I tried tying a hairwing "caddis" with yellow body and dun wing. The trout loved it, and since that time I have tied the same "caddis" pattern to imitate several varieties of stonefly. I must mention here, however, that reduced water quality on many streams is fast eradicating stonefly populations, and, sadly, anglers have far too few opportunities to fish these exciting hatches. The stonefly in many areas is facing the same future as the native brook trout for many of the same reasons. As a result of this my stonefly patterns are few, and I find that they generally have been tied for a specific application such as the one noted above.

WET FLIES

Oh, here among the nymph boxes are several examples of the traditional wet fly. I almost overlooked them because I think of them in the same category with nymphs; just a different pattern type because they have

The standard wet fly, a British tied Grouse and Claret in this case. (Photo courtesy of *Field and Stream.*)

wings. Because they are *the* traditional fly, however, they deserve a special mention. The wet fly may imitate either the emerging dun or the ovipositing spinner of the mayfly family. Likewise it may represent the emerging or ovipositing caddis. It may give the impression of the nymph of either family, and in larger sizes, it may even look to the fish like a minnow. Certainly any pattern type that does all this is worth a second look.

Well, I carry about three dozen wet flies whenever I fish for trout. In looking them over, they run from size 12 to size 18, and a good two-thirds of them have bodies of hare's ear. They have either gray, duck-quill wings or woodduck flank feather wings and either grizzly or dun hackle. This tells me that I generally fish them as imitations of emerging mayflies—when I fish them at all. And, that's the problem! Wet flies are extremely effective, but my thoughts are generally so preoccupied with the imitation of food forms that my mind always thinks, "nymphs" when considering sub-surface imitators. Each year I regret not using wet flies more often because I know that they have often produced either because analysis of fish and insect behavior showed that they would be the most effective imitation, or because, for whatever reason, I began fishing a wet fly "blind" (to no visible rises, insects or fish) and did well with it.

Arriving at a selection of wet flies to carry in your fly box may be the result of careful entomology study or it may reflect what you like in the way of patterns. In the former case you would select your flies based on insects that appear below the surface with fully developed wing structures, such as several of the mayflies and caddis. In the latter, you would simply select what appeals to the eye, and this is not to say that the selected patterns would always be different. The Leadwing Coachman, for instance, holds great eye appeal with its conservative dressing of shiny, bronze peacock herl body, slate-gray wings, and brown hackle, yet it is also a reasonable imitation of the *Isonychia* genus nymphs. But, as stated earlier, if there were but one wet fly to carry, I would select the Hare's Ear. I have them in every conceivable variation: with and without gold rib; with and without wings; and with and without hackle. I fish them upstream, and I fish them down, with action and dead drift. They are in the nymph section, and they are tied as true wet flies. Do I recommend them? Well, sort of!

The remaining insect imitating patterns that populate my fly box, and which should be carried by any serious trout angler, are the day savers—the terrestrial patterns. From the time the first ant appears on my patio in

Inch worm imitations used to be a regular resident of my fly box, but I don't seem to use them very often anymore. I do recall a period about 10 or 12 years ago when they provided the most exciting fishing of the year; and at that time my favorite pattern was a clipped deerhair version tied in brilliant green. I still have a few, but they have been used in recent years only in desperate cases to try to coax a rise, and then have met with singularly poor results.

Beetles are another story, however. Once again, my favorite pattern is the contribution of Larry Solomon. The tie is simple—a peacock herl body and a deerhair "shell." They reside in my fly box in sizes 12 down to 20, and I suspect they always will. They have proved themselves in several locations over the past 8 or 9 years, and they truly rate the name, day savers. Terrestrials are the flies that can turn a fishless day into a

The Adams, a reliable producer. (Photo courtesy of *Field and Stream.*)

the spring, I know I can count on daytime activity along my favorite meadow stream with no pattern other than the black ant. I have ants tied in sizes 12 to 24, and I consider them to be the most reliable producers I can carry. In the last 2 years, I can say with confidence that 20 percent of my trout have been taken on black or cinnamon ants. In addition, I carry several Letort Crickets and Letort Hoppers. The cricket is a marvelous exploring fly on summer days, and when the grasshoppers are out, the Letort Hopper is as reliable a pattern as I have tried. The hopper is another insect that seems to stimulate creative flytiers, and I am no exception. Several different hopper patterns are in my collection, and surprisingly all of them seem to generate equally good results. My only rationale for recommending the Letort Hopper above the others is the ease with which it is tied and its durability.

good day during the hot months of late summer. The beetles, hoppers and crickets can turn a rookie into an expert, because in most cases a sloppy (or splashy) presentation is the right one when imitating the clumsy land insects. The major requirement is for stealth in approaching the stream, because generally the locations where trout feed on terrestrials are still water locations where the slightest tremor will send trout fleeing for safety. Generally you'll be fishing the terrestrials close against the bank, but I've had luck with them right in the middle of some relatively large rivers. (I question why I was using them there to start with, but they worked nonetheless.)

The only flies tied in traditional "insect" style not covered in these discussions have been those that do not imitate anything, and there are some fairly consistent performers in this category. In fact, one of my favorite all-time patterns, the Adams, fits this description. I suppose it is unfair to say that the Adams is non-imitative, because it "sorta" imitates everything. Its buggy looking appearance has been the stimulus for a number of flies that have found a permanent place in my collection. The gray-brown tones of the Adams have led me to tie similar mixed tone flies in gray-cream and brown-light ginger combinations, using a variety of body colors and wing combinations. I have had enough good results using these flies that I am convinced I could probably "get by" with using them for all my mayfly imitations. I'd be missing out on the fun of tying close imitations if I were to do this, but I'm not at all sure that I would be sacrificing very many fish. The secret to the success of these flies is that they are impressionistic; they look like "bugs," and the trout respond to the stimulus. The patterns are not quite what the insect actually looks like, but they are close enough to force the fish to "give it a try."

The impressionistic premise does not explain the existence in my fly box of the Royal Coachman. I can perhaps best explain the reason for this fly's being by the following story. I had occasion a few years ago to be the subject for a brief film on fly-fishing for ABC television. I spent two enjoyable days with the crew filming, during the first of which I could not hook a fish with my best efforts until late in the day when a very large fish sucked in a number 28 fly on an 8X tippet. The results of that rise did not have a chance to be recorded on film as the trout's first run popped the tippet. Finally on the second day two nice trout were hooked and landed, and we completed the action filming. The producer wanted a casting sequence to end the film and asked that I tie on a bright fly and cast right at and as close to the camera as possible. A Royal Coachman served admirably for this purpose. We complted that sequence, and he asked that

I simply turn and wade up stream (into the sunset, as it were) casting to likely spots to close the film. As I turned and made the first cast, a 16-inch brown nailed the number 10, Royal Coachman! That's why it and several replicas are in my fly box.

STREAMERS AND BUCKTAILS

The remaining population of my fly boxes is comprised of streamers and bucktails. The patterns here span the range from the imitative to the fanciful—from Muddlers and Black-Nosed Dace to Mickey Finns, and yes, to more Royal Coachmen. I have tied and keep in my fly boxes several streamers from Keith Fulsher's Thunder Greek Series. I have Gray Ghosts and Black Ghosts, and Little Brown Trout, and Dark Tigers and Light Tigers, and Matukas and Marabous. I use them all, and so will you. They are fun to tie. They are pretty to look at. They allow you to express your creativity. And, they are supremely effective.

One of my favorite stories involving streamers took place one hot day in early September in the Catskills. I was hosting the expert angler from Pennsylvania's limestone country, Ed Koch, author of *Tying and Fishing the Midge*. He had guided and hosted me many times on Pennsylvania's wonderful Letort, Yellow Breeches, and Falling Springs streams, and I was trying to reciprocate on the Catskill streams. We had been meeting with frustration as a result of the heat in both air and water.

We were fishing a long, smooth stretch of the Beaverkill where many substantial trout could be seen "tipping and sipping" to something very small floating in the surface film. Both Ed and I had gone to tiny number 28's and hair-like tippets, but we still could not turn a fish. Ed decided to get out his seine net to see if he could collect some natural insects to try and concoct an

The Cardinelle, an excellent example of an attractor-type streamer.

imitation. I simply stayed frustrated, but decided that maybe if very small wouldn't work, perhaps very large would. I clipped off the number 28 and the 7X tippet and tied on a number 4 Black-Nosed Dace. My first cast landed about 4 feet in front of where Ed was diligently seining. A 14-inch brown nailed the streamer almost as it hit the water, showering Ed with its splash. The next cast pointed out one slight error I had made. I had clipped off the 7X, but had neglected to consider that the streamer was then tied to 6X. A good fish broke me off on the strike. I cut the leader back to 3X, tied on a different pattern and enjoyed continued success, while Ed insisted on continuing with his seining. After a couple more fish, he joined me with a streamer, and a point was proved. While the tiny midges were providing the greatest *quantity* of available food, imitating them precisely provided an almost impossible challenge. On the other hand, if something large in the way of food were presented to the same fish, their selection was not likely to be as critical.

MIDGES

The mention of midges draws my attention to a small pocket of my vest which contains the one fly box not yet discussed. This box is only about 2 inches x 3 inches, but it contains many, many very small flies. The hook sizes are 22, 24, 26 and 28. The colors of these flies are white, cream, gray, brown, black, and ginger. The experienced angler knows when these flies are used. They have their times from the start of the season right through the end, as midges along with tiny caddis or mayflies are always evident to some extent in trout streams. The patterns do not imitate anything specific, with the exception of some number 24's that imitate the black and white spinners of the *Tricorythodes* genus of mayfly. But all the tiny flies are essential.

Size is the most critical element involved in matching any insect. When the natural insects which you are trying to imitate are the size of a number 24 hook, using a number 22 means that your imitation is 25 percent larger than the natural, a discernible difference even to an organism with a brain the size of a chick pea.

It is worth noting that midge imitations should not only be carried in floating patterns. Nymphs or pupa imitations of the tiny flies should be part of the angler's bag of tricks as well. These need not be elaborate concoctions; a bit of quill or dubbing for a body, and a slightly heavier section of dubbing for the thorax is all the dressing that's needed. A light tippet, a soft action rod, some tiny nymphs and a delicate hand to hold the rod can provide some awfully exciting fishing.

In reviewing what I've written here I think I have begun to see the answer to my question raised at the start of this piece. I think I know why I carry so many flies. Part of the answer is that I need them, but I have to give equal weight to the fact that I like them. The variety of patterns gives me confidence that I'll be able to meet just about every angling situation I'm likely to encounter, and it is this variety of situations in trout fishing that has given birth to the number of fly patterns that exist.

I thank you for coming with me on this trip through the pockets of my fishing vest, and I hope that my mania for carrying so many flies has provided you with some guidance in stocking the pockets of your own fishing vest. Incidentally, something that I *did* discover while examining the collection of flies is that almost all of the flies are tied on barbless hooks or on hooks from which the barbs have been removed. I encourage you to do this with your own flies, because as Lee Wulff has so eloquently and briefly stated, "A trout is a resource too valuable to be used only once." It is far better to put them back alive to provide fun on another day than to bring them home.

Eric Peper

CHAPTER 6
Salmon and Steelhead Fishing With a Fly

THE AREA OF salmon fly-fishing is unique unto itself. For the first half of this century, if a fly-fisherman spoke of the salmon, he was usually referring to the Atlantic salmon. In recent years, however, the steelhead, the chinook and the coho have gained popularity in the fly-fishing world. Although they have been a popular sport fish on the West Coast for some time, their introduction to the Midwest and, more recently, to the eastern part of the country has opened new angling horizons. The Atlantic salmon, however, being the classic of them all, will be discussed separately from the others. The landlock salmon, which is actually the same fish as the Atlantic in a landlocked state will also be discussed.

THE ATLANTIC SALMON

To many enthusiastic fly-fishermen, the Atlantic salmon, (*Salmo Salar*), is the king of all sportfish. Each species of fish seems to have its own unique characteristics that make it appealing to the fisherman. The trout has its beautiful river environment, the selectivity with which it will take a fly and its magnificent colora-

The Atlantic salmon is the king of gamefish to many fly-fishermen.

This delicate "parr" is the first stage of the salmon's life.

tion. The bonefish has its lightning speed runs as he races off a shallow flat to the safety of deeper water and a 100-pound tarpon has its spectacular gill rattling jumps that seem to give it more control over you than you have of it. The Atlantic salmon has all of that. He is fished for in beautiful river systems where he may selectively take a fly; when hooked, he often makes long reel screaming runs and spectacular jumps; and last, but not least, the salmon is one of the finest delicacies to ever grace a dining room table. What also makes the Atlantic salmon attractive to the fly-fisherman is that the law restricts fishing for them only with a fly. This means that there is no competition from the bait or spin fisherman. Unfortunately, there is sometimes considerable poaching and illegal netting, which takes its share of many of the fish that should be available for the fisherman to cast his fly over.

Years ago, the Atlantic salmon was widely distributed in rivers up and down the New England coast and Canada. However, being extremely susceptible to pollution and environmental changes, the Atlantic all but disappeared from the New England waters. It has only been in recent years that sincere and progressive stocking and conservation efforts have reintroduced the Atlantic salmon to several rivers in Maine. Fishing is once again permitted in these rivers, and they are catching salmon. The progress that's been made is evidenced by the fact that in 1977 the total catch was 475 salmon, and in 1978 it was 797. The state of Connecticut has even reintroduced the salmon into the Connecticut River. They are starting to come back now. That's progress.

Many of you who are not familiar with salmon fishing may wonder what "coming back" means, so let's talk a bit about the life cycle and habits of the Atlantic salmon, (*Salmo salar*), a subject that has many mysteries and differences of opinion.

The salmon is anadromous. That is, he is one of the unique group of fishes that is able to make the transition from saltwater into freshwater and then back to saltwater. This transition would be fatal to most fish, but the salmon's system can adapt to this sudden change.

A fat 4½-pound grilse.

(Left) A bright 15-pound salmon that had just entered the river. (Photo Courtesy Mark Cabot.)

(Below) Mixed catch of salmon and grilse.

The mature salmon spawn in the freshwater rivers in the fall of the year. After the eggs hatch, the life of the small "parr," as the small salmon is called during its growing state in the freshwater river, is similar to that of the trout. It feeds voraciously on just about anything that it can fit into its mouth, often leaping high into the air to snatch insects that are flying close to the stream surface. These are the same acrobatics as an adult that make him so appealing to anglers.

It will usually take about 3 to 4 years of stream life for the parr to develop sufficiently to be ready for the journey to the sea. These small brightly colored fish are often caught in sizes of about 3 or 4 inches while fishing for the mature salmon. In fact, they can often be quite annoying when you are expecting the pull of a larger fish. The fisherman should take care to carefully unhook and return these parr so that they will not be injured. These are the same beauties that become 15- and 20-pound adults if given a chance.

As the spring thaw of approximately their third year in the freshwater river arrives, the parr lose their colorful appearance. Their spots mostly disappear and their sides and underbellies become silvery. They also get quite dark along their backs. This is the salmon's coloration for its life in the sea. As they swim and drift toward the sea with the spring floods, they are now known as "smolts," and will join thousands of cousins in their migration through the waters of the North Atlantic. The travels of the Atlantic salmon at sea are still one of nature's mysteries. It is during this period that

(Right) A healthy 12-pounder—typical size for the Matane River. (Photo courtesy of Sid Neff.)

The results here show that salmon do take flies. (Photo courtesy of Mark Cabot.)

they feed heavily and grow so rapidly, increasing from about 6 inches to about 24 inches (attaining an average weight of about 3 or 4 pounds) in a little over 1 year's time.

At this stage, the salmon is referred to as a "grilse," and averages about 3½ pounds in weight. The true meaning of "grilse" is a salmon that has spent 13 months at sea. These are the smallest fish that come up the river to spawn. It is their first return to the river that

they left as a smolt. However, not all of the salmon return to the rivers as a grilse. In some river systems, the fish may spend 2 years at sea. When they return for the first time, they will probably be in the 8- to 14-pound class.

The return to the parent river is a behavior pattern that is amazing. The salmon have an extremely well developed sense of smell or taste. Probably as a parr, spending several years in the river, the taste of the water becomes indelible in their sensory and memory system. They then can recognize the minute variations in that particular water system, the same as we can recognize the smell of a pine forest or a freshly cut lawn. Since no two river systems are exactly alike in their chemical makeup, the salmon is able to distinguish its own parent river.

The great mystery is how the salmon, after leaving the river and traveling thousands of miles to sea, is able to find its way back to the exact spawning area of its river. Similar to the mystery of the homing pigeon, the salmon has this unique homing instinct that guides it back. If the salmon just haphazardly selected a river in which to spawn by random chance or convenience, some rivers would be overcrowded and some would be barren of spawning fish. This would not be a sound ecological balance for the propagation of the salmon. Therefore, this homing instinct is essential to the survival of the species, and fortunately, they have it.

It is this return to the river to spawn that is the main attraction to the salmon fisherman. The rivers are in the best fishable condition and at the same time they usually have good numbers of fish present. That is if everything is right. The salmon is particular when he enters a river. He is concerned with water level and water temperature. If the water is too low, he might not come up. Deeper water offers the fish protection from its enemies. It also makes it easier for him to travel over shallow bars and riffles. The heavy water currents do not offer much of an obstacle to the salmon's great strength. Quite often, during low, warm water condi-

Two salmon from 8 to 14 pounds are barely visible as they move upriver in shallow water.

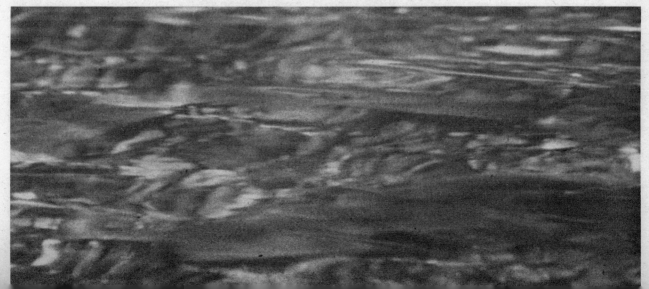

tions, salmon have been known to congregate at the mouths of the rivers by the hundreds, waiting for the water to rise so that they can move up.

Water temperature is equally as important to the salmon as it is to the trout. When the temperature of the water goes up around 70 degrees, the oxygen content begins to decrease. This would be the same as if we went to some high elevation where the air was thin. If you have ever done so without proper preparation, you may remember that you got sort of weak and dizzy. The effects are similiar with the salmon. He doesn't function well. When a dry spell hits a salmon river and the water temperature reaches high numbers with the low water, the fish that are already in the river will congregate at the places where cooler streams come into the main river or where natural springs come up from the bottom of the river. I have seen fish stacked up like cordwood at the mouths of streams during those conditions. If the conditions get too bad, the rivers are often closed to fishing in these areas until there is an improvement, so that poaching and illegal fishing or snagging methods are averted.

The salmon start to come into the rivers in June, in most areas, and may continue sporadically for several months. The fishing seasons open around June, but actual dates will vary with the different provinces or states. Different rivers reach their peak of migration at different times, so it is important to find out about that particular river you may want to fish to have an idea when it may be best. It is also important to know if an impediment on a river, such as a dam, could delay the run. For example, the Matapedia in Quebec is at its best for the size and quantities of fish around the middle to the end of June under average conditions, while the Matane River, only about 50 miles away but having a dam at its mouth, usually has its peak of good fish around the beginning to the middle of July. You will also find that the larger salmon may come in larger concentrations at one time and the smaller grilse at another. Many of the rivers in the Gaspe peninsula will have the larger salmon come first, then to be followed by the grilse, which will mix in with the larger fish.

The Miramichi River in New Brunswick, Canada, is one of the most popular rivers because of the large quantities of fish that come back each year. The first runs begin in the middle and end of June, while the water is fairly high. The majority of the run are larger fish, and then as the July run comes in, the size of the fish will be mixed, most of them being grilse. This will continue sporadically through July, August and September. However, once again in the latter part of September and into October, larger salmon will enter the river in increasing numbers just before spawning time.

Around late October the large male salmon will find a mate. The female will then make her nest in the gravel and will deposit her eggs. The male will then fertilize them with his milk, and the life cycle begins all over again. The fish will mate for about 1 week or until they are spent. Some of the salmon may return to the sea shortly after, but many will winter in the river and not return till the following spring.

The rigors of the spawning are quite strenuous. The fish are known to lose nearly half their weight by the time they return to the sea the following spring. The province of New Brunswick permits fishing for these "black" salmon in the spring. However, being spent and hungry, they do not offer the normally spectacular fight that can be counted on when the fish has just entered the river.

There is a considerable mortality rate of those salmon that journey to the sea after spawning. However, those that return to the river again are considerably larger the next time back. Salmon returning after 3 years at sea could be in the 25- to 30-pound range. There are rare occasions where fish have been recorded returning four and even five times. The largest salmon taken in the United States or Canada is around the 55-pound class. Fish up to 79 pounds have been recorded in Norway, and just under 70 pounds in the British Isles. The average size fish will vary greatly with different rivers. For example, one river that is known for its run of larger fish might have an average size of 16- to 18-pound fish with many in the 20-pound class, while another river may have an average of 8- to 10-pound fish with many grilse and an occasional salmon up to 20 pounds or so.

Although there are many mysteries with the Atlantic salmon, we know one thing for sure—he is one of the greatest challenges for the fly-fisherman and one of the most spectacular fighting fish that we could have the thrill of hooking. One of the great mysteries, and one that is most important to us as fishermen, is why the salmon takes the fly. If you can imagine a river system, ecologically balanced to sustain populations of trout and small parr, being invaded each year by thousands of large salmon with ravenous appetites, you can see that it would not take very long for the larger fish to totally upset the food supply and therefore upset the number of small fish in the river. Mother Nature in her miraculous way has arranged it so that the salmon, upon entering the river to spawn, will not eat until it returns to the sea. Personally, I can say that upon examining the stomach contents of many salmon over the years, I have never seen any particles of food in them. If this is the case, then why do the salmon take a fly?

Well, there are several schools of thought. The most logical is that the salmon spent its initial 3 years of life in this freshwater river system, and all of that time he fed continuously on just about any and every insect he could catch. Possibly, now that he has returned to the same river, there are those instinctive responses that cause him to rise to a properly presented fly now and then, even though he might not be taking it for food nourishment.

Another school of thought was expressed to me many

times by a man who I truly respected as a great flytier, salmon angler and gentleman—the late Charles DeFeo. He believed that salmon sometimes like to play with the insects. He also contended that the fish would come up, take the fly and squeeze out the juices of the insect. Now anyone who has fished for salmon for any period of time can attest to the fact that a salmon can be ever so gentle and tender in the way he takes a fly. Charlie felt that after the fish squeezed out the juices, he let the fly go, therefore, no evidence of an insect in the fish's stomach. Charlie also told me that he had hooked small 3- or 4-inch parr on his fly and then had large salmon come up and take the parr. This may be the reason why streamer flies or flies imitating small fish sometimes work very well.

Others feel that, like bass, a salmon can sometimes be coaxed into taking your fly by arousing its curiosity or by annoying or teasing him. Well, I don't know if we will ever really know the exact reasons why the salmon takes a fly, but sometimes the mystery of it makes it just a bit more appealing. The important fact is that they will take a properly presented fly, and there are certain basics that are important to know, even though there are quite a few variables. We will attempt to cover them in this chapter.

EQUIPMENT

Salmon fishing is done either from a boat on the large rivers or by wading. The type of situation that you are most likely to encounter is wading. Therefore, one of essentials is a decent pair of chest high wading boots. They are the same waders that are used for trout fishing or any other fishing where you will be walking in deep water.

For your walking stability, it is important that the bottom of the boots be of felt, which does not slip easily on the rocks, or hob nails, or other material that will grip the bottom and prevent you from taking an unexpected and unenjoyable bath.

Rods

Earlier in the book, I mentioned that an 8½-foot rod for a #6 and #7 line could be used to catch just about any species of fish with a fly. I also went on to say that it might not always be the most practical rod for certain situations. You can use this rod to catch salmon, and in many situations it might be perfectly adequate. However, for the majority of situations and conditions that you might encounter in fishing various salmon rivers, a slightly larger outfit will fish more comfortably and give you the flexibility to handle the larger waters and cast the larger flies as well as the smaller waters and smaller flies.

Unlike trout fishing, in which you are quite concerned with pinpoint accuracy and delicacy as important qualities of a rod's performance, salmon fishing is a game of line control and line speed, enabling you to cast longer distances when needed. Distance is not

The proper position for the rod and line together as the forward cast is started (below left). The follow through of the cast (below right) with the rod tip pointed at the target, is important for maximum distance and accuracy.

Three rods that will do the job: (top to bottom) bamboo, fiberglass, graphite.

always important, but there will be enough situations where you will want to get out just a bit farther, and you will want a rod that can reach out and still control the line. A strong rod is also an advantage when you hook into a large fish. This is especially true near the end of the battle when the salmon is close to the net. You want to be able to have as much control over the salmon at that time as possible so that you can lead him into the net. A soft or weak rod would not do the job as well as a stronger one.

If I was to have one rod for salmon fishing, it would be a 9-foot rod for a #8 and #9 line. This rod would cover just about any situation that I could encounter. In talking about larger rods, we are getting into a heavier weight outfit. Salmon fishing is a casting game. The average salmon angler probably makes from 300 to 400 casts a day, including his false casts. If your rod, reel and line are excessively heavy and not balanced correctly, you will surely know it by the end of the day. I can remember my first day on a salmon river. I had borrowed a friend's outfit for the occasion. I knew that it was not his favorite since it had spent much time in the back of his closet. A salmon rod was a salmon rod, so I thought. The rod was an old three-piece 9-foot bamboo club that weighed close to 7 ounces. It took a #8 or #9 line and had a reel that I know now was about three sizes too light for the rod. Being an enthusiastic fisherman, I was out there casting for probably 7 or 8 hours that day and did happen to catch two grilse. However, I remember remarking how tired my hand got now and then. I had been used to dainty 7- to 8-foot lightweight trout rods. When I woke up the following morning, my hand was in the shape of a claw. I had to soak it in hot water to relax the muscles before we fished again. A heavy, unbalanced outfit was the problem.

The vast majority of salmon fishermen are now using rods that are made of fiberglass, graphite or the new boron/graphite combination. The graphite rods, especially in the sizes above 8 feet have revolutionized large rod fly-fishing. A bamboo rod that weighs 6 ounces can now be replaced by a fiberglass rod weighing 4¾ ounces, or even better yet, a graphite rod weighing less than 4 ounces. In many instances, the lighter rod might get the job done better while being about 35 percent lighter. It just stands to reason that the lighter and better balanced your outfit is, the less tired your hand will be, and the less tired your hand and casting arm, the more effective and consistent your presentation can be over a longer period of time.

There are many differences of opinion and many theories when it comes to presentation of a salmon fly. I have seen so many occasions when a totally unorthodox, and often unintended, method or presentation was successful, that it would be a bit difficult to say that one particular way was the only right way. However, I believe that salmon usually prefer to take a fly that is swinging across the current at a certain speed. That speed preference can also vary from time to time. It is my opinion that if the angler can control the placement of his fly and line on the cast, he has a better chance of controlling the speed of the drift or swing. A slightly stronger or stiffer rod might enable you to have more control than a soft or weak rod. Also, the more line that you have to "shoot" on the cast, the less control you will have in the placement of the fly. A stronger rod will enable the competent caster to hold more line in the air for the false cast, therefore requiring less line to shoot for the cast itself.

The need to make long casts of 60 feet or longer are more pertinent to wet fly-fishing. Dry fly-fishing for salmon is usually done at distances of less than 40 feet in order to have maximum control of the cast, of the pick up of the line and the strike. A shorter rod of 8 or 8½ feet can often be used very effectively and with ease. Since many more casts are made with the dry fly than with the wet fly over a given period of time, the shorter, lighter rod will also not tire you as quickly.

One of the important points in selecting any rod is being comfortable with it and having it work with your casting ability. Again, it is important to buy your equipment at a place where people working with you know the equipment, its applicability and how to coordinate it with your needs. Or, take someone with you who knows. It does not matter how much a rod costs—if it doesn't work well for you, you might as well hang it up.

Fiberglass rods are the least expensive, ranging from around $40 up to $100. Graphite rods range from about $100 to $175 with the boron/graphite combination rods a bit higher. Bamboo is quite high going from $150 to $400. As I mentioned before, many of the rod manufacturers will sell rod blanks for approximately 40 percent of the finished rod price. If you are creative and like to do-it-yourself, the components to finish the rod are readily available through several distributors. A rod that might cost $100 ready-made, might only cost you $50 if you put it together yourself. It is fun work for the wintertime doldrums.

Reels

Once the salmon is hooked, the reel is the most important piece of equipment that you have. While you are casting, the purpose of the reel is to act as a counter-balance for the weight of the rod and the line in the air, and to hold a sufficient amount of line backing and flyline. However, when the action starts, the salmon reel is put to the test and is vital in the playing and landing of the fish.

When fishing for bass, panfish, small trout and other fish that do not run much, the reel does not have to do much more than balance the rod and hold the line. An inexpensive reel can often be quite adequate for the job. However, a salmon reel must be of superior quality, dependable and precisely made. Of the six parts of your salmon outfit—the rod, the reel, the backing, the line, the leader and the fly—you can get by with inferior quality with just about everything except the reel. Salmon make long, swift runs which puts maximum stress

A strong salmon will truly put a reel to the test. (Photo Courtesy of Sid Neff.)

on quality and performance. Any minor malfunction or inability to operate smoothly will surely result in a lost fish.

One of the requirements of a salmon reel is the ability to hold an adequate amount of backing along with the flyline. On the average, an adequate amount of backing would be about 150 yards of 18- to 20-pound test dacron (not nylon). For larger rivers having long stretches of rapids between pools or where you cannot follow a fish along the banks, you may want to have anywhere from 200 to 300 yards.

Another requirement is that the reel be the proper weight to balance the rod. It is a more common mistake to have a reel that is too light than too heavy. Many fishermen make the mistake of balancing the rod and reel without having any line out or in the air. They do not usually think of the additional amount of weight that 30 or so feet of line in the air will create.

The most important quality of a good salmon reel is the drag system. This is the device inside of the reel housing that puts resistance on the free spinning of the spool. This resistance is most commonly in the form of an adjustable tension spring and tooth, called a pawl, which works against the turning of a cogged wheel drag system attached to the spool. The tightening or loosening of the tension spring adjusts the amount of drag. The working of the pawl on the cogged wheel also makes a clicking sound when reeled slowly and sings a beautiful song as the salmon makes his run. Another drag system is one that has a screw adjustable pressure plate that works against a small smooth wheel attached to the spool. The tightening or loosening of the screw dial adjusts the amount of drag. The most important factor about the drag is that it must be smooth and able to respond properly to the varying pressures that occur during the fight with a good size fish.

Initially, the drag is set to prevent overspooling as the line is taken from the reel. While fishing, the drag should be adjusted to work smoothly and be no stronger than about 50 percent of the leader tippet strength. For example, if the tippet of your leader is 8-pound test, the drag should be no more than about 4 pounds of resistance. The heavier your tippet section is, the higher the percentage of drag you can possibly get away with. However, if you have the occasion to go to much lighter

A leaping salmon.

When this fish rolled, he became an easy target for a well presented fly.

tippets, you may find it necessary to have your drag as light as 20 percent of tippet strength. You are usually much safer having too light a drag rather than too heavy. The sudden rushes of salmon put great strain on the leaders, especially when the fish are close. That is quite often the time when they are lost. A properly adjusted smooth drag should absorb the shock of those rushes and allow you to play the fish confidently. Quite often experienced anglers use a rather light drag and apply additional pressure with their fingers on the line, or with their palm on the rim of the spool if the spool is of the revolving type.

If a little extra money is to be invested in any one piece of salmon equipment, make it in the reel. It will pay for itself many times over. I have often seen and heard too many stories about drags that froze or malfunctioned when big fish made long runs, or sudden bursts at the net, resulting in broken leaders and lost fish. That in turn results in a large ache in the pit of your stomach.

There are three types of retrieve systems available with reels—the single action, the multiplying and the automatic. The single action is the simplest and most popular. Single action means that one turn of the handle will make one turn of the spool. Multiplying means that there is an additional gear system that increases the ratio of the handle-to-spool turn. For example, a 3 to 1 retrieve means that one turn of the handle will result in three turns of the spool. Naturally, this will allow a faster retreive of the line with less effort. It will also cause the reel to be a bit heavier since there are extra gears involved. Multiplying reels are a bit more expensive than single action reels, and because they are more complicated may possibly be prone to more problems than the single action. The automatic reel should not even be considered for this type of angling. It has a spring system that winds up as the line is taken off the spool. However, the amount of line and backing that this reel can hold is quite limited. Then, when a lever is pressed, the wound spring automatically spins the spool to retrieve the line. This system is fine for bass, panfish or any type of fly-fishing where the drag and critical mechanics of a reel are not important for fighting the fish.

Lines

The vast majority of your salmon fishing will be done with a floating flyline. I would say that the most popular type of line is the weight forward, since it is the easiest to cast for most people. The weight forward also has another advantage. Since most of the casting weight is in the front of the line, the balance of the line, referred to as the running section, is considerably smaller in diameter. This means that you are able to put more backing on a spool using a weight forward line than if you were using a double taper, which has a relatively consistent larger diameter throughout the majority of its length.

The lady shows off her 17-pounder. It was better than the guys could do.

A guide can often be quite helpful in locating the fish for the angler.

The double taper line, in my opinion, has some advantages of its own. Many of the better casters and fly-fishermen I have known prefer the double taper for salmon. In my experience the preference is because of the control. Since you are able to hold a considerable amount of this even diameter line in the air, not requiring you to have to shoot too much, it is easier to turn or place the fly along with the line where you want it.

I also feel that the even diameter of the double taper allows the current to work more consistently on the swing of the line and fly. With the weight forward line, there is a larger diameter section up front for approximately 20 feet, then a considerably smaller diameter for the balance of the line. The current tends to push harder against the forward larger diameter than on the thinner running section. This could cause the line to belly quicker on the swing which could be a disadvantage with standard techniques. Keep this in mind for future discussion, since a bellying line could be an advantage for certain other fishing methods. Since the double taper line is level for the majority of its length and tapers equally at either end, it has the added value of two lines. When one end becomes worn, just simply reverse it and you have a new casting and high floating line.

In recent years, the Garcia Corporation, working with Lee Wulff, who has contributed so much to the world of salmon fishing, developed the long belly flyline. Rather than having only the first 20 feet with the significant casting weight, the long belly has a consistent diameter for the first 30 feet. It then tapers down to a smaller diameter running line. This line offers some of the benefits of both the weight forward and the double taper.

Leaders

As has often been said before, the chain is only as strong as its weakest link. The leader, being the weakest part of your tackle, needs the most careful attention to assure its security. It is extremely important to take extra care to make sure that each junction and knot is well made and secure. In fact, it is a good practice every time you go to the river to check the knots to make sure that they have not loosened. When a knot is loose, a sudden tightening, such as the violent tug of a large fish, could cut the leader much easier than if the knot was tight.

The first knot on a line is the juncture of the flyline to the leader. The Nail-less Nail Knot or Needle Knot and the Wedge Knot are the three most popular knots used for this purpose. (See Chapter 2 for illustrations and descriptions of these three knots.) The Nail and Needle knots are for a permanent juncture and should be coated with pliobond or epoxy to make an extra smooth connection, allowing the knot to slide through the guides with ease. The Wedge Knot allows the leader to be removed and replaced quickly and easily.

The most common knot for connecting two pieces of monofiliment and one used for joining leader sections together is the Blood Knot (see Chapter 4). Although one-piece leaders are often used, it is often necessary to attach new pieces of tippet to the end of them, even if you don't wish to build your own leaders from scratch. Every fisherman should know how to tie this knot.

A suggestion when tying knots with monofiliment is to wet or spit on them before pulling them tight. This lubricates the monofiliment, allowing it to tighten easier without causing too much friction on the crossing parts. The Surgeons Knot (see Chapter 4) is another popular knot that can be used for joining two pieces of leader.

Possibly the most important knot on the leader is the one that is used to attach the leader tippet to the fly. There are basically two knots that are used for this. For the down-eye hooks the Improved Clinch Knot (see Chapter 4) may be used. However, for all of the up-eye hooks and even for the down-eye hooks if you prefer, I recommend the Figure Eight Turle Knot illustrated here. I find it to be as strong as any other.

One of the main objectives of the salmon cast, at least for the wet flies, which account for about 90 percent of all salmon fishing, is to have your line lay out as straight as possible. For that reason, it is important to use a relatively stiff leader material. It is also very important to use leader material that has good knot strength. That means, when you tie a typical overhand knot in the leader, the strength of that piece will not be reduced too drastically. Some inferior materials will be reduced in strength by as much as 50 percent by tying a knot in it. Others, such as a brand called Maxima, have excellent knot strength. One of the main reasons for a leader to have good knot strength, is that during the course of casting so many times, it is inevitable that you will put what the salmon fisherman calls, a "wind knot" in the leader. The result is that if you are fishing an 8-pound leader tippet and you unknowingly get a wind knot, you will then be fishing with a tippet strength of anywhere from 4 to 6 pounds, depending on the quality of the material. It is important to check your leader quite often for these wind knots. If you don't detect them, the result is often a lost fish—and salmon don't usually come easily.

Other Equipment

Before we talk about the flies used for salmon, there are several other items that would be advisable to have along on a salmon trip.

First of all, if you are fortunate enough to hook a salmon, you will probably need something to land it—meaning either a large net or a tailer. Salmon, usually the grilse, are sometimes beached on a gradual shoreline without the aid of net or other device. However, this is often difficult, especially for the novice, and can result in a lost fish. It is a good idea to have a

THE FIGURE EIGHT TURLE KNOT

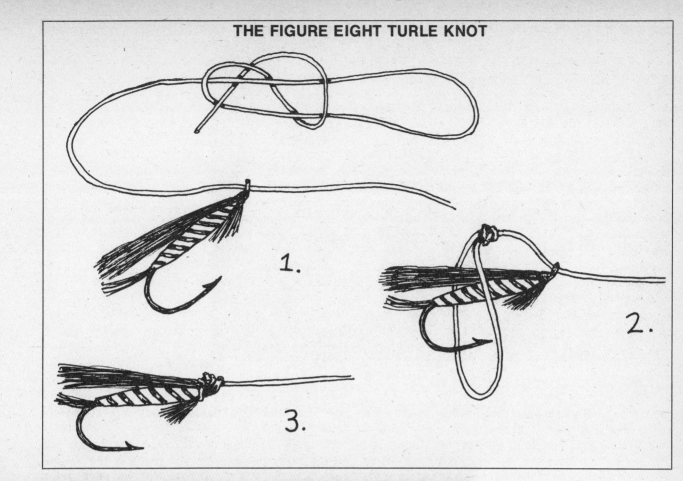

1.

2.

3.

A large net really comes in handy with a larger fish. (Photo courtesy of Sid Neff).

Typical fly books of an Atlantic salmon fisherman.

large net with a long handle. Bringing the fish to the net will be discussed later. If the netting material is made of nylon rather than cotton, it will last much longer and will not rot. I remember once seeing a guide lift an 18-pound salmon out of the water with an old net made of cotton. The rotten netting broke and the fish fell back to the water. Fortunately, the guide was quick. He reached down and grabbed the salmon by the tail before the fish knew what happened and could swim away.

A tailer is a device that puts a loop around the tail of a mature salmon. This will not work with a grilse since their tail bones have not yet developed enough to prevent the loop from slipping off. The tailer is usually made of a cable, a spring steel bow and a handle approximately 2 feet in length. When ready for use, the cable is set to hold the spring steel in a bent "U" position. This forms a snare which can be drawn over the fish's tail. The snare is rigged enough that it can be held in the current. When the fish is tired and close to you, the snare noose is carefully moved up over the tail of the salmon, trying not to touch him. The tailer is then lifted straight up. The weight of the salmon releases the snare, and the noose fastens securely around the tail. It is important to keep this upward pull so that the noose does loosen. With the noose secure, the salmon can then be dragged to shore or lifted into the canoe if that is the case. It is important, when using a tailer, to make sure that the snare loop is not brought up further than the middle of the fish before released. I have seen anglers lift the tailer with the noose around the head, only to have the embarrassing and difficult situation of the frightened fish streaking off on another run, only this time with the tailer loop now fastened around the line. The result of this fiasco is usually a lost fish and a dejected angler.

Naturally, it is important to have a vest or some item having many pockets for you to carry the various equipment that you should have with you on the river. These are items such as: extra spools of tippet material; fingernail clippers to trim the ends of your leaders after you tie knots; floatant for your dry flies; a small hook hone to sharpen the hook points of your flies; your various boxes of flies; a rainjacket; insect repellent; and any other items that you feel are important. A good item to carry in your vest is something to patch small holes in your waders. This could help prevent much discomfort.

SALMON FLIES

The true link between the salmon and the angler is the salmon fly that is attached to the end of the leader. Unlike most trout flies, which are tied to resemble specific insects, salmon flies are tied as a suggestion. It is often a wonder that they suggest anything, as the majority of salmon flies that I have seen are quite different, in their gaudy coloration, from any insect that Mother Nature has created. Yet they do catch salmon and that is what keeps them popular, along with a respect for the masterful talent that it takes to tie these patterns.

The Wet Fly

Salmon flies have a tradition that goes back over 200 years. The popular patterns were tied from beautifully colored feathers of exotic birds, pieces of shiny gold or silver tinsel and various colors of floss. It took great skill to construct them properly. Most of the flies had a

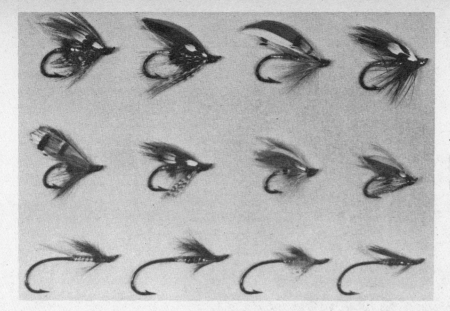

Top two rows—various heavily tied popular English salmon patterns. Bottom row—several "low water" patterns.

mixture and blending of many different colors in their makeup. A certain arrangement of these feathers and materials by an individual created a particular pattern which was named after or by that person. Names such as the Durham Ranger, Dusty Miller, Jock Scott and Green Highlander are a few of the patterns that have proved to be popular and successful over the years. Actually, the beauty of a salmon fly is probably more important in catching the fisherman's eye than the salmon's. Some of them are so beautiful that it is a shame to cast them into the water.

In more recent years, however, many of the new popular and successful patterns have been tied very simply from a few basic materials. They are easier to tie and are just as effective. Names such as the Rusty Rat, Green Butt, Butterfly and Oriole are several of the favorites. I guess someone along the line felt that if the flies are supposed to resemble insects, we might as well make them look a bit more like insects. Personally, I

believe that one of the most important features that a salmon fly can give you is confidence that you can catch a fish with it. With this confidence, you can fish the fly properly and the pool thoroughly. Without confidence in the fly that you have on, you will usually fish it poorly—most of the time thinking about what fly you should really have put on. With this in mind, you will seldom fish properly. I have a friend who, after having hooked probably 20 salmon on one particular fly during a week's time, hooked and landed his largest salmon ever (29 pounds) on that same fly even though all that was left of it was some sparce black wool on the shank as a body and a tiny red tail. It was almost a bare hook. However, my friend knew that the fly could catch fish so he fished it well and got the results.

Unfortunately, it is not quite as simple as that. There are times that the salmon seems to be selective to a degree. Certain color shades will take fish better one time and others another time. Sometimes a light fly is

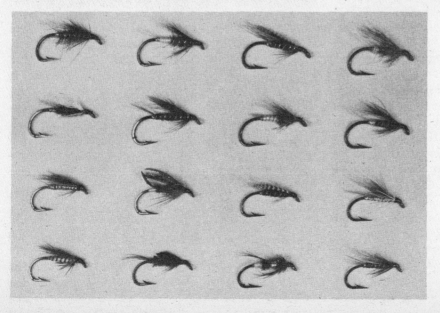

A small collection of more modern-day salmon wet fly patterns.

A feeling of confidence is important when selecting what fly to tie on to your leader.

best—sometimes a dark one does the trick. I have often heard the philosophy—bright day, bright fly; dark day, dark fly. Unfortunately, I have also heard the reverse philosophy. Who is right? Well, my feeling is that the fly that has hooked the fish is the one that is right.

The size of the fly is probably one of the most important considerations when making your selection of what to put on the end of your leader. Probably the most popular size for a salmon fly and one that is used on the majority of rivers is a size #6. However, some rivers require considerably larger flies up to size 2/0 or more. You will also find that a larger size fly will be necessary when the water gets high and dirty. Conversely, it is often necessary to go down to size #8 and #10 flies or smaller when the water gets low. Many times a salmon will roll to a certain size fly, but not take it. The most common procedure if you can not get him to come back is to change to a smaller fly. This technique often works and shows the occasional selectivity that salmon can have for size preference. I can remember many occasions when having the correct size fly did the trick. I think the one that will always be foremost in my mind was the first big salmon that I caught. I was fishing the Miramichi River in New Brunswick, Canada, in 1965 or 1966. There were several people fishing on each side of the run, but the only person who was doing well was Ted Williams, the baseball star. He had caught two grilse and had lost one salmon. One other man on his side of the river had also lost one fish. At one point, I was opposite him, just about in the hot spot of the spool. He must have known what I was thinking, because he

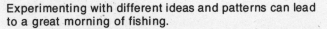

Experimenting with different ideas and patterns can lead to a great morning of fishing.

An 11-pounder that rose classically to a large dry fly. (Photo courtesy of Sid Neff.)

said, "They're taking a #10 Green Butt." I thanked him for the information, quickly removed the #6 Rusty Rat that I was using and tied on the #10 Green Butt. Since the river was relatively low at that time, and not too wide, each one of my casts landed pretty close to Ted. On the fourth cast I saw a flash shortly after my fly hit the water. I felt the heavy pull of the salmon just as Ted said, "I think you've got a big one." About 15 minutes later I landed my first salmon, weighing a bit over 11 pounds. I hooked one more fish that morning and several others were taken from the pool that morning, but only on #10 flies. Now that is not always the case, and who knows exactly why it happens. The important thing is to know what size fly the salmon are taking. It can often make the difference.

Charlie Defeo used to tell me that Ed Hewitt, a very famous trout and salmon fisherman, who he was fortunate to know, used to fish the low water with a light #5 line and a trout wet fly about size 16. He caught salmon when the fishing was tough. I'll have to admit that I have not tried it yet, but I hope to some day when I have those conditions again.

I also know a man who made an experiment using a fly tied on a #16 double hook. He called it the "Mighty Mite." This is a considerably small fly in the world of salmon fishing. I don't recall the period of time exactly. I think the fly was fished occasionally during low water conditions over six or seven seasons. The results were over 60 fish caught—about 40 percent salmon and 60 percent grilse. There were about another 12 fish that

took the fly but got off, meaning that very few fish that take the fly are lost, that is unless you are careless and they break off.

Besides hook size as an important consideration, I mentioned earlier that many anglers have preference to certain colors, or at least light shades under certain conditions and dark shades for others. In addition to color considerations is a belief that shiny silver, gold or copper flies (that is, flies that consist mainly of silver, gold, or copper tinsel) work best under certain conditions. For example, one of the best flies for dirty water conditions is the Copper Killer. Bright copper, gold and orange combination flies seem to work better than others when water visibility is low.

I had mentioned earlier that a good way to pick up a fish that refused your fly was to put on a smaller fly. Another technique is to put on a small silver fly after a salmon has refused or just rolled to your initial offering. After many experiences I feel quite strongly about the silver fly in certain situations. I had one experience with a pattern called the "Silver Rat." I was about to leave for a salmon trip one summer and was discussing the situation with Charlie DeFeo. He said that I should use a small silver fly each morning for the first hour or so. His logic was that at that time of year, a particular caddis insect hatches around the river during the night, and this insect has a silvery glisten to it. The fish would associate the silver fly with the caddis insect. Well, I knew there was no "matching the hatch" in salmon fishing, but I knew enough to put some value in Charlie's comments. On each of the first four mornings, I took one or two fish on that Silver Rat between 8 and 10 o'clock. They didn't seem to want it after that. Only one or two fish were caught by my friends during the entire day. I don't know if it was a coincidence or what, but it did register, and was put away in my personal stock of learning experiences. In fact, to show you how crazy this salmon game can be, one of my friends came to me just after I had caught my first fish on that fourth morning. He was the only one of the four of us on this trip that had not yet caught a fish. My friend said, sheepishly, "Would you show me what you're doing and let me fish down in front of you?" "Sure," I said. "Put on a #12 double Silver Rat, move down to where that stick is on the bank and make about a 40-foot cast at about a 45-degree angle to the current." I had taken two of my fish from that spot, and I thought that it would be

tending behind the actual tied fly. Since salmon are often known to take short in low water conditions, the low water hook can be an asset by having the hook point considerably behind the fly that the salmon will be rising to.

Another single hook that is commonly used is the down-eye offset hook. The point of this hook is offset at an angle. As the hook slides through the mouth of a fish, the point is more likely to take a good hold with this slight offset. Again, the choice of which hook to use, whether up-eye or down-eye offset is purely a matter of personal preference. If I want a fly to stay perfectly straight and not wobble at all, I will probably use the English hook. However, there are many times that I might want my fly to move a bit, looking more alive. The offset hook often makes the fly rock a bit as it is making its swing.

(Left) Single offset hook (left) and double hook (right).

(Below) A collection of salmon dry flies. Top row (left to right): Royal Wulff, Bivisible, Humpy. Middle row: MacIntosh, Irresistible, Bomber. Bottom row: Skater.

a good place for him to start, not really expecting anything to happen. For some reason, when he made his first cast, it just didn't seem quite right. I immediately said, "Pick it up and cast about 5 feet further." He did and asked, "Is that about right?" By the time I could say, "Yeah, that looks pretty good," a grilse had taken his fly and was 2 feet in the air. All he could say was, "I don't believe it, I just don't believe it." To tell you the truth, neither did I. But that's part of salmon fishing. Many times since that episode, I have used the small silver fly to pick up interested, but selective fish. You should keep this idea in your bag of tricks.

Salmon flies are tied on several different types of hooks. The English type salmon single hook has an up-eye and is made in both a standard and low water model. A low water hook is thinner and slightly longer shanked than the standard type. The flies on low water hooks are tied quite short, as though they were tied on a smaller size hook, with much of the hook shank ex-

The other type of hook that is popular is the double hook. This also is available in both the standard and low water models. A large double hook is quite heavy and can be an advantage when you might want your fly to sink a bit and swim deeper in the water. When the water gets a bit high and dirty, this is often advantageous.

The double hook can also be valuable during the summer months when the mouths of the salmon are quite soft. I have often seen the mouth of a fish fall apart while it was being carried by the jaw. Just imagine how easily a thin hook might pull out if it is not in just the right spot. A double hook can offer a better holding capacity than the single. Actually, the idea is to have the salmon hook himself in the corner of the mouth. Then it really doesn't matter whether it's a single or a double, it will usually hold.

The Dry Fly

Although the wet fly has been important for more than 200 years, it is only during the past 50 years that the dry fly for salmon has gained its popularity. While salmon will take a wet fly under just about every water and weather condition, the dry fly has a much more selective applicability. Usually lower water and warmer air conditions will be more conducive for the salmon to take a fly floating on the surface.

One of the great attractions, naturally, is the sight of a large fish, like the salmon, rising and taking your feathered offering. However, I would estimate that for every one salmon taken on a dry fly, there are probably 100 or more taken on a wet fly. One of the main reasons is that the dry fly is just not fished that much by many anglers although its popularity is gaining as fishermen are learning more of the techniques.

One of the most important features in a dry fly is that it must float well. Since dry flies for salmon are relatively large, many hackle feathers of good quality should be used. The other material that makes up the balance of the fly, such as the tail, body and wings should also be made of materials that will not easily absorb water and that will float well. A good example is a pattern designed by Lee Wulff back in 1929. Lee developed the "Wulff" series, which uses water resistant, high floating deer or bucktail for the wings and tail, animal fur for the body, and then, of course, several hackles for their great floating ability. The pattern is tied in several color combinations, such as the White Wulff, Gray Wulff and Royal Wulff.

Another excellent fly is the Bivisible, which is a fly that is hackled or "palmered" for the entire length of the shank. The hackle makes up the entire fly, and therefore floats quite well. It was originally tied with a white feather up front for visibility with the balance of the feathers of a dark shade. The Mackintosh is probably the most popular of the squirrel tail and hackle combination flies. It is an obvious suggestion of the stonefly that is prominent in most of the salmon rivers,

and it also floats quite well. One of the patterns that is quite popular as a trout fly and is also successful as a salmon fly in slightly larger sizes is the Humpy or Goofus Bug. It is made of hollow high floating deerhair that is folded over to form an air pocket body. Another fly using deer hair, but having the hair clipped as the body is the Irresistible.

One of the more recent patterns also using clipped deerhair is the Bomber. This torpedo shaped chunk of clipped deerhair with hackle palmered over has been one of the more successful fish locators. The salmon don't always take it, but after they rise, they are then vulnerable to the presentation of another pattern. Another excellent fly for locating fish, using a slightly unorthodox technique, is the skater. This type of fly has very long extra stiff hackles tied on a relatively small hook. When desired, they can easily be skittered across the surface, often stimulating a salmon to show himself. In order to obtain extra stiffness in the fly, Charlie DeFeo used to tie his skaters with a combination of grizzly hackle for coloration and woodchuck tail fibers for added stiffness.

It is not really necessary to carry a large variety of dry flies as is commonly done with wet flies. A selection of four to six different patterns and silhouettes, in different sizes, ranging from #10 up to #4, and in a few different colors—some light colors and some dark—will give you ample ammunition to experiment with.

WHERE TO FIND SALMON AND HOW TO FISH FOR THEM

As the salmon works its way from the sea into the river system, the first waters in which he is approachable by the fly-fisherman are the tidal pools. These are the pools at the mouth of the river that are influenced both by the incoming and outgoing tides, and the rise and fall of the freshwater river itself. In the spring when the rivers are quite high with a heavy flow of fresh water, the tidal pools are completely freshwater. However, as the season wears on and the waters become low, the incoming tide will create a brackish water environment. The effect of the freshwater river system extends farther out to sea than the eye can imagine. The fish follow this in and begin holding in these tidal pools. At this time, they can be fished for and caught.

Water temperature is a key factor as to when the salmon will move from these tidal pools into the river system itself. In the early spring, the high rivers, influenced by the melting snows, will have cold temperatures that will keep the salmon in the tidal pools. They will move in and out waiting for the proper temperature to induce their migration. In contrast, water that is too warm and low during the summer months will also detain the fish. They will gather in the brackish tidal pools waiting for the rains that will raise the river level, lower the temperature and invite them in. Both of these conditions present worthwhile fishing in the tidal pools.

Another bonus of fishing the tidal pools is that the fish are at their strongest. They have not yet expended any of their stored up energy which will be used for their up-river adventure. The tidal pool also is much more spacious than the normal river pool. The combination of these two conditions usually results in considerably longer runs and numerous spectacular jumps, when a fish is hooked. The disadvantage of the tidal pools, is that, because of their large size, they are often difficult to approach. It may be difficult to cover the most productive sections of water unless you have a boat.

As the salmon makes its way up the river, it tends to follow the main flow of current. There could be some exceptions to this during warm water periods, where the fish might follow a lesser current that had a cooler stream coming into it. Salmon prefer to do most of their moving at night or at times when the water is high. These conditions offer the fish maximum protection from its enemies and predators.

As the salmon works its way up the river, it will pause periodically to rest. This is what is known as "holding." Salmon will hold a position anywhere from several minutes up to many days. Unless there have been significant changes to the stream bottom or to any structures, salmon will hold the same lies year after year. The height of the water will also play an important part in where the fish will be. The most ideal fishing conditions are when the water is between 45 and 60 degrees and after the water has just risen to a normal average level and is dropping slowly. The fish will have been stimulated into moving by the rise in water and will start to hold as the level starts to drop.

A "lie" or "holding position" could be anything that enable the salmon to remain in that place with the minimum of effort. It may be a rock that they can lie behind, along side of or in front of. Most people are not aware how often good sized fish, whether they be trout or salmon, hold in front of large rocks. The current being backed up by the rock and diverted up and over enables the salmon to remain in that position quite easily.

I remember being at the mouth of the Matane River in Quebec, observing the river and the fishermen from a bridge that crossed the river in the middle of the town of Matane. Just slightly upstream from the bridge was a large submerged boulder, and it was easily visible at that time, as were the approximately 30 salmon that had gathered to hold around that rock. To my surprise, approximately 25 fish were in front of the rock, with the remaining few on either side. At that time there were no fish holding behind the rock. Most fishermen not knowing holding positions would probably work the side on down and in back of the rock. Unless they were aware of the fish, or of the potential for salmon to quite likely be in front of the rock, the angler might very well just pass by an excellent opportunity to hook a fish. Another good lie position is a hole or depression in the

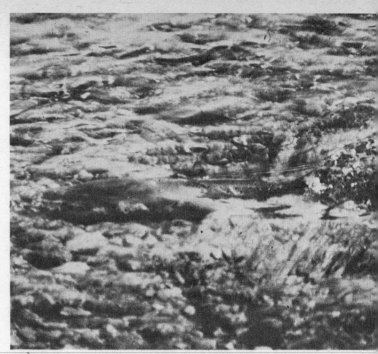
Salmon can often be found in the shallows.

river bottom. The area where a riffle drops into the depths of a pool or pocket is an ideal resting spot for a salmon. Anything that breaks the current, giving the fish an eddy, is a potential lie.

As salmon work their way up through the rapids and riffles, they take advantage of opportunities to rest if they are able to. There are two places that offer this to the salmon and have given me good fishing over the years. If there are rocks or holes at the tail of long pools just before the river goes into a long stretch of rapids, you should be sure to fish these lies the first thing in the morning when the fish are starting to hold. It is also a good idea to check them out periodically during a day when the water is a bit high or on a rainy and dark day. Salmon can do a lot of traveling on those dark days. When they have just traveled through 100 or 200 yards of heavy water, they often take the first opportunity to rest at the tail of those pools. Another spot that most fishermen pass by is what is referred to as the "bumps." This is where a long flat narrows down at its tail and forms a fast slick glide that turns into a stretch of rapids and is a place that very few anglers bother with, but which can offer some interesting fishing. These places are often where there is an island in the river that narrows the width of the flow.

During the season, eels often enter the river system and lay their eggs in "redds" that they create by piling stones in a mound. This is often done in those fast glides. As the glide comes down over the redds, it forms a bump on the water surface. These are areas where salmon can rest a while as they work up the heavy current. The idea is to make your cast so that your fly lands on the far side of the bump and swings through it.

It is important to work both the front and back of the bumps. The exciting part of fishing the bumps is that since the water is so slick, you can see every move that the fish makes. You can actually see him coming before he takes your fly.

When a salmon takes a lie, he may remain there for anywhere from several minutes up to several days, or even weeks on occasions. Usually, the fish coming into the river in the early season will be moving faster and farther and holding less than the fish that enter the river in the fall.

The fun of knowing exactly where a salmon is lying is that you can experiment with various techniques. Quite often, if the water is low enough, the salmon is visible while you are fishing for him. This is an added advantage, since you can watch for his reaction to your fly. I remember an old Canadian guide saying to me, "If I see the salmon make the slightest movement, even just twitch a fin, as my fly goes by him, I know that I can take that fish eventually, and I'll stay with him till I do."

If a salmon is caught from a particular spot or lie, you can be pretty sure that there are either more fish there now, or there will be more soon. Unless there is a drastic change in water conditions, a good lie is always used by other fish. It is extremely important to be observant and to make mental notes of where fish are caught, where they roll and where they may be seen lying. As you fish down through a pool, you should mark a place on the bank where you were standing if you should happen to raise or hook a fish. Also try to estimate the amount of line that you had out. This also pertains to other fishermen that you see hook fish. Mark the spot where they were standing. By doing this, you will be pinpointing the hot spots of the pool. You will then be able to concentrate your efforts as you reach these areas. I have seen many days where almost all of the salmon that were caught in a particular pool came from the same spot. Sometimes everything is just right at that spot. The flow of the current, the water depth and temperature create the perfect "taking" environment.

I remember a man on his first salmon trip. He could not cast too well, but apparently got the fly to the fish the way they wanted it. He fished through a particular pool four times. Each time that he was approximately 10 feet below a large rock in the water, he hooked a fish. It was uncanny. In fact, the last time down, his friends on the bank were kidding with him, saying, "Come on Charlie, just a few more feet and you'll have another one." Sure enough, two more casts and the fish was on.

The currents of the river are important as to where the fish will lie. Salmon would like to take the path of least resistance, but still follow the main current of the river. Therefore, they will often move and lie along the edges of the main current, in the slightly slack water. Early in the morning, and before the first anglers have worked through the pool, salmon can often be found lying in relatively shallow water. I have had fish take my fly when it was directly below me in no more than 15 inches of water. One of the most common errors that many salmon fishermen make is to wade much too deep the first time the pool is fished, when all that should be done is step a few feet off the bank, cast the fly into the edge of the current and let it swing into the slower water. Salmon will usually move upstream with the strongest current. If there is an island splitting a river, the fish will usually follow the strongest and deepest flow. They will also sometimes use both currents. As the level of the river rises and falls, one current may be more suitable than the other.

One factor that can often come into play, especially during the summer months when the river may get low and warm, is the water temperature of the currents. Many times when there are two currents converging one may have a small cold stream flowing into it upriver. If the main river is in a warm state, the salmon will usually follow the cooler current. In fact if the river system has exceptionally low and warm water conditions, the salmon will often stop and hold for a considerable period of time at the mouths of these small streams where the water temperature is often 15 degrees cooler. They will often wait there in large numbers until a rain makes it more suitable to move upriver. At times like these, fishing can be quite good in these small areas of cool water. Sometimes the river conditions become so bad and so many fish gather in a small area, that those sections have to be temporarily closed to fishing.

Salmon will often "show," that is they will jump or roll, as they move into and work their way up the river system. This is very exciting and stimulating to the fisherman. It gives him confidence that there are fish in the pool and encourages him to fish better and enthusiastically. There is nothing more frustrating than not having seen a fish for a considerable period of time. After a while you start to wonder whether there are any fish in the river at all. But the great thing about salmon fishing is that a day or two of a weather or water change can often turn those dead periods around and have the river alive with fish.

A jumping fish is not necessarily a "taking" fish (one that will take your fly at that time). Usually salmon will jump just as they enter the river system and will do so from time to time as they make their way up river. Just as there are many theories as to why salmon will take a fly, so there are just about as many as to why salmon jump. Many believe that upon entering the freshwater system the change that takes place in their body stimulates the jumping activity. Another theory includes sea lice. One of the ways that you can tell if a salmon has recently entered the river is by the sea lice that will still be on its body. The theory is that these sea lice annoy the salmon when he enters the fresh water, and the jumping is an effort to get rid of them. One of the significant times that this jumping activity can be informative to the angler is when the fish are moving. Usually an hour or so before dark on fair weather days, or at almost any time on very dark days or when the water is a bit high and slightly discolored, salmon will jump as the school is about to move out of the slow part of the pool and up into the run. The angler should take this as a signal to get his fly into the water, because a school of fish might be moving through. A good place to be fishing at that time is at the head of the pool or run where the run of water is the narrowest. This way you can be sure to cover all of the water easily.

Many fishermen get very excited when they see a jumping salmon and immediately try to cast for that fish if it is close enough. This effort is usually fruitless, since the jumping fish is rarely a taking fish at that time. The fish that can be taken with the fly when he shows is the classic rolling fish. When a fish "rolls" first the head appears, then the dorsal fin followed by the tail, all in a gentle rolling motion. The angler has good reason to get excited by that activity, because that is a fish that he can catch. The rolling fish is often holding a position in the river. He will often roll periodically, making it easy to mark his position exactly. If you see a salmon roll more

than once, or better yet, several times, you should stay with that fish, whether it be with dry fly or wet fly, until he is caught or until you get too frustrated working him.

Charlie DeFeo told me that he feels the best way to take a salmon that is rolling periodically is to take a position with a wet fly up above the fish. Let out exactly the amount of line that will cast your fly to where the fish came up, and stand there waiting for the fish to come up again. What you are doing is anticipating the rise. As soon as the fish rolls again, you pick up the line and make your cast, landing the fly about 2 feet on the far side of the fish, so that it swings over him slowly. Charlie said that if done correctly, the salmon will take it almost every time. I have found it successful on the few occasions that I have had the opportunity to try it.

The vast majority of your salmon fishing will not be to the rolling fish, but to the water itself. Therefore, since you do not know exactly where every fish is, you must have confidence that there are fish in the pool and fish away enthusiastically. Under these circumstances, it is important to work the entire pool systematically in a pattern so you present your fly to every possible lie.

Fishing the Wet Fly

Wet fly-fishing for salmon goes back hundreds of

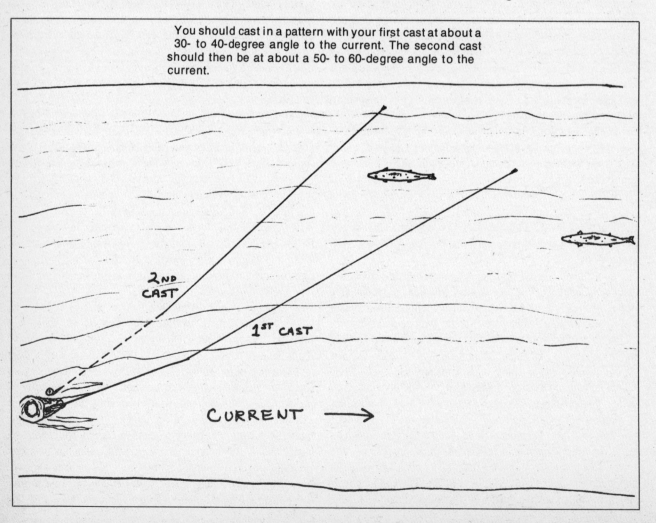

You should cast in a pattern with your first cast at about a 30- to 40-degree angle to the current. The second cast should then be at about a 50- to 60-degree angle to the current.

2ND CAST

1ST CAST

CURRENT →

years. The modern technique of wet fly-fishing is referred to as "greased line" fishing—fishing with a line that floats.

Salmon will take a wet fly under just about all water conditions, while the dry fly requires more selective conditions to be effective. A fish that will take a dry fly will almost always take a wet fly. However, the fish that will take a wet fly might not have any interest in the dry. You can see that the wet fly is generally more productive.

The standard way to fish the wet fly is to make a down and across stream cast, trying to lay the line, leader and fly in as straight a line on the water as possible. The idea is to have the fly "swim" sideways across the current. There are many variations to this basic technique, and no one can really say that there is only one right way to do it, since there is no particular logic in feeding as there is with trout fishing. What I will describe is the general concept that is practiced. If you can master the basics, then you can experiment with any variations you wish.

The first objective is to take your position at the head of the run or pool and analyze the water as to what line or path in the water you are going to follow and start fishing. You should try to get a feel for what part of the current the fish are most likely to follow, how much line you will casting, and what angle to the current you wish to cast your fly and line. If you are the first one through the pool, or if the people who have fished through before you have been wading shallow, then you should wade shallow and fish your side of the current first. Do not attempt to cast to the far side of the river—at least not the first time through the pool.

Select a particular fly that you have confidence in and fish the pool through completely with that particular fly. A mistake that many anglers make is that they continuously change flies if they don't get immediate results. That doesn't help, it just takes time away from your fly being in the water, and that's where you're going to catch the salmon. If you don't have the confidence to give that fly a full chance, you shouldn't have selected it.

It is important to fish a definite pattern. For example, make two casts from where you are first standing, take two or three steps and make two more casts, take two or three more steps and repeat this process all the way through the pool or run. At each position, the two casts that you make should also have a pattern. A good variation would be: the first cast at about a 30- to 45-degree angle to the current; the second cast would then be at about a 50- or 60-degree angle to the current. This same pattern and angle to the current will be made at each position. Remember I said angle to the current—

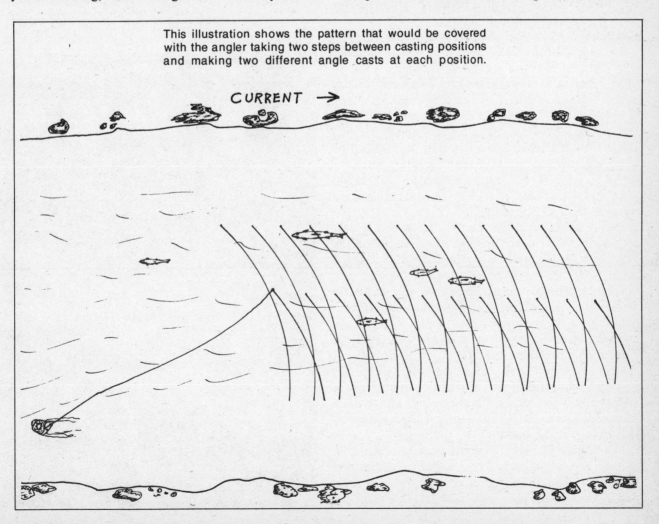

This illustration shows the pattern that would be covered with the angler taking two steps between casting positions and making two different angle casts at each position.

CURRENT →

not to the river itself. You have to look at the water and see if the current is coming straight down the river, or if it is working at an angle away from or toward you. The reason for this is that the speed that a fly swings across the current is one of the factors that a salmon can be selective to. Sometimes they want it at just a certain speed. A bit too fast or too slow and they might reject it or not even bother to move to it. That speed selectivity is a very fickle thing. It could be one speed one day or week and another the next. Also, the fish in one river system might be known to prefer a fly at basically a certain angle and speed to the current and another will be known for a different preference. As strange as it may seem, that's the way it is. When you are making one cast at a 45-degree angle, and another at 60 degrees, you are making casts that will swing the fly at two different speeds. The smaller the angle of the cast to the current, the slower the speed of the swing.

In making your casts, it is most important not to cast any more line than you can control. If you cannot control the placement of the fly with 60 feet of line, then you should only cast 50 or 45 feet, or whatever length you can control consistently. You should be able to lay the line, leader and fly in a straight line. In fact, if you can turn the fly so that it lands downstream from the line, in most cases you will be better off. However, for starters, try for the straight line.

When you make your cast, point the tip of your rod where you want the fly to land. If you make a proper cast, and the line is straight, the fly will swim sideways to the current at a moderate rate of speed. This is usually the action that you want. If you make a sloppy or uncontrolled cast and the fly lands upstream of the line, you will have created an instant belly in the line. When the current works on that cast, the fly will be dragged across the current at a much greater speed than with a proper cast. There might be times when that will work, but you will be better off if you wait until you are trying to do it intentionally.

Larger salmon usually do not like to chase a rapidly moving fly. The slower you can move the fly on the swing, usually the better your chances of attracting the larger fish. Grilse will be more apt to take a faster moving fly than the larger fish. When you let the fly swing, let it swing all the way below you and then let it hang there a few seconds before you pick it up to make another cast. The end of the swing is sometimes the point at which a salmon will take your fly. A fish will not always take your fly above where they were lying. They will often follow the fly and take it in a certain depth of water or at a certain point in the swing. I have often wondered how many fish followed and inspected my fly that I never knew about.

If you have worked the entire pool systematically with no results, and you know or feel confident that there are salmon there, then you might try another fly pattern or size, and possibly a different angle sequence or technique until you find some combination that gets results. If someone else is getting results and moving fish, you might ask what he is doing. Although salmon fishermen are often quite secretive, they will usually be willing to help with some information.

What happens if on your way down the pool you are fortunate enough to raise a fish, but he doesn't take your fly? Well, you might proceed as follows. Immediately mark the exact spot where the fish rose, then make an identical cast to the one you made when the fish rose. Quite often you will take the fish on that cast, so be ready. One thing I should say at this time; actually I should have mentioned it earlier. When a salmon takes a wet fly, you DO NOT STRIKE. The worst thing that you can do is strike when you feel the salmon take the fly. It may take a bit of discipline, but the thing to do is NOTHING. Just hold your rod in the same position as for the swing, which should be your arm at your side, the rod parallel to the water with the rod tip pointing at the fly and following it as it makes its swing. What will happen, is that the salmon will come up casually, will take the fly and will start to go down. As he does so, the current acting on the line will pull the fly into the corner of the salmon's mouth. The salmon will then feel the

Salmon hooked where it should be—in the corner of the mouth.

180

International Atlantic Salmon Foundation logo.

pressure and will shake his head—he will actually be hooking himself at that time. This is probably what you will first feel. The fish will then panic and make his runs and jumps. Another point to remember is to never hold the line tight against the rod with your fingers or hand as the fly is making its swing. You might get a hard take by a fish which could break your leader if the reel is not free and able to let out line smoothly.

Now back to that fish that rose to your fly. If the fish was moving up the river after he rose to your fly, he may have moved up a foot or so by the time you have made your second cast. Therefore, if you do not get him to come again to the second cast, strip in, DO NOT REEL IN, about 3 feet of line and make a third cast that is 3 feet shorter than the first two. If no results, make a fourth cast the same length as the first two. If you get no response at that time, you may want to switch to a smaller or a silver fly as a pickup attempt. This is when the game gets interesting, with great anticipation each time the fly swings through the spot where the salmon first came up. If you cannot get that fish to come back, make sure that you mark where the salmon came up and where you were standing, so that the next time you work through the pool you can concentrate on that area.

There are times that salmon will take a fly ever so gently. In fact, it almost seems like the hook just grazed a piece of weed. However, being that the fly is only several inches below the water you know there are no weeds there. As you fish a salmon river, you will expe-rience numerous times the strike of 3- or 4-inch paar. They hit it pretty hard, and the strike usually feels like a sharp "rap." The soft releasing take by the salmon almost feels the same, but it's softer as though the fly grabbed on to something, then let go. If you are not aware of the possibilities of a large fish doing this, you will never know it and will probably keep on fishing through the pool. However, if you are aware of this, you will wisely stop and work that fish. Sometimes you may actually be working and fishing to a paar, but once you get that heavy pull, you'll be amazed.

Again, this was knowledge given to me by Charles Defeo one July as I was about to head for Canada. He told me to be aware of the gentle pull, and described the sensation to me. The whole idea is to anticipate this possibility so that you don't pass it by when it occurs. On that summer trip, two of the fish that I caught were comebacks to that gentle take, and I can tell you that I was quite astounded when I picked up the first one. I believed enough in it that I had changed to a smaller fly after I got no response to the second cast. I am sure that 99 percent of salmon fishermen pass this by. It en-hances your concentration and anticipation while per-forming the casting ritual.

Another extremely important point is to follow your fly from the time it hits the water until you're about to pick it up for another cast. Now naturally, you cannot actually see your fly because it is under the water, but you can follow the speed of the swing and concentrate at the spot where your fly would be. This is important because there will be many times when a salmon will come up and roll behind your fly without actually touching it. If you do not see this, you will never know it happened and will probably pass up an opportunity to pick up a fish. Quite often the angler fishing behind you will pick up that fish if you passed it by.

Fishing High Water Conditions

Many salmon pools and runs that are good under normal water levels are quite difficult to fish when the water gets high. On the other hand, there are other pools on the river that are usually passed by under normal conditions, but become the places to go when the water rises. This is one of the values of having a knowledgeable guide if you are not familiar with the river system yourself.

When the water gets high, it also gets dirty. However, it usually gets dirty on the surface first. If you are fishing the river during a rain, and it starts to get a bit muddy, the thing to do is switch over to a large, heavy hooked fly and possibly a sinking tip line if you have one. If the water is dirty on the upper 3 or 4 inches of the surface, your fly can still be seen well if it is a foot or so deep. You may be able to get in ½-hour or more of fishing before the river gets dirty enough to get you thinking of other strategies. It also may be just enough time to hook another fish.

As the level of the river rises, the currents take on a different image. They become less and less affected by the rocks and terrain on the bottom. Rather than showing the character of the pools and runs, the current will be one powerful force working down river. The key of knowing where to fish or where the salmon would be is in remembering that they will try to seek the paths of least resistance. With the exception of the outside part of a turn or bend of the river, the easiest parts of the currents will be right against the banks or on the inside of any turns. If you examine the banks of a river, you will see that there is a great deal of irregularity in the form of rocks, grass clumps, depressions, etc. These formations cause the current to form eddies right against the banks. The salmon follow these eddy pockets and periodically hold in them. You can easily see the significance of these eddies if you step into the river and stand against the bank. The current pressure will not be too bad there. However, just step a foot or two out into the river, and you will surely be able to feel why the salmon prefer to stay in close. If there are large rocks in the river that create obvious eddies, these will also be spots that you can work a fly through.

There are many times during these high water conditions when you may not even be wading in the river. You may be limited to walking the banks. It is not necessary to cast a long line—working with about 30 to 40 feet and casting at about a 30- to 45-degree angle downstream is all that is needed. It is very important to let the fly hang for 5 to 10 seconds right against the bank at the end of the swing. I have had many salmon take at that time.

The variation in tackle, if you desire, would be to use a sinking or sinking tip line to help get your fly deeper. Using slightly larger flies on heavier hooks might also be an asset. The most popular colors for flies used when the water is dirty are orange, red, copper, gold combinations.

You will find that as the water starts dropping and clears, the salmon will start holding more. A dropping water level after a good rise in the river is quite often the best time for good fishing action.

Fishing Low Water Conditions

When the water level gets low, the areas where the salmon will hold are reduced in size and are relatively

A "low water" fly.

easy to cover properly at that time. However, if the low water is accompanied by high water temperatures, it creates a fishing problem. When the water temperature jumps above the 70-degree mark, the salmon do not respond well to the fly. The oxygen content is reduced to a point where the fish become very concerned about moving to a cooler environment. Though many people think that in warm water conditions the fish's activity slows down, the fish in actuality, increase their pace in search of that cooler water. This is a time when the salmon will stop and hold at the mouths of small, cooler feeder streams, spring holes and spring fed bogens. If the angler or his guide know the river and where these areas are, they can surely find fish.

If the water is low and the temperature is respectable, the fishing can be extremely interesting. This is the time when you can locate those holding fish and try to work them with various techniques and flies. You can also

THE "RIFFLE" HITCH

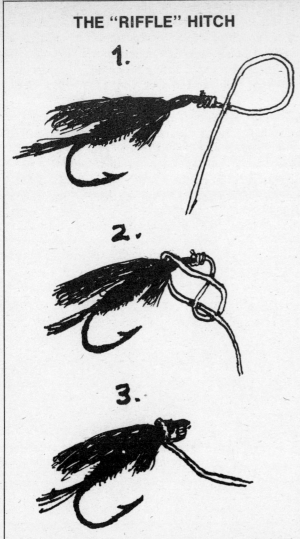

1.

2.

3.

For a single hook fly, the knot is made so that the leader will come out from one side of the fly. Which side depends on which side of the river you are fishing. For a double hook, the leader should come directly underneath from the throat.

see fish roll from time to time and have an opportunity to work them. This is one of the best times for the dry fly. Personally, I prefer slightly low, cool water because of its visual aspect.

The trend in low water is to use smaller flies. If normal conditions warranted size #6 or #4, you might go down to #8, #10 and even #12 flies. Many flies that are specifically tied for low water conditions are tied small in silhouette for the size hook they are tied on. For example, a fly tied on a size #6 low water hook will have the body size that might normally be tied on a #8 or #10 fly.

During low water conditions you can also take the opportunity to fish with lighter weight tackle. If you are normally fishing with a 9-foot rod for a #8 line, you will find it comfortable to fish with an 8½-foot rod for a #7 line, or even smaller if the conditions permit. Regardless of the size outfit you use, make sure that you can still control the placement of the fly on the cast. You may find it a bit more strenuous fighting a salmon with a lighter outfit, and it might take longer to get the fish to the net, since you will not be able to apply the same pressure, but it is an additional challenge and another aspect of the game.

As I mentioned before, low water is a good time to experiment if you know where the salmon are. It is quite often advantageous to use a very small fly. The famous Edward Hewitt showed Charles DeFeo how to work with a small #16 dark wet fly. He used a light #5 and #6 line with about 4- to 6-pound leader, and made casts of no more than 30 to 35 feet at a rather short angle of about 30 degrees or less.

Riffling

An unorthodox technique that gained its popularity on Portland Creek in Newfoundland, involves the use of a Half-Hitch Knot on the fly. The knot is referred to as the "Portland Hitch" or the "Rifle Hitch." The tech-

Here is the proper position of leader and fly for the "Riffle Hitch."

nique itself is called riffling.

What it involves is making a half-hitch knot over the head of the fly after the initial tying of the leader to the fly with a conventional knot. For a single hook fly, the half-hitch is made so that the leader will come out from one side of the fly or the other, depending on which side of the river you are fishing. Looking from the rear of the fly, if you are fishing the right side of a river (looking downstream), the leader should come out of the right side of the fly, and vise versa. When the fly is swinging, its head will always be pointing toward the side of the river that you are fishing from. For a double hook, it is best if the leader comes directly underneath the throat of the fly.

that is the norm. Quite often the fish will miss the fly and come back for it again during the same swing, so never pick up your fly from the water until it has fully completed the swing. It is not too uncommon to have a fish come three or four times to a riffled fly. It can be quite unnerving, and keeps you on your toes with anticipation.

This type of fishing is always interesting, since everything takes place on the surface, and you can see all the action. You should always follow your fly as it riffles across the current, to make sure that you don't miss a short strike. You may have to readjust the Half-Hitch Knot on the fly if you no longer see the "V" wake on the water.

Skaters are heavily hackled flies that are tied on small lightweight hooks.

Because the current hits the fly at an angle, the fly is forced to the surface and makes a "V" wake in the surface film as it makes its swing toward shore. The cast is not as critical with this type of fishing, although the angle that you cast across the current should be taken into consideration. The more your cast is across the current, the faster the swing. The swing must be just fast enough to keep the fly on the surface and make the riffle wake. If the current is quite slow, you may have to cast almost directly across the current and maybe even lift your rod a bit to get the action desired.

This surface activity is often enticing to fish that are otherwise uninterested in routine presentations. The strike may be quite sharp in contrast to the casual take

When to Use the Dry Fly for Atlantic Salmon

Dry fly-fishing for Atlantic salmon can be very exciting. Quite often you are seeing large fish come up to take your offering, and it gets your nerves on end. In contrast to trout fishing, however, you are not really trying to match any particular hatch or any specific insect. You are merely presenting a suggestive surface imitation.

Since the dry fly is not as effective as the wet fly for all conditions, you have to be more selective as to when you will use it. Like so many things in Atlantic salmon fishing, there is a saying, that a salmon will not stick his nose out of the water when the air is cooler than the water temperature. Therefore, he will supposedly not take a dry fly under these conditions. Personally, I can't remember having taken any fish on a dry when the air was cooler, so I'll have to go along with the philosophy.

High water conditions are not at all conducive to dry fly-fishing—even if the water is clear. The best conditions are when the water is anywhere from moderate to low level with the water temperature under 70 degrees.

Fishing the dry fly is most effective when you see a fish roll and can cast to that spot, or when you know where fish are or might likely be and you work that area in an attempt to bring them up. For the majority of dry fly-fishing for salmon, the fly should be fished dead drift, making sure that it does not have any unnatural drag. This does not mean that a dragging fly will not catch fish—anything will at times or if you work it long enough. However, for your basic presentations to rolling or holding fish, work the fly drag free, dead drift initially. If you wish to experiment after that, by all means do so. One particular dry fly technique that requires movement of the fly is skating—a means of locating fish and getting them to show themselves.

There is not the major concern with the size of the dry fly that there is with the wet fly. It is important, however, to have an assortment of several different patterns in several different sizes and colors. A salmon may come several times to a particular fly or to several different flies, but not take one. If you are patient and persistent, changing flies and sizes, allowing the fish to rest now and then, you will usually be able to get the salmon to take a fly that suits his fancy.

I can remember the first salmon that I caught on a dry fly. He was no monster—just about 6 pounds—but the incident taught me a lot. I was working down a pool with a wet fly and noticed a fish roll about 100 feet below me in a shallow run only about 15 feet from the bank. Before I got down to it, the fish rolled again. I was really expecting it to take when I presented the wet fly. However, I was quite disappointed when my offering of several different flies received no response. I began to think about using a dry fly since the water was just right for it, and stepped out of the river to take a good position along side of the fish and to ponder over a choice of flies. I was just tying on a #8 Humpy when the fish rolled again about 20 feet in front of me. I quickly marked the exact spot where the fish was and began casting. On about the fifth float over it, the salmon came up and took the fly in a classic head and tail roll. I was so startled that I struck immediately and felt the fly pull out of his mouth. At that time I really wasn't sure if I should have waited until the fish disappeared. I made another 30 casts or so with that same fly, but got no response. However the second cast with a smaller fly, after allowing the fish to rest for about 5 minutes, brought him up—only this time he didn't take the fly. Well, to make a long story short, it took about ½-hour of casting, resting the fish and changing flies, until I finally

got the salmon to come up a third time. It was to the same #8 Humpy that I had first brought it up with. This time I waited when the fish rolled on it and then just lifted the rod tip. The fish was on, and I was thrilled.

Personally, I prefer to be directly across from the fish when I use the dead drift float. I use the upstream hold or reach cast, which enables me to get a long drift, yet have contact with the line and fly at all times. Some anglers favor casting upstream. Whatever works best for you, you should use. It is extremely important to float your fly directly over the lie of the salmon. Quite often a float of 6 inches to either side will go unheeded, while the cast right on target will bring a rise. Again another reason to mark exactly where the fish came up. If you are just working fish that you see or know are holding in a particular lie, make a series of casts and dead drift floats in a pattern over the water, so that you are sure you covered the lie with at least a few favorable casts.

It is usually more advantageous to search or prospect with a large bushy fly rather than a small sparse one. If you raise a fish, you can often be quite successful if you come back with a smaller fly. There are basically two types of rises that you will get to a dry fly, and each rise form requires a different strike. First, there is the classic head and tail or "porpoise" roll. With this rise, the fish casually comes up to the fly, gently takes it in his mouth, then turns to go back down. If you strike right away, you will most often take the fly away from the fish. The idea is to keep your wits about you, allow the fish to disappear under the surface, then lift your rod. He should be on. The other type of rise form is when the fish comes up under the fly and takes it, either in a sharp swirl or by just simply sucking it under. With this type of rise, if you wait, the salmon will probably spit out the fly. You must strike immediately, just as you would to most rising trout.

A very successful technique was originated by Roger Desjordins, superintendent of the Matane River. It was made popular by George Maul, who runs a fishing camp and tackle shop on the Matane River, in St. René, Quebec, on the Gaspe peninsula in Canada. It is called the 10-second dry fly technique. What this means is that from the time that the fly lands on the water surface for one cast, until it lands on the water for the next cast will be about 10 seconds. The fly will only stay on the water for about 4 seconds, then is picked up, false cast a time or two, then put down again.

Once again, it is important to know just where the fish is. Your cast should place the fly, not in front of, but along side of or even slightly behind the fish. It is allowed to drift for 3 or 4 seconds, then immediately picked up. This is repeated several times. The principle is that the fish never gets a good look at something that comes down to the surface then leaves again quickly. This stimulates its interest. The idea is to never give the salmon a good look at the fly. A slight variation of this is to make four or five of these presentations, landing the fly just behind the fish, then making a cast so that the fly lands about 1-foot in front of the fish and drifts right over it. The object here is to get the fish thinking—what was that?—for four or five times, and the next time—hey, there it is—and hopefully, the fish will take it. When salmon fishing it is best to have several concepts in your bag of tricks, and to experiment with them until you get results. You will find this exciting.

Another technique, mentioned before, that works both for trout and salmon as a searching method, is "skating." The principle of this is to present a fly to the water and to periodically give it a gentle twitch. This gives the illusion of something alive that might just be ready to fly away. It often arouses the curiosity of a salmon and entices him to come up and give it a look. You usually do not hook the fish when he comes to a skater, but it locates an interested fish that you can mark and come back to with another fly.

Skaters are heavily hackled flies that are tied on small lightweight hooks. They should be made so that they can be skittered on the surface without sinking. Unless you are working a specific fish, you can fish the skater in a pattern similar to the wet fly. This way you will cover most of the likely holding water. The procedure would be to make your cast somewhat across stream, let it drift several feet, then skitter it a few inches, allow it to drift a few more feet, then skitter it again, and so on. Make two or three of these casts for each position, then take two or three steps downstream and repeat the

activity. Again, if you raise a fish and he doesn't take the skater, get another fly back to him as fast as you can.

Fighting the Salmon

One of the greatest thrills of any salmon trip that I have been on has always been the first "pull" or fish hooked. By "pull" I mean when a salmon takes hold of your wet fly as it is swinging. The feeling is the sudden sensation of weight pulling at the end of your line, followed by the shaking of the fish's head when he realizes that something is wrong. This is usually followed by a reel screeching run, and quite often cartwheeling jumps.

The nature of Atlantic salmon fishing is that you usually do not catch large quantities of fish. In fact, over the long run, if you can average one fish for every day fished, you will be quite successful. You have to be prepared to have days when you will not even have a pull. It is the anticipation that the next cast will be the one. Because of this, you want to make sure that you fish each fish properly so that you can have the best chance to land most of those you hook.

Personally, I was spoiled the first time that I went salmon fishing. We happened to hit it just right that day, and I had caught my limit of four fish by 11:30 that morning, as did the friend that I was with. In fact I can remember being so casual with the third and fourth fish that I all but horsed them to the shore. I thought that this was an easy game. Unfortunately, I was in for a rude awakening. The second day I blanked out—not

Angler properly "bowing" to a leaping fish.

even a pull. The third day I hooked one fish and lost it. I remember being really upset about that. Each day after, and ever since, I have cherished each salmon that I hooked and made sure to play it carefully.

As your fly is swinging, when fishing a wet fly, you should not hold any loose line in your hand. Whatever line is off the reel should be in the guides of the rod and on the water. The arm that is holding the rod should be down along your side, and your hand should be holding only the rod handle. You should not be holding the line. The rod should be pointing along the path of the line with the rod tip just inches above the water. As the line swings toward the shore, you should move the rod tip along with it. In fact, it is sometimes a good practice to move the rod tip slightly ahead of the line. This is called "leading the swing."

When a fish takes your fly, it will immediately be pulling against the drag of the reel without interference and there will be no possibility of the line hanging up on your finger or the reel handle. Any hangup can cause immediate loss of the fish by a break in the leader or a pulled out fly. I still remember two instances when I was holding the line against the rod handle and had hard taking fish break off my fly. It's a lesson you don't forget easily.

With the dry fly you do not want to have a lot of loose line dangling in the water. Whatever you are not going to cast, put back on the reel. In this way, when the fish takes and you strike, you can have the fish running line off the reel right away. You want the fish playing off the

reel immediately. As soon as a fish knows that it is hooked, it will bolt away quickly. Any tangle or complication will result in a lost fish.

Once the salmon is on and running, the first thing you want to do is lift your rod up at about a 45-degree angle. If you lift it too high, you will be severely increasing the drag and will put excess pressure on the leader. With the rod up at this angle, any sharp moves or jerks by the fish will be softened somewhat. This position will also allow you to "bow" to the salmon when it jumps. Bowing to the fish means throwing your rod tip forward and down to the water at the moment you see the fish come out of the water. Any time you are fishing for large fish, you should execute this movement. A fish of 10 pounds coming out of the water and then down on an 8-pound test leader could be coming down with a force of 20 pounds or more. If the leader is kept tight, it will easily break. When you throw your rod down, you are throwing slack in the line which will absorb the shock. For some reason, most people instinctively lift their rods up when a fish jumps, as though to pull the fish off balance. This is the worst thing you can do. Then when the heavy fish comes down and breaks the leader, these same people are at a total loss of how it could have happened. So just remember, when a large fish comes out of the water, bow to him—not just in its honor, but in order to keep it on your line.

Now that you have the fish on, and it has made its initial run, you want to get out of the river, if you are wading, and work down the shore to get along side of

Angler with salmon just hooked, with net in preparation. (Photo courtesy of Sid Neff.)

the fish. In order to tire the fish the fastest, you must put side pressure on it. Standing up above a salmon after it has run downstream does not tire it too much. In fact you are even holding it up in the current. Side pressure takes its toll on the fish's muscles. This is also where you want to be when you are ready to land the fish.

As you work down river, your guide or a friend should come with you with a net if you have one. There are three basic techniques in landing a salmon—beaching, netting and tailing. It is often difficult to beach a large salmon because of its strength and weight. However, beaching is often done with grilse. First you must have a shoreline that is gradual enough so that you can slide the fish up onto the shore. When the fish is tired and you have it about 20 feet from you, keep yourself slightly downstream from it, apply pressure with your rod at about a 45-degree angle, and try to get the fish heading toward the shore. Once you get it coming, just keep the pressure on, holding the rod at that same angle (don't pick it up too high) and just back up, pulling the fish out of the water. Any movement that the salmon makes when you have it pointing toward shore will help you get it out.

The one thing you have to be aware of any time you have a salmon close to you, whether you are using a net, beaching it or whatever, is that this is the time most fish are lost. The fish has just been through a battle and is scared. The fly that is in its mouth may have worked a bit loose, and any sharp run, jump or movement that it makes will accentuate the stress on your tackle because of the fish's closeness. Therefore, you always have to be aware of any sudden move and bow to it, allowing the fish to work on slack and off the reel.

If you are using a net, which I feel is the most advisable, it should be a big one. You can never be sure when you may hang into a big fish. I'm never embarrassed to have a really big net for a smaller fish, but I sure would be embarrassed if I had a skimpy net for a large fish and had problems with it. The man with the net should get into the river, downstream from the fish, and should hold the net in the water. He should not make quick lunges at the fish, but should wait until you bring the salmon over or into the net. At that time he simply lifts up sharply. The angler should manipulate the salmon so that the fish is about 6 feet upstream from the net. Then, keeping himself a bit downstream from the fish, should exert sufficient pressure to get the fish to turn downstream. As soon as the fish turns, he will be just upstream from the net and facing into it. The critical move is to keep the pressure on and pull the fish down into the net. If you keep the fish facing downstream after you have turned it, any swimming movement that it makes will carry it right into the net.

The third method is with the use of a tailer. The tailer, as mentioned earlier, utilizes a 30-inch handle and a wire snare loop. The angler can tail a fish himself or have another do it. When the salmon is tired, it should be brought close to you while you are standing in approximately knee deep water and should be held in position with the rod and line. Whoever is using the

Salmon about to be netted after 20-minute battle. (Photo courtesy of Sid Neff.)

Angler admiring his prize. (Photo courtesy of Sid Neff.)

pressure will now be from directly downstream. The fish will usually work upstream, and all you have to do is reel in the slack line as it comes. Once you get it back up stream, it's off to the races again.

Where to Fish for Atlantic Salmon

Atlantic salmon, as the name implies, are found on the northern Atlantic coast of this continent. Canada has the vast majority of fishable rivers at this time. The only state in the U.S. that has available fishing is Maine.

See the 1978 Catch Statistics chart on page 191 for a listing of rivers that are open to fishing in Maine and Canada. For more detailed information, you can contact the Atlantic Salmon Association. They have a map available that can help you with river location.

THE LANDLOCK SALMON

The landlock is the same fish as the sea going Atlantic salmon. It is believed that during the ice age, certain rivers became sealed off from the sea, preventing the salmon from leaving the freshwater system.

Proudly displaying catch. (Photo courtesy of Sid Neff.)

tailer sticks it into the water behind the fish and carefully slides the noose over the salmon's tail. It is important not to touch the fish while doing this or he will dart forward. When the noose is just forward of the tail, lift upward sharply and continue the upward pull until you are holding the fish's tail out of the water. This does not work well with smaller grilse, since their tail bones are not adequately developed to hold the noose.

A point that you may want to remember if you ever get in a position where you cannot follow the fish down river, is that rather than trying to pull the fish back up river, give it slack and let it come up by itself. If a salmon runs 100 yards or so down below you and stops, it can stay there all day while you try to pull from directly above it. There is no lateral pressure to tire it. The fish will also naturally try to swim away from the direction of the pull. If you don't panic and give the fish slack, you can get it to come to you. Strip out about another 20 to 30 feet of line, then wait. What happens is that the line will now be pulled below the fish, and the

Lifted net holds salmon securely.

Hand-tailed salmon. (Photo courtesy of Sid Neff.)

Adult salmon larger than 5 pounds can be carried with a loop over its tail.

1978 CATCH STATISTICS*

QUEBEC rivers

NORTH SHORE

	1977	1978
Saint Paul	239	102
du Vieux Fort	132	96
Gros Mecatina	186	169
Etamamiou	415	370
Olomane	130	59
Washicoutai	92	126
Musquanousse	81	138
Musquaro	110	192
Kegashka	98	30
Natashquan	803	564
Petite Watshishou	60	76
Watshishou	205	195
Piashti	27	11
de la Corneille	122	125
Romaine	22	16
Mingan	37	64
Saint-Jean	390	457
Jupitagon	42	14
Moisie	1180	1380
Petite Trinite	7	20
de la Trinite	355	303
Godbout	361	442
Mistassini	60	61
des Anglais	8	9
Laval	14	26
Ste-Marguerite	167	252
Saint-Jean	167	209
Petti Saguenay	59	144
du Gouffre	8	5
TOTAL	5577	5562

GASPESIE

	1977	1978
Ouelle	40	65
Rimouski	90	110
Mitis	41	75
Matane	1118	1432
Cap Chat	58	98
Sainte-Anne	261	251
Madeleine	163	201
Dartmouth	186	352
York	814	540
Saint-Jean	1161	617
Grande Rivière	386	207
Grand Pabos	11	7
Grand Pabos O.	10	2
Bonaventure	683	394
P. Cascapedia	38	35
Cascapedia	725	739
Matapedia	1590	1708
Restigouche	1923	1259
Patapedia	250	103
Kedgwick	40	37
TOTAL	9588	8232

ANTICOSTI

	1977	1978
aux Saumons	126	287
à la Loutre	74	51
Jupiter	1276	662
(others)	206	–
TOTAL	1682	1000

QUEBEC overview

North Shore	1977	5,577
	1978	5,562
Gaspésie	1977	9,588
	1978	8,232
Anticosti	1977	1,682
	1978	1,000
Totals	1977	16,847
	1978	14,794

THE MIRAMICHI SYSTEM, N.B.,
Northumberland County Only

RIVER	SPECIES	NO.
Main Southwest	Black-large	4798
Miracmchi R.	Black-grilse	1189
	Bright-large	2024
	Bright-grilse	2832
	TOTAL	10,843
Cains	Black-large	161
	Bright-large	12
	Bright-grilse	27
	TOTAL	200
Renous	Black-large	127
	Bright-large	70
	Bright-grilse	53
	TOTAL	250
Northwest	Black-large	345
Miramichi	Black-grilse	430
	Bright-large	289
	Bright-grilse	443
	TOTAL	1507
Sevogle	Bright-large	545
	Bright-grilse	499
	TOTAL	1044
Dungarvon	Bright-large	67
	Bright-grilse	35
	Total	102
Little	Black-large	100
Southwest	Black-grilse	180
Miramichi	Bright-large	289
	Bright-grilse	219
	TOTAL	668
GRAND TOTAL for Northumberland County		14,614
TOTAL for York and Carleton Counties		2,506
GRAND TOTAL		17,120

MAINE

	1977	1978
Penobscot	188	360
Narraguagus	134	136
Machais	50	117
East Machais	50	48
Dennys	26	75
Sheepscot	24	34
Pleasant	3	16
TOTALS	475	797

We wish to thank Leon Tremblay and Jack Fenety for their invaluable help in compiling these statistics.

*Taken from the *Atlantic Salmon Journal*, January, 1979.

Landlocks were first discovered in Maine's Sebago lake, hence the name *Salmo salar sebago*. Around the turn of the century, specimens in the 20- to 30-pound class were occasionally caught, with fish of 10 to 12 pounds not too uncommon. Unfortunately today, a catch of a 6- or 7-pound salmon is considered a prize. Landlocks can be found in three northern New England states—Maine, New Hampshire and New York—and in the Maritime Provinces of Canada. Strangely enough, efforts to introduce them into other parts of the country have not been very successful.

Since the landlock is structurally the same fish as the Atlantic salmon, it has the same fighting capabilities and is known for its spectacular cartwheeling jumps. The landlock is known to eat a wide variety of foods and has been caught on worms, spinning lures, shiners, insects, plugs and various types of artificial flies. However, one of their favorite foods is the smelt, a small fish

acrobatic routine. There are times when you can see the salmon feeding on a hatch of some sort. This is not uncommon in many of the pools on the West Branch of the Penobscot River in Maine and other waters in the area. Most of this surface activity takes place in late spring and early summer. The fish are not as particular as trout if they are working the surface. Standard patterns such as the Adams, Hair Wing Coachman, Light or Dark Cahill and Quill Gordon in sizes #8, #10 and #12 will produce.

The majority of the action, however, will be to bait fish imitations, especially in the fall when the fishing is exclusively with streamers or bucktails. During the early season, after the ice-out the landlocks will be relatively shallow in the lakes and ponds, feeding on the smelt that have just returned from spawning in the tributary rivers. Working the shorelines with boats or canoes and casting or trolling your streamers can pro-

(Above) Beautiful 3½-pound landlock taken from a Maine river with a streamer. (Photo courtesy of Sid Neff.)

(Right) A nice day's catch of landlocks ranging from 1½ pounds to 4½ pounds.

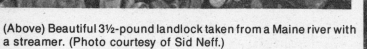

that is indigenous to their habitat. Where the schools of smelt go, so go the salmon. The object of the fisherman is to use an imitation that resembles these bait fish. Most of the popular streamer patterns work fairly well. The sizes can vary from #6 to #10. The same type of outfit that you would use for Atlantic salmon would be perfectly adequate here—8½-foot to 9-foot rod for a #7 or #8 line. The leader should be approximately 9 feet long tapering down to about 1X or 2X, which is about a 6-pound test.

There are even times when the landlock can be taken on dry flies. This is some of the most exciting fishing of all since you can see the fish take the fly, then go into its

duce. You should experiment fishing your flies at different depths unless you see fish working the surface here or there. It is also important to experiment with the speed of your retrieve or your trolling speed until you hit the rate that the fish want. This can vary from time to time. Since your fly is lifeless, you have to make an extra effort to impart an irregular action to it to give it life. Materials like marabou help in making the streamers look alive.

As the season moves into summer, the salmon will be deep in the lakes, and you will have to get down there with sinking lines. Many trollers even use wire lines with their flies on the end. The wire gets them down

A small collection of landlock streamers. Top row (left to right): Demon, Smelt, Silver Doctor. Bottom row (left to right): Six-Pounder, Mickey Finn, Warden's Worry.

Successful angler displays his prize—a beautiful 5-pound landlock that took a Marabou Streamer. (Photo courtesy of Stanley Bryer.)

Square Lake, in northern Maine, is good for spring fishing around the beginning of or in mid June. Another excellent spring lake is Lake Memphremagog, from mid May to mid June. This lake straddles the U.S.-Canada border from northern Vermont into southern Quebec.

Some of the better fall fishing can be had in Cross Lake and Mud Lake in northern Maine. The West Branch of the Penobscot River, in central Maine, is very good around an area called "Fox Hole Rips." This is above where it enters Chesuncook Lake. The end of the season is the best. The Roache River north of Moosehead Lake in Maine, is also worthwhile to fish in the fall with streamers.

OTHER SALMON SPECIES

The other salmon species that may be of some interest to the fly-fisherman are the chinook and the coho. They have been popular gamefish on the West Coast for many years. Unfortunately, their reputation for fly-fishing is not as productive as with spinning, casting or trolling with lures or bait. Although their popularity was originally from northern California up through British Columbia, they have been introduced in recent years to the Great Lakes and have provided some enthusiastic fishing on the Michigan peninsula and in the Salmon River area in Polaski, New York.

The times that the coho and chinook are most accessible to the fly-fisherman is in the late summer through the winter. The coho will usually come into the river a bit earlier, from late August into the fall. The chinook will often come in through September, October and November.

Although it is quite difficult to get them to take a fly, it is quite a sight to see them in numbers working their

deeper, but takes away some of the aesthetics of the game. You might also want to go to weighted flies at this time. With the end of summer comes the fall—the spawning season for the salmon. This is the time when good sized fish can be taken in the rivers that empty into the lakes. You should work the river with streamers just as you would for trout fishing, casting and working the likely looking runs and holding pockets. As I mentioned, this is streamer fishing activity and the results are literally "smashing."

Some of the good areas to fish are listed below, but there are many others. There are many camps that cater to the fisherman. Inquiry with a state's Chamber of Commerce can help. There are often advertisements by these camps just before the seasons open in the popular outdoor magazines such as *Field & Stream*, *Outdoor Life*, *Sports Afield* and *Flyfisherman*.

way up the rivers to spawn. Coho have been caught up to around the 30-pound range, but 6 to 8 pounds would be closer to the average. The chinook runs a bit larger, averaging about 16 to 18 pounds.

The fact that these fish do not feed when they enter the freshwater system to spawn, similar to the Atlantic salmon, is one of the reasons it is so difficult to get them to take a fly. One important characteristic that sets the chinook and coho apart from the Atlantic salmon, is that, contrary to the Atlantic salmon which usually returns to sea after the initial spawning run, the chinook and coho only have one chance and then die. Because of this fact, many areas permit the snagging of these fish with lures and hooks since they will die anyway. Some areas on certain river systems have regulations that limit the fishing to single hooks only, or even to flies only. This gives the fisherman, who wants to be a bit more sporting, a chance to escape the masses who will take the fish by any means.

Rivers such as the Big Manistee, White, Pere Marquette, and Muskegon on the lower Michigan peninsula, and the Salmon River in Polaski, New York, draw large crowds from late September through November to fish for these monsters. Most of the time if the rivers aren't too high, you can see the numbers of fish in the river. At times there can be so many fish in an area, that it is difficult not to snag one accidently with even a single hooked fly. If you don't think that a foul hooked 12- to 16-pound salmon doesn't give one heck of a fight, you should try it some time.

The tackle that is used is pretty strong. Rods should be from 8½ feet to 9½ feet and be able to handle a #8, #9 or #10 weight line. It is necessary to fish on the bottom, therefore sinking lines or at least sinking tips are advisable. Naturally weighted flies would be in order. I have seen anglers fishing with flies the way I used to fish bait with a fly rod. They would put about 100 yards of monofiliment line (about 10-pound test) on their fly reel in place of the flyline. To the end of the line, which served as the leader, they would attach ¼-ounce sinker. About 1-foot up from that they would attach a 4-inch dropper to which they would attach the fly. To cast it

A proud angler with a 16-pound chinook salmon. (Photo courtesy of Bob Linsenman.)

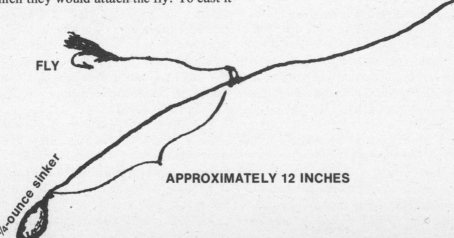

FLY

¼-ounce sinker

APPROXIMATELY 12 INCHES

would be easy. About 30 feet or so of the monofiliment was stripped from the reel and allowed to hang loose. The rod was simply flipped as though you were casting a spinning lure. The weight of the ¼-ounce sinker made the cast. It's not typical fly-fishing, but it helps get the fly to where the fish are. If the sinker is not bouncing on the bottom it will be necessary to add more weight.

THE STEELHEAD

Although the steelhead is simply a rainbow trout that has gone to sea and not a salmon, I have included it in this chapter since it is anadromous, as are the salmons (making the transition from fresh to salt water then back to fresh water to spawn).

The steelhead in many respects is the equivalent on the West Coast to the Atlantic salmon on the East Coast. They will both spend from one to several years at sea before returning to their freshwater environment. It is during this journey that they develop great strength, evidenced by their powerful fins and spectacular jumps.

Although it gained its initial popularity on the West Coast and is one of the more important freshwater gamefish from northern California up through British Columbia, the steelhead's introduction to the Great Lakes has made them a great attraction in that area, especially on the Michigan peninsula.

The steelhead will spend its first 1½ to 2 years in the freshwater river system before it migrates to sea. The next 1 to 3 years that they spend at sea is where their

(Below) Mixed bag of salmon and steelhead that took deep fished weighted nymphs in the fall. (Photo courtesy of Bob Linsenman.)

(Above) A 14-pound October salmon being untangled from net on the Pere Marquette river in Michigan. (Photo courtesy of Bob Linsenman.)

Two nice steelhead that liked the offerings in the angler's fly box. (Photo courtesy of Bob Linsenman.)

rapid growth takes place. Although they have been caught over 30 pounds, a more realistic average in a good river system could be from 8 to 14 pounds. The fish returning after only 1 year at sea will be relatively small, in the 2- to 4-pound range. The fish that stay longer will be considerably larger upon their return.

On the West Coast, there are steelhead returning from sea almost every month of the year. This varies with the different systems, and local knowledge is the key to knowing when the fishing is best. Those fish that enter the river in the fall and winter are referred to as winter fish—these are the most abundant. Those that enter in the spring and summer are called summer fish. Each new freshet or raise in the river level brings in new schools of fish.

Although the summer runs of steelhead are in the minority, fishing for them in the fall can often be the most interesting and exciting. At those times, the waters are often at a moderate level and quite clear. The techniques for fishing for these summer fish are quite similar to those used for the Atlantic salmon—both wet fly and dry fly. The tackle and fly patterns used are also about the same.

The majority of steelhead fishing, however, done

This fine 11-pound steelhead would be a good average anyplace. (Photo courtesy of Bob Linsenman.)

(Right) Steelhead fishing is often the best when there is snow on the ground. (Photo courtesy of Bob Linsenman.)

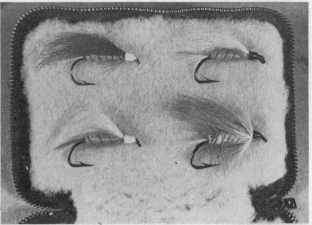

(Left) Four typically large #2 heavily weighted steelhead flies for big rivers.

(Right) A sinking tip #11 weight line was used to get the fly properly down to this waiting steelhead. (Photo courtesy of Bob Linsenman.)

Patience and persistence pay off with a fat steelhead by bouncing the fly on the bottom. (Photo courtesy of Bob Linsenman.)

under less favorable water conditions from late fall through the winter and into the spring. During these seasons the rivers are high and quite roily much of the time. This requires the usual steelhead technique which is getting the fly right down to the bottom. Since river conditions can change quickly, it is advisable to keep in touch with a tackle shop or a friend in the local area where you intend to fish. If you are thinking about going and they say that the conditions and fishing is good, you should get there right away before the conditions change.

The rods used are 8 to 9 feet long and handle #6 to #8 lines for the summer fishing. The winter fishing will usually require slightly heavier outfits of 8½ feet to 9½ feet that handle #8 to #10 lines. The lines used for the winter steelhead will usually be of the sinking type in order to get and keep the fly on the bottom of the river.

The flies that are used for the summer steelhead are pretty much the same as those used for Atlantic salmon with one major variation. The dry flies could be easily interchanged, as could most of the wet flies, if you were going to fish the greased line method of the across and

East, Midwest, or West, the steelhead will always be a prize to catch. (Photo courtesy of Bob Linsenman.)

198

downstream swing technique. The difference is that much steelhead fishing is done with flies fished on the bottom of the stream. Where it is illegal to fish with weighted flies for Atlantic salmon, it is almost the expected technique for steelhead. The flies used to bounce the bottom are usually made to imitate or suggest a cluster of salmon eggs, or a large nymph. The egg imitations are tied in bright colors of orange, yellow or red. The large nymphs or wet flies are sometimes tied with bright colors, but most often utilize the colorations of the naturals.

The flies used for the winter steelhead fishing are all wet flies and large nymph patterns. Since they are all designed to be fished on the bottom, they are heavily weighted. Naturally these flies are fished with sinking lines. In fact, more and more fly-fishermen are using sinking shooting heads for this type of fishing. They find that they can cast farther using about 30 feet of a #8 or #9 head with a monofiliment running line of about 20-pound test. This line will also sink faster and stay down easier, since there is less drag of the current on the smaller diameter shooting line than there would be on the regular flyline.

The fly sizes used on the larger rivers for their wet fly patterns, especially on the northern rivers and into British Columbia are fairly large. . . . #4's up to #1/0. However, the smaller rivers will usually produce very well on flies tied on #10 to #4. The technique in fishing a weighted fly on the bottom can sometimes be tricky. The problem when the water is high is knowing where to cast and how to manipulate your line so that you get the fly down as deep as possible. If the water is not too high and has some character to it, you can read the holding water similar to the way you would for regular

trout fishing. Then work your fly through those runs or pools. If you can feel your fly bouncing on the bottom, you know that you're getting down to where the fish are. Using as short a line as possible will give you the most control. Many times the water will be clear enough that you will be able to see the fish in their holding positions, or you may know from other information that there are steelhead in a particular location. This is where patience and persistence can pay off. Try to take a position for a good presentation and make sure your fly is bouncing on the bottom. Keep working the fish and periodically change flies, sometimes even going back to one that you had on before. You will hang up on a lot of rocks, but you will also hook some fish. If you are not having too much success with the standard flylines, try the monofiliment and sinker rig illustrated earlier for chinook and coho salmon. It will surely get your fly down.

I remember one early spring fishing for winter steelhead on the lower Michigan peninsula. The Little Manistee River was relatively clear, and I could spot several good sized fish that other anglers had worked for a while, then abandoned unsuccessfully. I started bouncing my flies down the run and could see that several casts went right by the fish. I also saw one good fish turn slightly to look at one fly as it went by. Well, I'm sure that I made close to 50 presentations to those fish, and many of my flies managed to get wedged in the rocks, costing me a couple of them. After a while I was getting a bit bored and was not concentrating fully. When my fly would get caught in the rocks, I would just give it a pull, pick it up and make another cast. On one cast, however, I felt a rock, and gave a tug, but the "rock" tugged back. I would have liked to have seen

Knowing where the fish lie makes it easier to get one to the net. (Photo courtesy of Bob Linsenman.)

the expression on my face when that 10-pound steelhead vaulted into the air and came down with a crash only 15 feet from me with my fly in the corner of its mouth. It taught me to be patient, and it has often paid off. There are times when you should cover a lot of water to try to cover the most fish, but if you can pinpoint them, it pays to work them well.

On the West Coast, steelhead can be found as far south as the Russian River north of San Francisco, California. Their range then extends north into Oregon, Washington and up into British Columbia. Northern California has the Eel River, the Klamath and Trinity Rivers which have good fall runs, and the Smith River near the Oregon border that has good winter fishing, to name a few.

Oregon has many excellent river systems that boast excellent steelhead angling—some summer fish and most winter fish. Most of the Columbia River system and its tributaries are good producers. The summer runs peak in October and November. Near Portland are the Kalama, Lewis, Willamette and Cowlitz Rivers. The Deschutes in north central Oregon also boasts of respectable summer fishing around August and September. The Rogue River in the southern part of the state, and the North Fork of the Umpqua River are famous for their fly-fishing for steelhead and have excellent summer runs of fish. In the Umpqua, fish are coming in sporadically throughout the entire year. There is a 36-mile stretch of the North Fork of the Umpqua that is regulated to fly-fishing only, for those who wish a bit more solitude and sport.

The state of Washington has over 150 rivers open to winter steelhead fishing. The best may possibly be the Skagit. Some of the others that are equally famous are the Kalama, Klickitat, Skykomish, Green, Cowlitz, Columbia, Wind and Sol Duc Rivers to name a few. These are only a few of the many good steelhead rivers that are available on the northern West Coast, not to mention British Columbia which also has many excellent rivers.

The Michigan peninsula provides some excellent steelhead fishing. Surprisingly, steelhead runs occur in almost every river that empties into the Great Lakes— even the Detroit River. The major rivers in the lower

An 8-pound female steelhead being released in the Little Manistee River, Michigan. (Photo courtesy of Bob Linsenman.)

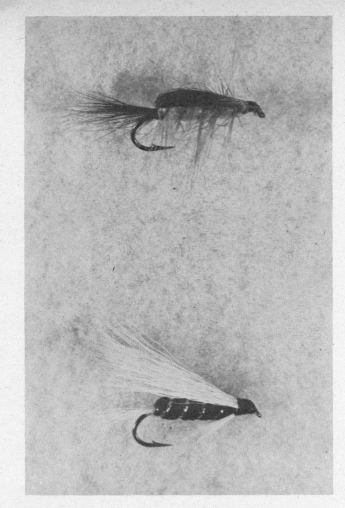

A Michigan Wiggler (top) and Michigan Skunk (bottom).

The flies used in the Michigan peninsula might be a bit smaller than the average used out West. The size range would probably be from #4 to #10. If there were two patterns that I could give you that are known to be good producers, they would be the Michigan Wiggler and the Michigan Skunk. These flies are probably the most popular on the peninsula and have accounted for many big fish. The materials for these two patterns are listed below. One important point is that you should be sure to use very strong hooks when tying flies for steelhead or salmon. Popular hook models are Mustad #7948A, #3407 saltwater and #36890 salmon hooks.

MICHIGAN WIGGLER
BODY: Yellow chenille with brown hackle tied palmer
TAIL AND WING CASE: For squirrel tied in for the tail and laid over the entire top length of the fly, then tied in again at the head.

MICHIGAN SKUNK
TAIL: White bucktail
BODY: Black chenille ribbed with medium silver tinsel
WING: White bucktail
THROAT: White bucktail

Over the past 10 years, the Salmon River that flows through Pulaski, New York, north of Syracuse, has become extremely popular as a salmon and steelhead fishery. The best time to have a chance at the really big steelheads is in January and February. At that time you have a chance to get one over 20 pounds. Unfortunately, the weather conditions at that time of year might not be the most comfortable. The flies used would be about the same as for the Michigan peninsula.

peninsula are: Muskegon, Grand, Rogue, White, North Branch of the White, Pere Marquette, Big Manistee, Little Manistee, Betsie and the Platte. Many of these rivers are relatively small and offer the opportunity to see the fish that you are working for. Lake Huron also has many good streams in its system. The better producers being the Ausable, AuGres and the Rifle.

BIBLIOGRAPHY

Bates, Joseph D. Jr. *Atlantic Salmon Flies and Fishing.* Harrisburg, PA: Stackpole, 1970.

Jorgensen, Poul. *Salmon Flies, Their Character, Style and Dressing.* Harrisburg, PA: Stackpole, 1979.

Wulff, Lee. *The Atlantic Salmon.* New York: A.S. Barnes, 1958.

Larry Solomon

CHAPTER 7
Fly-Fishing for Bass and Panfish

THOUGH MOST BLACK BASS anglers would, I think, agree that the use of a fly and some sort of an artificial fly, bug or popper has long been a most exciting and thrilling method of taking bass, no one has really been able to establish when the first bass were caught with long rods. We do know only that the first fly rods, designed originally for salmon and trout and not specifically for black bass, were early cane rods made entirely of split bamboo somewhere around the turn of the century.

While researching some early records of fly rod fishing for bass, it was particularly interesting for me to discover that some of the very first bamboo rods were ironically built by an angler named Green. Now my family tree of fishermen goes back a few generations, but to the best of my knowledge E.A. Green, the rod builder, was never a distant relative, as much as I'd like to have claimed that he was. But E.A. Green's first all-cane rods eventually led to the development of other better quality cane rods which ultimately in turn included fly rods.

Now the first of these fly rods was actually designed and constructed for the European market where a few sophisticated anglers wanted to try long rodding with greased flyline for Atlantic salmon, even then considered by most Europeans a gamefish fit for royalty.

Most of this information is according to Dr. J.A. Henshall, a distinguished writer/angler, who published a book in the year 1881 entitled *The Book of the Black Bass*. Dr. Henshall's book was the first of such writings totally dedicated to a single warm water gamefish species, in this case the black bass. Since the black bass was Henshall's favorite fish and since Henshall was adept at using the long cane fly rods, it might be justified to say that Dr. Henshall was, in part, the father of fly rod fishing for the black bass. In those early days the use of long rods for bass was almost unheard of until Henshall published his book.

Through *The Book of the Black Bass*, Dr. Henshall planted the seed of enthusiasm for the sport of fishing for bass with a fly rod. Soon others would pick up the long rod and discover for themselves that this was indeed a highly contagious way to catch not only bass but all species of warm water gamefish. As interest grew over the years, so did the technology and an understanding of the fishery, both of which have raised fly-fishing in general to the high place it now holds as a tradition of superlative sport for anglers the world over. In my opinion, fly-fishing is simply a grand way to catch bass and panfish.

(Above) The fly rod is adaptable to live bait fishing as well as artificials.

(Right) A beautiful stringer full of black and white crappie taken on a fly rod.

Bass respond to artificial flies, bugs, and poppers unlike any other fish. Unlike the cautious delicate approach of the trout, the black bass is a noisy, gluttonous predator who shows no mercy, especially when attacking artificials that are fished on the surface. Often with seemingly reckless impulse it attacks suddenly and viciously without any prior warning. I have taken literally countless numbers of both largemouth and smallmouth bass on various flotables, yet still after more than 25 years there is that sense of tension and expectation that mounts as you creep; crawl, hop or pop some artificial creation on the surface, when you know that at any given second a bass may explode out of nowhere to engulf the offering. Watching your creation execute its seductive dance on the surface heightens one's pulse and sharpens the senses, for you know something is bound to happen, yet you cannot predict when or where. Thus when it does happen, you jump instinctively and the hackles raise on the back of your neck, just as though each bass was your first on a flotable. If that great expectation and thrill ceases to happen, I'll put my fly rod in moth balls and hang it up

for good! Fly rodding for bass is that kind of sport. I can still feel this sense of excitement after 25 years of fly rodding for bass.

Surface fishing for bass with a fly rod and artificials is only one form of bass fishing, but it's one you're not likely to pass by easily without being caught up in the offerings. The take, as sudden and as spectacular as it may be, is merely the final curtain to the proceeding moments when the angler's long rod becomes an extension of himself as he peers down the rod like a rifle and manipulates the line to make his flotable do a dance that will cure the curious and harvest the hungry.

To complete the picture you can add such aesthetics as a placid pond in summer, painted in yellow hues from the low light of a sun rising to meet the dawn or fading to close out the dusk—for this fishing I will waive all others. Yet, surface fishing is only one form of the sport. Sub-surface fishing for bass with artificials offers great sport and the variety of creations tied and used on black bass alone are even more diverse than artificials used by fly-fishermen in pursuit of cold water gamefish, anadromous gamefish or saltwater gamefish. Sub-

Fly rodding for smallmouth bass is increasing in popularity all over the United States.

These 12-inch smallmouth are more common in small tributary streams.

surface fishing permits the fly rodder to catch bass from any depth at any time of year, with a variety of offerings so unusually diverse that they stagger the imagination.

Yet, for all that fly rodding for bass offers, bass fly rod fishermen are still in the minority by a considerable percentage when compared to the total number of bass fishermen today. It's a puzzling fact to anyone who has ever caught a single bass with fly tackle. Yet because we are still in the minority, we can enjoy our form of sport in solitude, and perhaps that in some respects is a blessing.

DISTRIBUTION AND RANGE OF SPECIES

The black bass is classified as a warm water gamefish, which means simply that its metabolism is such that it functions in warm water better than it does in colder waters. Temperature, depending on the species (largemouth, smallmouth, or spotted bass) plays a most significant role in the catching of bass, and this holds true whether you're a fly, spin, or conventional caster. The general acceptable fishing range for most warm water gamefish is above 60 degrees, preferably 68 degrees. This does not mean that a fly rodder cannot catch bass in waters of less than these

204

(Above) This is a setting in every bass bugger's brain.

(Below) Author lands a river smallmouth with a fly rod.

temperatures because you can, but the metabolism of the bass is such that when the water temperature drops below 60 degrees, bass are noticeably less aggressive in behavior than in water above 60 degrees. In water temperatures less than 50 degrees, bass as well as most other warm water gamefish become so sluggish that they become almost semidormant in state. Unlike trout, salmon, steelhead, and other cold water gamefish, the black bass is a solitary fish not a free roaming migrant. Once a bass locates a suitable feeding or nesting area within the habitat, it will quickly establish a territory and defend it.

Temperature change, especially on the downward trend, is about the only variable that will drive a bass out of an established feeding or nesting area. Most habitats will vary in temperature from deep cold waters to more shallow, warmer waters. Thermoclines (a temporate layer between cold and warm water) are usually established at given depths within most big bodies of water. Whatever the layer is, for that given period of time, it will hold at one constant depth throughout the lake.

Bass then, are known to move about within limiting ranges of their habitat seeking the warmer temperatures that are more conducive to their metabolism. Temperature then, becomes a principal key to fishing success, which suggests simply—find the right depth and temperature and you'll find bass. Modern technology with respect to sophisticated electronic fishing aids have proven this theory to be a positive one time and time again. The serious fly-fisherman would do well to keep these facts in mind when comtemplating which artificials he will fish and at which depths. Some of the most successful bass fly rodders that I fish with today use the same sophisticated electronic fishing aids that the conventional bass fishermen use when fishing the tournament trials.

The black bass has become the most popular of all the species of warm water gamefish over the years for two very sound reasons. For one, black bass are basically nonselective feeders, which means that they can feed on a very wide variety of prey that ranges from birds, rodents and reptiles down to tiny aquatic insects that land on the top of the water. Bass also eat the smaller fish and crustaceans that swim beneath the surface. In contrast to this, when food is scarce, bass can go for weeks, sometimes months, without feeding at all.

As species of freshwater fish go, the black bass is extremely hardy and shows little susceptibility to diseases that so adversely affect many other fish. For all these reasons this species of bass will increase rapidly given any opportunity at all.

The second reason for the popularity of bass is its wide range and distribution throughout the entire North American continent. Bass of one species or another are found in every state including Alaska and Hawaii. They

The author and his guide compare a brace of largemouths.

have populated large reservoirs, small lakes, rivers, creeks, farm ponds, irrigation ditches, and canals. The fertilized egg (zygote) of the black bass is of a sticky nature. Wading birds such as egrets, flamingos, herons, bitterns, cranes, storks, and such, not to mention a host of other migratory waterfowl, accidentally pick up fertilized eggs while wading the shallows where bass have spawned. The sticky eggs cling to the birds' feathers

This husky largemouth inhaled a big black popper.

206

(Above and left) The float tube and one man rubber raft are ideal for the fly rodding bass fisherman. You can manuever into areas where boats cannot.

and legs, and when these birds migrate to other waters, the eggs drop off, hatch, and thus populate waters that never before had been introduced with bass. The same holds true for other warm water species of gamefish whose eggs are also susceptible to these airborne drops. This is nature's way of aerial restocking.

In many areas the bass (because of its predatory nature) soon becomes the top of the food chain order, thus it becomes the dominant species. The bass is also a cannibal, so if its food supply becomes depleted for any reason, it merely preys upon its own kind. In fact, some fishery biologists claim that big bass sometimes show a preference for little bass over other species sharing the same habitat. This may serve more of a biological benefit than given credit to. If a bass eliminated much of its competition among equal predators, it is, in fact, insuring itself of more forage upon which it can then prey. If too many little bass were allowed to survive and become big bass, then soon few prey would be left. If the source became completely exhausted, the bass would then himself be facing slow growth for lack of food, or in some cases, complete starvation.

But since bass will eat just about anything it can stretch its jaws over, the latter usually does not occur except in some isolated incidences. These are good things for fly-fishermen to remember, because knowing the many things that bass will eat broadens the range of artificials by which fly-fishermen can experiment with and use as acceptable baits for catching bass. Avid bass fly rodders usually become avid fly and bug tiers.

All those days of early trial and error experimentation with respect to what bass *will* or *will not* eat are long behind us, yet praise be to those early experimenters. Today's highly thought out, technically advanced, fly-fishing tackle—encompassing rods, reels, lines, leaders, and a seemingly inexhaustible variety of artificials— has been so beneficially constructed that the bass fly rodder has virtually no limitations or restrictions with regards to tackle. Fly-fishing tackle suitable for bass today is probably as advanced as I'm ever going to see it get in my lifetime.

Anglers can find or tie their own artificials (depending on their skills) to closely represent every known prey of all the species of warm water gamefish. To that artificial they can tie a leader of any desirable taper, length, and breaking strength, and to that they can attach a flyline of any design or specific weight of gravity to fish anything and everything from the surface to the bottom and everything else in between. To cast that line, the fly rodder can obtain any number of fly rods of numerous materials, weights and lengths that will accomplish precisely what the angler wishes to do, providing of course that his own skills are proficient enough to permit him to accomplish his goals.

And last but not least, to that fly rod the angler can attach any *number* of fly reels to hold any size and weight flylines. Personally I feel the reel is the least important piece of equipment. I consider the reel first as a storage spool for your flyline and only second as a functional necessary part of the actual playing of a bass. But I'll cover this under proper fly-fishing equipment later in the chapter.

As to the bass itself, though great fighters they are, great distance runners they are not. What this equipment phrasology really means in essence is this: If you cannot catch a bass, it is no fault of the design or manufacture of your fly-fishing equipment. Though each of the four principal species of bass—the Florida largemouth, the Northern largemouth bass (*Micropterus salmoides*), the smallmouth bass (*Micropterus dolomieui*), and the spotted bass (*Micropterus punctulatus*)—varies slightly in its feeding moods, the fly-fisherman need only remember that any and all of these four species of bass (including some hybrid subspecies) are aggressive predators that will respond only too willingly to artificials that in any way closely resemble those creatures lower on the food chain than they but sharing the same habitat. Matching the hatch is much a part of this game, and it's a superb fascination to those fly rodders who tie their own artificials.

Bass have their moods like any other fish and at any given time may display uncooperative moods, even when everything seems to be correct and going in your favor. I call these uncooperative periods biological

(Below) Bass engulf bugs with a sucking sound that raises the hackles on the back of any fly rodder's neck.

(Above) A 4-pound largemouth is all you can ask for on a fly rod. Anything above that is a bonus.

shutdowns, and when they occur, you might as well hang up your fly rod and wait it out. Shutdowns may be caused by a change in barometric pressure, water clarity, temperature, phases of the moon or whatever. But whatever the reason is, it's a biologically inherited one which neither man nor machine can change. Even the most skilled of fly rodders has to respect the laws of nature even when they are against him, and when it comes to moods, few freshwater gamefish I know of are as moody and unpredictable as the black bass. Yet it's this part of the character of the bass that makes it such a refreshing challenge even to the well seasoned black bass fisherman.

Finding and catching black bass with fly tackle is no different than finding and catching bass with any other kind of tackle. Strong winds that drastically curtail fly casting may be the only thing that would keep a fly rodder off waters still fished by conventional anglers. A factor to remember when searching for black bass is that all bass are fond of substrate. Substrate is a very general term which identifies anything above or beneath the surface that a bass can take refuge in, find shade under, or catch food on. Substrates include rocks, trees, brush, lily pads, grass—you name it.

This does not mean that bass are only found on these substrates because bass are often found schooled at various depths in open water with no substrate within hundreds of yards. But if you were to spend any number of hours fishing bass with a fly rod and artificials, you

(Above) Fly rodder, Dick Gaumer plays a farm pond largemouth.

(Left) Three-pound smallmouth are considered good size in most western rivers.

would, I think, ultimately come to find that better than 75 percent of your catch will consist of bass that were caught on or near some kind of substrate.

I fish bass with a fly rod a great portion of the year, yet seldom do I catch bass on flies in open waters void of substrates. My greatest percentage of fish come from shorelines, dense with brush, trees, limbs, logs, and other ideal substrates. Even when I'm fishing big rivers or small streams for smallmouth or largemouth bass, I'll always try to find some shoreline brush, overhanging trees, or shady substrates where I can place my offering.

Bass do not like very swift water so I concentrate on those slower moving backwaters, eddies and shorelines out of the main stream of a river's current. It doesn't seem to matter if I'm fishing streamer flies, nymphs or wet flies beneath the surface or popping bugs, deerhair sliders or dries on the surface, the best catches of bass from rivers and streams always seem to come from

209

places where some kind of substrates are near and always in those slower stretches of the stream.

Though water temperature is very important, an avid fly rodder willing to experiment with a wide range of surface and sub-surface artificials can catch bass anytime of year, anywhere in this North American continent. The difference between success and failure usually is proportionate to how much time the fly rodder is willing to give to experiment on new or strange waters known to be inhabited with bass. The species responds pretty much the same to artificials anywhere, providing that water temperatures are taken into consideration.

Regardless of where you live, if it's on the North American continent, you're probably within a short drive to some piece of water that is inhabited by some species of warm water bass or sunfish. Take the opportunity to investigate even the most unlikely looking spots. You may find a surprise waiting in store for you.

BASS AND PANFISH—PREDATOR/PREY RELATIONSHIP

To speak about any one species of fish in any given habitat, one must also include other species that share the same habitat. To exclude neighboring predators and prey alike from the environment of the black bass would be as much of an injustice to the fishery as it would be to the fishing. The black bass shares its habitat with a wide variety of other warm water gamefish of which the largest group of fish living in a predatory/prey yet commensal relationship with the black bass are the panfishes.

The term panfish is rather general terminology for a broad range of species of flat-sided fish of the freshwater sunfish family. Depending on where you live and fish on the North American continent, panfish are more specifically referred to as perch, bluegill, pumpkinseeds, crackers, warmouths, bream, green sunfish,

The secret of catching crappie and panfish during midday hours is to fish in the shade.

This angler works a sunken tree for black crappie.

red-earred sunfish, nesters, rock bass, and a host of other local or regional references. Though most are separate species, all fall under the general classification of freshwater perch, so designated because of their rather stubby, broad, yet flat-sided perch-like torsos. The name panfish is significant of the fact that one of these delicious eating species fits perfectly into a fry pan.

Included in this group are two other principal species that also are very much a part of the black basses' common habitat. These are the white crappie and the black crappie, also true members of the sunfishes.

I really think it quite impossible for an ardent black bass fly rod angler not to catch panfish, if only by accident, during the course of several black bass outings, unless of course, one should be fishing in a controlled environment purposely void of panfish. In natural environments panfish greatly outnumber the bass in most warm water habitats.

Panfish are aggressive little gamefish that will eagerly attack most all offerings of artificial bugs, poppers, and flies. On occasions too numerous to count, I have hooked panfish barely larger than the artificial bug or fly I'm using. Though panfish lack the large hinging jaws of the bass, panfish will try to eat anything that they can stretch their tiny mouths around. Many a bass fisherman has responded to a vicious surface strike only to discover a panfish has eaten his offering.

Black bass fly-fishermen in particular will at one time or another come in contact with some species of panfish, and if any one of these perch-like species had the capability of developing into the size that bass grow to, the bass would soon take a back seat to panfish. Size is the one limiting factor that dampens the enthusiasm of some. Yet, despite the fact that any and all of the aforementioned species rarely exceed 12 inches in length, they are each and every one a fine fighting fish (unquestionable game), and a fine match of the fly rodders who pursue panfish with the kind of light fly tackle that permits this fish to display its character against properly proportioned tackle.

Crappie have rather large mouths, and although considered a sunfish they have been known to attain weights exceeding 5 pounds. Yet, pitted against one another of equal size, I personally believe that the common bluegill can out-match either black or the white crappie in fighting ability.

Panfish offer a greater range of fly rod challenges than do crappie for two principal reasons. First, is the fact that in North America there are only two species of crappie but there are numerous species of panfish. Secondly, and perhaps more relevant to fly-fishing, is the fact that panfish feed well off of the surface, whereas crappie rarely feed off the surface. This can be substantiated by the fact that 90 percent of the crappie's diet consists of minnows, whereas 90 percent of the panfish's diet consists of aquatic as well as non-aquatic insects.

Plump bluegills like this one inhabit farm ponds all across North America.

A young boy poses with his first fly-caught crappie.

Once you locate a school, you can usually catch panfish two at a time.

The split caudal fin on this crappie indicates that it was on a spawning nest.

This is particularly true in the spring, summer and fall months when insect life around fresh, warm water habitats greatly intensifies. This is not to say that a crappie will not take a deerhair bug, floating popper or dry fly, because occasionally they will, but for the most part crappie confine their feeding to sub-surface.

All panfish, including the crappie, share one common trait that fly-fishermen would do well remembering, and that is that panfish, like the basses, feed principally on live, moving creatures. Again I must cover myself by stating that panfish have also been known to eat things that range from dough balls and salmon eggs to cheese and canned corn, but these are for the most part isolated incidents. A lot depends upon the panfishes' metabolism. Like the bass, panfish are basically warm

Lucky Lloyd holds up the author's string of bass and panfish.

212

water fish, therefore their metabolism and feedings intensify as the water temperatures increase. In midwinter when water temperatures are at their lowest, panfish (like bass) become almost semidormant to the point that even a live, dangling red worm (better known in fly-fishing circles as a garden hackle) won't often stimulate a strike even when it's dropped on their nose. With some exceptions, fly-fishing for panfish certainly is at its minimum during these extremely cold water periods.

(Left) The shade beneath bridges, wharfs, and piers are hot spots for panfish.
(Below) A plump sided crappie struck the author's fly.
(Below left) In most California lakes, anglers are urged to keep all the crappie they catch in order to thin the populations to prevent stunting.

But from spring's earliest thaw through fall's first frost, fly-fishermen and panfish coexist quite well. Panfish are exciting because they are such diverse feeders. Most any offering that simulates an insect will most assuredly be challenged. Because panfish feed on insects they are real patsies for artificial flies resembling insects. Panfish will feed sub-surface, and standard patterns of wet flies, or comparatively small streamer flies are naturals for most all panfish including crappies. Crappie, though, seem most fond of small feather and hair jigs, but in sizes small enough and light enough to be effectively fished with the fly. Short quick jerking movements of an artificial fly or jig will bring a crappie to immediate attention, especially during the spring spawning months.

Panfish feed best though off the surface during the warmer periods of the year, and the dry fly trout purist who has yet to experience the challenge of putting his artificial trout flies to work over schools of panfish have missed a part of living as essential as breathing. It's not that panfish take dries so spectacularly, because generally they don't. But they'll take most *any* dry fly you can offer so long as the angler gives the artificial that sudden little twitch that indicates life.

Generally the panfish will stalk its prey, rise slowly beneath, and with sudden sucking motion inhale the offering from the surface. That sound of a panfish inhaling an insect or artificial fly from the surface can be easily duplicated, as it is the same sound you get when you pucker your lips together and suck in air sharply, as if you were to blow a kiss to someone across the room. It's that sound that often makes an ardent bass angler bite off a large bass popper and stick on a small dry fly fitting of the panfish. Often when bass are not on the feed, panfish are.

Like the basses, sunfish of numerous species are found throughout most all of the freshwater rivers, streams, lakes, ponds, sloughs and other warm water habitats on the North American continent. Sunfish are a particular joy to catch on light tackle which makes these scrappy little fighters a natural for the fly rodder. Sunfish are schooling fish, so where you find one you generally find dozens if not hundreds.

You can catch sunfish all year long and even through the ice in mid-winter months with a variety of subsurface offerings. But my favorite time of year to fish sunfish with the fly rod is during the spring spawning periods when sunfish build nests in shallow waters along the sand or gravel bottom close to shore. Sunfish

Once the fly rodder locates a spawning bed, it's a fish on every cast.

The author poses with a 2½-pound crappie.

214

will then strike savagely at any intrusion that invades the territory of their nesting sites. I've sat in a float tube or boat many times and caught and released sunfish on artificial flies hours on end. It's truly as interesting a fishery as the bass fishery.

PROPER FLY-FISHING EQUIPMENT

There really is no such thing as the perfect fly outfit for catching bass and panfish. The word perfection addresses an absolute, and when it comes to the subject of fishing, I've learned that there are few, *if any*, absolutes. The perfect outfit is purely in the eyes of the beholder. There are, however, certain standards regarding the rigging of fly rods, reels, and lines for bass fishing and panfish which the beginner or novice fly-fishing enthusiast would be wise to pay close attention to. In order to carry out any form of casting (especially fly casting), some attention should be directed to balancing or matching the outfit—that is the proper fitting of rod, reel and line.

A matched or balanced fly outfit permits the angler to

The author with 100 crappie which will make 200 delicious fillets.

accomplish his casting goals with grace and efficiency. This is not to advocate any premise that you simply cannot catch bass or panfish with an improperly matched or balanced fly outfit. Again, what may be considered a perfectly matched, well-balanced outfit by one angler may well be rejected by another. I look upon proper fly casting as an art form. Casters, like all artists, range from good to poor, but seldom will you find a good caster using improperly matched or unbalanced fly tackle. Any good caster knows the benefits of a properly rigged fly rod, reel and line.

Many teachers of fly casting more bluntly preach that there is *only* right from wrong, and few in betweens. For the benefit of this chapter I choose to use more lenient terminologies like "efficient" and "inefficient," with room for those that fall somewhere in between. What I'm saying in essence is that it's alright to use improper fly tackle, but you should know that you're facing a definite disadvantage by doing so. This is especially true to the newcomer or novice fly caster. Remember that a good fly caster can pick up a poorly mismatched, unbalanced fly outfit and make it perform. The angler does this by improvising with his own skills at casting. But it is tough enough for a newcomer to make a well balanced fly outfit work for him, let alone try to fight poor tackle while also trying to learn the art of fly casting.

When I tell you that picking up a #5 weight 7½-foot ultra light fly rod and attaching a #12 weight forward taper to it is inefficient, I mean just that. Each fishing situation with respect to the various artificials calls for a specific kind of tackle. Knowing the different combinations will benefit not only your casting, but your fishing

Author and wife with strings of crappie and catfish taken on a fly rod.

(Above) Fly rodders should remember that bass are non-selective feeders and will eat just about anything.

(Below) The author with a limit of bug caught large-mouths.

as well. To simplify matters we will examine the different flylines and fly rods that specifically fit the various ways to present a wide variety of artificials for first the bass, and then the panfish.

Fly Rods

Since the fly rod serves as the angler's principal casting instrument, we will discuss the rod first. From the earliest years to present day we have witnessed a major transition in fly rod design from the earliest split canes to the modern graphites. Ironically, in action at least, we are back to the originals, though alot of well gained technology has been learned and put to good use in between. The early cane rods were quite rigid (stiff) to the feel, yet when loaded with a proper weight line, they flexed and cast beautifully. This is principally what we're finding in some of the newer graphite fly rods of today. When you pick a graphite fly rod off the rack and flex it without load, it feels quite rigid. But once loaded with the proper line weight, we see the graphite flex and perform beautifully. Both the modern split cane fly rods and the graphite fly rods share this hidden aspect. Today's graphites, like today's split cane fly rods, share yet another similarity—both are expensive.

Though fly-fishing, like everything else around us, seems to be progressing constantly, many fly-fishing professionals believe that with the advent of the graphites we have advanced our technology about as far as we ever will with respect to fly rods. Perhaps. Perhaps not. Now we're experimenting with boron and who knows what's next?

But in between we went through several fly rod trends that included everything from solid fiberglass, tubular steel, and aluminum, to hollow fiberglass. We saw slow, parabolic actions, and fast tapered actions, all of which worked either to the likes or dislikes of fly-fishermen, many of which were fanciers of bass and panfishing. In those early days most all emphasis was put on rod design, while in comparison little emphasis was placed on new flyline concepts. Today, of course, line technologies as well as selections has equalled, if not exceeded, fly rods.

Personally at the present time I'm partial to using the graphite fly rods over standard fiberglass for *one* specific reason. I fish to relax, which means I don't want to rush at anything, particularly casting. I like to fish slowly, which also means I like to cast slowly, something you really cannot do with those quick responding, fast-tapered fly rods.

Graphites are fast *if* you fish the recommended line weight. However, since graphites are so powerful, they take well to overloading. I purposely overload my graphite fly rods with lines one to two sizes greater than the rod calls for. If my 8½-foot graphite calls for a #7 weight line, I purposely fish a #8 or #9 line on that rod. Overloading a graphite one to two line sizes slows its action considerably without affecting the rod's performance, and that makes the graphite perform like an expensive cane fly rod. Overloading (with respect to one or two line sizes) is a misleading word because you really *do not* overload a good graphite by just a minimal increase of one or two line sizes. It still makes for a well balanced outfit, but the novice fly caster should stick with the recommended line weight as indicated on the rod.

The size line and rod I use is governed entirely by the waters I fish just as much as the choice of artificials I choose to present to the bass are also geared to the waters I fish. Fortunately, I have a number of fine fly rods to choose from which I find helps to induce the maximum pleasure out of the sport. I use ultra light fly rods and light lines for certain artificials fished over certain waters, and other large longer fly rods with heavier lines for different waters and larger artificials. But for years, I fished bugs for bass with only one fly rod and realized that the majority of fly casters also do the same. Knowing what I know now, if I were to go back to choosing just one fly rod to serve all needs, it would probably be a 9-foot length graphite that is capable of handling line sizes that range from a #7 through #10.

There are numerous graphite fly rods on the market today, many of which I own and fish exclusively for bass. I have my personal preferences based on performance for this particular kind of fishing. The brand name graphite fly rods I personally fish bass with most are Fenwick-Woodstream, Orvis, Skyline, and Scientific Anglers System rods. Since I have several of each

(Above) Lloyd Eiserman at the paddle, Larry Green at the fish.

(Left) The ultimate end of a great beginning.

in various lengths and line specifications, my choice varies with each fishing situation.

I fish largemouth and smallmouth bass with dry flies, wet flies, nymphs, streamers, deerhair bugs, sliders, fluff bugs, serpent flies, and floating poppers. All forms of artificials invoke their own sense of excitement and sport, but to me, there is no thrill like that of enticing a largemouth to rise to the surface. I am most fond of fishing balsa wood popping bugs with concave faces such as the great master bug builder, Lucky Lloyd Eiserman, of Turkey Creek, Missouri, builds. I've caught more largemouth and smallmouth bass than I care to count on poppers, and always, there is the same intense anticipation and excitement as if each were my first bass all over again.

Flylines

The lines I match to my graphite fly rods are either forward tapers or double tapers, but occasionally I'll

217

A good rod and a good line are the only basic necessities for bass bugging.

variety of weights, sizes, and colors to fit any bass or panfish fly rodder's needs. Sunset and Cortland as well as Berkley also offer many fine lines for this kind of fishing.

For my own bass fishing needs I use Scientific Anglers special bass bug taper lines for 95 percent of all my surface fishing with artificials. This bass bug line has a heavier, shorter front taper which is ideal for accuracy in the short cast. I've caught both bass and panfish on all of the various colored lines including bright orange, but my preference is to the light green line. Regardless of the line you ultimately choose, make sure it is a brand name and that its weight or size fits your fly rod.

Leaders

Little need be said about leaders, though I'm a strong advocate of the tapered leader for any and all fly-fishing. *Turnover* is a very important part of fly-fishing. A proper turnover means simply that your fly ends up at the end of your cast and not somewhere in the middle. On any cast you want the leader to fully unfold and your artificial to snap to attention at the end of your leader upon presentation. To accomplish this you must have a

Here the old master, Lloyd Eiserman, lands a good one.

also use level lines. Lines I feel, are really more important than the choice of fly rod, since it is the line that actually delivers your artificial to its intended target and not the rod. The rod serves merely as the casting instrument to propel the line. Modern flylines have come a long, long way in just a few short years. Taking the lead in new flyline technology are several principal flyline manufacturing companies, like Scientific Anglers, Sunset, and Cortland, though others are following suit.

At present Scientific Anglers offers a greater range and variation of modern flylines than any other company. They offer sinking lines of four different classifications to achieve four specifically different wet line fishing situations. Aside from sinking lines, they manufacture level flylines, double tapers, weight forwards, shooting tapers, and a special bass bug taper that I'm particularly fond of. All of these lines come in a good turnover. I've found a way to insure a good turnover on practically every cast. A poor turnover can result not only from a poor cast but from using too light of leader at the line end. To insure a good turnover I always make certain that the diameter (thickness) of my leader at the point where it attaches to the end of my flyline, is *no* less than the same diameter of the end of the flyline.

If a purchased tapered leader is not of the same diameter as the end of my flyline, I will add a 20-inch piece of good, stiff monofilament that is of that same diameter, and then to this 20-inch piece, I'll attach my regular tapered leader of 7½-feet or 9-feet. Unless I get off a really poor cast, I'll be insured of a good turnover. This is very important if, for example, you have but one shot to try and place a fly, bug, or popper in a small opening in thick surface weeds. You'll need a good cast and a perfect turnover.

Fly Reels

Purposely, I have left fly reels to the last, simply because in most cases concerning bass and panfishing, a fly reel serves little purpose other than storing your

The lower lip hold temporarily paralyzes a bass.

Fitting of the stringer is this 3½-pound bass which we used for camp meat.

line when you're not actually casting. Occasionally though I have hooked a big bass that has taken me into deep water, and then, and only then, has the reel and the drag feature of the reel played an important role in assisting in the taking of that fish. But since I'm such an advocate of the short cast for bass fishing, it makes my dependency upon a good fly reel even less important than those bass anglers who work their artificials at greater distances. I play 95 percent of my warm water gamefish on flylines I manipulate with my hands rather than with the handle of the fly reel.

Just the opposite is true when I'm fishing a fly for anadromous or saltwater gamefish; then the reel becomes *the* most important part of my tackle. But not with bass or panfish. Though I have a number of really fine, sophisticated fly reels, when it comes to bass and panfish, I prefer just a simple single action reel of moderate size. I use Scientific Angler's System reels numbered to fit my matching rods or Pfleuger's 1495 and 1495½ single action fly reels 100 percent of the time, and feel that nothing more important need be said about fly reels as it relates to still water fishing for bass and panfish. If the reel holds your flyline, it's accomplishing 85 percent of its job on or off the water. There are those exceptions, but with the short cast they are few.

SHORT CASTS AND CAUTIOUS STALKS

With relatively few exceptions, the use of the fly rod for black bass requires rather short casts of 50 feet or less. The exceptions might be long-lining for smallmouths on some big fast moving rivers, or a shorebound angler who tries to reach out to a particular distant piece of structure known to hold bass. In either case, the use of a float tube, rubber raft, or boat will eliminate the necessity of any long cast.

It's a practical statement, why should you execute long casts when you do not absolutely have to? The shorter the cast, the more control the angler has over his line, his artificial, and ultimately his fish. Long casts place the angler at a definite disadvantage pertaining to the hooking and landing of any fish. A black bass can rise, strike, inhale, and reject an offering from the surface with such surprising speed that by the time the angler has regained his senses and responds to the strike, the fish might already be long gone.

The more line you have played out between the tip of your fly rod and the artificial, the slower the response time, and the greater your chances are at missing strikes. It is, I think, appropriate about here to say something about the stalking of a bass in connection with short casts. Approach is an important part of fly rodding for bass when implementing the short cast. As effective as it can be, the short cast is of no use at all if you come storming into the intended fishing spot like a

The author and Lucky Lloyd with a husky stringer of fat, western largemouth bass, all of which were taken on a fly rod.

The take of a floatable by a bass comes swiftly and suddenly.

I never pass up a good looking shoreline.

(Below) For a bass fly rodder, nothing beats a placid shoreline in those early morning hours.

bull in a china shop. Always make your stalk or approach a slow, quiet, cautious one, regardless if you're in a pair of waders, a float tube, or a boat. Any sharp noise or ripple on the water can, and usually does, put surface feeding bass down. In the shallows a noisy approach will make bass retreat to deeper water. A cautious approach is an absolute must for bass fishing in still water sloughs, lakes, ponds, or backwaters and eddies of large waters. Remember that your quest is the black bass, and not some free swimming migrant that is constantly on the move, and therefore somewhat accustomed or desensitized to water movements, color change or other variables.

When it comes to travel, the black bass is a real stick-in-the-mud. Once a bass locates a decent feeding and resting area in any piece of still water, he will generally take up residence and defend this territory against all other intruders. The larger and meaner the bass, the better it is able to defend its claimed territory. Consequently, the biggest bass usually holds the best feeding zones in any given body of water. These are usually constants that vary little from one season to the next, although changes within the habitat will be noted due to changes within that season such as water temperature, fluctuation, light penetration, and water color.

When a big bass is removed from a particularly ideal feeding area, it does not take long for another bass of equal size and dominance to move into that same spot. Any angler would do well to remember this fact. Bass, like many creatures, follow a sort of pecking order by which according to size and stature, larger more domi-

221

to exercise good common sense and always use a quiet stalk. If you fly-fish from a boat, always wear soled shoes like tennis or boating shoes, carpet the bottom of your boat (particularly aluminum boats), and quiet your oar locks. If you use a motored boat, keep the speed constant, do not switch from low to medium to high and back again, as bass are easily spooked by this change, more than the running of the motor itself.

WHICH ARTIFICIALS WORK BEST FOR BASS

There really are few limitations pertaining to the makeup of artificials that the black bass will strike. Remember that unlike certain other freshwater species all species of bass are nonselective predators that will usually try to eat just about anything they can stretch their jaws over. There is only one criterion—the prey *must be* alive. It's a good point that fly-fishermen should remember. I have taken various species of bass with the fly rod on a wide range of artificials that include streamer flies, dry flies, wet flies, nymphs, woolly

This is the kind of water fly rodding bass men love best.

Tule ladden shorelines in those late evening hours will provide good and fast fishing.

nant bass keep moving smaller, less dominant bass out of the more suitable habitats.

As a dominant bass on or near the top of the pecking order becomes eliminated from its choice spot, the next bass in order of its dominance moves in, and this is reflected right on down the line. Each bass in a particular school sort of moves up a notch, causing a slight change in territories, but still within the same general territory. What all this jargon means to the angler is really a very logical explanation of why it is that certain spots always seem to yield bass of a certain size.

Removing one good bass from a certain location practically guarantees that the angler will *again* find a bass of equal size back in that same spot a few days, weeks, or months later. Sometimes the new occupancy takes place within hours. For this reason I make a visual list of any spot that yields a really good bass. I have a number of spots like this on waters I fish often, and over the years these spots have given up dozens of good bass, all pretty much equal in size. Making notes of the time, of the season, water color, temperature, etc. helps me to repeat my performance in each of these known big bass hot spots from time to time.

But the best advice of all in the stalking of any bass is

worms, deerhair sliders, fluff bugs, serpent flies, and regular poppers, not to mention artificial lures, spinners, and spoons and even certain natural baits that are adaptable to the fly rod.

I could write a lengthy chapter of my experience with each of these separate categories, but I won't. Instead, I'll write in general my own preferences as to which artificials I feel can produce the maximum thrill out of fly rodding for bass. To me, bass and surface fishing are synonymous. I've already mentioned my preference to surface fishing. Although once thought to be a mid-summer *only* sport, any fly rodder can take bass off the surface year long if they are willing to put in the necessary hours to experiment with bass in various habitats during cold water periods.

Regardless, whether the fly-fisherman chooses to fish the surface or sub-surface, a lot about how you present your artificial has to do with water temperature. Each species of bass in its known special habitat reacts a little differently, but basically the metabolism of the bass is triggered by changing temperatures. Each species like the largemouth, smallmouth, Kentucky spotted bass and Florida bass, responds best to different temperature ranges. Bass respond most aggressively to warming trends. On a temperature rise, say, coming out of the cold winter months into spring, smallmouths are the first to stir, then the Kentucky spotted, then finally the largemouths. I'll make a flat statement that applies to all these species by saying

(Above) Bugs in his hat—the identifiable trademark of a bass bugger.

(Below) A full color selection of balsa wood poppers handmade by Lucky Lloyd Eiserman of Turkey Creek, Mo.

simply that all bass become more and more active as the water temperature steadily rises from spring through the fall. Then again bass will become less and less active as temperatures begin to drop again from fall through winter. Remember that the bass is a warm water gamefish, I can't state it often enough.

The bass' metabolism does not necessarily govern which artificials you should choose to use as much as it governs how you work those same artificials. Here is where the angler should try to think like a bass, or at least get your mind on the same general wave length. I use a very simple formula for success when presenting artificials (particularly surface bugs) in direct accordance with the water temperatures. If the water is cold I fish S-L-O-W. As the water warms I begin to speed up the actions of my artificial. An old master bug tier and bass artist with a fly rod, Mr. Lloyd Eiserman of Turkey Creek, Missouri, taught me this many many years ago, when we fished together in California.

"Lucky Lloyd," as he is called, proved to me that he could catch bass on a surface popper in 40-degree water in the dead of winter. He did so many times by working his bass surface popper so slow that he'd often roll a Bull Durham cigarette between "pops," letting his bug stand motionless for several minutes on end. This same old bug fishing master fishes his same home-tied poppers so fast in the heat of summer that I often wonder how a bass could catch up with his bug—but they do, and by the thousands I might add. Speed then is a considering factor geared to water temperature.

Another good point to remember about fishing the surface pertains to the depth of the water you're fishing. Bass (for as aggressive and predaceous as they are) can be as spooky as an old, sore-jawed brown trout in a chalk stream. The shallower the water, the spookier a bass may become. A bass that has some deep water close at hand where he can quickly retreat to in the face of a threat, is at least a little less spooky.

Noise, the kind the angler creates with his artificial offerings, can work for you or against you. For this, I also have a simple, productive formula you may want to remember and try for yourself. The deeper the water, the more noise and action I put into my artificial. The shallower the water, the quieter and least action I put into my offering. If you plop a big surface popper down in only a foot or so of water and give it a big loud pop, you're very likely to send even these concealed bass scampering off to deep water. That same noisy surface commotion, though, worked in deep water, may be very necessary to lure and in fact steer bass onto your bug from deep water or muddy waters.

On the other hand, the gentle presentation of a small, lightweight surface bug like a silent deerhair slider, dry fly, or feathered bug, carefully, quietly, and slowly eased across the surface of some bass inhabited shallows, usually will induce a non-suspicious bass and produce an immediate pounce from a bass feeding the shallows. Use common sense and this simple formula. In shallow waters use quiet stalks, and small offerings, and fish quietly and slowly. In deep water or murky water also use a quiet stalk but use larger bugs, preferably hollow-faced poppers, worked with added life and commotion. In some cases you may find the opposite to be true, but if so, these occasions will be rare.

Surface Bugs Fitting for the Avid Bass Fly Rodder

Regardless of their descriptions, surface bugs are the most exciting to fish over bass for all of the obvious reasons. My personal choice above all of the many surface artificials used for bass is the hollow-faced poppers usually made of balsa wood or cork.

Second only to these hollow-faced popping bugs I prefer the silent, slider head, deerhair bugs, and last but not least, the dry fly. The three principal species of bass (largemouth, smallmouth, and Kentucky spotted) will respond favorably to most all artificial surface bugs. The productivity of each, of course, depends purely on the angler's skills at presenting these artificials to bass in such a manner that the fish is without any suspicion, and that what it sees and hears is a live creature that somehow found itself on the surface in unfriendly territory.

Many things can be interjected into a bass' mind in the period of the offering. It is the angler's job through his skills to remove all suspicion and compel the bass to attack the offering. Done correctly, the bass will come to the bug, not gently, but with a savage splendor that will startle any living thing in the surrounding environment, most of all the angler. That's what surface fishing for bass with a fly rod is all about.

Fishing Sub-Surface Artificials for Bass

Though far less than 50 percent of my own personal fly-fishing exploits for black bass involve the use of sub-surface artificials, I should make it clear that my preference is slanted to surface purely because I like to see the take. However, I must admit that the majority of large bass I catch, in say a year's time, do come on sub-surface artificials. Sub-surface artificials are of as great or greater range of diversity than surface artificials.

An experienced tier can duplicate any one of dozens of small fish with streamer flies, all of which represent natural prey for bass. In addition nymphs, wet flies, and all sorts of imitations of amphibians, bugs, eels, frogs, waterdogs, crayfish, and what have you, are at times deadly on all species of bass on all warm water habitats.

I would rate the streamer fly at the top of the list with exception to only one other artificial, that being the serpent fly. Serpent flies, tied with 5- to 7-inch long saddle hackles represent eels or snakes. I needn't remind any ardent bass angler how effective the plastic worm is on black bass. Well the serpent fly bears close resemblance to a plastic worm when it's retrieved

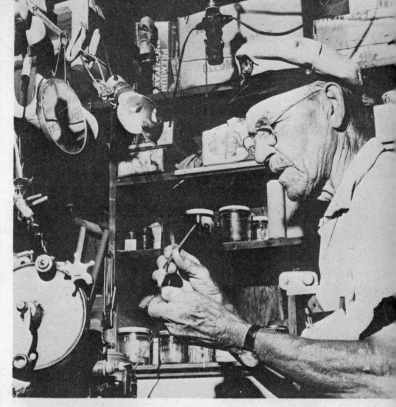

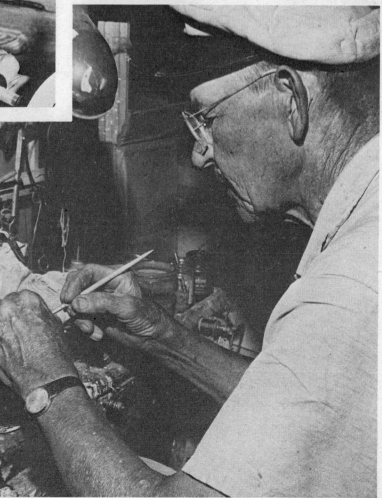

(Above) Master craftsman and bug builder, Lucky Lloyd Eiserman, at work.

(Above right) Here, Lloyd creates his masterpieces in his humble shop.

(Right) Each bug is hand-crafted and hand-painted.

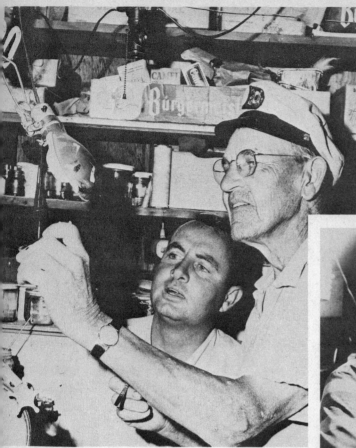

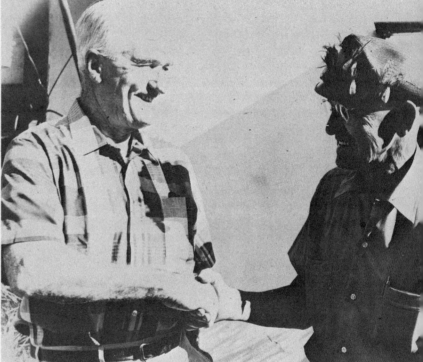

(Left) Author is amazed at this old gentleman's works.

(Right) Here, the late great Joe Brooks congratulates Lucky Llody Eiserman for his works.

(Below) Author admires Lloyd's full color line of bugs.

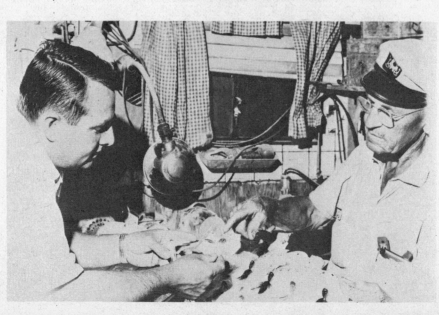

slowly through the water. Tied in a variety of colors and lengths serpent flies have been my singlemost effective artificial (fished sub-surface) for big bass.

The color or style of any artificial fished sub-surface is more to the fisherman's preference than the fish's, although bass, like most fish, can clearly distinguish colors. If I were made to choose only one or two colors based on my own personal experiences, I would choose either black or purple. I should state, however, that I have caught most all species of bass on a variety of sub-surface artificials that at one time or another cover the entire color spectrum and in this respect your guess is probably as good as mine on any one habitat.

WHICH ARTIFICIALS WORK BEST FOR SUNFISH

One of the beneficial things about all the species of sunfish in general is their willingness to attempt to eat a wide variety of offerings. Sunfish are very predaceous little gamesters whose aggressive nature is restricted only by its size and not by its temperament. In comparison to a bass of equal size, sunfish have small, short hinging mouths, yet sunfish will attack things much larger than they can possibly swallow.

Fly-fishermen are no less restricted to the range of artificials they can use on sunfish than for the use on black bass. The only mandate is that the angler must think in smaller terms. Any artificial with a hook too large to fit into the tiny mouth of the sunfish may be batted around a bit, but it can't possibly be eaten, therefore the sunfish can't be hooked. The only exception to this family of fish are the black and white crappie which have rather peculiarly large mouths.

Since I've already clearly stated my preference to surface fishing with the fly rod throughout this chapter, it's only fitting that I start talking about surface artificials adaptable to the sunfish. All of the surface creations mentioned for bass are equally effective on sunfish when tied and fished in smaller sizes. Artificials from as small as a size #16 hook up to about a size #4 hook will catch sunfish.

Of all the surface artificials mentioned earlier in this chapter including poppers, dry flies, sliders, etc., there is one very unique type of artificial specifically designed for sunfish with the fly rodder in mind and in my opinion one that far exceeds any other. These are the soft,

The author's pocket selection of woolly worms, sponge flies, and beetles for bluegill and other members of the sunfish family.

sponge bodied imitations with soft rubber legs protruding from the sides. These artificials are usually flotables tied in a variety of colors and shapes, but most are cut or tied to represent some sort of six- or eight-legged creature like a water walker or a spider. I have caught more species of sunfish on these lively looking creations than all the other artificials combined.

Why I believe they are so effective is because the long soft rubber legs give the imitation insect or spider such realism. The slightest touch of your line or sudden soft pulse with the tip of your fly rod sets these rubber legs into action. Sometimes the artificial will roll or spin almost as if it were truly struggling to escape its fate. That action drives sunfish right out of their tree, and to tell you the truth, I haven't found a breed of sunfish yet that could resist the antics performed by one of these soft rubber legged bugs in the hands of a skilled fly rodder.

As effective as they are, the rubber legged sponge bugs are only one of many, many artificials that panfish in general will strike. This is no secret as evidenced by the shelves of the sporting goods retailers today. You'll probably see 10 panfish poppers or bugs to every one popper or bug tied and designed specifically for black bass. Leading fly tackle manufacturers like the Gaines Company of Pennsylvania, the Weber Tackle Company of Wisconsin, the Glen L. Evans Company of Idaho, and many, many others, that all make an almost endless variety of poppers and bugs incorporating every known color pattern.

When fishing these artificials in search of panfish, choose the same general areas that you would normally expect to find bass. The depth at which you're most likely to find schools of sunfish will vary according to the season. Think in terms of temperatures rather than depths, and you'll ultimately find the right depth. Remember that those spring spawning periods are the times when sunfish are most aggressive, and this is also the time that you find most sunfish in sandy or rocky bottomed shallows, sitting over nests.

These six artificials are colored, sponge-bodied insects with soft rubber legs which no panfish can resist.

(Above) Crappie like rocky areas as well.

(Right) The only difference between black and white crappie is a slight change in coloration.

Regardless of the pattern or style of submersibles you fish, remember that the best retrieve is a short snappy jerky motion that brings the artificial along in inch long snappy jerks. Panfish, including both species of crappie, cannot resist this snappy life-like movement in an artificial.

FLY-FISHING'S PRESENT AND FUTURE

It has taken the better part of 70 years for fly-fishing to establish itself with any solidarty in North America, but now that fly-fishing is more than just the "in" thing for sportsfishermen to do, we must look to the future to insure its stability.

Aside from the technological advances in fly-fishing tackle, we must become equally strong in perpetuating fly-fishing sports to the degree that we recognize the importance of the fishery itself. After all, what would fly-fishing (or for that matter any fishing) be without fish to fuel our fascination in the first place. This may sound silly, but it should be a sobering thought. My philosophy regarding any fishing sport is that the more we can do to gain popularity of the sport, the more we do to increase an individual's support to insure that sport's survival, and in insuring the survival of the sport, we insure the survival of the species.

In the case of the freshwater bass we have only recognized the full potential of this species in the last 10 years. Black bass and black bass fishing may have been fashionable from the beginning in portions of the deep South and midwestern states, but before the late 1960s freshwater bass were considered a nongame species of little interest in many of the remaining states. In a few areas the black bass was actually considered a trash fish. Today we know better, and because we know better, the fishery has gained such nobility that it is in better shape ecologically than it has ever been.

There are presently populations of bass as well as panfish firmly established in more North American waters than ever before. Yet, numbers alone do not necessarily indicate stable fisheries. There are constant threats upon this fishery; threats that every avid bass angler should be fully aware of.

Threats Upon the Fishery

Within any living environment there are natural checks and balances which tend to control all species in a manner that attempts to insure survival. Left alone, nature takes care of itself quite well. We can see nature at work in the world of fish with something as basic as the predator/prey relationship of fish coexisting in the same habitat.

There are enough natural forces at work in nature to regulate the population density of most all aquatic environments and its living organisms. The thinning or reduction of any species by natural causes usually serves some biological purpose, either short-range or long-range, even though man may not fully understand what these purposes are at the time. For instance, it seems

A selection of poppers, jigs, streamers, and wet flies, all suitable in size and design for the taking of sunfish.

totally senseless that porpoises and whales beach themselves time and time again, even when they are led back to sea by man, until they finally die. Do they beckon to a call so strong that the will to die supersedes the will to live? These are questions we may never know answers to, yet the porpoise continues to survive quite well in spite of such things, just as they have for thousands of years.

Though we do not always understand such purposes of nature, they are in fact natural and with purpose, and that makes even the strangest of acts acceptable. What I find totally unacceptable are threats upon the species from unnatural causes, principally by the hand of man, not by fishing mind you, but by careless acts like the dumping and over-spraying of chemicals into streams, rivers, and lakes, or the manipulation of water levels during critical spawning periods. Man, it seems, for all the beneficial things we are capable of doing for fish and fishing, does not always manage the resource to the best of his capabilities. Personally, I think that on an individual basis, one of the smartest things any avid bass fisherman can do to fulfill his part is to join an active bass club, one that has a conservation officer. Bass club conservation officers should be kept well informed about legislative moves that may pose threats upon the fishery in their particular area. A well informed conservation officer can in turn inform his club members, and as an organization, the total membership can become involved in changing improperly posed legislation into proper legislation, which does not hamper, but rather enhances the fishery.

Keeping on top of current proposals, even in small areas is the best way to insure good fishing in the future. Many active bass clubs now work very closely with various state fish and game departments, U.S. forestry departments, and other government, state, and regional agencies. A bass club with an active membership can provide money, manpower, or both to help correct or establish better fishing by working on various habitat problems. Bass memberships in various bass organizations are doing this all over North America now. You might even think about starting a bass fly-fishing club in your own area. You'll probably be very surprised to find how many fly rodding bass fishermen you'll drag out of the woodpile.

Since I am an avid fly-fisherman who believes that the most sporting way to catch a bass or panfish is with a fly rod, I'm very interested in doing whatever I can to help perpetuate the species whenever and wherever I can. Hopefully in this manner I can save at least a piece of the fishing I love best for my son and daughter, and hopefully their sons and daughters.

Larry Green

This photograph shows the author's preference to both bass and panfish artificials.

CHAPTER 8
Saltwater Fly-Fishing

HISTORY

"**THE EEL SKIN** used mainly along New England shores is attached to a hand-line, and cast into and drawn rapidly through the boiling surf of the ocean; the squid is towed with trolling tackle behind sail or row boat in the quiet waters of the Middle States; *while the fly is used with stout rod and long line wherever the fresh current of some river haunted by fish falls directly into the salt water of the sea.*" This is an excerpt from the chapter on striped bass fishing in the book *Superior Fishing,* by Robert B. Roosevelt, 1865 (italics by the author).

The above 1865 reference to fly-fishing on the Potomac River for striped bass is ample evidence that fly-fishing in salt water is not the new sport that we sometimes would like to think. The nature of the three pages of description that follow in the book indicate further that even at this early date, saltwater fly-fishing was widely followed by some anglers.

According to Roosevelt, fly-fishing for striped bass was common along many rivers in the mid-Atlantic, particularly in the South, and that standard salmon fly-fishing rod, reels, lines and leaders were used. Flies consisted of simple (like those of today apparently) patterns of red, yellow, and red/white to take striped bass of up to 20 pounds or more. Fly-fishing technique was similar to that practiced today for salmon—drifting

a fly in the current so that it would swim in the surface, but not on it as with a dry fly.

There are other records of fly-fishermen, primarily well-to-do Englishmen on trips to America, bringing their fly-fishing tackle with them to take tarpon and sea trout in Florida in the mid 1800s. Their tackle then was long fly rods of up to 16 feet made of ash or hickory, and later of a "new material," greenhart.

The 1878 book, *Camping and Cruising in Florida,* by Dr. James A. Henshall, more widely known today for his book on black bass fishing, contains references to the author taking tarpon, redfish, snook, sea trout, jack crevalle, bluefish and other species with his freshwater fly-fishing tackle. Bonefish were likely first taken in the early 1900s in Miami.

In 1912, Henry Flagler had completed his Florida east coast railway from Miami to Key West to further open access to the Keys for fishing, including fishing with the fly rod. The Long Key Fishing Club kept records on fishing for eight species, and considering its membership of Zane Gray, Andrew Mellon, Herbert Hoover, and the wealthy and elite from England, it is probable that some fly-fishing was practiced. Any records of such which might have existed, however, were lost when the club was destroyed in the Florida Keys hurricane of 1935.

Later on, in the 1930s the Rod and Reel Club of Miami, Florida, began to keep records on catches with the fly rod of popular species of gamefish, including tarpon and sea trout. The book *Florida Fishing*, by Stewart Miller, published in 1931, also recounts that fly-fishing at that time was extremely popular for such species as tarpon, barracuda, snook, jack, channel bass, sea trout, bluefish, mackerel, dolphin and grouper, using streamer flies and feathered minnows. Howard Bonbright developed his still famous and popular tarpon fly early in the 1900s, and it was sold by Abercrombie and Fitch in the 1920s. Preston Jennings, more famous for his classic freshwater fishing books, *The Dry Fly and Fast Water*, and *The Salmon and the Dry Fly*, also fished for tarpon on the fly rod in Florida in the 1930s.

Flies of the early pioneers were simple at best. Bluefish flies were tied at the turn of the century or before with the wing at the bend of the hook to keep the toothy-fish as far from the leader as possible. Flies for striped bass were simple, often full bodied with plain simple colors not unlike the most popular patterns today. Some of the early flies for bonefish, first taken on the fly about the 1930s, even contained pork rind in them, much to the dismay of fly-fishing purists. It was initially thought that bonefish would not take a fly at all, and must only be fished for with some type of bait or bait attractant added to a fly.

Unfortunately, saltwater angling with a fly rod was not properly recognized until recently, and early writings seem to have been widely scattered in newspapers, magazines, and only in some cases, in books. No doubt, newspaper morgues on all three coasts might still today contain articles which would shed light on the saltwater fly-fishing accomplishments of early anglers. Even with any scattered angling records which might exist, it seems that the main thrust of saltwater angling interest came in the 1920s and 1930s and then immediately after World War II in the Florida area. The area was rich for exploration, rich with untapped angling resources on the flats, in the cuts and canals, and offshore during a period when the population perhaps for the first time had time and money for experimenting with a new sport and recreation.

Obviously, then as now, fly rodding attracted anglers in a way that other methods of saltwater fishing have yet to match. The light rod more typically thought of as a proper match for bluegills instead of bluefish, trout instead of tarpon, brought out the challenge in many. The climate of the subtropical south Florida area along with the thrill of stalking and sight fishing for so many species, the possibility for experimentation in flies, tackle, methods, approaches and techniques and the development of the skills necessary to take large fish on light rods, single action reels and fine tippets, was as appealing then as it is today.

TACKLE—RODS, REELS, LINES

While freshwater fishermen are cognizant of the need

Leon Martuch with a fly rod caught bluefish taken in the Chesapeake Bay. Fish was caught from Captain Bruce Scheible's boat, chumming with medhaden. A Lefty's Deceiver fly was used to take the fish.

for different fly outfits for different species of freshwater fish under different conditions, the myth seems to persist that only one outfit is needed for all types of saltwater fly-fishing. While this might be true for you if you are only after one type of fish under one set of conditions, a change of coastline, species or type of fishing might dictate something radically different from what works well in your own backyard.

Another tackle myth believed by many is that anyone even considering saltwater fly-fishing must lay out a few hundred for the tackle—a Fin Nor or Seamaster quality reel, a specially custom built rod to take the

233

Only inexpensive tackle is required for much fly-fishing as shown by this catch of shad.

into about four different categories, based on line weight, that will take care of anything that can be caught in the salt water on flies. These include:

1. A 7½- to 8-foot long rod to take a 6-weight line, single action reel with a weight forward line and 50 yards of backing. This outfit is suitable for white perch, shad on both coasts, and similar small species that are easy to take with a small fly and which won't run far when hooked. The same outfit will be ideal for bonefish, provided the reel is changed to accommodate 100-150 yards of backing. Consider it for all fish in the 1- to 6-pound range.

2. An 8½-foot rod balanced for an 8-weight line, single action reel, spooled with a suitable weight forward line and 100 yards or more of 20-pound Dacron backing. Such an outfit will present a larger fly and also have the power to cope with medium size bluefish, medium size striped bass, small tarpon, large bonefish, snook, small dolphin, flounder, small barracuda, small jack crevalle. Use it for any fish in the 5- to 15-pound range.

3. A 9- to 9½-foot rod balanced to take a 10-weight line, and matched with a single action reel, weight forward line, and 150-200 yards of backing. Such an outfit is ideally suited for fish in the 15- to 20-pound range including large bluefish, large striped bass, medium size tarpon, big snook, medium size dolphin, big barracuda and big jack crevalle.

4. A 9-foot rod designed with a strong butt and good

Fly and striped bass.

heavy lines that are frequently associated with saltwater fly-fishing, bulk spools of Dacron backing, an assortment of flylines or shooting tapers, and a few gross of flies to suit all occasions.

Both myths can be torpedoed pretty quickly. First, saltwater fly-fishing is just that—fly-fishing in salt water for any species that you fancy. Thus, if you practice all aspects of the sport, it quickly becomes obvious that it takes different tackle for white perch, sea trout, bonefish, tarpon and shark, just to name a few. Some saltwater fly-fishermen will be outfitted with one outfit; others will need several for their different fishing; and others end up with broad range collections of tackle suitable for everything from ½-pound white perch to 150-pound tarpon. But to say that only one outfit will suffice for all saltwater fly-fishing is as foolish as saying that one fly outfit will take all freshwater species from small stream 6-inch brookies, to lunker largemouths or large pike.

Generally, saltwater fly outfits can be broken down

234

Example of tackle—rods, reels and flies for small inshore species of gamefish like shad, white perch, sea bass, others.

lifting and control power, matched with a 12- to 13-weight line, large capacity single action reel of high quality, and spooled with a weight forward line, and 200 yards or more of 20- or 30-pound backing. Such outfits are tough and designed for big fish exclusively. Fortunately, they are usually used only for "sight fishing" for fish, so that they are not cast all day long, but instead cast only when a fish or the suspected presence of fish is spotted by the angler, guide or captain. These outfits are designed for fish over 50 pounds and ranging to 150 pounds including really big tarpon, billfish, sharks and big dolphin.

Obviously, there are chinks in this line of armament, and some areas and some fish might be more adequately fished for with say a 7-, 9- or 11-weight outfit that would fit in between some of the above categories. And, for a real challenge on smaller species or bonefish, there is no reason why a 4- or 5-weight outfit can't be used under appropriate conditions of fly size and wind.

As mentioned above, species and size of fish is not the only criteria for choosing a certain size outfit. For example, in the Chesapeake Bay, bluefish and striped bass in the 1- to 5-pound range are ideal fly rod fare in the fall when they school on the surface chasing bait. If size and species alone were the criteria, they could be easily handled on a size 5- or 6-weight outfit. But two

conditions frequently exist, either of which would force going to a heavier size 8 or 9 outfit. First, when the fish are schooling on the surface, they are actively chasing small bait fish in the 2- to 3-inch length. Thus, a large fly that will closely match the size of the bait is required to get any interest out of the fish. And a large fly that will imitate the bait just can't be cast effectively with too light an outfit. Secondly, wind is always a factor in the Chesapeake Bay, as it often is in many other coastal areas. The wind conditions often gust to 15 knots or more and a line lighter than a size 8 just couldn't cope with the wind and get a fly—even if a small fly could be used—out to the fish. Sometimes, it is even difficult with a size 8 or larger line. Thus, for careful selection of any saltwater fly-fishing outfit, four factors—species, size of the fish, size of the fly required to take the fish and wind conditions—are all equally important and must be equally considered.

Even when the size of the outfit is determined, the use in salt water forces other considerations in tackle choice as well. Salt spray, and for that matter, even salt air is corrosive and tackle must be chosen that will stand up to this constant exposure.

Rods
Choose an action that is best for the fishing. Some fly rods are either too soft or too fast taper (stiff butt and

flexible tip) and either of these extremes are poor choices. Often you will be required to pick up long lengths of line. For this a rod that is parabolic bending, but with a strong butt section is a must. This becomes even more important in the really large outfits which should be chosen more for their power and lifting capacity than for their casting ability.

Guides should be noncorrosive wherever possible. There are several types of guides available today. The snake guides are traditional and still found in the majority of saltwater fly rods. But be sure to insist on, or if you are building your own, be sure to purchase, guides that are stainless steel with a hard chrome plating. Aetna foul proof guides and similar flex foot guides sit higher on a rod and some prefer them since they reduce line friction against the rod blank. Most of these are hard chrome plated over stainless steel. The Fuji ceramic guides such as the BSPHG (black), SPHG (bright) and the BZG guides all have stainless frames,

Ed Given with a large tarpon taken in Costa Rica at Casa Mar Camp. Note the heavy tackle extension butt on the fly rod and also the forward grip on the fly rod for extra comfort when lifting big fish.

A 21-pound blackfin tuna taken on the fly by Lefty Kreh.

are lightweight and suitable for saltwater fly-fishing.

One, two, or in the case of the really large saltwater rod, three of the butt guides are stripping guides similar to spinning guides. They can be ceramic (most often preferred today) or wire, but should have a stainless steel frame. An important factor in all guides and matching tip tops is that they should be large—often far larger—than those found on freshwater rods. The larger fish caught in salt water will run line far more rapidly through the guides, and the knots connecting line-to-backing and line-to-leader will often run back and forth through the guides several times in the course of a fight. A hang up due to a small guide can cost a fish or a rod.

Grips should be comfortable, either of cork or the new synthetic materials of hypalon, cellite or foamlite. I

Large tarpon taken on the fly. Note the typical Florida tarpon fly of hackle and wing tied in at the bend of the hook.

Suitable reels for saltwater fly-fishing include the Pflueger (left top) and Zebco (right top) and the Scientific Anglers (left bottom) and Fin Nor (right bottom). Quality and size of reel is determined by the type of fishing.

still prefer cork for fly rods, since it is firmer and makes it easier to put the final "punch" into a forward cast for maximum distance and a tight loop for control.

Reel seats should be large enough to take the foot of any fly reel to be matched with the rod, anodized to resist corrosion and with double locking nuts to hold the reel firmly in place through a long day of fishing. For larger fish and fishing, consider reel seats with either permanent or detachable extension butts to aid with leverage while fighting a fish. If you are considering records, make sure that the extension is not too long since some organizations prohibit extension butts longer than 2 inches, while others allow butts to 6 inches long.

Reels

Wherever possible, saltwater fly reels should be made of corrosion resistant materials. Also, unlike many freshwater fly reels, they should have a relatively large capacity (line plus backing) and a good drag system. This doesn't mean, however, that less expensive

reels are unsuitable in salt water. It just means that the reel must be chosen with care considering the above three attributes. And the first—corrosion resistance—is not that important provided that the reel is carefully washed after each trip (each day) and sprayed with WD40, CRC, LPS-1 or similar antimoisture sprays and lubricants.

Using the above criteria, it is entirely possible to go saltwater fly-fishing for smaller species using the relatively inexpensive Pflueger Medalist. It has long been considered a staple of the freshwater fly-fisherman, but in the larger sizes is also suitable for saltwater fishing for the lightweight species.

When considering any fly reel for salt water use, consider the following:

Construction—It should be of anodized aluminum or similar noncorrosive material where possible, and with brass or stainless steel innards for maximum long life.

Action—Automatic reels have no use in salt water since the drags are poor and the many parts are almost sure to corrode and freeze up in a short time. Single action reels, in which one turn of the handle retrieves one turn of the spool, are the most popular and found in most of the fly reels today. Multiplying reels are those with gearing that retrieves two or more turns of the spool with one turn of the handle. Orvis and several other companies make such models, usually in the high price range.

Drag—A smooth drag with no roughness or unevenness during the fight is a must for any fish over 5 pounds and an absolute must for the bonefish, big tarpon, sharks, and similar species that will take out more line on one run than a freshwater angler will find trout taking in a decade of fishing. Most of the better drags are large composition cork or Teflon combinations. They do require periodic checking and oiling to prevent them from getting glazed and useless.

Durability—All saltwater fly reels will be subject to more knocks and hard wear than freshwater models so that construction should be sturdy. Reels with lots of screws to hold posts, reel feet, etc., in place should be checked frequently to make sure that they are tight. Also be sure to check these points for corrosion

that sometimes builds up there first. Reels that of this date work well in the salt include:

Pflueger Medalist 1498—Inexpensive, sturdy, large line capacity and suitable for a majority of fly-fishing for smaller species.

Daiwa 732 and 734—Flanged spool for hand drag control; adjustable click drag, enough capacity for light saltwater fly-fishing, sturdy construction and priced right. Double handles prevent vibration with the run of a fish.

Zebco 178 Cardinal—On the small side, but features a flanged spool for hand control, adjustable drag, adjustable click, and suitable for small species.

Pflueger 577 and 578—Designed for saltwater fly-fishing, good drag, enough line capacity, higher priced than the above, but as a medium priced reel, suitable for all but the really big stuff in salt water.

Shakespeare 1898 model—Similar in features to the above, but a little bulkier. Good drag, well made, will take all fish but the real biggies.

Scientific Anglers Reels System 6 through 11—All will perform well in salt water, good click drag, flange spool for hand control, good line capacity. Medium priced.

Typical example of saltwater fly-fishing. The guide poles from the bow of the boat, one angler sits in the middle waiting his turn, while the other casts from a casting platform in the stern. Sometimes poling is done from the stern and the casting from bow platforms.

The wide range of models makes it imperative to pick the model best suited to your fishing, fish and line.

Fin Nor—Available in several sizes and with the Sea Master ranked as the best available. Spools and frames are out of bar stock aluminum, superb drags, excellent construction, high priced.

Sea Master—Also available in several sizes and ranked with the best available today. Like the Fin Nor, they have excellent construction, super drags, and are high priced.

In addition to the above, there are several other new reels on the market which are proving to be super in salt water, but all are high priced and any angler should be

Shooting heads and long casts with large streamers are used to take big striped bass in San Francisco Bay, such as this striper caught by angler Dan Blanton.

prepared to drop several hundred in buying one. All are excellent and in high demand among the top saltwater fly rodders of the world today. They include the John Emory Fly Reel, and the Orvis Multipliers.

Lines

Today, it sometimes seems like there are more flylines available than there used to be saltwater fly-fishermen. And many of the vast assortment of lines available are suitable for saltwater fly-fishing.

Flylines come in different sizes to match rods, in different tapers for different types of fishing and floating, and different sinking lines for these specialized forms of fishing. Obviously, the line must match the rod, or as mentioned before, the line should be suited to the fish, fishing conditions, wind conditions, fly used and then the rod matched to the line and fly combination. It is my firm belief that only the weight forward line and the shooting tapers have any place in saltwater fly-fishing. Both will cast quicker (less false casts), further (more weight in the belly and smaller running line) and can still make for a delicate presentation when needed by using the proper leader for the line and fly.

Many companies now have special, shorter belly saltwater tapers that are designed for saltwater fly-fishing, and are far better than the longer belly weight forwards that were originally designed for bass bug fishing in fresh water.

Shooting heads are another type of flyline, originated and, until recently, used on the West Coast, but now gaining acceptance everywhere. They consist of a 30-foot long flyline to which is attached a 100-foot long shooting line of small diameter designed to run freely on a cast for maximum distance. Both floating and sinking shooting heads are available, and for running lines, anglers use either 30-pound monofilament, or the special very thin level flylines made expressly for running lines by the flyline companies.

Floating, intermediate, sinking, fast sinking and extra fast sinking lines are all suitable for various types of saltwater fly-fishing. The floating probably finds use in 90 percent of the saltwater fly-fishing situations, since in many cases fish are cast to while breaking on the surface, schooling in the shallows, cruising on the flats or when staked out in a boat and sight fishing for them. But for bonefish on a deep flat, an intermediate or regular sinking line will get the fly down in a hurry to present it to the fish before they change direction in their often rapid zigzag course of picking up bottom food.

Fast sinking or extra fast sinking lines will get the fly down deeper, quicker and are ideally suited for fishing blind in those situations where fish are known to be. An example would be fishing the mid-Atlantic for sea trout where the fish are schooled each spring in the bays and estuaries and where a slow strip of a fly down deep is the only way to get the fish. The extra fast sinking lines are best not only for getting down extra deep, but also getting to moderate depths in a fast moving current or tide.

While all flyline manufacturers make a wide variety of lines, perhaps the best for the saltwater fly rodder in terms of maximum selection is Scientific Anglers. Their selection includes lines of all sizes, and tapers (including Air Cel Salt Water Tapers) and floating, sinking and intermediate lines. The sinking lines, in terms of sink rate, include the Wet Cel I, Wet Cel II, Wet Cell Hi-D, and the Wet Cel Hi-Speed Hi-D shooting tapers and weight forward tapers. The latter sinks especially fast and deep, and compares favorably with the lead core lines that are particularly favored by West Coast anglers.

For virtually all saltwater fly-fishing, except for the smallest fish, backing is needed behind the 90- to 100-foot long flyline. The best choice is Dacron. Other lines, such as monofilament and nylon braided line will stretch and, under the pressure of fighting a fish, can build up pressure and damage the side plates of the reel. Dacron will not stretch (to any appreciable degree), is strong, fine and can usually be easily spliced for connecting loops.

For most saltwater fly-fishing use 20-pound test, although you might want to consider 30-pound test for really big fish insurance, or 12-pound test for small reels, light outfits and smaller species.

LEADERS, KNOTS, FLY BOXES

Leaders

Leaders and flies are just as specialized in saltwater fly-fishing as they are in freshwater fly-fishing. But they are specialized in different ways. For example, for freshwater fishing you are most often concerned with presentation and the long, delicate leader necessary to do the job. The saltwater fly rodder might have the same concern with some species such as bonefish and permit, but for toothy fish such as shark, barracuda, bluefish and the like, a shorter stouter leader with a shock tippet will be a must to keep the fish from cutting off.

While there are endless leader formulas, combinations and theories for saltwater fishing, just as there are for freshwater fishing, leaders can be broken down into general categories that will serve most fishing needs or serve as a starting point for any needed changes that specific fishing conditions warrant.

1. A 7½- to 10-foot leader tapered down to a fine tippet—appropriate to the fish, water and fishing conditions.

2. An 8-foot tapered to a tippet and ending with a shock tippet of wire or heavy monofilament.

3. Three feet or 4 feet of level leader ending with a tippet and fly for sinking lines. The short leader prevents or minimizes any floatation or upward bellying of the fly

Typical white perch catches and small flies and light tackle.

to keep the fly down close to the level of the sinking flyline.

4. A 7-foot to 9-foot level leader, but ending with a tippet (to comply with record requirements) and a shock tippet.

Basically the above leaders would apply to saltwater fly-fishing as follows:

Leader #1—Bonefish, redfish, permit, jack crevalle, baby tarpon, any other small to medium size fish on the flats or in shallows.

Leader #2—For any toothy fish, such as bluefish, shark, barracuda, king mackerel. Light short shock tippets or mono are often used for flounder, weakfish, and other species with small teeth that could wear away a regular tippet in the course of a fight.

Leader #3—Can be used with a regular or shock tippet, for use with any sinking or sink tip flyline, to get the fly down close to the line depth, for maximum rapid sink rate of the fly.

Leader #4—Specialized leader used for big gamefish only. The heavy level mono keeps the leader from wearing through on the skin of the fish in the course of a long fight, while the short tippet qualifies for any records, and the shock tippet prevents the fly from being cut off. Used for shark, billfish, etc.

Knots

Knots are extremely important in saltwater fly-fishing. The right knot is required at several points—including the backing to flyline, flyline to leader, sections of leader and leader tippet or shock tippet to fly. The reel-to-backing connection is nothing more than an overhand knot around the standing part of the line. Strength is not important here since, if a fish takes that much line, it's all over anyway.

Backing to Line Connections: Interconnecting loops make it possible to keep the same backing, yet change flylines easily. This can be done in the field, as in changing from floating to sinking lines for different

Example of connections possible from flyline to backing. Possibilities include, top to bottom: wrapped and spliced fly line loop; interconnecting loops; Uniknot in flyline and Pfeiffer's End Loop in flyline. The end loop should be covered with pliobond before using.

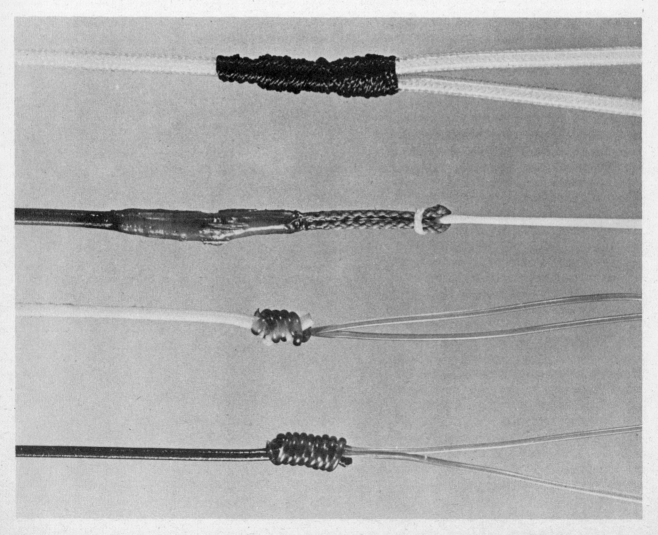

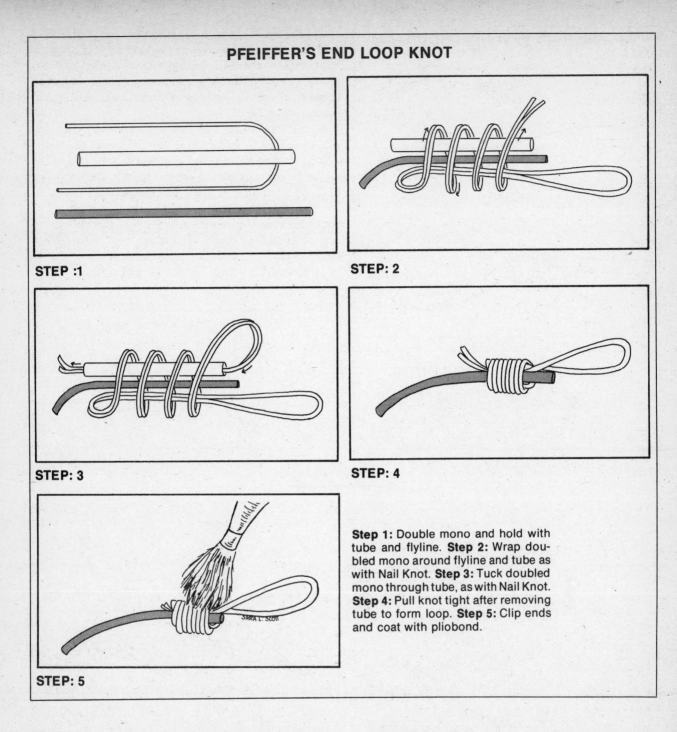

PFEIFFER'S END LOOP KNOT

STEP :1

STEP: 2

STEP: 3

STEP: 4

STEP: 5

Step 1: Double mono and hold with tube and flyline. **Step 2:** Wrap doubled mono around flyline and tube as with Nail Knot. **Step 3:** Tuck doubled mono through tube, as with Nail Knot. **Step 4:** Pull knot tight after removing tube to form loop. **Step 5:** Clip ends and coat with pliobond.

fishing conditions, or at your tackle bench at home to keep from retying knots. With Dacron, it is easy to splice a loop in the end with a splicing needle that is supplied with the line by some companies, or available from any good tackle shop. It is possible to form a loop in the flyline by several means:

A. You can use *Pfeiffer's End Loop* with mono to form a strong loop in the end of the flyline. This consists of a doubled monofilament tied in a Nail Knot directly onto the end of the flyline. This is nothing more than a regular Nail Knot, but tied with two ends of the line to make a loop.

B. *Spliced Flyline Loop.* Strip 1-inch of the coating off the end of the flyline, and fray out the braided core. Fold it over the flyline. Wrap with size A rod wrapping thread securely all along the frayed portion of the flyline. Finish as with a guide wrapping by wrapping the thread over a separate loop of thread, cord or mono. Cut the end of the thread, run through the loop and pull the loop through the wrapping. Cut any excess and coat with Pliobond or other thin, flexible waterproof coating.

Line To Leader Connections: A. The standard connection here is the Nail Knot. (See Chapter 2.) It is fast, secure, small and will pass easily through guides at the

SPLICED FLYLINE LOOP

1

2

end of the fight. Using this method it is possible to tie 3 to 4 feet of your leader butt section as a permanent attachment to the flyline. Generally 30- to 40-pound test mono is ideal for this butt section and will allow for easy transfer of energy from the flyline to the leader and ultimately to the fly.

B. Another connection that will allow easy changing of the leader is to splice a loop into the leader and to use a Surgeon's or Perfection Loop Knot at the end of the leader to connect with a spliced loop in the line. The obvious advantage is the interchangeability of entire leaders; the disadvantage is that the loops are more bulky than the Nail Knot and will not go through the tip top or guides as easily. It makes it easy to change leaders, but the bulk of the spliced loop (doubled fly line) makes this a poor choice for salt water.

SURGEON'S END LOOP KNOT

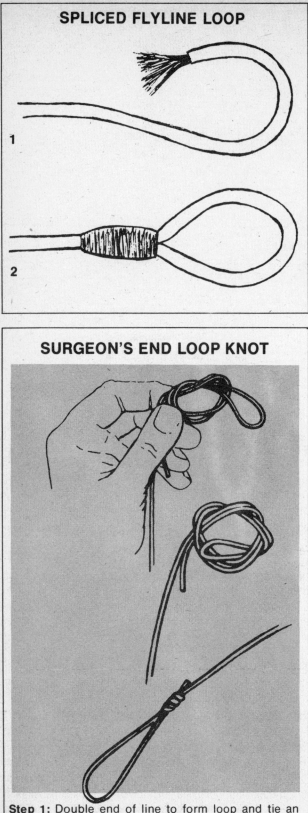

Step 1: Double end of line to form loop and tie an overhand knot at base of double line. **Step 2:** Leave loop open in knot and bring doubled line through once more. **Step 3:** Hold standing line and tag end and pull loop to tighten knot. Size of loop can be determined by pulling loose knot to desired point and holding it while knot is tightened. Clip end ⅛-inch from knot. (Illustration courtesy of DuPont Stren.)

PERFECTION LOOP KNOT

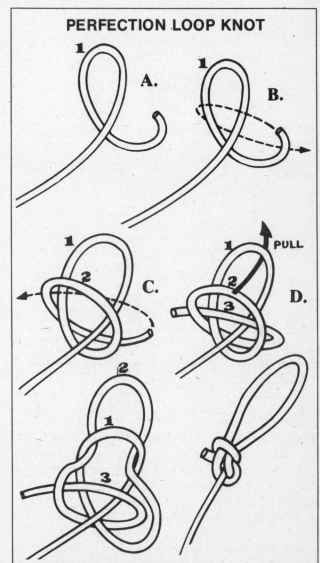

For making a loop on the end of the leader using the Perfection Loop Knot, **(A)** make a loop from behind, **(B)** come round in front, **(C)** come around again in the middle and **(D)** pull the second loop through the first one. (Illustration courtesy of Scientific Anglers.)

C. The same interconnecting loop arrangement can be accomplished with the same loop in the leader, using a Pfeiffer's End Loop knot. The mono loop is thinner and slicker to travel through the guides easily.

Leader Knots: A. For most leader connections, the common Blood Knot (see Chapter 2) is preferred. It is quick to tie, easy, and when trimmed properly, makes for a small compact knot of high strength.

B. When connecting sections of leader that are quite different in diameter, one solution is to double the end of the smaller mono and use the doubled line to tie the Blood Knot. This gives more bulk to the knot and less possibility of slippage when the knot is pulled up. Be sure to leave the doubled section long enough so that you can use both strands to pull up the knot securely.

C. A third way preferred by many experienced saltwater anglers is to connect the main portion of the leader and the tippet with interconnecting loops. This allows flies to be ready rigged on shock leaders and tippets, and it only takes seconds to change a fly when needed.

The loops are easily made by using a Perfection Loop Knot or Surgeon's Loop Knot in the mono at the end of the leader and at the tippet. To preserve the strength in the tippet, usually it is tied with a Bimini, and the doubled end of the Bimini (a 100 percent knot) used to tie the loop that will fasten to the rest of the leader.

Leader to Shock Tippet Knots: A. The standard here is the Albright. This makes for a relatively small knot (at the shock leader, it won't be going through the guides) with maximum strength.

B. Another good leader-to-shock leader knot is the Surgeon's (see Chapter 4) which is nothing more than a doubled overhand knot. Leave plenty of excess leader on both sides of the knot so that when you pull it up, you can do so evenly without the smaller mono slipping and pulling through. Good for attaching tippets to mono shock leaders of up to 60-pound test.

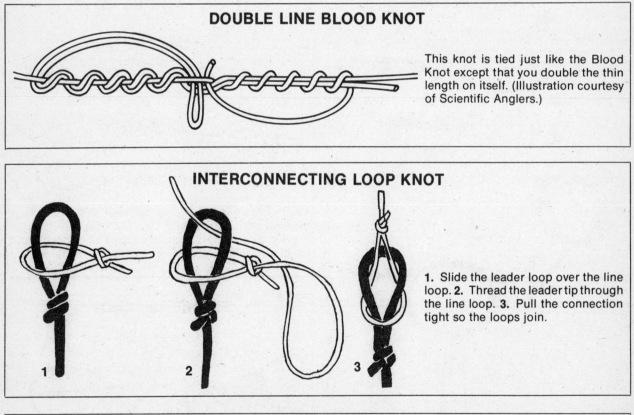

DOUBLE LINE BLOOD KNOT

This knot is tied just like the Blood Knot except that you double the thin length on itself. (Illustration courtesy of Scientific Anglers.)

INTERCONNECTING LOOP KNOT

1. Slide the leader loop over the line loop. **2.** Thread the leader tip through the line loop. **3.** Pull the connection tight so the loops join.

1   2   3

ALBRIGHT KNOT

This knot is easily tied if you think of it as two interlocking loops. Bend a "U" in the heavier line and make at least 12 wraps with the smaller strand. Draw both small strands tight to insure a firm knot. (Illustration courtesy of Scientific Anglers.)

Leader to Fly Knots: **A.** The Improved Clinch Knot (see Chapter 2) is a standard for attaching a fine tippet to a fly. It is easy to tie, has high degree of strength and will not slip.

B. Jansik Special—Good for fine tippets and relatively easy to tie.

C. Homer Rhode Loop—This knot is a must to tie large mono shock tippets to a fly to give the fly some action in the water. A regular tight knot with heavy mono will keep the fly from moving or swimming naturally in the water and will decrease the number of possible strikes or interest of fish. The Homer Rhodes loop knot provides for a free connection to the fly and allows it to swim in the water and react to jerks, strips, currents, etc. The size of the loop can be controlled by the position of the loops and to be sure, the knot should be pulled up tight with pliers.

D. Figure 8 Knot—Used with wire only. Gives the same loose connection as with Homer Rhodes loop knot.

"Fishing For Record" **Knots:** Fishing for records requires a leader tippet of at least a certain length, and not testing more than that leader class. For example, for the Saltwater Fly Rodders records (recently turned over to the International Game Fish Association), record classes are kept for 6-, 10-, 12- and 15-pound test leader tippet sizes. The leader tippet must measure at least 12 inches, and any shock leader used must measure not more than 12 inches from knot to fly. Since fishing for records frequently involves a lot of time, preparation and expense, serious fly rodders will use knots that test 100 percent of the line test wherever possible to give every possible edge in fishing. Thus, a typical leader will be tapered to the tippet, where special knots are used.

A. Bimini Twist—This knot is 100 percent when tied correctly and is the usual choice for tippets where records are expected or hoped for. The procedure in use is to tie two Biminis in the leader tippet (the weakest point in line), so that the leader tippet is only slightly

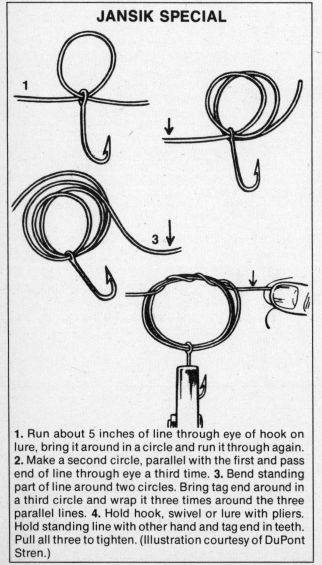

JANSIK SPECIAL

1. Run about 5 inches of line through eye of hook on lure, bring it around in a circle and run it through again. **2.** Make a second circle, parallel with the first and pass end of line through eye a third time. **3.** Bend standing part of line around two circles. Bring tag end around in a third circle and wrap it three times around the three parallel lines. **4.** Hold hook, swivel or lure with pliers. Hold standing line with other hand and tag end in teeth. Pull all three to tighten. (Illustration courtesy of DuPont Stren.)

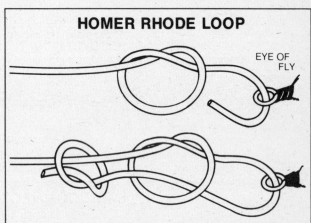

HOMER RHODE LOOP

Tie overhead knot with the tag end. Insert tag end through eye of lure. Pass the tag end back through the overhand knot. Close overhand knot and, with tag end, tie a second overhand knot and close using pliers. (Illustration courtesy of Scientific Anglers.)

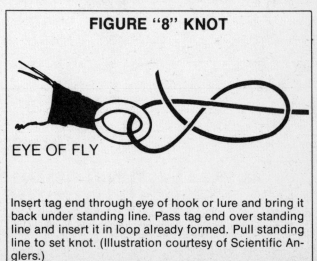

FIGURE "8" KNOT

EYE OF FLY

Insert tag end through eye of hook or lure and bring it back under standing line. Pass tag end over standing line and insert it in loop already formed. Pull standing line to set knot. (Illustration courtesy of Scientific Anglers.)

BIMINI TWIST

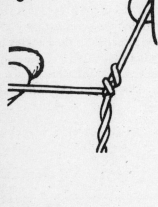

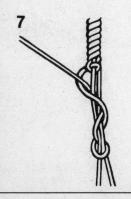

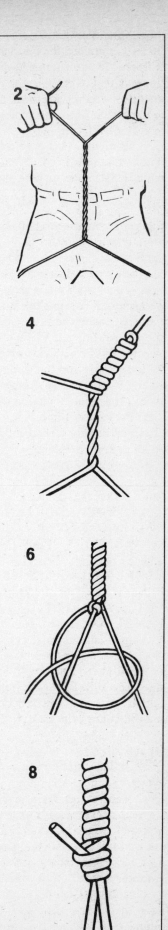

Step 1: Measure a little more than twice the footage you'll want for the double-line leader. Bring end back to standing line and hold together. Rotate end of loop 20 times, putting twists in it.

Step 2: Spread loop to force twists together about 10 inches below tag end. Step both feet through loop and bring it up around knees so pressure can be placed on column of twists by spreading knees apart.

Step 3: With twists forced tightly together, hold standing line in one hand with tension just slightly off the vertical position. With other hand, move tag end to position at right angle to twists. Keeping tension on loop with knees, gradually ease tension of tag end so it will roll over the column of twists, beginning just below the upper twist.

Step 4: Spread legs apart slowly to maintain pressure on loop. Steer tag end into a tight spiral coil as it continues to roll over twisted line.

Step 5: When spiral of tag end has rolled over column of twists, continue keeping knee pressure on loop and move hand which has held standing line down to grasp knot. Place finger in crotch of line where loop joins knot to prevent slippage to last turn. Make half-hitch with tag end around nearest leg of loop and pull up tight.

Step 6: With half-hitch holding, now release knee pressure but keep loop stretched out tight. Using remaining tag end, make half-hitch around both legs of loop, but do not pull tight.

Step 7: Make two more turns with the tag end around both legs of the loop, winding inside the bend of line formed by the loose half-hitch and toward the main knot. Pull tag end slowly, forcing the three loops to gather in a spiral.

Step 8: When loops are pulled up neatly against main knot, tighten to lock knot in place. Trim tag end about ¼-inch from knot. (Illustration courtesy of DuPont Stren.)

longer than that required by the regulations if a shock tippet is required for the fish. Otherwise, one Bimini will serve for connecting the tippet to the leader, and the tippet is tied directly to the fly. This knot is most frequently used for tying the doubled strands of the Bimini to the leader, or to a shock leader of up to 60-pound test mono or light wire.

B. Albright—This knot is the best one for attaching doubled strands from a Bimini to very large (over 60-pound) test mono or wire shock leader.

Connecting Loop Knots: Since the connections for any one leader and fly combination can be complicated and sometimes difficult to tie in a rocking boat, some fly rodders have gone to making up their fly and tippet combinations beforehand and connecting them to a basic leader with interlocking loops. The interlocking loops make it possible to change flies frequently should a pattern change be required, a leader become frayed, or a breakoff occur. The loop must be large enough to pass the fly for a quick connection. And, even though the loop knots and this connection is not as strong as others, it will still be stronger than the tippet which is always the weakest link in the chain.

A. Perfection Loop Knot—This will work well for single or double strand mono coming from a single tippet or from a Bimini.

B. Surgeon's Loop Knot—This accomplishes the same as the above and is tied the same as the Surgeon's Knot, except that double leader is used to form a loop at the end. THE IMPORTANCE OF USING THESE TWO KNOTS OVER A REGULAR OVERHAND LOOP KNOT IS THAT THE LOOPS WILL BE IN LINE WITH THE LEADER OR TIPPET, RATHER THAN OFF AT AN ANGLE AS WITH A REGULAR OVERHAND LOOP KNOT. AN ANGLED LOOP CAN CAUSE TWISTING OR TANGLING. In all cases for leaders, it is important to have the smallest strongest knot possible. Further, with those knots which are running through the guides such as those at the backing-to-line and line-to-leader, be sure to coat the knot with waterproof pliobond or some similar glue that will remain flexible, but provide a smooth coat to the knot.

Fly Boxes

When fish start hitting, or when a fly or leader change is required in a hurry, it pays to be prepared—to have flies, leaders and spare leader material at the ready. There are several ways to do this. While leaders should be made up in advance, there are times when you run out or when a leader requires rebuilding or modifying for a particular fishing situation. One way to solve this is to keep spare spools of leader material on a closed loop of monofilament, old flyline, or heavy cord. To keep them organized, keep all spools in order of the pound test, and all the identifying decals facing the

same direction. This way, it is easy to find the leader material that you want in a hurry, spool off the required amount and clip what you need. Many anglers wear holsters with Sportmate or G-96 fisherman's pliers on their belts at all times, and use the wire cutters for cutting mono. If you don't wear such pliers, thread a pair of nail clippers in the loop of leader spools for this purpose so that you have them ready at all times.

Ready made leaders can be kept in small polyethylene envelopes, marked as to the type, length and tippet size. Be sure to mark the envelope with a permanent felt tip marker so that it won't wash or wear off.

Spare lines, and especially shooting heads of 30-foot lengths are best kept in 4- to 5-inch coils held together with pipe cleaners or the twist ties used by gardeners or for trash bags. Label them and make sure that they are spooled so that the end to be attached to the backing is on the outside to prevent tangles.

While you won't need the vast assortment of sizes and patterns of flies often carried by freshwater trout

Ray Smith with a typical school striped bass caught in Rhode Island.

Striped bass with examples of typical striped bass flies and popping bugs.

anglers, you will need a sufficient assortment of colors, patterns and sizes for the fish that you are after. There are several solutions to prevent them from tangling with each other.

First, you can separate each type and size of fly into different compartments of a small lure box. Use the kind that has six to eight long compartments, in a box 6 x 4 inches to 8 x 6 inches in size. Another solution is to keep each fly in 2- x 8-inch poly envelopes and store them in a lure box or separate larger envelopes as to type, size and color.

A third solution is to rig the flies with the leader tippet (using the interconnecting loop method of attaching them to the leader) and coil this up carefully with the fly in an envelope.

Fourth, snelled hook holders work well for those flies that you want to keep with a wire or mono shock tippet attached. I like the long, round plastic snelled hook holders that will take shock leaders up to 12 inches or more, although shorter ones are available if required.

SALTWATER FLIES

Freshwater anglers are concerned primarily with size and pattern in their choice of flies. Saltwater anglers have these same considerations, but also must consider color, sink rate, hooking qualities and durability. And while the freshwater angler is usually concerned with the imitation or appearance of an aquatic or terresterial insect, the saltwater angler is also most always concerned with imitating some form of bait fish (although some shrimp and crab patterns are notable exceptions).

Size

Size is perhaps the single most important factor in many types of saltwater fishing, as for bluefish, striped bass, bonefish, small tarpon, etc. It is definitely the most important consideration for any species of fish

Typical simple saltwater flies that will take a variety of fish. These simple body and wing patterns developed by the author can be tied in any color and on any size hook.

that is feeding or breaking on the surface, or has been goaded into a feeding mood through the use of chum, teaser baits or other attractants. Fish are just like people, only wetter. If you are driving down the road looking for a steak house, you will automatically pass up anything else, including restaurants featuring sea food, Chinese dishes, Japanese dishes, Italian food, hamburgers, etc. Fish are the same. If they are breaking on the surface and into a school of 2½-inch bait fish, they want only 2½-inch bait fish. Something a little

all the same size. Generally they are around 1½ to 2 inches long. Thus any large fly patterns will almost always get a refusal.

An example at the other extreme are the needle fish flies used to take barracuda in the Florida Keys and Central America. These flies are generally tied with long strands of thin nylon to imitate the needle fish that are a favorite meal for barracuda. Longer is better and too short a fly will not interest the fish, because it will not closely resemble the shape and size of the bait.

Bluefish flies (and flies for other toothy fish) can often be tied in at the end of the shank so that the chance of a cut-off is lessened.

smaller might take a fish or two, but larger flies will almost always be met with immediate rejection. Any pattern can be tied to any size by varying the size of the hook, or the size of the wing of the fly.

A good example of the importance of size can be found in the fall fishing for breaking striped bass and bluefish in the Chesapeake Bay. These schools feed on large pods of bait fish that within fractions of an inch are

Color and Pattern

Color is important, but usually only as far as a general impression of the color of the bait fish. White and yellow are perhaps the two most popular base colors, but there are variations for specific patterns tied for specific species.

Pattern ties in closely with color, since the pattern of a fly is determined by both shape and color. While there

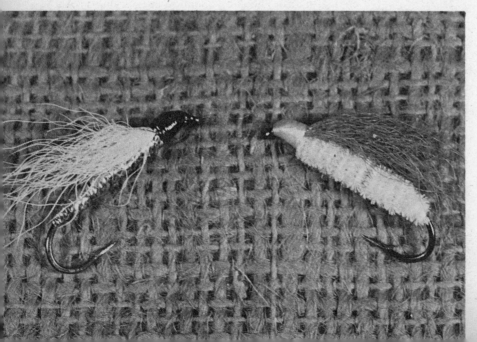

Example of small flies tied on freshwater hooks for shad, white perch, small striped bass, etc.

Example of big gamefish flies by Bob Popovics, surrounded by normal saltwater flies and popping bugs.

are patterns, such as the popular Blonde series, the Hi-Ties, Keel Flies, Stu Aptes Tarpon Flies, Lefty's Deceiver, Pfeiffer's Simple Fly and others, these are patterns of a general nature and do not come close to the highly detailed and complex patterns of mayflies, caddisflies, stoneflies and terresterials of the freshwater troutman. The important thing to remember is that any saltwater fly should in pattern resemble as closely as possible the size, color and shape of a bait fish popular with the species that you are after.

Sink Rate

A factor seldom considered in freshwater fly-fishing is the sink rate of the fly. It is highly important in some forms of saltwater fly-fishing since the sink rate of the fly will determine how rapidly a fly will get down to deep fish, or whether or not a fly will get to a channel cruising fish in time for the fish to see and take it. An example would be tarpon fishing, where the tarpon are spotted by the angler or guide from a staked out boat.

Usually these fish are several feet below the surface. A fly must be cast far enough ahead of the fish so that it will sink enough to be right in front of the fish by the time the fish reaches the fly. If it sinks too fast (or if the cast is too far in front of the fish) it will be below the fish when reached. If it sinks too slowly, (or if the cast is too close to the fish) it will be above and out of sight of the tarpon as it swims by. For this reason, often tarpon flies are tied sparsely with only a few feathers for wings, and a sparce hackle tied in at the bend of the hook.

Hook Quality and Sharpening

Hooks for saltwater fly-fishing must obviously be strong, sharp and corrosion proof or resistant. Good choices are stainless steels such as the Eagle Claw 254SS hooks or Mustad 34007, the Eagle Claw hooks with a tinned finish (available in several hook styles) and the VMC Perma Plate hooks by the French company VMC and distributed by FisHair Inc. in this country.

No hook, regardless of the style or manufacturer, is sharp enough as it comes from the factory. If you don't believe this, take any new fly hook and hold the point against your thumb nail. Use very slight pressure and see if the hook will grab or bite into the nail. For comparison, take a sharpened hook (using the instructions that follow) and do the same test. If sharpened properly it will immediately bite into the nail and will not slide across the nail as will a factory fresh hook.

To properly sharpen a hook, it must be triangulated. This means that the round point must be shaped into a triangular cross section. To do this, use a flat file such as a Red Devil #15 or a Nicholson Power Mower file against both sides of the hook. Usually I like to hold the hook (the best grip is with a small 4-inch Vise Grip), by the bend and run the file along the point parallel to the direction of the point. Do this on both sides and then finish with a light filing on the base of the point. The point should be sharp from barb to point for quick easy penetration. If you tie your own flies, be sure to file the hooks before placing them in the vice, to minimize any possible damage to materials.

Durability

Flies fished in the salt are subject to far more abuse from fish than any freshwater fly will get. Anything with teeth—which includes about half of the fish that you'll take—will shred a fly quickly. And, if the fishing is fast, it is important to make flies as durable as possible to eliminate fly changes between fish.

The solution to this seemingly insurmountable problem is to make flies as simple as possible, tie them with an eye to the fish that they will take, and reduce body materials as much as possible. Any body material will shred when cut, and it only takes one fish to cut right through a chennille, mylar, wool or tinsel body. One solution is to tie a fly body with fine monofilament. This will give it durability and also give it a translucency very similar to small bait fish.

Wing material is also subject to cutting, and feathers are cut more easily than fur. FisHair, a synthetic fur that is very like natural polar bear, but which comes in a variety of lengths and colors, is very durable and holds up well in saltwater flies. Saran or fine nylon crimped or straight wing material is also good since it will hold up well for many fish and has a good color and shine in the water. Its one disadvantage is that it lacks the bulk of the natural or artificial fur or feathers.

Some toothy fish like bluefish will cut right through a fly on the strike. One solution to this is to use a long shank hook and tie in the fly at the bend of the hook. That way, the fish will take the fly, but won't have any body to cut through. Also, on small fish such a tie will take the place of a wire leader, although a short leader will be necessary on big fish. I tie a fly like this for bluefish using a Eagle Claw 266SS hook on which I have straightened out the offset bend.

A final tip for making flies durable in the salt is to use epoxy cement instead of regular fly head cement to seal off the thread at the head of the fly. Fly head cement is quickly cut through, but the epoxy will hold up for fish after fish.

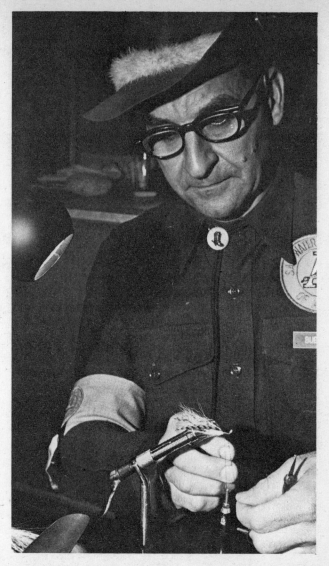

Saltwater fly rodder, Bub Church, tying a saltwater fly.

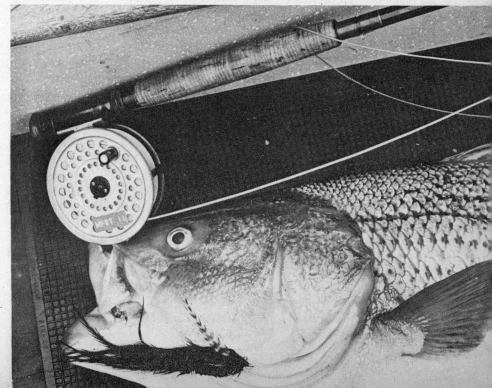

Large striped bass taken on a fly. Note the heavy tackle and large streamer fly used to take the 32-pound fish in San Francisco Bay.

252

Selected Flies

Saltwater flies are always in a state of flux and change, far more so than those used in freshwater. For some fish like permit, a truly successful fly has yet to be developed. For other fish, flies are constantly being modified and changed in the search for even more effective patterns. The following have proved to be standard, have produced over the years, and will continue to produce for years to come. Don't however, regard any of them as sacred, and don't be afraid to modify any basic pattern to your own needs or fancy. The fish will be the ultimate judge of the success or failure of any modification you make, any fly you tie.

BLONDE PATTERNS: Originated by Joe Brooks, this fly is basic to any saltwater fly box. It can be made in a wide range of sizes and solid or two tone wing color combinations.

HACKLE: None.
WINGS: Two of bucktail, tied on top of the hook shank, one tied in at the rear of the shank and the other tied in at the head. Both wings extend behind the hook about 1 to 1½ times the shank length.
BODY: Silver tinsel or silver mylar.
HOOK: 8 to 4/0
COLOR: Any color or color combination.

KEEL FLY: Used on Keel hooks for fishing close to the bottom or around obstructions since the wing of the fly serves as a weak guard for the hook point. White and yellow are popular, but any color or color combination of body and wing can be used.
BODY: Chenille tied in the length of the hook shank.
WING: Bucktail tied in on top of the hook shank so that the point is covered, and about 1½ times the length of the hook shank.
HOOK: 6 to 2/0
COLOR: Any color combination.

HI-TIE FLY: Because of its construction of tying 6 to 10 separate wings along the top of the shank of the hook, this fly gives the appearance of a larger bulkier fly and thus is good for gamefish feeding on larger bait fish. Good tied with any color wing, but white and yellow most popular.
WING: 6 to 10 separate bucktail wings (sparse) tied on top of the hook shank beginning at the rear of the hook and working forward to the eye.
THREAD: Any color—can contrast or match the bucktail color, since it will give body color to fly.
HOOK: 6 yo 4/0.
COLOR: Any color.

Shark flies on wire leaders. Note the chum in the chum bag to attract the fish to the boat when fishing in deep water.

MONO FLY: A good durable fly because of the body of monofilament. Gives the transluscent appearance of a bait fish.

BODY: Tinsel or mylar, over wrapped with 20- to 30-pound clear or light mist blue monofilament to cover and protect the tinsel.

WING: Blue or green over white, using bucktail, calftail or FisHair.

HOOK: 6 to 3/0

STU APTE TARPON FLY: Developed by fisherman Stu Apte especially for big tarpon.

WING: (Tied in at tail position at the end of the shank) two orange saddle hackles 3 inches long over wrapped with two bright yellow saddle hackles also 3 inches long.

HACKLE: Tied in at the bend of the hook right in front of the wing or tail. Two to four turns of a mix or orange and yellow saddle hackle.

Note: Shank of the hook is left bare or sometimes painted with orange paint.

LEFTY'S DECEIVER: Named for the developer, Lefty Kreh, one of the finest fly casters and saltwater fly-fishermen around today.

TAIL: 6 to 20 saddle hackles (depending upon the size of the hook used)—tied in at the bend. Over wrapped with two to six strands of thin (1/64- to 1/8-inch) silver or gold mylar.

BODY: Mylar

HACKLE: White polar bear, calftail or bucktail, laid on the hook near the eye so that it encircles the hook shank.

HEAD: Red or white with painted eye.

HOOK: 6 to 7/0

A versatile fly for a wide variety of fish, Lefty's Deceiver can be modified with a dark topping over the wing of peacock herl or long bucktail. White and yellow popular, but different color combinations also used.

PFEIFFER'S SIMPLE ONE: I developed this fly to fill the need for a very simple-to-tie fly that can be tied in less time than any other saltwater pattern and will take a wide variety of saltwater fish, including striped bass, bluefish, sea trout, bonefish, etc. It can be tied in a wide variety of colors, and a wide range of sizes.

BODY: Silver or gold mylar.

WING: White bucktail or FisHair (or other colors as desired) wrapped in at the eye of the hook and wrapped so that it encircles the hook shank completely.

HOOK: 6 to 4/0

PFEIFFER'S BLUEFISH STREAMER: Another simple fly tied especially for mid-Atlantic bluefish and incorporating a long, bare shank so that in most cases a wire leader is not needed. For very large bluefish, a short 3-inch wire leader will still be needed.

WING: White or yellow bucktail or FisHair tied in at the rear of the hook shank.

HOOK: 266SS Eagle Claw, straightened out, or similar long shank stainless steel hook, sizes 6-3/0.

Note: Another version involves a short body of mylar, with the wing tied in about two-thirds back from the eye of the hook.

SKIPPING BUG: A saltwater popping bug originated by Joe Brooks for striped bass.

BODY: 1½-inch long balsa or cork body, red head and white body, yellow eye with black center.

TAIL: Yellow bucktail.

HOOK: Long shank, 1 to 3/0 sizes.

SWIMMING BUG: A bug with tapered end towards the eye, so it doesn't pop, but swims on the surface.

BODY: 1- to 1½-inch long balsa or cork body, painted white or yellow.

TAIL: Flared saddle hackles or saddle hackles and bucktail mixed.

HOOK: Long shank 1 to 3/0 sizes.

Close-up of Pfeiffer's Simple One, saltwater fly.

Examples of West Coast shad flies. They are tied in very bright colors.

CASTING IN SALT WATER

The following might make saltwater fly casting seem both easier than it really is and harder than it really is. First, let's assume that you have never fly cast, or never fly cast in salt water before. Even with a complete lack of experience, you can take fish. Obviously you won't be able to stand in the bow of a guide boat, make one false cast and drop a fly 100 feet away in front of a cruising tarpon. But you will be able to flail out (and I use the word advisedly) a cast to take breaking bluefish or striped bass in the mid-Atlantic. On the other hand, saltwater fly casting does impose certain problems that at first almost seem insurmountable for the freshwater trout fisherman used to dropping a size 16 fly in front of a rising trout 25 feet away on a small stream.

First, the tackle will be heavier. The rods are longer and have more mass to push against the air, and the rod, reel, backing and line combination will weigh several times more than that of a freshwater outfit. Second, you will be handling far more weight in the air than in fresh-water fishing. For example, 30 feet of a light 4-weight line will weigh about ¼-ounce when in the air; 30 feet of 9-weight line will weigh ⅝-ounce; and 30 feet of a 12-weight line will weigh ¾-plus-ounce. Couple this with the fact that 60 feet of line are often cast while saltwater fishing, add the weight and air resistance of a heavy 3/0 streamer fly, and you have a whole new ball game.

Obviously, casting these lines and flies isn't impossible or so many fly casters wouldn't be traveling to coastal areas. But it does mean that your casting will have to be modified from freshwater techniques to take advantage of the rod power to control the line. The best way to accomplish this is to practice in your backyard with a typical saltwater outfit including a full leader and practice fly (hook point and bend cut off).

Longer casts are often required in salt water and casts of 60-70 feet are no longer uncommon with modern fly tackle. In fact, the further that you can cast well, (up to or over 100 feet, if possible) the better and easier your casts of 50, 60, 70 and 80 feet will be. The answer again is proper technique and enough practice before you get to the water and the breaking fish.

Norm Bartlett double hauling a saltwater fly outfit to get out maximum distance in casting.

The importance of good casting can't be overemphasized. First, it is essential to get a fly out to the fish, even if it requires an extra long cast. Second, it is important to be able to cast accurately to get the fly to the proper position for the fish to take when casting to a specific fish or to a school. Third, it is important to be able to cast well under wind conditions of up to 15- to 20-knot gusts which are common when fishing coastal and ocean waters.

While there is not sufficient space here to cover all fly casting properly (see the excellent book, *Fly Casting with Lefty Kreh,* by Lefty Kreh; Lippincott, 1974.) two problems stand out for most beginning saltwater fly casters.

1. *Dropped Back Cast.* Fly casting is not just flailing the line back and forth and hoping for the best. It is a definite accelerated power motion to pick the line up off the water, accelerating the cast to a position slightly beyond vertical, waiting for the line to straighten out, and then a slowly increasing accelerated push forward culminating with a quick snap and follow through that will mark the forward cast of the line.

Unfortunately, too many anglers think of a back cast as one in which the rod should be thrown further back for longer and more powerful casts. The result is that the line is constantly slapping the water and killing the cast. The cast must be high and lifted up to make a proper cast.

Several years ago when giving a private fly casting lesson to a client, I explained all this in an effort to correct his poor back cast. "Oh, what you really mean is a back lift," he said, suddenly realizing the problem

Joe Zimmer casting from a small skiff in the Turniffe Islands off Belize.

Below are fly rod caught striped bass.

that he had been having. With this realization he lifted his backcast high in the air, watched it straighten out and then made the proper forward snap to make an excellent cast. The term "back lift" is an excellent way to think of the back cast if you are having this problem.

2. *Loop Control*. The second problem is in loop control and involves the forward cast. Too many anglers come forward in a wide sweep that drives the cast down and kills the cast. At the end of the snap the rod should be high, at about a 45-degree angle to propel the line out and slightly up and to keep the loop of uncoiling line as small or tight as possible.

The angle of the snap is the key to loop control. A wide snap will make for a wide loop, and a small angle of snap will make for a narrow loop. The wide loop will kill the cast, causing it to drop prematurely on the water, and present a wide area of line to the wind. The narrow loop, which you want in all your fly casting, will present a small area to the wind, won't cause the cast to drop, and will give you maximum distance—especially important in saltwater fly-fishing.

Solve both of these problems through practice, and you will have done a lot to increasing your casting distance tremendously. The important thing to realize is that you should work on one problem at a time, solve it and then work on the next. Once your casting technique is perfected, then work on increased distance. But don't try to work on increasing your distance all in one casting practice session. Work on it in 5-foot or 10-foot increments. Become good and proficient at each distance before moving on to a longer cast. The 100-foot cast for the average angler is no longer an unattainable goal and only a little work will attain it for you and make you comfortable in any angling situation in saltwater.

3. *Wind*. One problem encountered in practically all saltwater fly fishing is wind. And there is no one solution to the wind problem, since it can be from the right, from the left, behind you, or from in front of you, or for that matter at any angle. But there are some ways to cope with wind. It is easy to adjust for any angle if need be by slightly modifying the following techniques:

Wind behind you: When using normal casting techniques, a wind behind you will blow down your cast everytime before you can make the forward cast. But there is a solution to this.

If you think about it, the wind decreases the closer you are to the water level. Using this knowledge, make a back cast with the rod held horizontal (you might have to pick up at a slight angle to get the line off the water and then throw back horizontal to the water) to keep the line as close to the water as possible and to minimize any wind effect on the line.

As soon as the line straightens out, bring the rod vertical and throw a high forward cast. The wind will catch the line and enable you to make as long or longer a cast as you can under calm conditions.

Wind in front of you: Here, the back cast is no problem since the wind will carry the line and straighten it out quickly. Because of the wind, you might find that your timing on your back cast is a little quicker than it normally is.

To make the forward cast, put far more power into the cast than you would normally and drive the cast down as close to the water as possible. The result is that

Fly casting for tarpon in Costa Rica.

you can cut under the wind to get the cast out. It is true that the line will slap down harder than under a no-wind situation, but fish hitting in the choppy water that results from such a wind will not be bothered by this.

Wind from the left: Assuming that you are a right-handed caster, this will not present too much of a problem since the wind will only tend to blow the cast away from your body. You may have to compensate on the forward cast some to keep the fly from being blown off course by the wind.

Wind from the right: Assuming that you are a right-handed caster, a wind from the right will tend to blow the forward cast into you unless you take corrective action. The solution is to make an angled side cast to the back, then move the rod to a vertical angle over your left shoulder so that the line is carried by the wind to the left of your body. Failure to make this correction will cause the line or fly to be blown into you while punching out the forward cast—a dangerous situation.

Note: If you are a left-handed caster, the solution to the last two problems will be reversed, for obvious reasons. Also, make sure when casting from a boat that you are always aware of the position of your angling partner, guide, boat captain or others around, and cast accordingly, so that the line or fly won't endanger them. Failure to do so, particularly when the wind is from the side, could result in driving a saltwater fly into a friend and a serious wedge in any friendship.

CASTING TECHNIQUES

Obviously casting from a boat or casting from a salt marsh is far different from casting in your own backyard for practice, or casting on a freshwater trout stream with only a minimum of line out. Most saltwater fly-fishing is done from a boat. On smaller boats you will probably have a casting platform at the bow or stern as are found on the Florida guide boats. Ideally, a casting platform should be completely clear of any obstructions that could catch the flyline on a cast, or when a fish is making its first run and taking line off the deck.

But there are some tips which will make your fishing easier. First, strip off all the line that you will need for a cast, and then make a long cast, even if you are not yet ready to fish. Retrieve the line in loose coils on the deck. This will insure that the line is coiled in the same direction that it will go out when a fish hits. If this isn't done, the line that goes out first will be on the bottom of the coil, increasing the possibility of a tangle that can break off the fish when it clogs in the guides.

Wind can be a problem, even on a clear casting platform. One way to keep your line stationary is to use Astroturf or a similar artificial grass on the platform to keep the flyline from blowing around. Another solution is to use a mesh weave plastic laundry basket—and strip the line into it while fishing. If the boat lacks a clean casting platform, there are still some things that you can

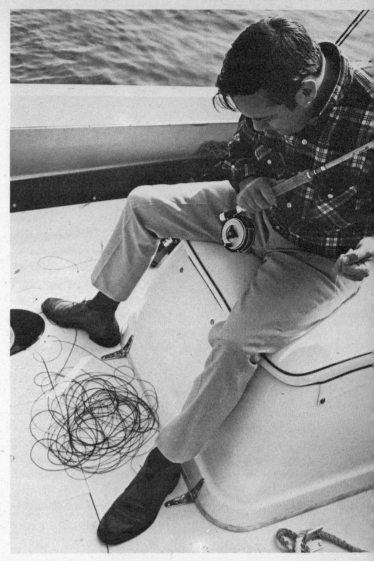

Line must be stripped from the reel before getting ready to cast to a fish and must be reversed so that the line going out through the guide will be on top of the coil to prevent tangles.

do to make your fly casting easier. First, carry along a roll of duct or masking tape and cover any cleats, antenna brackets, anchor holders, etc. with it. You don't have to cover each item completely, just run the tape from any projections to the deck so the line won't catch. Some anglers accomplish the same purpose with a fine mesh net that they carry just for throwing over a casting area. This is ideal if you have a lot of other rods, tackle boxes, etc., which could catch flylines.

Two additional tips will help in your casting. First, if you are sight fishing, you won't make a cast until you spot the fish. To get your cast out as quickly as possible after spotting the fish, hold the rod in your hand, have line stripped out on the deck as previously described, and have enough line outside of the rod tip for you to make a quick false cast. Usually 10 to 15 feet of line is enough. Hold a loop of leader close to the line-leader connection and hold the fly by the bend of the hook or the tail. Then, when a fish is spotted, drop the leader coil and make your first false cast. The fly will be pulled from your fingers and you can have the fly in the water seconds later.

Saltwater Fly-Fishing Tactics

There are still a few loose ends to consider even after you have your equipment, terminal tackle, have bought or tied your flies, and have mastered casting. While the fishing techniques for every species and every area can differ, there are basics to all of them. These basics are the retrieve, the strike, the fight and landing of fish.

Retrieve: With the exception of Florida, much of saltwater fly-fishing is to breaking fish such as bluefish, striped bass and similar species. For this the retrieve should be a fast strip right through the school of fish, giving the fly a short strip, jerky action. The method is to run the line through the index or middle finger of the rod hand and pull with the line hand at the rate and length of retrieve desired. Sometimes you will have to let the fly sink slightly to get it to stay in the surface film of bait fish, rather than on top.

The same stripping action will control the fly in almost any situation, including fishing down deep. One technique that you'll want to use here is to count between the time the fly hits the water and the time you start to retrieve, so that you can repeat a retrieve at the right level if you hit fish. Often when blind fishing for deep fish, the technique is to make several retrieves at each count to be sure that you are giving the fish a good look at the fly before counting more for a deeper retrieve. When fishing deep, the slow strip seems to be best, with about a 6- to 8-inch strip of the line, pause and repeat, all the way back to the boat. One way to vary

this is to start with a fast strip and end slower so that the fly imitates a bait fish suddenly startled into movement, but slow enough to be an easy prey for any gamefish.

For sight fishing to feeding or cruising fish, the retrieve will be different still. Here you will want to cast so that the fly is in place when the fish comes by. In some cases if you cast too far, or if the fish changes direction, you might have to retrieve rapidly to get the fly into position, pause until the fish sights the fly and then give a twitch or series of short strips to pique the fish's interest and provoke a hit. The sink rate of the fly and distance cast in front of the fish is also important here to make sure that the fly ends up on the same level as the fish.

In some cases you might have to retrieve extra fast. One example is the barracuda, which won't be interested in anything other than a needle fish fly traveling just under the speed of sound. And they can catch it, no matter how fast you retrieve it. One way to get the fastest possible retrieve is to cast, hold the rod between your legs and retrieve with both hands until the fish hits. I had to use this method for the first barracuda I ever took on a fly, a 15-pounder caught in the Florida Keys years ago.

Naturally, for any fishing like this, you'll need your longest cast to get the maximum retrieve for the 'cuda to hit before it sees the boat.

Strike: For maximum efficiency on any strike, the rod should always be pointed at the fish, or at the direction of the line (if there is a belly in the line due to current or tide, this may be different). By keeping the rod tip low and pointed at the fish or line, you will get maximum leverage when you lift up on the rod to strike the fish.

Usually the best strike is accomplished by a combi-

(Left) Tarpon in white sand. Cast should be ahead of fish and stripped in front of him. Rod tip should be pointed at the fish in preparation for the strike. (Middle and right) The reaction when a large fish feels the hook.

Jumping fly rod caught tarpon caught and photographed by the author. Note the slack line thrown to the fish to prevent it from breaking the leader.

nation of two actions—lifting the rod sharply, and pulling back on the line simultaneously. In some cases you might feel the fish and have the fish hook itself without any action on your part. If so fine, but it is usually best to strike anyway, to make sure that the hook is driven in past the barb.

When fishing with a light tippet, I prefer a slightly different action, since a hard strike with a heavy rod may snap the tippet. The best way to strike a fish in this case is to pull back on the line firmly, but not enough to break the tippet. Repeat this two to three times to make sure that the fish is hooked well. The action is firm—like coaxing a dog on a leash—not sharp, as in a regular strike.

In some cases a fish will miss a strike. If fishing deep you may or may not get another hit (from the same fish or another fish in the area) on the same retrieve. The secret here is to continue retrieving the fly at the same rate, after the missed strike and not to hurry it in for another cast.

The same applies when fishing in a breaking school. Here, missed strikes are not at all uncommon, and a continued retrieve at the same speed of retrieve will usually get another strike. I've had as many as a half dozen missed strikes from fish in breaking schools of bluefish and striped bass before one finally connected solidly.

Immediately after the strike of any large fish, the fish will run. There is nothing that you can do at this point except hold the rod high and pointed toward the fish, and hold your finger and thumb of your line hand in a circle to help clear any slight tangles of line as it comes off the deck. Once the line is off the deck and the line is running from the reel, you are ready to fight the fish.

Fighting the Fish: Obviously, the drag should be set on the reel before making the first cast. Assuming that the drag is set properly (*no more* than $\frac{1}{3}$-$\frac{1}{2}$ of the tippet test), you have additional control by adding drag with your hand. Many reels today have flanged spools which will allow you to hold the reel in your palm and add additional pressure. Or, you can push the reel against your shirt to add drag. The angle of the rod will also control drag (high angle more drag; lower angle or pointed at the fish, less drag). If your reel does not have a flanged spool, you can add drag by cupping the reel with your hand and adding finger pressure on the inside of the spool.

One mistake that many beginning anglers make (in all fishing—not just fly-fishing) is that they see a fish taking line and want to add drag, either through increased hand pressure or increasing the reel drag setting. When a fish has a lot of line out, this is exactly the *wrong* thing to do. First, the flyline and any backing has a lot of water resistance so that the drag is constantly increasing as the line is running out. Second, a long run will decrease the amount of line on the reel spool, increasing the torque and increasing the reel drag, even though the setting has not been touched. The solution is that on any long run of a fish, *decrease* the drag.

Some of the best saltwater fly rod fish are jumpers. The tendency when a fish jumps is to rear back on the rod to hold it tight. This again is the *wrong* approach. The correct solution is to "bow" to the fish—to throw slack line to it. There are two reasons for this. First, the violent shaking that most fish do out of the water exerts far greater shock on a tippet than the same shaking when cushioned by water. Thus a shake of the head out of the water is much more likely to break a tippet than the same shake in the water. Two, with some fish such as the tarpon, the hook can come out and be rehooked in the bony mouth several times before landing—or loosing—the fish. A tight line on a tarpon in the air will tend to pull the hook out of the fish's mouth, whereas with a loose slack line, a loose fly has a better chance of rehooking in the mouth.

In some situations, you might have to follow a big fish with your boat. When you expect this, for such a fish as big tarpon and sharks when fishing from a small boat staked out on a flat, be sure that you have a way to slip the anchor rope so that it can be picked up later. A definite no-no is to stay behind a big fish with the boat while chasing. I did this years ago on a big shark hooked on a fly rod off Ocean City, Maryland. Norm Bartlett and I were fishing out of his 17-foot Mako and chumming sharks up around the boat to where we could take them on a fly. One big shark that I hooked headed for Florida and was well into the backing when we got the boat in gear and ready to chase. Neither of us were experienced at the time, and we ran directly behind the fish. The result was that we overran the line, and while we didn't cut it, there was so much slack that by the time that I got a tight line again, the fish had shaken the hook and gone.

For this reason, fight any big fish from the side of a

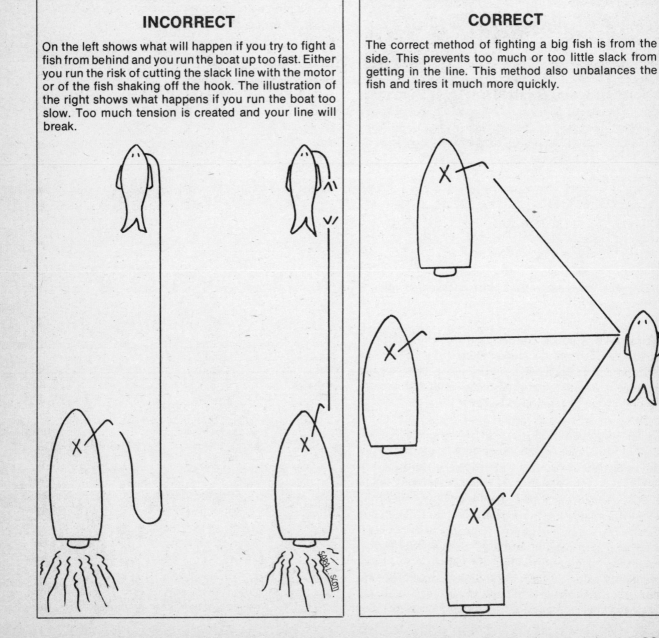

INCORRECT

On the left shows what will happen if you try to fight a fish from behind and you run the boat up too fast. Either you run the risk of cutting the slack line with the motor or of the fish shaking off the hook. The illustration of the right shows what happens if you run the boat too slow. Too much tension is created and your line will break.

CORRECT

The correct method of fighting a big fish is from the side. This prevents too much or too little slack from getting in the line. This method also unbalances the fish and tires it much more quickly.

Joe Zimmer with a catch of white perch taken on light fly tackle.

wears out the fish faster.

After the first long run of the fish, fighting it is usually a see-saw battle with you regaining some backing or line, the fish taking it out again, you regaining it, etc., until the fish is ready to land or release. The secret of regaining line with the fly rod (or for that matter any outfit) is in pumping the fish. Pumping is a simple procedure of raising the rod to pull line in towards you and then dropping the rod rapidly while at the same time reeling in line. At all times the line is kept tight. And since the drag may slip when raising the rod to regain line, use your hand on the reel or reel flange to, in effect, tighten the drag. Using your hand for additional drag also allows you to release the drag (hand drag) instantly should the fish suddenly take a lunge away from the boat or begin another run.

Landing the Fish: Any fish, and particularly big fish, must be completely tired out before attempting to land them. Failure to do so can result in a broken leader and lost fish, broken tackle, or injury to the angler or assistant landing the fish.

Lefty Kreh with a Key West, Florida cobia which took a popping bug cast near a buoy.

moving boat. Here, if you run 20 feet ahead or behind the fish, you are still at about the same distance from the fish and can maintain a tight line. The same erratic movement directly behind a fish can result in a screaming drag or a slack line and lost fish.

There are two other reasons why you should fight a big fish from the side. First, side pressure on a fish will tend to unbalance it, and keep it making corrective moves to right itself. This will tire the fish and get it to gaff quicker. Pressure directly behind a fish will not tire it. Also, a leader and line running directly behind the fish will create another serious problem. The long leader used in fly-fishing will come directly in contact with the fish throughout much of the fight. Gill plates, dorsal fins, pectoral fins and tails will wear against it, eventually cutting it through. And on a shark, the skin alone is enough to wear through any leader. Fighting a fish from the side eliminates all these problems and

Offshore fishing with the fly rod requires cooperation. Here in the lower right, Larry Kreh casts a streamer fly for big amberjack, while the mate standing on the transom teases up the big fish with bait.

Dolphin caught off shore on a fly.

Norm Bartlett with a fly rod caught shad.

Author with a fly rod caught jack crevalle.

On big fish you will need the lifting power of the rod to get the fish with its head up and to lead it around the boat or to an optimal landing position. Ideally, the fish would be on or very near the surface, and parallel to the boat.

To land the fish with a net, have your assistant hold the net with the bag under water and lead the fish head first into the net. The reason for this is that when the fish touches the net, it will become violent, and the natural direction for any fish to go is forward, thus driving the fish deeper into the net bag. Trying to land a fish tail first is like trying to catch a playful dog by the tail—it can always go faster than you can.

To gaff a fish, use a suitable gaff with a long handle. Gaffing techniques differ from angler to angler, but the best rule is to try to gaff the fish near the middle so that it will be unbalanced. If gaffed at either end, it will have the other end to thrash about and possibly break tackle or injure someone. Usually, the best spot is just behind the pectoral fin, which is near the center balance point for most fish.

If you plan to release the fish, do not gaff or net it, but instead remove the fly or in the case of some toothy fish, cut the leader. For smaller fish, grab them behind the gills, hold them in the water and remove the fly. If the

Large tarpon taken on the fly.

Lefty Kreh unhooking fly rod caught sea trout.

fish is a big one or toothy, lip gaff the fish by running the gaff through the bottom of the mouth. Hold the fish against the gunnel of the boat, and remove the fly by hand, or in the case of a mouth full of teeth, with long nose pliers. And if there is any question about the safety of this, cut the leader and sacrifice the fly. Big bluefish have a habit of lunging at their captors and sharks are just too powerful, dangerous and nasty to even consider unhooking.

CONSERVATION

While landing fish is the proof and cuimination of fly-fishing in salt water, anglers should always be concerned with the conservation of the species and of preserving the ecology of the resource. Unfortunately, some anglers feel that they have to keep every fish that they land, or have in a landing situation. But to do so will only ultimately ruin the fishing. One of the salvations of both tarpon and bonefish is that they are inedible. Trophy fish and the maximum in angling thrill in both quantity of catches and size of the fish is the ultimate for any saltwater fly-fisherman in any area, and in fishing for any species. But there are only limited numbers of big tarpon, schools of bonefish, runs of shad, and breaking schools of striped bass.

Even those species which seem in unlimited supply are affected by natural cycles of abundance, and fishing pressure. Recently, the Chesapeake Bay has seen the sharp reduction of striped bass, as a result of overfishing and reduced reproduction, according to biologists. While fly-fishermen in the Chesapeake Bay have exerted only a miniscule of fishing pressure over the past years, fishing for breaking striped bass in the Chesapeake is at its lowest in recorded history, and will probably remain that way for years to come.

Similarly, the seemingly abundant bluefish at this

writing is the subject of some fisheries management surveys whose members are worried about the future of this fish from overfishing pressure both commercial and sport. Again, fly-fishing takes only a small fraction of the bluefish caught, and any loss of these fish in the future certainly cannot be attributed to fly-fishermen. But by the same token, saltwater fly-fishermen can be in the vanguard of showing their fellow anglers that you don't need fish in the cooler to make for an exciting day on the water.

Similarly, conservation should be practiced while fishing. In Florida, wheel tracks across flats made from the outboard props of small high speed boats have helped to destroy the flora and fauna of the fragile bottoms, and have reduced the amount of aquatic life in those areas. And since all fishing is based on a biological chain of large fish feeding on smaller fish, which in turn eat crustaceans, plant life and microscopic plankton, such a loss ultimately affects the gamefish and the game fisherman.

If you are concerned about bringing back a trophy, try pictures instead, or restrict your fish kept for possible mounting to that one fish that you can be truly proud of—a 100-pound tarpon, 10-pound bonefish, 10-pound or larger bluefish, 20-pound striped bass. One way to do this is to decide beforehand your criteria for a trophy fish. And for those lesser fish, pictures will prove to the world your prowess as an angler, if you like.

Unlike freshwater fish which can be landed, held up for a quick photo and released, saltwater fish are far more fragile and stand a good chance of dying if taken from the water. Confine your photos to fish fighting shots, fish photographed near the boat, or the fish as you cut the leader or remove the fly to release them. Such pictures will be far more appealing than static shots of you holding a fish. For proof of this, just examine the outdoor magazines and books to note the number of action shots compared to those static shots of dead fish.

To preserve good saltwater fly-fishing such as you know now and to know that your youngsters will enjoy the same fishing, it is necessary to preserve the fish and the fishery. The best way to do this is to set your own personal goals and standards to preserve the fragile saltwater environment and to release as many fish as possible for others to enjoy, or to serve as stock for further generations of fish.

A mackerel taken by Lefty Kreh on a large fly outfit. Note the extension butt, large precision fly reel, and the forward grip above the regular grip for additional leverage in lifting fish.

FISH FOR SALTWATER FLY-FISHING

The basics of fly casting, fly-fishing and angling techniques for handling the tackle and hooked fish are basic for all species, but each different type of fish does require specific tactics in terms of finding the fish, approaching them, hooking them and handling them once hooked.

Striped bass

Striped bass are strictly a coastal fish found along both the Atlantic and Pacific coasts. Prime areas on the East Coast are from the New England area through North Carolina, and in the San Francisco area on the Pacific coast.

They are highly migratory and ascend freshwater rivers to spawn. It is on their spawning runs that fly-fishermen will get the best chance for the big ones, although sizeable fish can be found year-round along shorelines, salt marshes, and around jetties and piers. Their principal food is eels, small bait fish, etc., which makes simple streamer flies the best bet for the fly rodder. As with most saltwater fish, moving tides are best, since a strong tide will move around bait fish and make a moving cafeteria for a striped bass finning along a jetty, behind a piling or along the edge of a current.

Much fishing is from boats, but it doesn't have to be.

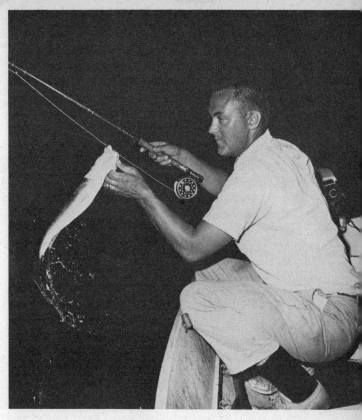

Joe Zimmer with a striped bass caught at dusk when the fishing is often at its best.

Striped bass caught with fly rod while fishing from shore along a salt marsh bank.

267

Salt marshes usually have sharp drop off edges, and any fly rodder can run a boat to an island, step out and walk the bank or cover any salt marsh on the mainland. When fishing a salt marsh from shore, walk quietly, since any vibration will be transmitted into the water where the fish will pick it up and move out.

The best method is to cast along the shore. If you are right-handed, start to the right of a shoreline and cast ahead and across your body to cover the shoreline to your left. Streamers and rapidly retrieved popping bugs both work best, although I lean to the popping bugs.

Boat fishing tactics will depend upon when and how you are after the fish. If fishing a spawning run, stake out or drift in a likely spot, one where previous success of other anglers (spin fishermen, etc.) has proven that fish will be in the area. Then, blind cast across the current or tide with Blondes, Simple Ones, Lefty's Deceiver, or your favorite striper fly and wait for the hit.

Fall often brings excellent fishing all along the estuaries of the East Coast when breaking schools of 1- to 5-pound striped bass start to drive bait to the surface. Diving gulls feeding on bait fish that the stripers miss are often the best sign of a feeding school. Small fast boats are needed to get to the fish before they go down.

Once you spot the fish, don't run into them with the boat. Cut the engine up tide or up wind (whichever will move the boat) of the school of fish if they are stationary. If they are moving, cut the engine so that your boat movement and the direction of the school will intersect.

(Below) Fly rod and striped bass.

(Above) Typical areas in the mid-Atlantic for striped bass and white perch include areas like this salt marsh where Norm Bartlett is fishing.

Tony Lorch and Leon Martuch with a fly rod caught bluefish taken by Tony on a fly. Note extension butt on rod handle to help in landing large fish.

ocean fish, coming into coastal waters only during the summer months. In southern waters they can be found all year-round and December fishing for bluefish off North Carolina and further south is not uncommon. While bluefish are sometimes close in shore, they are constantly on the move, which makes boat fishing the only practical way to fish for them.

In some areas, big blues will come into shallow areas early in the spring and fly casting with popping bugs or large streamers can provoke some vicious strikes and fights. They fight hard and will jump when hooked and near the boat. Tides are nearly as important as when fishing for striped bass. Like the stripers, fall fishing for breaking bluefish is excellent. Use the same tactics as for striped bass. A fast, jerky erratic retrieve is best, but missed strikes are not uncommon.

Another excellent way to take them on fly tackle is to anchor and chum with menhaden (or a local favorite

Author with a fly rod caught bluefish taken while chumming.

Danny Kipnis removes the fly from a ladyfish. These fish provide great night fishing sport on small white streamer flies around the lighted docks in the southern half of Florida.

As long as the engine is off, the fish won't be skittish. In fact, I've done this and minutes later been completely surrounded by feeding, slashing striped bass. The only problem then is deciding in which direction to cast! Once hooked, striped bass will make one long run and several shorter runs. Release them where possible, or if you must land them, net the small ones and gaff the larger ones.

West Coast fishing around San Francisco Bay, differs from East Coast fishing in that much of the fishing is made with long casts, using shooting heads. Popping bugs or streamers are good with the best fishing at dawn and dusk.

The best temperatures to fish bass are from the high 50s to the low 70s, which means that fishing in the mid-Atlantic area is good from late May through mid fall, with a longer season further south and a shorter one further north.

Bluefish

Bluefish, found along the entire Atlantic coast, are an

bait) to bring the fish to the boat where they can be taken on long streamer flies. Use a fly tied in at the bend of the hook, like Pfeiffer's Bluefish Fly, or use a short wire leader. If you wish to release them, a longer leader will make it easier to hold the fish at the boat while removing the fly with longnose pliers.

Sea Trout and Weakfish

These two similar fish are excellent fly rod quarry all along the Atlantic coast, with the mid-Atlantic areas the best. In recent years, Delaware Bay has been excellent in late May and early June. In areas like these where there are large concentrations of sea trout, the best fishing is blind casting in an area, using Keel Flies to keep the hooks from hanging up on bottom rocks or weeds.

Yellow is the best color, with white a close second choice, but sometimes the fish are fickle and will want other colors. A slow strip is best, after allowing the fly to sink to or near the bottom, using a sinking or sink tip flyline. To keep the fly down with the line, use a short leader.

Another good method is to fish the mid-Atlantic salt marshes, either from shore or from a boat, blind casting over weedy bottom in shallow waters.

Since sea trout have several canine teeth, a long shank hook for flies or a short heavy mono leader for big fish is a must. Best fishing is from late spring through early fall.

Author with sea trout caught in Delaware Bay on a keel fly and sinking line.

The guide poles boat in search of rolling tarpon, while angler stands ready to make a quick cast.

Larry Solomon and guide display 85-pound tarpon before releasing it.

Shad

Shad are perhaps questionable for inclusion in a section on saltwater fly-fishing. True, they are a saltwater fish, and like the striped bass, do ascend rivers to spawn, although they go much further inland. Your fly-fishing might be in saltwater, in brackish water or in freshwater. White shad (also called American shad) are prevalent all along the East Coast and the northern West Coast, smaller but more aerial hickory shad are found only in the mid-Atlantic area.

Both fish take small brightly colored flies of red, orange, white, yellow, etc., fished with light fly outfits. For hickory shad floating lines are OK, but for the deeper running whites, a sinking or sink tip line will be necessary. The line should have a sink rate sufficient to get it near the bottom when cast across current to allow the fly to drift downstream. Both fish are capable of taking line off a reel and into the backing, but their tendency to run upstream (remember, this is a spawning run), makes this unlikely most of the time.

Tarpon

The many inlets and canals of southern Florida make it an ideal area for fishing from shore for baby tarpon of up to 10 pounds. Light fly outfits and popping bugs or streamer flies work best, fishing along the shore and throwing flies along and under the mangroves. Accuracy casting is a must, since many of the fish are right in the mangroves and a fly more than a foot away from the roots just won't interest them.

272

Boats are a must for the bigger tarpon, and the standard method is to pole along, searching for the dorsals and tails of surfacing fish, or to stake out and wait for fish to come down a channel. The boat would be positioned on a flat, but near enough to the channel to cast a fly, and in a position to spot the fish well in advance so that the fly can be cast with the sink rate of the fly and the speed of the fish calculated to intersect.

Tackle for tarpon will vary widely, since the little ones can be taken on a light 4- to 6-weight outfit and small streamer flies, while the big ones will require the heaviest and best of saltwater fly-fishing tackle. For the big fish, use an 11-weight fly outfit, a rod with suitable lifting power to control the fish, a heavy reel with a good drag, spooled with a suitable flyline, and at least 200 yards of 20- to 30-pound Dacron backing, a short leader tapered to your choice of tippet and shock leader and the fly.

Flies will be streamers, varying between 2 to 6 inches, depending upon the size of the fish and the area fished. Some parts of Florida require the big flies, while others can be fished effectively with smaller patterns.

While most of the fishing will be with floating or intermediate sinking lines to get to the fish that are only a little under the surface, there are some exceptions. Tarpon are a tropical fish and, as such, are found

(Left and above) Tarpon almost always take to the air once hooked.

throughout Central America. One of the best places to fish for big tarpon is at Casa Mar in Costa Rica, where the fishing is done up in the ocean at the mouth of the Rio Colorado River, fishing sinking lines and typical streamer flies.

Here, one cast will last a long time, and you'll be blind fishing rather than fishing to individual fish. Keep your rod in your hand at all times, since a hit can come when least expected. Sometimes, the fish will roll on the surface where you can cast to individual fish, but deep blind fishing is the rule.

Once hooked, a tarpon will go immediately into the air. You must bow to it—throw it slack line to keep it from breaking the leader. After that, depending upon the size of the fish, the area, the depth of the water and the individual temperament of the fish, you will be in for a combination of long runs and aerial battles. Lifting power will be needed to land the fish for a quick admiration of their beauty or a quick photo of the tarpon in the water before releasing it.

Tarpon jumping in the deep, water of the Rio Colorado River at Casa Mar camp in Costa Rica.

Charley Wells with a tarpon from the backcountry of the Florida Everglades.

(Above) A small school of bonefish search the flats for food.

(Left) Lefty Kreh with a fly rod caught bonefish taken in the Turniffe Islands off Belize, Central America.

Bonefish

Fly-fishing for bonefish is flats fishing—fishing the shallow waters that can be found around the Keys in Florida and through Central America and Caribbean waters. It has been said by the bonefish experts that practically any flat will hold bonefish at some time during a tide. While the tides will vary the amount of water on a flat, bonefish like it shallow—so much so that one standard way to spot these bottom feeders is to look for tailing as they feed on the bottom. The shallow waters also makes them extremely skittish and nervous as they zigzag across a flat looking for food.

Except for very large bonefish, light tackle is ideal, although the reel must have a good drag (bonefish are known for their long runs) and sufficient capacity to hold the line and enough backing—about 100 to 200 yards of 20-pound Dacron.

Since the fish are feeding on the bottom, Keel Flies are best, particularly when fishing over coral or turtle grass that is found on some flats. In fact, some of the best fishing in the world in terms of numbers of bonefish and opportunities of casting to hundreds of bonefish can be found on the coral and turtle grass flats of the Turniffe Islands 30 miles offshore of Belize, in Central America. Belize is only a short hop from Miami and some excellent camps there—among them Kellers Caribbean Sports run by Fred Keller and Turniffe Island Lodge, run by Andre and Phillipe Job—make the

Typical casting for bonefish over the turtle grass flats in the Turniffe Islands is shown by Joe Zimmer. Fish can't be seen in photo, but are schooled and moving in the patch of clear water just beyond the turtle grass.

fishing ideal for a beginner.

Since bonefish everywhere are so nervous, a careful noiseless approach is necessary, along with accurate careful casting from a crouched position. Bonefish will rapidly change their course of direction while feeding so that repeated casts are sometimes necessary in front of a school before a hook up.

The secret of the fishing is to cast the fly far enough ahead and beyond the fish so that it doesn't scare them, yet close enough so that you can retrieve it to place the fly in front of the school, and skim it across the bottom as they pass by.

Snook

Snook are also a tropical fish found throughout southern Florida and in Central America. They are an ideal fish for freshwater fly-fishermen to start on, since in their habits, habitat, effective fly rod lures, and even in fight, they closely resemble fly rod caught largemouth and smallmouth bass.

The best spots to find them are around the mangroves that line the Keys, mainland and canals inshore along south Florida and Central America. Since they are usually hiding right in the mangroves, a large outfit (capable of casting big Keel Flies and popping bugs) is necessary to throw the fly with accuracy tight into the brush. Loop control is a must in this type of fishing to get under the brush, and accuracy is a must to cast up to but not into the mangroves.

Best flies are bright colors like those for bass and skipping popping bugs that will attract their attention.

Some shoreline fishing is possible along the canals of south Florida, as is bridge and pier fishing (especially at night) where big snook will congregate on the uptide side of a bridge to watch for bait fish washing along with the current. They fight like bass, only much harder.

Larry Kreh with a large snook taken on a streamer fly.

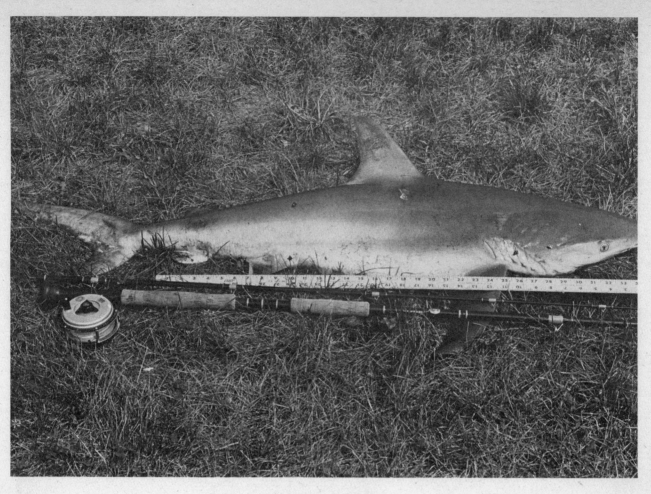

Shark and fly tackle.

Sharks

Sharks present a unique challenge to the fly rodder. They are large, strong, wary, with very poor eyesight and difficult to present a fly to so that it will be taken. There are two basic ways to fish for them. Along all three coasts where there aren't any shallow flats to find them as in Florida, the best way is to anchor, chum with a suitable oily fish to get them close to the boat, and throw flies to individual fish as they cruise by. They won't be wary at all and will only concentrate on the free lunch that you are passing out.

Usually the sharks will be deep—2 to 5 feet down—so that a sinking or sink tip line is best to get the fly to the fish as rapidly as possible. Use a short leader for the same reason, and you might want to go with weighted flies. The problem is like that of tarpon fishing—casting the fly so that with the retrieve and the sink rate of the fly, the shark and fly will end up at the same place at the same time. Unlike other fish where you will present the fly to the front, you must have the fly at the side of the fish so that it comes in close to their eye as they swim by, see it, and hopefully turn on it to take it.

The same presentation is necessary when fishing Florida, Caribbean or Central American flats, only here sharks will be far more wary and skittish. Any sudden movement or noise can scare them right off a flat. Use a floating line for flats fishing, since the fish will be right under the surface, often with their dorsal fins out of the water.

Once hooked a shark will make a long run and be well into your backing in seconds. Depending upon the size of the fish, you might be able to fight it from a dead boat, or might have to take off after it.

Your heaviest rod and best tackle is a must for sharks. You will need the best drag for the long runs and the strong rod for the lifting power to get the fish near the boat. If you plan to release the shark, cut the leader well away from their mouth. If you plan to land them, gaff them, *BUT DO NOT BRING THEM INTO THE BOAT!* This is a must, even if you have gaffed the fish, beat it to death with a priest, or hit it with a bang stick (a special stick loaded with a 12 gauge shotgun shell), since there are too many horror stories of "dead" sharks coming to life minutes or hours later and causing injury and costly damage to tackle and boats. If you want to keep the shark, hold it securely with a gaff near the pectoral fin, get another gaff in near the tail and lasso around the tail to drag it to the weighing dock.

278

Author with shark taken on the fly rod, using chummed flounder entrails to attract the fish to the boat.

Barracuda

Barracuda present two major problems for the fly rodder. First, the rapid retrieve that is necessary to get the fish to take, and second, the immediate long runs that will threaten to tangle line if you don't have all the coils of line in order on the casting platform.

Like sharks, barracuda are found cruising the flats. A long needle fish fly is best to take them with yellow and chartreuse the best colors. Since the flies are large and have a lot of wind resistance, a large outfit is best. Use as long a cast as possible, since this will give the 'cuda more time to see and follow the fly before being scared

Author with catch of white perch and crappies caught in brackish water in the mid-Atlantic.

off by the boat. Throw the fly in front of the fish and beyond it so that it crosses in front of the 'cuda at a high rate of speed.

Once hooked, the 'cuda will run and jump at the same time. Like sharks, don't bring them into the boat when landed, although you can dispatch them if necessary and drop them into a large cooler.

Dolphin

Dolphin are an excellent ocean gamefish but usually thought of as a fish that can only be taken with trolling techniques. While this is true for bigger bull dolphin, it is not true of small school dolphin.

Dolphin are habitually found near flotsom and most skippers, seeing any floating object will steer a course for it with the idea of taking dolphin. Dolphin are a school fish, and once one is hooked, others will stay in the same area. Thus, once a dolphin is hooked on trolling tackle, any others in the area will stay near the fish as long as it is in the water.

This makes for an ideal chance for the fly rodder with a ready rigged outfit to throw a fly to the other fish. Using this method, you can take one fish after another, provided that you cast and hook a fish before removing the one previously caught from the water.

The best place for casting from the large sport fishing boats from which most dolphin are caught, is from the port transom if you are a right-handed caster. This will allow you to cast almost astern from a dead boat, to drag the fly through the school of dolphin. You will have to modify your cast to a side, low-to-the-water cast, to avoid any outriggers, antennas, etc. Since dolphin can be big and are quite strong, use your heaviest outfit and use a shock leader on the fly. Large bright streamer flies are best, but the fish usually aren't that particular.

Billfish

Billfish require specialized techniques for fly rodders. Those experts who pioneered it, soon realized that it takes three persons to take the fish—one fly rodder, one at the controls of the boat, and a mate to handle the teasers that will attract the fish.

The technique is to have trolling teasers out from both flat lines and outriggers. Once a fish is raised, the mate must try to tease the fish up as close to the boat as possible. In some cases this will prove impossible, while other fish will run right under the transom. Once the fish has been teased into a feeding mood, the technique is for the captain to throw the engine out of gear (record keeping organizations and some tournaments usually require fly casting from a dead boat to prevent any possibility of trolling with fly tackle). The mate pulls the teaser out of the water and into the cockpit and the fly rodder casts the fly to the fish.

Most experienced billfishermen recommend throwing the fly somewhat to the side and behind the fish, so that it will see it, but have to turn to take it. The reason

Bonita taken on a streamer fly.

is that a fish facing the boat and close to it, might run or jump into the cockpit upon feeling the hook. Throwing the fly to the side and behind it, assures that the fish will be facing away from the boat when it starts its run or jump.

Obviously, the largest, heaviest, best tackle in terms of lifting power of the rod, drag and capacity of the reel and sufficient backing are necessary for such large fish.

Other Species

Fish that can be taken in saltwater on the fly rod would make an endless list, as more and more techniques are being developed each season to catch fish previously thought of as uncatchable on the fly rod. Keel Flies fished along the bottom sloughs will take *flounder* and *fluke,* and *channel bass* can be sight cast to off North Carolina waters, or in the Gulf of Mexico.

Cobia will take a fly cast around piling and buoys offshore, while *permit* prove among the most difficult and prized of fly rod catches with their almost constant refusal of any type or pattern of fly.

Perch can be taken in numbers, once you locate a

school and fish small flies with a quick retrieve at the right depth. *Bonito, tuna* and other pelagic species can be occasionally taken when these fast moving strong fish cross your path, and you are ready with a rigged outfit to throw a fly to them.

In short, don't restrict your thinking to only those familiar fish taken by others and constantly written about in the magazines. Virtually any fish that can be found within casting range, reasonably close to the surface (within 30 feet), that will take any form of artificial (spoon, plug, skirt lure, soft plastic, bucktail or hose lure), will also take a fly—if it is the right fly, in the right size, the right color and presented correctly. Finding out all of the right answers for new species, is much of the fun of saltwater fly-fishing, where pioneering new ideas and techniques is still possible on every trip.

CONCLUSION

Too many freshwater fly-fishermen or conventional saltwater fishermen avoid trying saltwater fly-fishing, feeling that they must fish only with a fly rod throughout

Lefty Kreh with a fly rod caught little tuna (false albacore).

a day of fishing. While some types of fly-fishing, such as fishing for striped bass in San Francisco Bay or sight fishing for bonefish or tarpon in Florida or Central America do require a single-minded dedication to the sport, other types of saltwater fly-fishing do not.

Obviously it is difficult for the beginning saltwater fly rodder to forego the sport that he knows he will get with casting and spinning tackle to fish exclusively with a fly rod. One solution around this is to continue to take and fish with your casting and spinning gear on saltwater trips, but to always carry a completely rigged (right down to tippet, shock leader and fly) saltwater fly outfit for those times that you get into breaking schools of striped bass or bluefish, tailing bonefish, schools of small tuna, hit an abundance of white perch, begin to take sea trout with your other tackle, fish a run of shad, or find a cruising shark. The result is that you can easily switch from your conventional tackle to fly tackle. It is important to keep your fly outfit rigged at all times for the appropriate species. After all, when you hit the fish, it is too late to start making up leaders, running line through guides and tying on flies.

Use this method, and the first saltwater fish taken on a fly rod will make a convert of you. The rest is just experience, dedication to learning the fish, tackle and sport, and the fun of enjoying the finest light tackle saltwater fishing available today.

BIBLIOGRAPHY

General Saltwater Fly-Fishing
Kreh, Lefty. *Fly Fishing in Saltwater*. Crown.
Waterman, Charley. *Modern Fresh and Saltwater Fly-Fishing*. Winchester.

Connections and Knots
Kreh, Lefty and Mark Sosin. *Practical Fishing Knots*. Crown.

Flies
Bay, Ken. *Saltwater Flies*. Lippincott.
Jorgensen, Poul. *Dressing Flies for Fresh and Saltwater*. Freshet.

Casting
Kreh, Lefty. *Fly Casting with Lefty Kreh*. Lippincott.
Gerlach, Rex. *The Complete Book of Casting*. Winchester Press.
Netherton, Cliff. *Angling and Casting*. Barnes.

Boyd Pfeiffer

Fishing Tackle Manufacturer's Directory

A

ABU-Garcia Inc.
21 Law Dr.
Fairfield, NJ 07006

Academy Broadway Corp.
5 Plant Ave.
Smithtown, NY 11787

Accardo Tackle Co.
3708 Conrad Dr.
Baton Rouge, LA 70805

Tony Accetta & Son Inc.
932 Ave. E.
Riviera Beach, FL 33404

Acme Tackle Co.
69 Bucklin St.
Providence, RI 02907

Action Lure Co.
P.O. Box 10529
Jackson, MS 39056

Action Products Co. Inc.
P.O. Box 100
Odessa, MO 64076

Airlite Plastics Co.
13724 Industrial Rd.
Omaha, NE 68137

Al's Goldfish Lure Co.
P.O. Box 13
Indian Orchard, MA 01151

American Clearwater Corp.
100 Sixth Ave.
Paterson, NJ 07524

American Tackle Corp.
7610 Coral Dr.
W. Melbourne, FL 32901

A-M Sport/Akro-Mills Inc.
1293 S. Main St.
Akron, OH 44309

Angler Prod. of Porcupine Inc.
210 Spring St.
Butler, PA 16001

Apple Mfg. Inc.
P.O. Box 1025
Havertown, PA 19083

AQUACONE Inc.
Box 197, 1033 Lakeshore Dr.
Port Orford, OR 97465

Fred Arbogast Co.
313 W. North St.
St. Akron, OH 44303

Axelson Fishing Tackle Mfg. Co. Inc.
17351-B Murphy Ave.
Irvine, CA 92714

B

Jim Bagley Bait Co.
P.O. Box 110
Winter Haven, FL 33880

Bass Buster Inc.
301 Main
Amsterdam, MO 64723

Bass Handler Products Co.
P.O. Box Drawer 6465
Lake Charles, LA 70606

Bass Hunter Boats
P.O. Box 1514
Valdosta, GA 31601

Bay De Noc Lure Co.
800 Railway Ave., Box 71
Gladstone, MI 49837

Bead Chain Tackle Co.
110 Mountain Grove St.
Bridgeport, CT 06605

Bear Paw Tackle Co. Inc.
Rte. 2, Box 494
Bellaire, MI 49615

Berkley & Co. Inc.
Hwy. 9 & 71
Spirit Lake, IA 51360

Betts Tackle Ltd.
P.O. Box 57
Fuguay Varina, NC 27526

Big-Jon Inc.
14393 Peninsula Dr.
Traverse City, MI 49684

Bingo Bait Co.
P.O. Box 30093
Houston, TX 77009

Black Marine Products
P.O. Box 3172
Marathon Shores, FL 33052

Blakemore Sales Corp.
Box 505, Hwy. 65 N.
Branson, MO 65616

B & M Co. Inc.
P.O. Box 231
West Point, MS 39773

Bob's Fly Tying
RR 2, Hazlett Lane
Springfield, IL 62707

Bomber Bait Co. Inc.
326 Lindsay St., Box 1058
Gainesville, TX 76240

Boone Bait Co. Inc.
P.O. Box 4009
Winter Park, FL 32793

The Brinkmann Corp.
4215 McEwen Rd.
Dallas, TX 75234

Brown Bear Bait Co.
Millvale Ind. Park
2100 E. Ohio
Pittsburgh, PA 15212

Brownell & Co. Inc.
Main St.
Moodus, CT 06469

Browning (Mitchell Reels)
Rte. 1
Morgan, UT 84050

Bullet Weights Inc.
P.O. Box 1186
Grand Island, NE 68801

Burke Fishing Lures
1969 S. Airport Rd.
Traverse City, MI 49684

Bystrom Brothers
2200 Snelling Ave. So.
Minneapolis, MN 55404

C

Camel Mfg. Co.
P.O. Box 835
Knoxville, TN 37901

Cast Craft/Chill Plastics
2278 Westside Dr.
Rochester, NY 14624

Lew Childre & Sons Inc.
P.O. Box 535
Foley, AL 36535

Coburn Corp.
1650 Corporate Rd. W.
Lakewood, NJ 08701

Coghlan's Ltd.
235 Garry St.
Winnipeg, Manitoba CANADA R3C 1H2

Columbia Co./CFT
Hwy. 52 West
Columbia, AL 36319

Continental Leisure Prod. Inc.
P.O. Box 1661
Meridian, MS 39301

Cossack Caviar Inc.
101 S. Dakota St.
Seattle, WA 98134

Crankbait Corp.
23500 Merchantile
Beachwood, OH 44122

Creme Lure Co.
P.O. Box 87
Tyler, TX 75710

Cuba Specialty Mfg. Co.
P.O. Box 38
Houghton, NY 14744

Ed Cummings Inc.
P.O. Box 6186
Flint, MI 48508

Cunningham & Co.
1316 N. Mill St.
Bowie, TX 76230

Cutter Laboratories Inc.
4th & Parker Sts.
Berkeley, CA 94710

D

Daiwa Corp.
14011 S. Normandie Ave.
Gardena, CA 90247

The Danielson Co.
755 N. Central
Kent, WA 98031

Dart Mfg. Co. Inc.
1724 Cockress Ave.
Dallas, TX 75215

Davco Fishing Products
1026 Linden
Texarkana, AR 75502

Les Davis Inc.
1674 Lincoln Ave.
Tacoma, WA 98421

De Long Lures, Inc.
85 Compark Rd.
Centerville, OH 45459

Den Mfg. Co.
13025 Old Hwy. 11, Box 537
Sturtevant, WI 53177

DuPont Co.
Wilmington, DE 19898

Dura Park Corp.
P.O. Box 1173
Sioux City, IA 51102

Dyer Specialty Co., Inc.
9901 Alburtis Ave.
Santa Fe Springs, CA 90670

E

Electric Fishing Reel Systems
1700 Sullivan St.
P.O. Box 20411
Greensboro, NC 27420

Emco Specialties, Inc.
2121 E. Walnut
Des Moines, IA 50304

Eppinger Mfg. Co.
6340 Schaefer Hwy.
Dearborn, MI 48126

Epsco Marine
411 Providence Hwy.
Westwood, MA 02090

Ero Leisure
189 W. Madison
Chicago, IL 60602

Eska Co.
2400 Kerper Blvd.
Dubuque, IA 52001

Ettinger Ent. Inc.
5310 Lance Dr.
Knoxville, TN 37919

Glen L. Evans
P.O. Box 850
Caldwell, ID 83605

E-Z Sales & Mfg. Inc.
1418 W. 166th St.
Gardena, CA 90247

F

Feldmann Engineering & Mfg.
633 Monroe St.
Sheboygan Falls, WI 53085

Fenwick/Woodstream
14799 Chestnut St.
Westminster, CA 92683

F.I.E. Corp.
4530 N.W. 135th St.
Opa-Locka, FL 33054

Fin-Wall Ent.
P.O. Box 1888
Ontario, CA 91762

FisHair
1484 W. County Rd. C.
St. Paul, MN 55113

Fisherman's Magi-Co-Lure
8356 79th St.
Cottage Grove, MN 55016

Fish Hawk Electronics Corp.
P.O. Box 340
Crystal Lake, IL 60014

Flambeau/Vlchek
P.O. Box 97
Middlefield, OH 44062

Don Fosher, Inc.
Box 16667
Clayton, MO 63105

Frabill Mfg. Co.
2018 S. First St.
Milwaukee, WI 53207

G

The Gaines Co.
P.O. Box 35
Gaines, PA 16921

The G. & C. Products Co.
1325 Macbeth St.
McLean, VA 22102

Gentex Corp.
P.O. Box 315
Carbondale, PA 18407

Gladding Corp. Fishing Line Div.
441 Stuart St.
Boston, MA 02116

Gott Corp.
1616 Wheat Rd.
Winfield, KS 67156

Grierson Industries Inc.
P.O. Box 945
Tucker, GA 30084

G & S Bait Mfg. Co.
Rte. 5, Box 890
Pell City, AL 35125

Gudebrod Inc.
12 S. 12th St.
Philadelphia, PA 19107

Gutmann Cutlery Co. Inc.
900 S. Columbia Ave.
Mt. Vernon, NY 10550

H

Harkins Tackle Inc.
P.O. Box 64
Carterville, IL 62918

Harrison Hoge Ind. Inc. Leisure Import
104 Arlington Ave.
St. James, NY 11780

James Heddon's Sons
414 W. St.
Dowagiac, MI 49047

Helin Tackle Co.
4099 Beaufait
Detroit, MI 48207

H & H Lures
10874 N. Dual St.
Baton Rouge, LA 70814

John J. Hildebrandt Corp.
817 High St.
P.O. Box 50
Logansport, IN 46947

Boyd Hinton Co.
508 S. Fannin
Amarillo, TX 79106

Hoots Inc.
404 S. Vine St.
P.O. Box 73
Mead, NE 68041

Hopkins Fishing Lures Co. Inc.
1130 Boissevain Ave.
Norfolk, VA 23507

HyPark Specialty Co.
P.O. Box 1413
5800 High Park Dr.
Minnetonka, MN 55343

I

Indian Head Sporting Goods
Ripley, MS 38663

IPCO Inc.
331 Lake Hazeltine Dr.
Chaska, MN 55318

Irving Weather-Rite Inc.
P.O. Box 1452
Secaucus, NJ 07094

J

J & L Tool & Machine Inc.
State Rd. 44 West
Shelbyville, IN 46176

Ray Jefferson
Main & Cotton Sts.
Philadelphia, PA 19127

Luhr Jensen & Sons Inc.
400 Portway Ave.
Hood River, OR 97031

Jenson Fishing Tackle
P.O. Box 9587
Austin, TX 78766

Jet-Aer Corp.
100 Sixth Ave.
Paterson, NJ 07524

Louis Johnson Co.
Box 21
Amsterdam, MO 64723

Johnson Reels Inc.
1531 Madison Ave.
Mankato, MN 56001

Jorgensen Bros.
4225 Stanley Blvd.
Pleasanton, CA 94566

K

Kencor Sports Inc.
2184 W. 190th St.
Torrance, CA 90504

Kennex Sports Corp.
2140 S. Yale St.
Santa Ana, CA 92704

Ketchum Co.
P.O. Box 729
Broken Arrow, OK 74012

Keystone Div. Star Products Ltd.
2633-43 W. Chicago Ave.
Chicago, IL 60622

Kimberly Rose Co.
2211 N. Elston Ave.
Chicago, IL 60614

Kingfish Tackle
1004 4th St. S.
Safety Harbor, FL 33572

Knight Mfg. Co.
P.O. Box 6162
Tyler, TX 75703

Kodiak Corp.
100 Mill St.
Bessemer, MI 49911

L

Lake King Rod Co. Inc.
820 N. Kansas
Topeka, KS 66608

Lakeland Industries
Isle, MN 56342

Lake Products Co.
P.O. Box 116
Utica, MI 48087

Lamiglas Inc.
P.O. Box 148
Woodland, WA 98674

Land-O-Tackle Inc.
4650 N. Ronald St.
Chicago, IL 60656

Lazy Ike Corp.
2221 E. Ovid
P.O. Box 4827
Des Moines, IA 50306

Leisure Lectronics
1220 Luke St.
Irving, TX 75061

Bill Lewis Bass Lures
P.O. Box 4062
Alexandria, LA 71301

Lindy-Little Joe Inc.
P.O. Box 27, Main St.
Isle, MN 56342

Lineminder Products
P.O. Box 552
Olathe, KS 66061

Lorie International Inc.
101 U.S. Hwy. Rt. 46
Saddle Brook, NJ 07662

Lowrance Electronics
12000 E. Skelly Dr.
Tulsa, OK 74128

M

Magic Worm Bedding Co. Inc.
Hwy. 10 & Cty. Trunk Q
Amherst Jctn., WI 54407

Magnuflex Rod
3923 N.W. 24th St.
Miami, FL 33142

Mann's Bait Mfg. Co. Inc.
P.O. Box 604
Eufaula, AL 36027

Marathon Rubber Products
510 Sherman St.
Wausau, WI 54401

Marine Metal Products
1222 Range Rd.
Clearwater, FL 33515

Markwort Sporting Goods
4300 Forest Park Ave.
St. Louis, MO 63108

Martin Reel Co.
30 E. Main St.
Mohawk, NY 13407

Mason Tackle Co.
G11273 N. State Rd.
Otisville, MI 48463

R.D. Massey Cheese Co.
521 League St.
P.O. Box 335
Muscatine, IA 52761

Master Fishing Tackle Corp.
1009 E. Bedmar St.
Carson, CA 90746

McCollum's Lunker Bass Lures
611 19th St.
Tuscaloosa, AL 35401

Medalist Cut'N Jump
11525 Sorrento Valley Rd.
San Diego, CA 92121

Mengo Industries Inc.
4611 Green Bay Rd.
Kenosha, WI 53142

Metalcrafts Inc.
27770 S.W. Parkway Ave.
Wilsonville, OR 97070

Mid-Lakes Manufacturing Co.
3304 Rifle Range Rd.
Knoxville, TN 37918

Mildrum Manufacturing Co.
230 Berlin St.
E. Berlin, CT 06023

Miltco Products Corp.
139 Emerson Pl.
Brooklyn, NY 11205

Minn Kota Inc.
1531 Madison Ave.
Mankato, MN 56001

MIRRO Corp.
1512 Washington St.
Manitowoc, WI 54220

Bruce B. Mises Inc.
1122 S. Robertson Blvd.
Los Angeles, CA 90035

Mister Twister Inc.
P.O. Box 996
Minden, LA 71055

Mold Craft Inc.
4848 N.E. 10th Terr.
Ft. Lauderdale, FL 33334

Morrow Electronics, Inc.
4740 Ridge Dr. N.E.
Salem, OR 97303

O. Mustad & Son (USA) Inc.
247-253 Grant Ave.
Auburn, NY 13021

Mylon Slonek KG
Ringweg 20-22
Saal/Donau
W. Germany D-8424

N

Nash Mfg. Co.
315 W. Riply St.
Ft. Worth, TX 76110

National Fiber Glass Products Inc.
979 Saw Mill River Rd.
Yonkers, NY 10701

Nelson Recreation Products
14760 Santa Fe Trail Dr.
Lenexa, KS 66215

Neosho Products Co.
P.O. Box 622
Neosho, MO 64850

Carl W. Newell Mfg.
940 Allen Ave.
Glendale, CA 91201

Norman Mfg. Co.
P.O. Box 580
Greenwood, AR 72936

Normark Corp./Blue Fox
1710 E. 78th St.
Minneapolis, MN 55423

Nova Products Inc.
P.O. Box 116, 220 Ave. C
Carrollton, GA 30117

O

Old Pal/Woodstream
Front & Locust Sts.
Lititz, PA 17543

O.L.M. International Corporation
868 Cowan Rd.
Burlingame, CA 94010

Optronics Inc.
350 N. Wheeler
Ft. Gibson, OK 74434

Outdoor Venture Corp.
P.O. Box 337
Stearns, KY 42647

P

Padre Island Co. (PICO Lures)
2617 N. Zarzamora St.
P.O. Box 5310
San Antonio, TX 78201

Palco Products
3017 San Fernando Rd.
Los Angeles, CA 90065

Penn Fishing Tackle Mfg. Co.
3028 W. Hunting Park Ave.
Philadelphia, PA 19132

J.F. Pepper Co. Inc.
P.O. Box 445
Rome, NY 13440

Perfection Tip Co.
4550 Jackson St.
Denver, CO 80216

Pflueger Sporting Goods
P.O. Drawer P
Columbia, SC 29260

PLANO Molding Co.
113 S. Center Ave.
Plano, IL 60545

Plas/Steel Products Inc.
Industrial Park
Walkerton, IN 46574

Plastilite Corp.
P.O. Box 12235
Omaha, NE 68112

Powerscopic Inc.
1111 E. El Segundo Blvd.
El Segundo, CA 90245

Pride Plastics Inc.
575 Glaspie St.
Oxford, MI 48051

Proos Mfg. Co.
1037 Michigan St. N.E.
Grand Rapids, MI 49503

Pro-Rod Mfg. Inc.
145 Fairmount Ave.
Jamestown, NY 14701

G. Pucci & Sons
480 Princeton St.
San Francisco, CA 94134

Q

Quality Tool & Mfg.
1022 S. 12th St.
Watertown, WI 53094

Quick Corp. of America
620 Terminal Way
Costa Mesa, CA 92627

R

Ranger Rubber Co.
1100 E. Main St.
Endicott, NY 13760

Rebel Lures
P.O. Box 1587
Ft. Smith, AR 72902

Reliance Products Ltd.
1830 Dublin Ave.
Winnipeg, Manitoba CANADA R3H 0H3

Rettinger Importing Co.
70 Caven Point Ave.
Jersey City, NJ 07305

Ridge Runner Lure Inc.
5025 Flournoy Lucas Rd.
Shreveport, LA 71109

Riviera Marine & Tackle Co.
3859 Roger Chaffee Blvd. S.E.
Grand Rapids, MI 49508

Rod Caddy Corp.
3153 W. 31st St.
Chicago, IL 60623

Rome Industries, Inc.
1703 W. Detweiller Dr.
Peoria, IL 61614

Royal Red Ball
8530 Page Ave.
St. Louis, MO 63114

Ruff'N Ready Mfg. Co.
6 Andrews St.
Greenville, SC 29610

Ryobi America Corp.
1555 Carmen Dr.
Elk Grove Village, IL 60007

S

Sampo Inc.
North St.
Barneveld, NY 13304

Seaway
7200 N. Oak Park Ave.
Niles, IL 60648

T.R. Seidel Co.
P.O. Box 268
Arvada, CO 80001

Seneca Tackle Co. Inc.
P.O. Box 2841
Providence, RI 02907

Sevenstrand Tackle Corp.
5401 McFadden Ave.
Huntington Beach, CA 92649

Sevylor
213 Louisville Air Park
Louisville, KY 40213

Shakespeare Co.
P.O. Drawer S
6111 Shakespeare Rd.
Columbia, SC 29260

Sheldon's Inc.
P.O. Box 508
Antigo, WI 54409

Shimano American Corp.
1133 Ave. of the Americas
New York, NY 10036

Skyline Industries, Inc.
P.O. Box 821
Ft. Worth, TX 76101

Hiram Smith Whetstone Inc.
1500 Sleepy Valley Rd.
Hot Springs, AR 71901

Smithwick Lures Inc.
P.O. Box 1205
Shreveport, LA 71163

Sportfish Treasures
RR 1, Box 856, Duck Key
Marathon, FL 33050

Sportline Div. of Beatrice Foods
3300 W. Franklin Blvd.
Chicago, IL 60624

St. Croix of Park Falls Ltd.
Hwy. 13 N., P.O. Box 279
Park Falls, WI 54552

Stearns Mfg. Co.
P.O. Box 1498
St. Cloud, MN 56301

Stillfish Corp.
3631 Marine Rd.
Toledo, OH 43609

S & T Industries My Buddy Div.
P.O. Box 32480
Louisville, KY 40232

Storm Mfg. Co.
P.O. Box 265
Norman, OK 73070

Strike King Lure Co.
2906 Sanderwood
Memphis, TN 38118

Strike Master Inc.
411 N. Washington Ave.
Minneapolis, MN 55401

Sundridge Tackle Ltd.
26 Marischal Rd.
London, England S.E. 13

Sunset Line & Twine Co.
P.O. Box 691
Petaluma, CA 94952

Symonds & Co.
333 N. Michigan Ave. Ste. 1125
Chicago, IL 60601

T

T's Bass Lures Inc.
7 Timothy Lane
Somerset, KY 42501

Techsonic Industries
One Hummingbird Lane
Lake Eufaula, AL 36027

3M Co./Leisure Time
3M Center 224-5N.
St. Paul, MN 55101

Trimarc Div. of Phoenix Int.
High Point Plaza
Hillside, IL 60162

Trophy Tackle Box Co.
9714 Old Katy Rd.
Houston, TX 77055

Tru-Turn Inc.
1120 Federal Dr.
Montgomery, AL 36107

Tucker Duck & Rubber Co.
2701 Kelley Hwy.
Ft. Smith, AR 72914

U

Uncle Josh Bait Co.
524 Clarence St.
Ft. Atkinson, WI 53538

Uniroyal Inc.
1230 Ave. of the Americas
New York, NY 10020

V

Varmac Mfg. Co. Inc.
4201 Redwood Ave.
Los Angeles, CA 90066

Vexilar Inc.
9345 Penn Ave. S.
Minneapolis, MN 55431

Vibrax-MCA Inc.
36 Pleasant St.
Watertown, MA 02172

VMC Peche
90120 Morvillars, France

Fritz Von Schlegell
1407 Santa Fe Ave.
Los Angeles, CA 90021

W

Walker International
1901 W. Lafayette Blvd.
Detroit, MI 48216

Water Gremlin Co.
4370 Otter Lake Rd.
White Bear Lake, MN 55110

Weed Master Inc.
249 N.E. 32nd St.
Ft. Lauderdale, FL 33334

Wenzel Co.
1280 Research Blvd.
St. Louis, MO 63132

Western Cutlery Co.
1800 Pike Rd.
Longmont, CO 80501

Whopper Stopper/Fliptail
P.O. Box 1111
Sherman, TX 75090

C.S. Williamson & Co.
261 Seminole Ave.
Orangeburg, SC 29115

Wilson Allen Corp.
P.O. Box 64
Windsor, MO 65360

Worm-A-Live Co.
3316 E. Morris
Cudahy, WI 53110

The Worth Co.
P.O. Box 88
Stevens Point, WI 54481

Wright & McGill Co.
4245 E. 46th Ave.
Denver, CO 80216

Wynn Mfg. Co. Inc.
568 Burgess St.
St. Paul, MN 55103

Y

Yakima Bait Co.
P.O. Box 310
Granger, WA 98932

Z

Zebco Div. Brunswick Corp.
6101 E. Apache, P.O. Box 270
Tulsa, OK 74101

Zeke's Floating' Bait Co.
P.O. Box 187
La Canada, CA 91011